The Scapegoat:
Ritual and Literature

HOUGHTON MIFFLIN COMPANY

BOSTON

NEW YORK

ATLANTA

GENEVA, ILL.

DALLAS

PALO ALTO

The Scapegoat: Ritual and Literature

EDITED BY

John B. Vickery

UNIVERSITY OF CALIFORNIA, RIVERSIDE

J'nan M. Sellery

HARVEY MUDD COLLEGE, CLAREMONT

Printed in the U.S.A.

Library of Congress Catalog Card Number: 70–166472
ISBN: 0–395–11256–7

for Anne and Meg
with Hope and Love

Preface

This collection of literature, criticism, and discursive prose presents a vital cultural phenomenon—the figure and the rituals of the scapegoat—from two vantage points. The first is that of scholars of anthropology, psychology, and comparative religion; the second is through drama and fiction from ancient Greece to modern England and America. The concept of the scapegoat is found in many cultures and times. Since it involves complex issues of group and individual dynamics, the idea is studied and utilized interpretively in a number of disciplines, particularly religion, psychology, anthropology, classical studies, sociology, and literature. To differentiate fully all the possible meanings and expressions of the term lies beyond the aims of this volume. Yet it does seek to suggest something of the range of functions with which man has invested the scapegoat since the earliest times and the extent to which these functions have been utilized by creative artists in a variety of times and places. In this sense, the thrust of this collection is emphatically interdisciplinary. Literature is profitably read in the light of religion and anthropology, for example, just as those subjects are enriched and made more vivid by the creative resources of literature.

The scapegoat has traditionally been one of the chief means by which men have imaginatively acted out the preservation of society, the honoring of the gods, and their own psychic release. The paradox that a figure destined for punishment and sacrifice should also be honored and even worshipped is fraught with tragic, ironic, and even comic possibilities. Creative artists have seized upon these eagerly and exploited them with subtlety and variety. As the selections indicate, cruelty, desire, self-preservation, witting and unwitting sacrifice, jealousy, hope, and fear all help to shape the scapegoat as he appears both in reality and in imagination.

The book is divided into two major parts: a series of perspectives on the scapegoat drawn from a variety of cultures and historical periods; and a group of literary works—drama, short story, and novella—that embody the scapegoat pattern. Brief biographical, critical, and bibliographical headnotes precede each artist's selection in Part II. Accompanying most of the selections in this part are critical essays relating the works to the scapegoat ritual. To provide the student with an unrestricted opportunity of testing his capacities for comparative and interdisciplinary interpretation, no essays dealing with Shirley Jackson's "The Lottery," James Baldwin's "Going to Meet the Man," and Strindberg's *The Scapegoat* are included. Both parts of the book are followed by a series of "Issues for Discussion." These raise representative questions of fact and interpretation that encourage comprehension and appreciation. The issues presented may also serve as topics for further research and writing assignments. At the end of the book there is a list of "Literary Works for Further Study," which can be used in augmenting the texts included here for a full term's work, and in suggesting works for research or critical papers.

Acknowledgements to authors and publishers to reprint their works appear on the first page of each selection. Throughout we have shared equally in choosing, organizing, and editing all the materials.

John B. Vickery
J'nan M. Sellery

Contents

PART ONE

The Scapegoat
and His Rituals

The Scapegoat

Sir James Frazer

The Transference of Evil

. . . The notion that we can transfer our guilt and sufferings to
some other being who will bear them for us is familiar to
the savage mind. It arises from a very obvious confusion
between the physical and the mental, between the material
and the immaterial. Because it is possible to shift a load of
wood, stones, or what not, from our own back to the back of
another, the savage fancies that it is equally possible to shift
the burden of his pains and sorrows to another, who will
suffer them in his stead. Upon this idea he acts, and the
result is an endless number of very unamiable devices for
palming off upon some one else the trouble which a man
shrinks from bearing himself. In short, the principle of
vicarious suffering is commonly understood and practised by
races who stand on a low level of social and intellectual culture. In the following pages I shall illustrate the theory and
the practice as they are found among savages in all their
naked simplicity, undisguised by the refinements of meta-
physics and the subtleties of theology.

The devices to which the cunning and selfish savage resorts
for the sake of easing himself at the expense of his neighbour
are manifold; only a few typical examples out of a multitude
can be cited. At the outset it is to be observed that the evil
of which a man seeks to rid himself need not be transferred

From Chapters I, II, IV, V, and VI of *The Golden Bough* by Sir James G.
Frazer. Reprinted by permission of Trinity College, Cambridge, England.
The Golden Bough is also published by Macmillan & Co., Ltd., and St.
Martin's Press, Inc.

to a person; it may equally well be transferred to an animal or a thing, though in the last case the thing is often only a vehicle to convey the trouble to the first person who touches it. In some of the East Indian islands they think that epilepsy can be cured by striking the patient on the face with the leaves of certain trees and then throwing them away. The disease is believed to have passed into the leaves, and to have been thrown away with them. In the Warramunga and Tjingilli tribes of Central Australia men who suffered from headache have often been seen wearing women's head-rings. "This was connected with the belief that the pain in the head would pass into the rings, and that then it could be thrown away with them into the bush, and so got rid of effectually. The natives have a very firm belief in the efficacy of this treatment. . . .

The Omnipresence of Demons

In the foregoing . . . the primitive principle of the transference of ills to another person, animal, or thing was explained and illustrated. A consideration of the means taken, in accordance with this principle, to rid individuals of their troubles and distresses led us to believe that at Rome similar means had been adopted to free the whole community, at a single blow of the hammer, from diverse evils that afflicted it. I now propose to shew that such attempts to dismiss at once the accumulated sorrows of a people are by no means rare or exceptional, but that on the contrary they have been made in many lands, and that from being occasional they tend to become periodic and annual.

It needs some effort on our part to realise the frame of mind which prompts these attempts. Bred in a philosophy which strips nature of personality and reduces it to the unknown cause of an orderly series of impressions on our senses, we find it hard to put ourselves in the place of the savage, to whom the same impressions appear in the guise of spirits or the handiwork of spirits. For ages the army of spirits, once so near, has been receding further and further from us, banished by the magic wand of science from hearth and home, from ruined cell and ivied tower, from haunted glade and lonely mere, from the riven murky cloud that belches forth the lightning, and from those fairer clouds that pillow the silver moon or fret with flakes of burning red the golden eve. The spirits are gone even from their last stronghold in the sky, whose blue arch no longer passes, except with children, for the screen that hides from mortal eyes the glories of the celestial world. Only in poets' dreams or impassioned flights of oratory is it given to catch a glimpse of the last flutter of the standards of the retreating host, to hear the beat of their invisible wings, the sound of their mocking laughter, or the swell of angel music dying away in the distance. Far otherwise is it with the savage. To his imagination the world still teems with those motley beings whom a more sober philosophy has discarded. Fairies and goblins, ghosts and demons, still hover about him both waking and sleeping. They dog his footsteps, dazzle his senses, enter into him, harass and deceive and torment him in a thousand freakish and mischievous ways. The mishaps that befall him, the losses he sustains, the pains he has to endure, he commonly sets down, if not to the magic of his enemies, to the spite or anger or caprice of the spirits. Their constant presence wearies him, their sleepless malignity exasperates him; he longs with an unspeakable longing to be rid of them altogether, and from time to time, driven to bay, his patience utterly exhausted, he turns fiercely on his persecutors and makes a desperate effort to chase the whole pack of them from the land, to clear the air of their swarming multitudes, that he may breathe more freely and go on his way unmolested, at least for a time. Thus it comes about that the endeavour of primitive people to make a clean sweep of all their troubles generally takes the form of a grand hunting out and expulsion of devils or ghosts. They think that if they can only shake off these their accursed tormentors, they will make a fresh start in life, happy and innocent; the tales of Eden and the old poetic golden age will come true again. . . .

Public Scapegoats

. . . Occasionally the scapegoat is a man. For example, from time to time the gods used to warn the King of Uganda that his foes the Banyoro were working magic against him and his people to make them die of disease. To avert such a catastrophe the king would send a scapegoat to the frontier of Bunyoro, the land of the enemy. The scapegoat consisted of either a man and a boy or a woman and her child, chosen because of some mark or bodily defect, which the gods had noted and by which the victims were to be recognized. With the human victims were sent a cow, a goat, a fowl, and a dog; and a strong guard escorted them to the land which the god had indicated. There the limbs of the victims were broken and they were left to die a lingering death in the enemy's country, being too crippled to crawl back to Uganda. The disease or plague was thought to have been thus transferred to the victims and to have been conveyed back in their persons to the land from which it came. So, too, after a war the gods sometimes advised the king to send back a scapegoat in order to free the warriors from some evil that had attached itself to the army. One of the women slaves, a cow, a goat, a fowl, and a dog would be chosen from among the captives and sent back to the borders of the country whence they had come; there they were maimed and left to die. After that the army would be pronounced clean and allowed to return to the capital. In each case a bundle of herbs would be rubbed over the people and the cattle, and would then be tied to the victims, who would thus carry back the evil with them. A similar use of scapegoats, human and animal, was regularly made after a King of Uganda had been crowned. Two men were brought to the king; one of them he wounded slightly with an arrow shot from a bow. The man was then sent away, under a strong guard, as a scapegoat to Bunyoro, the enemy's country, and with him were sent a cow, a goat, and a dog. On his sad journey he took with him the dust and ashes of the sacred fire, which had burned day and night at the entrance to the late king's enclosure and had been extinguished, as usual, at his death. Arrived at their destination, the man and the animals were maimed and left to die. They were believed to bear away with them any uncleanness that might cleave to the new King or Queen.

Some of the aboriginal tribes of China, as a protection against pestilence, select a man of great muscular strength to act the part of scapegoat. Having besmeared his face with paint, he performs many antics with the view of enticing all pestilential and noxious influences to attach themselves to him only. He is assisted by a priest. Finally the scapegoat, hotly pursued by men and women beating gongs and tom-toms, is driven with great haste out of the town or village. In the Punjaub a cure for the murrain is to hire a man of the Chamar caste, turn his face away from the village, brand him with a red-hot sickle, and let him go out into the jungle taking the murrain with him. He must not look back. When disease breaks out among a herd, the Oraons take the herdsman himself, tie a wooden bell from one of the cows round his neck, beat him with sticks, and drive him out of the village to a cross-road, where the bell and sticks are deposited. In the territory of Kumaon, lying on the southern slopes of the Western Himalayas, the custom of employing a human scapegoat appears to have taken a somewhat peculiar form in the ceremony known as Barat. First of all a thick rope of grass is stretched from the top of a cliff to the valley beneath, where it is made fast to posts driven into the ground. Next a wooden saddle, with a very sharp ridge and unpadded, is attached by thongs to the cable, along which it runs in a deep groove. A man now seats himself on the saddle and is strapped to it, while sandbags or heavy stones are suspended from his feet to secure his balance. Then, after various ceremonies have been performed and a kid sacrificed, he throws himself as far back in the saddle as he can go, and is started off to slide down the rope into the valley. Away he shoots at an ever-increasing speed; the saddle under him, however well greased, emits volumes of smoke during the greater part of his progress; and he is nearly senseless when he reaches the bottom. . . .

The scapegoat by means of which the accumulated ills of a whole year are publicly expelled is sometimes an animal. For example, among the Garos of Assam, "besides the sacrifices for individual cases of illness, there are certain ceremonies which are observed once a year by a whole community or village, and are intended to safeguard its members from dangers of the forest, and from sickness and mishap during the coming twelve months. The principal of these is the Asongtata ceremony. Close to the outskirts of every big village a number of stones may be noticed stuck into the ground, apparently without order or method. These are known by the name of *asong*, and on them is offered the sacrifice which the

Asongtata demands. The sacrifice of a goat takes place, and a month later, that of a *langur* (*Entellus* monkey) or a bamboo-rat is considered necessary. The animal chosen has a rope fastened round its neck and is led by two men, one on each side of it, to every house in the village. It is taken inside each house in turn, the assembled villagers, meanwhile, beating the walls from the outside, to frighten and drive out any evil spirits which may have taken up their residence within. The round of the village having been made in this manner, the monkey or rat is led to the outskirts of the village, killed by a blow of a *dao*, which disembowels it, and then crucified on bamboos set up in the ground. Round the crucified animal long, sharp bamboo stakes are placed, which form *chevaux de frise* round about it. These commemorate the days when such defences surrounded the villages on all sides to keep off human enemies, and they are now a symbol to ward off sickness and dangers to life from the wild animals of the forest. The *langur* required for the purpose is hunted down some days before, but should it be found impossible to catch one, a brown monkey may take its place; a hulock may not be used." Here the crucified ape or rat is the public scapegoat, which by its vicarious sufferings and death relieves the people from all sickness and mishap in the coming year.

Again, on one day of the year the Bhotiyas of Juhar, in the Western Himalayas, take a dog, intoxicate him with spirits and bhang or hemp, and having fed him with sweetmeats, lead him round the village and let him loose. They then chase and kill him with sticks and stones, and believe that, when they have done so, no disease or misfortune will visit the village during the year. In some parts of Breadalbane it was formerly the custom on New Year's Day to take a dog to the door, give him a bit of bread, and drive him out, saying, "Get away, you dog! Whatever death of men or loss of cattle would happen in this house to the end of the present year, may it all light on your head!" It appears that the white dogs annually sacrificed by the Iroquois at their New Year Festival are, or have been, regarded as scapegoats. According to Mr. J. V. H. Clark, who witnessed the ceremony in January 1841, on the first day of the festival all the fires in the village were extinguished, the ashes scattered to the winds, and a new fire kindled with flint and steel. On a subsequent day, men dressed in fantastic costumes went round the village, gathering the sins of the people. When the morning of the last day of the festival was come, two white dogs, decorated with red paint, wampum, feathers, and ribbons, were led out. They were soon strangled, and hung on a ladder. Firing and yelling succeeded, and half an hour later the animals were taken into a house, "where the people's sins were transferred to them." The carcases were afterwards burnt on a pyre of wood. According to the Rev. Mr. Kirkland, who wrote in the eighteenth century, the ashes of the pyre upon which one of the white dogs was burnt were carried through the village and sprinkled at the door of every house. Formerly, however, as we have seen, the Iroquois expulsion of evils was immediate and not by scapegoat. On the Day of Atonement, which was the tenth day of the seventh month, the Jewish high-priest laid both his hands on the head of a live goat, confessed over it all the iniquities of the Children of Israel, and, having thereby transferred the sins of the people to the beast, sent it away into the wilderness.[1]

The scapegoat upon whom the sins of the people are periodically laid, may also be a human being. At Onitsha, on the Niger, two human beings used to be annually sacrificed to take away the sins of the land. The victims were purchased by

[1] Leviticus xvi. The word translated "scapegoat" in the Authorised Version is Azazel, which appears rather to be the name of a bad angel or demon, to whom the goat was sent away. "In later Jewish literature (Book of Enoch) Azazel appears as the prince of the fallen angels, the offspring of the unions described in Gen. vi. 1 ff. The familiar rendering 'scapegoat,' *i.e.* the goat which is allowed to escape, goes back to the *caper emissarius* of the Vulgate, and is based on an untenable etymology" (Professor A. R. S. Kennedy, in his commentary on Leviticus xvi. 8, in the *Century Bible*). There is some ground for thinking that the animal was killed by being thrown over a certain crag that overhangs a rocky chasm not far from Jerusalem. See *Encyclopaedia Biblica*, ed. T. K. Cheyne and J. S. Black, vol. i. (London, 1899) coll. 394 *sqq.*, *s.v.* "Azazel." Modern Jews sacrifice a white cock on the eve of the Day of Atonement, nine days after the begining of their New Year. The father of the family knocks the cock thrice against his own head, saying, "Let this cock be a substitute for me, let it take my place, let death be laid upon this cock, but a happy life bestowed on me and on all Israel." Then he cuts its throat and dashes the bird violently on the ground. The intestines are thrown on the roof of the house. The flesh of the cock was formerly given to the poor. See J. Buxtorf, *Synagoga Judaica* (Bâle, 1661), ch. xxv. pp. 508 *sqq.*

public subscription. All persons who, during the past year, had fallen into gross sins, such as incendiarism, theft, adultery, witchcraft, and so forth, were expected to contribute 28 *ngugas,* or a little over £2. The money thus collected was taken into the interior of the country and expended in the purchase of two sickly persons "to be offered as a sacrifice for all these abominable crimes—one for the land and one for the river." A man from a neighbouring town was hired to put them to death. On the twenty-seventh of February 1858 the Rev. J. C. Taylor witnessed the sacrifice of one of these victims. The sufferer was a woman, about nineteen or twenty years of age. They dragged her alive along the ground, face downwards, from the king's house to the river, a distance of two miles, the crowds who accompanied her crying, "Wickedness! wickedness!" The intention was "to take away the iniquities of the land. The body was dragged along in a merciless manner, as if the weight of all their wickedness was thus carried away." Similar customs are said to be still secretly practised every year by many tribes on the delta of the Niger in spite of the vigilance of the British Government. Among the Yoruba negroes of West Africa "the human victim chosen for sacrifice, and who may be either a free-born or a slave, a person of noble or wealthy parentage, or one of humble birth, is, after he has been chosen and marked out for the purpose, called an *Oluwo.* He is always well fed and nourished and supplied with whatever he should desire during the period of his confinement. When the occasion arrives for him to be sacrificed and offered up, he is commonly led about and paraded through the streets of the town or city of the Sovereign who would sacrifice him for the well-being of his government and of every family and individual under it, in order that he might carry off the sin, guilt, misfortune and death of all without exception. Ashes and chalk would be employed to hide his identity by the one being freely thrown over his head, and his face painted with the latter, whilst individuals would often rush out of their houses to lay their hands upon him that they might thus transfer to him their sin, guilt, trouble, and death. This parading done, he is taken through a temporary sacred shed of palm and other tree branches, and especially of the former, the Igbodu and to its first division, where many persons might follow him, and through a second where only the chiefs and other very important persons might escort and accompany him to, and to a third where only the Babalawo [priest] and his official assistant, the Ajigbona, are permitted to enter with him. Here, after he himself has given out or started his last song, which is to be taken up by the large assembly of people who will have been waiting to hear his last word or his last groan, his head is taken off and his blood offered to the gods. The announcement of his last word or his last groan heard and taken up by the people, would be a signal for joy, gladness, and thanksgiving, and for drum beating and dancing, as an expression of their gratification because their sacrifice has been accepted, the divine wrath is appeased, and the prospect of prosperity or increased prosperity assured."

In Siam it used to be the custom on one day of the year to single out a woman broken down by debauchery, and carry her on a litter through all the streets to the music of drums and hautboys. The mob insulted her and pelted her with dirt; and after having carried her through the whole city, they threw her on a dunghill or a hedge of thorns outside the ramparts, forbidding her ever to enter the walls again. They believed that the woman thus drew upon herself all the malign influences of the air and of evil spirits. In Japan the "*tsuina* or *oni-yarahi*, that is to say, demon expelling, is a sort of drama in which disease, or more generally ill-luck, is personified, and driven away with threats and a show of violence. Like the *oho-harahi*,[2] it was performed on the last day of the year. This association is only natural. The demons of the *tsuina* are personified wintry influences, with the diseases which they bring with them, while the *oho-harahi* is intended to cleanse the people from sin and uncleanness, things closely related to disease, as well as from disease itself. Though probably of Chinese origin, the *tsuina* is a tolerably ancient rite. It is alluded to in the *Nihongi* under the date A.D. 689. It

[2] The *oho-harahi* or "Great Purification" is a ceremony, which used to be performed in the Japanese capital twice every year, namely on the last days of the sixth and twelfth month. It included a preliminary lustration, expiatory offerings, and the recital of a *norito* or formula (not a prayer), in which the Mikado, by virtue of an authority transmitted to him from the Sun-goddess, pronounced to his ministers and people the absolution and remission of their sins. . . .

was at one time performed at Court on an imposing scale. Four bands of twenty youths, each wearing a four-eyed mask, and each carrying a halberd in the left hand, marched simultaneously from the four gates of the palace, driving the devils before them. Another account of this ceremony says that a man disguised himself as the demon of pestilence, in which garb he was shot at and driven off by the courtiers armed with peach-wood bows and arrows of reed. Peach-wood staves were used for the same purpose. There was formerly a practice at Asakusa in Tokio on the last day of the year for a man got up as a devil to be chased round the pagoda there by another wearing a mask. After this 3,000 tickets were scrambled for by the spectators. These were carried away and pasted up over the doors as a charm against pestilence." The Battas of Sumatra offer either a red horse or a buffalo as a public sacrifice to purify the land and obtain the favour of the gods. Formerly, it is said, a man was bound to the same stake as the buffalo, and when they killed the animal, the man was driven away; no one might receive him, converse with him, or give him food. Doubtless he was supposed to carry away the sins and misfortunes of the people.

Human scapegoats, as we shall see presently, were well known in classical antiquity, and even in mediaeval Europe the custom seems not to have been wholly extinct. In the town of Halberstadt, in Thüringen, there was a church said to have been founded by Charlemagne. In this church every year they chose a man, who was believed to be stained with heinous sins. On the first day of Lent he was brought to the church, dressed in mourning garb, with his head muffled up. At the close of the service he was turned out of the church. During the forty days of Lent he perambulated the city barefoot, neither entering the churches nor speaking to any one. The canons took it in turn to feed him. After midnight he was allowed to sleep in the streets. On the day before Good Friday, after the consecration of the holy oil, he was readmitted to the church and absolved from his sins. The people gave him money. He was called Adam, and was now believed to be in a state of innocence. At Entlebuch, in Switzerland, down to the close of the eighteenth century, the custom of annually expelling a scapegoat was preserved in the ceremony of driving "Posterli" from the village into the lands of the neighbouring village. "Posterli" was represented by a lad disguised as an old witch or as a goat or an ass. Amid a deafening noise of horns, clarionets, bells, whips, and so forth, he was driven out. Sometimes "Posterli" was represented by a puppet, which was drawn on a sledge and left in a corner of the neighbouring village. The ceremony took place on the Thursday evening of the last week but one before Christmas.

In Munich down to about a hundred years ago the expulsion of the devil from the city used to be annually enacted on Ascension Day. On the Eve of Ascension Day a man disguised as a devil was chased through the streets, which were then narrow and dirty in contrast to the broad, well-kept thoroughfares, lined with imposing buildings, which now distinguish the capital of Bavaria. His pursuers were dressed as witches and wizards and provided with the indispensable crutches, brooms, and pitchforks which make up the outfit of these uncanny beings. While the devil fled before them, the troop of maskers made after him with wild whoops and halloos, and when they overtook him they ducked him in puddles or rolled him on dunghills. In this way the demon at last succeeded in reaching the palace, where he put off his hideous and now filthy disguise and was rewarded for his vicarious sufferings by a copious meal. The devilish costume which he had thrown off was then stuffed with hay and straw and conveyed to a particular church (the Frauenkirche), where it was kept over night, being hung by a rope from a window in the tower. On the afternoon of Ascension Day, before the Vesper service began, an image of the Saviour was drawn up to the roof of the church, no doubt to symbolize the event which the day commemorates. Then burning tow and wafers were thrown on the people. Meantime the effigy of the devil, painted black, with a pair of horns and a lolling red tongue, had been dangling from the church tower, to the delight of a gaping crowd of spectators gathered before the church. It was now flung down into their midst, and a fierce struggle for possession of it took place among the rabble. Finally, it was carried out of the town by the Isar gate and burned on a neighbouring height, "in order that the foul fiend might do no harm to the city." The custom died out at Munich towards the end of the eighteenth century; but it is said that similar ceremonies are observed to this day in some villages of Upper Bavaria.

This quaint ceremony suggests that the pardoned criminal who used to play the principal part in a solemn religious procession on Ascension Day at Rouen may in like manner have originally served, if not as a representative of the devil, at least as a public scapegoat, who relieved the whole people of their sins and sorrows for a year by taking them upon himself. This would explain why the gaol had to be raked in order to furnish one who would parade with the highest ecclesiastical dignitaries in their gorgeous vestments through the streets of Rouen, while the church bells pealed out, the clergy chanted, banners waved, and every circumstance combined to enhance the pomp and splendour of the pageant. It would add a pathetic significance to the crowning act of the ceremony, when on a lofty platform in the public square, with the eyes of a great and silent multitude turned upon him, the condemned malefactor received from the Church the absolution and remission of his sins; for if the rite is to be interpreted in the way here suggested, the sins which were thus forgiven were those not of one man only but of the whole people. No wonder, then, that when the sinner, now a sinner no more, rose from his knees and thrice lifted the silver shrine of St. Romain in his arms, the whole vast assembly in the square broke out into joyous cries of *"Noel! Noel! Noel!"* which they understood to signify, "God be with us!" In Christian countries no more appropriate season could be selected for the ceremony of the human scapegoat than Ascension Day, which commemorates the departure from earth of Him who, in the belief of millions, took away the sins of the world.

Sometimes the scapegoat is a divine animal. The people of Malabar share the Hindoo reverence for the cow, to kill and eat which "they esteem to be a crime as heinous as homicide or wilful murder." Nevertheless the "Bramans transfer the sins of the people into one or more Cows, which are then carry'd away, both the Cows and the Sins where-with these Beasts are charged, to what place the Braman shall appoint." When the ancient Egyptians sacrificed a bull, they invoked upon its head all the evils that might otherwise befall themselves and the land of Egypt, and thereupon they either sold the bull's head to the Greeks or cast it into the river. Now, it cannot be said that in the times known to us the Egyptians worshipped bulls in general, for they seem to have commonly killed and eaten them. But a good many circumstances point to the conclusion that originally all cattle, bulls as well as cows, were held sacred by the Egyptians. For not only were all cows esteemed holy by them and never sacrificed, but even bulls might not be sacrificed unless they had certain natural marks; a priest examined every bull before it was sacrificed; if it had the proper marks, he put his seal on the animal in token that it might be sacrificed; and if a man sacrificed a bull which had not been sealed, he was put to death. Moreover, the worship of the black bulls Apis and Mnevis, especially the former, played an important part in Egyptian religion; all bulls that died a natural death were carefully buried in the suburbs of the cities, and their bones were afterwards collected from all parts of Egypt and interred in a single spot; and at the sacrifice of a bull in the great rites of Isis all the worshippers beat their breasts and mourned. On the whole, then, we are perhaps entitled to infer that bulls were originally, as cows were always, esteemed sacred by the Egyptians, and that the slain bull upon whose head they laid the misfortunes of the people was once a divine scapegoat. It seems not improbable that the lamb annually slain by the Madis of Central Africa is a divine scapegoat, and the same supposition may partly explain the Zuni sacrifice of the turtle.

Lastly, the scapegoat may be a divine man. Thus, in November the Gonds of India worship Ghansyam Deo, the protector of the crops, and at the festival the god himself is said to descend on the head of one of the worshippers, who is suddenly seized with a kind of fit and, after staggering about, rushes off into the jungle, where it is believed that, if left to himself, he would die mad. However, they bring him back, but he does not recover his senses for one or two days. The people think that one man is thus singled out as a scapegoat for the sins of the rest of the village. In the temple of the Moon the Albanians of the Eastern Caucasus kept a number of sacred slaves, of whom many were inspired and prophesied. When one of these men exhibited more than usual symptoms of inspiration or insanity, and wandered solitary up and down the woods, like the Gond in the jungle, the high priest had him bound with a sacred chain and maintained him in luxury for a year. At the end of the year he was anointed with unguents and led forth to be sacrificed. A man whose business it was to slay these human victims and to whom practice had given dexterity, advanced from the crowd and thrust a sacred spear into the victim's side, piercing his heart. From the manner in which the slain man fell, omens were drawn as to the welfare of the commonwealth. Then the body was carried to a certain spot where all the people stood upon it as a purificatory ceremony. This last circumstance clearly indicates that the sins of the people were transferred to the victim, just as the Jewish priest transferred the sins of the people to the scapegoat by laying his hands on the animal's head; and since the man was believed to be possessed by the divine spirit, we have here an undoubted example of a man-god slain to take away the sins and misfortunes of the people.

In Tibet the ceremony of the scapegoat presents some remarkable features. The Tibetan new year begins with the new moon which appears about the fifteenth of February. For twenty-three days afterwards the government of Lhasa, the capital, is taken out of the hands of the ordinary rulers and entrusted to the monk of the Debang monastery who offers to pay the highest sum for the privilege. The successful bidder is called the Jalno, and he announces his accession to power in person, going through the streets of Lhasa with a silver stick in his hand. Monks from all the neighbouring monasteries and temples assemble to pay him homage. The Jalno exercises his authority in the most arbitrary manner for his own benefit, as all the fines which he exacts are his by purchase. The profit he makes is about ten times the amount of the purchase money. His men go about the streets in order to discover any conduct on the part of the inhabitants that can be found fault with. Every house in Lhasa is taxed at this time, and the slightest offence is punished with unsparing rigour by fines. This severity of the Jalno drives all working classes out of the city till the twenty-three days are over. But if the laity go out, the clergy come in. All the Buddhist monasteries of the country for miles round about open their gates and disgorge their inmates. All the roads that lead down into Lhasa from the neighbouring mountains are full of monks hurrying to the capital, some on foot, some on horseback, some riding asses or lowing oxen, all carrying their prayer-books and culinary utensils. In such multitudes do they come that the streets and squares of the city are encumbered with their swarms, and incarnadined with their red cloaks. The disorder and confusion are indescribable. Bands of the holy men traverse the streets chanting prayers or uttering wild cries. They meet, they jostle, they quarrel, they fight; bloody noses, black eyes, and broken heads are freely given and received. All day long, too, from before the peep of dawn till after darkness has fallen, these red-cloaked monks hold services in the dim incense-laden air of the great Machindranath temple, the cathedral of Lhasa; and thither they crowd thrice a day to receive their doles of tea and soup and money. The cathedral is a vast building, standing in the centre of the city, and surrounded by bazaars and shops. The idols in it are richly inlaid with gold and precious stones.

Twenty-four days after the Jalno has ceased to have authority, he assumes it again, and for ten days acts in the same arbitrary manner as before. On the first of the ten days the priests again assemble at the cathedral, pray to the gods to prevent sickness and other evils among the people, "and, as a peace-offering, sacrifice one man. The man is not killed purposely, but the ceremony he undergoes often proves fatal. Grain is thrown against his head, and his face is painted half white, half black." Thus grotesquely disguised, and carrying a coat of skin on his arm, he is called the King of the Years, and sits daily in the market-place, where he helps himself to whatever he likes and goes about shaking a black yak's tail over the people, who thus transfer their bad luck to him. On the tenth day, all the troops in Lhasa march to the great temple and form in line before it. The King of the Years is brought forth from the temple and receives small donations from the assembled multitude. He then ridicules the Jalno, saying to him, "What we perceive through the five senses is no illusion. All you teach is untrue," and the like. The Jalno, who represents the Grand Lama for the time being, contests these heretical opinions; the dispute waxes warm, and at last both agree to decide the questions at issue by a cast of the dice, the Jalno offering to change places with the scapegoat should the throw be against him. If the King of the Years wins, much evil is prognosticated; but if the Jalno wins, there is great rejoicing, for it proves that his adversary has been accepted by the gods as a victim to bear all the sins of the people of Lhasa. Fortune, however, always favours the Jalno, who throws sixes with unvarying success, while his opponent turns up only ones. Nor is this so extraordinary as at first sight it might appear; for the Jalno's dice are marked with nothing but sixes and his adversary's with nothing but ones. When he sees the finger of Providence thus plainy pointed against him, the King of the Years is terrified and flees away upon a white horse, with a white dog, a white bird, salt, and so forth, which have all been provided for him by the government. His face is still painted half white and half black, and he still wears his leathern coat. The whole populace pursues him, hooting, yelling, and firing blank shots in volleys after him. Thus driven out of the city, he is detained for seven days in the great chamber of horrors at the Samyas monastery, surrounded by monstrous and terrific images of devils and skins of huge serpents and wild beasts. Thence he goes away into the mountains of Chetang, where he has to remain an outcast for several months or a year in a narrow den. If he dies before the time is out, the people say it is an auspicious omen; but if he survives, he may return to Lhasa and play the part of scapegoat over again the following year.

This quaint ceremonial, still annually observed in the secluded capital of Buddhism—the Rome of Asia—is interesting because it exhibits, in a clearly marked religious stratification, a series of divine redeemers themselves redeemed, of vicarious sacrifices vicariously atoned for, of gods undergoing a process of fossilization, who, while they retain the privileges, have disburdened themselves of the pains and penalties of divinity. In the Jalno we may without undue straining discern a successor of those temporary kings, those mortal gods, who purchase a short lease of power and glory at the price of their lives. That he is the temporary substitute of the Grand Lama is certain; that he is, or was once, liable to act as scapegoat for the people is made nearly certain by his offer to change places with the real scapegoat—the King of the Years—if the arbitrament of the dice should go against him. It is true that the conditions under which the question is now put to the hazard have reduced the offer to an idle form. But such forms are no mere mushroom growths, springing up of themselves in a night. If they are now lifeless formalities, empty husks devoid of significance, we may be sure that they once had a life and a meaning; if at the present day they are blind alleys leading nowhere, we may be certain that in former days they were paths that led somewhere, if only to death. That death was the goal to which of old the Tibetan scapegoat passed after his brief period of licence in the market-place, is a conjecture that has much to commend it. Analogy suggests it; the blank shots fired after him, the statement that the ceremony often proves fatal, the belief that his death is a happy omen, all confirm it. We need not wonder then that the Jalno, after paying so dear to act as deputy-deity for a few weeks, should have preferred to die by deputy rather than in his own person when his time was up. The painful but necessary duty was accordingly laid on some poor devil, some social outcast, some wretch with whom the world had gone hard, who readily agreed to throw away his life at the end of a few days if only he might have his fling in the meantime. For observe that while the time allowed to the original deputy—the Jalno— was measured by weeks, the time allowed to the deputy's deputy was cut down to days, ten days according to one authority, seven days according to another. So short a rope was doubtless thought a long enough tether for so black or sickly a sheep; so few sands in the hour-glass, slipping so fast away, sufficed for one who had wasted so many precious years. Hence in the jack-pudding who now masquerades with motley countenance in the market-place of Lhasa, sweeping up misfortune with a black yak's tail, we may fairly see the substitute of a substitute, the vicar of a vicar, the proxy on whose back the heavy burden was laid when it had been lifted from nobler shoulders. But the clue, if we have followed it aright, does not stop at the Jalno; it leads straight back to the pope of Lhasa himself, the Grand Lama, of whom the Jalno is merely the temporary vicar. The analogy of many customs in many lands points to the conclusion that, if this human divinity stoops to resign his ghostly power for a time into the hands of a substitute, it is, or rather was once, for no other reason than that the substitute might die in his stead. Thus through the mist of ages unillumined by the lamp of history, the tragic figure of the pope of Buddhism—God's vicar on earth for Asia—looms dim and sad as the man-god who bore his people's sorrows, the Good Shepherd who laid down his life for the sheep.

On Scapegoats in General

The foregoing survey of the custom of publicly expelling the accumulated evils of a village or town or country suggests a few general observations.

In the first place, it will not be disputed that what I have called the immediate and the mediate expulsions of evil are identical in intention; in other words, that whether the evils are conceived of as invisible or as embodied in a material form, is a circumstance entirely subordinate to the main object of the ceremony, which is simply to effect a total clearance of all the ills that have been infesting a people. If any link were wanting to connect the two kinds of expulsion, it would be furnished by such a practice as that of sending the evils away in a litter or a boat. For here, on the one hand, the evils are invisible and intangible; and, on the other hand, there is a visible and tangible vehicle to convey them away. And a scapegoat is nothing more than such a vehicle.

In the second place, when a general clearance of evils is resorted to periodically, the interval between the celebrations of the ceremony is commonly a year, and the time of year when the ceremony takes place usually coincides with some well-marked change of season, such as the beginning or end of winter in the arctic and temperate zones, and the beginning or end of the rainy season in the tropics. The increased mortality which such climatic changes are apt to produce, especially amongst ill-fed, ill-clothed, and ill-housed savages, is set down by primitive man to the agency of demons, who must accordingly be expelled. Hence, in the tropical regions of New Britain and Peru, the devils are or were driven out at the beginning of the rainy season; hence, on the dreary coasts of Baffin Land, they are banished at the approach of the bitter arctic winter. When a tribe has taken to husbandry, the time for the general expulsion of devils is naturally made to agree with one of the great epochs of the agricultural year, as sowing, or harvest; but, as these epochs themselves naturally coincide with changes of season, it does not follow that the transition from the hunting or pastoral to the agricultural life involves any alteration in the time of celebrating this great annual rite. Some of the agricultural communities of India and the Hindoo Koosh, as we have seen, hold their general clearance of demons at harvest, others at sowing-time. But, at whatever season of the year it is held, the general expulsion of devils commonly marks the beginning of the new year. For, before entering on a new year, people are anxious to rid themselves of the troubles that have harassed them in the past; hence it comes about that in so many communities the beginning of the new year is inaugurated with a solemn and public banishment of evil spirits.

In the third place, it is to be observed that this public and periodic expulsion of devils is commonly preceded or followed by a period of general license, during which the ordinary restraints of society are thrown aside, and all offences, short of the gravest, are allowed to pass unpunished. In Guinea and Tonquin the period of license precedes the public expulsion of demons; and the suspension of the ordinary government in Lhasa previous to the expulsion of the scapegoat is perhaps a relic of a similar period of universal license. Amongst the Hos of India the period of license follows the expulsion of the devil. Amongst the Iroquois it hardly appears whether it preceded or followed the banishment of evils. In any case, the extraordinary relaxation of all ordinary rules of conduct on such occasions is doubtless to be explained by the general clearance of evils which precedes or follows it. On the one hand, when a general riddance of evil and absolution from all sin is in immediate prospect, men are encouraged to give the rein to their passions, trusting that the coming ceremony will wipe out the score which they are running up so fast. On the other hand, when the ceremony has just taken place, men's minds are freed from the oppressive sense, under which they generally labour, of an atmosphere surcharged with devils; and in the first revulsion of joy they overleap the limits commonly imposed by custom and morality. When the ceremony takes place at harvest-time, the elation of feeling which it excites is further stimulated by the state of physical wellbeing produced by an abundant supply of food.

Fourthly, the employment of a divine man or animal as a scapegoat is especially to be noted; indeed, we are here directly concerned with the custom of banishing evils only in so far as these evils are believed to be transferred to a god who is afterwards slain. It may be suspected that the custom of employing a divine man or animal as a public scapegoat is much more widely diffused than appears from the examples cited. For, as has already been pointed out, the custom of killing a god dates from so early a period of human history that in later ages, even when the custom continues to be practised, it is liable to be misinterpreted. The divine character of the animal or man is forgotten, and he comes to be regarded merely as an ordinary victim. This is especially likely to be the case when it is a divine man who is killed. For when a nation becomes civilized, if it does not drop human sacrifices altogether, it at least selects as victims only such wretches as would be put to death at any rate. Thus the killing of a god may sometimes come to be confounded with the execution of a criminal.

If we ask why a dying god should be chosen to take upon himself and carry away the sins and sorrows of the people, it may be suggested that in the practice of using the divinity as a scapegoat we have a combination of two customs which were at one time distinct and independent. On the one hand we have seen that it has been customary to kill the human or animal god in order to save his divine life from being weakened by the inroads of age. On the other hand we have seen that it has been customary to have a general expulsion of evils and sins once a year. Now, if it occurred to people to combine these two customs, the result would be the employment of the dying god as a scapegoat. He was killed, not originally to take away sin, but to save the divine life from the degeneracy of old age; but, since he had to be killed at any rate, people may have thought that they might as well seize the opportunity to lay upon him the burden of their sufferings and sins, in order that he might bear it away with him to the unknown world beyond the grave.

The use of the divinity as a scapegoat clears up the ambiguity which, as we saw, appears to hang about the European folk-custom of "carrying out Death." Grounds have been shewn for believing that in this ceremony the so-called Death was originally the spirit of vegetation, who was annually slain in spring, in order that he might come to life again with all the vigour of youth. But, as I pointed out, there are certain features in the ceremony which are not explicable on this hypothesis alone. Such are the marks of joy with which the effigy of Death is carried out to be buried or burnt, and the fear and abhorrence of it manifested by the bearers. But these features become at once intelligible if we suppose that the Death was not merely the dying god of vegetation, but also a public scapegoat, upon whom were laid all the evils that had afflicted the people during the past year. Joy on such an occasion is natural and appropriate; and if the dying god appears to be the object of that fear and abhorrence which are properly due not to himself, but to the sins and misfortunes with which he is laden, this arises merely from the difficulty of distinguishing, or at least of marking the distinction, between the bearer and the burden. When the burden is of a baleful character, the bearer of it will be feared and shunned just as much as if he were himself instinct with those dangerous properties of which, as it happens, he is only the vehicle. Similarly we have seen that disease-laden and sin-laden boats are dreaded and shunned by East Indian peoples. Again, the view that in these popular customs the Death is a scapegoat as well as a representative of the divine spirit of vegetation derives some support from the circumstance that its expulsion is always celebrated in spring and chiefly by Slavonic peoples. For the Slavonic year began in spring; and thus, in one of its aspects, the ceremony of "carrying out Death" would be an example of the widespread custom of expelling the accumulated evils of the old year before entering on a new one.

Human Scapegoats in Classical Antiquity

We are now prepared to notice the use of the human scapegoat in classical antiquity. Every year on the fourteenth of March a man clad in skins was led in procession through the streets of Rome, beaten with long white rods, and driven out of the city. He was called Mamurius Veturius, that is, "the old Mars," and as the ceremony took place on the day preceding the first full moon of the old Roman year (which began on the first of March), the skin-clad man must have represented the Mars of the past year, who was driven out at the beginning of a new one. Now Mars was originally not a god of war but of vegetation. For it was to Mars that the Roman husbandman prayed for the prosperity of his corn and his vines, his fruit-trees and his copses; it was to Mars that the priestly college of the Arval Brothers, whose business it was to sacrifice for the growth of the crops, addressed their petitions almost exclusively; and it was to Mars, as we saw, that a horse was sacrificed in October to secure an abundant harvest. Moreover, it was to Mars, under his title of "Mars of the woods" (*Mars Silvanus*), that farmers offered sacrifice for the welfare of their cattle. We have already seen that cattle are commonly supposed to be under the special patronage of tree-gods. Once more, the consecration of the vernal month of March to Mars seems to point him out as the deity of the sprouting vegetation. Thus the Roman custom of expelling the old Mars at the beginning of the new year in spring is identical with the Slavonic custom of "carrying out Death," if the view here taken of the latter custom is correct. The similarity of the Roman and Slavonic customs has been already remarked by scholars, who appear, however, to have taken Mamurius Veturius and the corresponding figures in the Slavonic cere-monies to be representatives of the old year rather than of the old god of vegetation. It is possible that ceremonies of this kind may have come to be thus interpreted in later times even by the people who practised them. But the personification of a period of time is too abstract an idea to be primitive. How-ever, in the Roman, as in the Slavonic, ceremony, the repre-sentative of the god appears to have been treated not only as a deity of vegetation but also as a scapegoat. His expulsion implies this; for there is no reason why the god of vegetation, as such, should be expelled the city. But it is otherwise if he is also a scapegoat; it then becomes necessary to drive him be-yond the boundaries, that he may carry his sorrowful burden away to other lands. And, in fact, Mamurius Veturius appears to have been driven away to the land of the Oscans, the enemies of Rome.

The blows with which the "old Mars" was expelled the city seem to have been administered by the dancing priests of Mars, the Salii. At least we know that in their songs these priests made mention of Mamurius Veturius; and we are told that on a day dedicated to him they beat a hide with rods. It is therefore highly probable that the hide which they drubbed on that day was the one worn by the representative of the deity whose name they simultaneously chanted. Thus on the fourteenth day of March every year Rome witnessed the curious spectacle of the human incarnation of a god chased by the god's own priests with blows from the city. The rite becomes at least intelligible on the theory that the man so beaten and expelled stood for the outworn deity of vegetation, who had to be replaced by a fresh and vigorous young divinity at the beginning of a New Year, when everywhere around in field and meadow, in wood and thicket the vernal flowers, the sprouting grass, and the opening buds and blossoms testified to the stirring of new life in nature after the long torpor and stagnation of winter. The dancing priests of the god derived their name of Salii from the leaps or dances which they were bound to execute as a solemn religious ceremony every year in the Comitium, the centre of Roman political life. Twice a year, in the spring month of March and the autumn month of October, they discharged this sacred duty; and as they did so they invoked Saturn, the Roman god of sowing. As the Romans sowed the corn both in spring and autumn, and as down to the present time in Europe superstitious rustics are wont to dance and leap high in spring for the purpose of making the crops grow high, we may conjecture that the leaps and dances performed by the Salii, the priests of the old Italian god of vegetation, were similarly supposed to quicken the growth of the corn by homoeopathic or imitative magic. The Salii were not limited to Rome; similar colleges of dancing priests are known to have existed in many towns of ancient Italy; everywhere, we may conjecture, they were supposed to contribute to the fertility of the earth by their leaps and dances. At Rome they were divided into two colleges, each composed of twelve members; and it is not impossible that the number twelve was fixed with reference to the twelve months of the old lunar year; the *Fratres Arvales*, or "Brethren of the Ploughed Fields," another Roman college of priests, whose functions were purely agricultural, and who wore as a badge of their office a wreath of corn-ears, were also twelve in number, perhaps for a similar reason. Nor was the martial equipment of the Salii so alien to this peaceful function as a modern reader might naturally suppose. Each of them wore on his head a peaked helmet of bronze, and at his side a sword; on his left arm he carried a shield of a peculiar shape, and in his right hand he wielded a staff with which he smote on the shield till it rang again. Such weapons in priestly hands may be turned against spiritual foes; in the preceding pages we have met with many examples of the use of material arms to rout the host of demons who oppress the imagination of primitive man, and we have seen that the clash and clangour of metal is often deemed particularly effective in putting these baleful beings to flight. May it not have been so with the martial priests of Mars? We know that they paraded the city for days together in a regular order, taking up their quarters for the night at a different place each day; and as they went they danced in triple time, singing and clashing on their shields and taking their time from a fugleman, who skipped and postured at their head. We may conjecture that in so doing they were supposed to be expelling the powers of evil which had accumulated during the preceding year or six months, and which the people pictured to themselves in the form of demons lurking in the houses, temples, and the other edifices of the city. In savage communities such tumultuous and noisy processions often parade the village for a similar purpose. Similarly, we have seen that among the Iroquois men in fantastic costume used to go about collecting the sins of the people as a preliminary to transferring them to the scapegoat dogs; and we have met with many examples of armed men rushing about the streets and houses to drive out demons and evils of all kinds. Why should it not have been so also in ancient Rome? The religion of the old Romans is full of relics of savagery.

If there is any truth in this conjecture, we may suppose that, as priests of a god who manifested his power in the vegetation of spring, the Salii turned their attention above all to the demons of blight and infertility, who might be thought by their maleficent activity to counteract the genial influence of the kindly god and to endanger the farmer's prospects in the coming summer or winter. . . .

The ancient Greeks were also familiar with the use of a human scapegoat. In Plutarch's native town of Chaeronea a ceremony of this kind was performed by the chief magistrate at the Town Hall, and by each householder at his own home. It was called the "expulsion of hunger." A slave was beaten with rods of the *agnus castus*, and turned out of doors with

the words, "Out with hunger, and in with wealth and health."
When Plutarch held the office of chief magistrate of his native
town he performed this ceremony at the Town Hall, and he
has recorded the discussion to which the custom afterwards
gave rise. The ceremony closely resembles the Japanese, Hindoo, and Highland customs already described.

But in civilized Greece the custom of the scapegoat took
darker forms than the innocent rite over which the amiable
and pious Plutarch presided. Whenever Marseilles, one of the
busiest and most brilliant of Greek colonies, was ravaged by
a plague, a man of the poorer classes used to offer himself as
a scapegoat. For a whole year he was maintained at the public
expense, being fed on choice and pure food. At the expiry of
the year he was dressed in sacred garments, decked with holy
branches, and led through the whole city, while prayers were
uttered that all the evils of the people might fall on his head.
He was then cast out of the city or stoned to death by the
people outside of the walls. The Athenians regularly maintained a number of degraded and useless beings at the public
expense; and when any calamity, such as plague, drought, or
famine, befell the city, they sacrificed two of these outcasts as
scapegoats. One of the victims was sacrificed for the men and
the other for the women. The former wore round his neck a
string of black, the latter a string of white figs. Sometimes, it
seems, the victim slain on behalf of the women was a woman.
They were led about the city and then sacrificed, apparently
by being stoned to death outside the city. But such sacrifices
were not confined to extraordinary occasions of public calamity; it appears that every year, at the festival of the
Thargelia in May, two victims, one for the men and one for the
women, were led out of Athens and stoned to death. The city
of Abdera in Thrace was publicly purified once a year, and one
of the burghers, set apart for the purpose, was stoned to death
as a scapegoat or vicarious sacrifice for the life of all the
others; six days before his execution he was excommunicated,
"in order that he alone might bear the sins of all the people."

From the Lover's Leap, a white bluff at the southern end of
their island, the Leucadians used annually to hurl a criminal
into the sea as a scapegoat. But to lighten his fall they fastened live birds and feathers to him, and a flotilla of small
boats waited below to catch him and convey him beyond the

boundary. Probably these humane precautions were a mitiga-
tion of an earlier custom of flinging the scapegoat into the sea
to drown, just as in Kumaon the custom of letting a man slide
down a rope from the top of a cliff appears to be a modifica-
tion of an older practice of putting him to death. The Leu-
cadian ceremony took place at the time of a sacrifice to Apollo,
who had a temple or sanctuary on the spot. Elsewhere it was
customary to cast a young man every year into the sea, with
the prayer, "Be thou our offscouring." This ceremony was
supposed to rid the people of the evils by which they were
beset, or according to a somewhat different interpretation it
redeemed them by paying the debt they owed to the sea-god.
As practised by the Greeks of Asia Minor in the sixth century
before our era, the custom of the scapegoat was as follows.
When a city suffered from plague, famine, or other public
calamity, an ugly or deformed person was chosen to take upon
himself all the evils which afflicted the community. He was
brought to a suitable place, where dried figs, a barley loaf, and
cheese were put into his hand. These he ate. Then he was
beaten seven times upon his genital organs with squills and
branches of the wild fig and other wild trees, while the flutes
played a particular tune. Afterwards he was burned on a pyre
built of the wood of forest trees; and his ashes were cast into
the sea. A similar custom appears to have been annually celebrated by the Asiatic Greeks at the harvest festival of the
Thargelia.

In the ritual just described the scourging of the victim with
squills, branches of the wild fig, and so forth, cannot have
been intended to aggravate his sufferings, otherwise any stick
would have been good enough to beat him with. The true
meaning of this part of the ceremony has been explained by
W. Mannhardt. He points out that the ancients attributed to
squills a magical power of averting evil influences, and that
accordingly they hung them up at the doors of their houses
and made use of them in purificatory rites. Hence the Arcadian
custom of whipping the image of Pan with squills at a festival,
or whenever the hunters returned empty-handed, must have
been meant, not to punish the god, but to purify him from the
harmful influences which were impeding him in the exercise
of his divine functions as a god who should supply the hunter
with game. Similarly the object of beating the human scape-

goat on the genital organs with squills and so on, must have been to release his reproductive energies from any restraint or spell under which they might be laid by demoniacal or other malignant agency; and as the Thargelia at which he was annually sacrificed was an early harvest festival celebrated in May, we must recognize in him a representative of the creative and fertilizing god of vegetation. The representative of the god was annually slain for the purpose I have indicated, that of maintaining the divine life in perpetual vigour, untainted by the weakness of age; and before he was put to death it was not unnatural to stimulate his reproductive powers in order that these might be transmitted in full activity to his successor, the new god or new embodiment of the old god, who was doubtless supposed immediately to take the place of the one slain. Similar reasoning would lead to a similar treatment of the scapegoat on special occasions, such as drought or famine. If the crops did not answer to the expectation of the husbandman, this would be attributed to some failure in the generative powers of the god whose function it was to produce the fruits of the earth. It might be thought that he was under a spell or was growing old and feeble. Accordingly he was slain in the person of his representative, with all the ceremonies already described, in order that, born young again, he might infuse his own youthful vigour into the stagnant energies of nature. On the same principle we can understand why Mamurius Veturius was beaten with rods, why the slave at the Chaeronean ceremony was beaten with the *agnus castus* (a tree to which magical properties were ascribed), why the effigy of Death in some parts of Europe is assailed with sticks and stones, and why at Babylon the criminal who played the god was scourged before he was crucified. The purpose of the scourging was not to intensify the agony of the divine sufferer, but on the contrary to dispel any malignant influences by which at the supreme moment he might conceivably be beset.

Thus far I have assumed that the human victims at the Thargelia represented the spirits of vegetation in general, but it has been well remarked by Mr. W. R. Paton that these poor wretches seem to have masqueraded as the spirits of fig-trees in particular. He points out that the process of caprification, as it is called, that is, the artificial fertilization of the cultivated fig-trees by hanging strings of wild figs among the boughs, takes place in Greece and Asia Minor in June about a month after the date of the Thargelia, and he suggests that the hanging of the black and white figs round the necks of the two human victims, one of whom represented the men and the other the women, may have been a direct imitation of the process of caprification designed, on the principle of imitative magic, to assist the fertilization of the fig-trees. And since caprification is in fact a marriage of the male fig-tree with the female fig-tree, Mr. Paton further supposes that the loves of the trees may, on the same principle of imitative magic, have been simulated by a mock or even a real marriage between the two human victims, one of whom appears sometimes to have been a woman. On this view the practice of beating the human victims on their genitals with branches of wild fig-trees and with squills was a charm intended to stimulate the generative powers of the man and woman who for the time being personated the male and the female fig-trees respectively, and who by their union in marriage, whether real or pretended, were believed to help the trees to bear fruit.

The theory is ingenious and attractive; and to some extent it is borne out by the Roman celebration of the *Nonae Caprotinae*, which I have described in an earlier part of this work. For on the *Nonae Caprotinae*, the ninth of July, the female slaves, in the attire of free women, feasted under a wild fig-tree, cut a rod from the tree, beat each other, perhaps with the rod, and offered the milky juice of the tree to the goddess Juno Caprotina, whose surname seems to point her out as the goddess of the wild fig-tree (*caprificus*). Here the rites performed in July by women under the wild fig-tree, which the ancients rightly regarded as a male and employed to fertilize the cultivated female fig-tree, can hardly be dissociated from the caprification or artificial marriage of the fig-trees which, according to Columella, was best performed in July; and if the blows which the women gave each other on this occasion were administered, as seems highly probable, by the rod which they cut from the wild fig-tree, the parallel between the Roman and the Greek ceremony would be still closer; since the Greeks, as we saw, beat the genitals of the human victims with branches of wild fig-trees. It is true that the human sacrifices, which formed so prominent a feature in the Greek celebration

of the Thargelia, do not figure in the Roman celebration of the
Nonae Caprotinae within historical times; yet a trace of them
may perhaps be detected in the tradition that Romulus himself
mysteriously disappeared on that very day in the midst of a
tremendous thunder-storm, while he was reviewing his army
outside the walls of Rome at the Goat's Marsh (*"ad Caprae
paludem"*), a name which suggests that the place was not far
distant from the wild fig-tree or the goat-fig (*caprificus*), as the
Romans called it, where the slave women performed their
curious ceremonies. The legend that he was cut in pieces by
the patricians, who carried away the morsels of his body
under their robes and buried them in the earth, exactly describes the treatment which the Khonds used to accord to the
bodies of the human victims for the purpose of fertilizing their
fields. Can the king have played at Rome the same fatal part in
the fertilization of fig-trees which, if Mr. Paton is right, was
played in Greece by the male victim? The traditionary time,
place, and manner of his death all suggest it. So many coin-
cidences between the Greek and Roman ceremonies and
traditions can hardly be wholly accidental; and accordingly I
incline to think that there may well be an element of truth in
Mr. Paton's theory, though it must be confessed that the
ancient writers who describe the Greek custom appear to
regard it merely as a purification of the city and not at all as a
mode of fertilizing fig-trees. In similar ceremonies, which combine the elements of purification and fertilization, the notion
of purification apparently tends gradually to overshadow the
notion of fertilization in the minds of those who practise the
rites. It seems to have been so in the case of the annual expulsion of Mamurius Veturius from ancient Rome and in the
parallel processions of the *Perchten* in modern Europe; it may
have been so also in the case of the human sacrifices at the
Thargelia.[3] . . .

---

[3] Mr. Paton ingeniously suggests that in the Biblical narrative of Adam
and Eve, who for eating a particular fruit were condemned to death and
driven out of the happy garden with aprons of fig-leaves about their loins
(Genesis iii.), we have a reminiscence of a custom of fertilizing fig-trees
by a pair of human scapegoats, who, like the victims at the Thargelia,
assimilated themselves to the tree by wearing its foliage or fruit. See
W. R. Paton, "The φαρμακοί and the Story of the Fall," *Revue Arché-
ologique*, iv. Série, ix. (1907) pp. 55 *sq.*

The Day of Atonement
E. O. James

THE ANCIENT SYMBOLISM of the blood as the life was retained (after the Exile), but it was re-evaluated in terms of the teaching of Ezekiel and the Deutero-Isaiah so that the need of atonement was felt to be an act of reconciliation, alike for the nation and the individual. This reached its climax in the rites performed on the tenth day of the seventh month when the annual expiation was made for the temple, the priesthood and the whole congregation of Israel. According to Ezekiel the sanctuary was cleansed ritually twice a year—on the first day of the first month, and on the first day of the seventh month— but no mention of this twofold purification occurs elsewhere in the Old Testament. After the time of Ezra (i.e. *c.* 397 B.C.), when the high priesthood was definitely established and the priestly legislation was in full operation, the Day of Atonement described in Leviticus xvi was instituted. In the present Levitical narrative three observances, or stages in the development of the rite, can be detected. The first, belonging to the middle of the fourth century and recorded in Lev. xvi. 3, 5–10, comprised the priest taking a bullock for a sin-offering to make atonement for himself and the priesthood. A ram was then offered and two he-goats were "set before Yahweh." Upon them lots were cast to determine the goat to be assigned to Yahweh as a sin-offering and the one to be presented to Azazel as a sin-receiver, to carry away the iniquity to the demon of the waste in the wilderness. After Yahweh's victim had been slain, the one selected for Azazel was "set before Yahweh alive" and despatched to the desert.

From *The Nature and Function of Priesthood* by E. O. James. Reprinted by permission of Thames and Hudson Ltd.

In the next stage (11–28) this relatively simple cleansing of the sanctuary was transformed into an elaborate atonement ritual with minute details concerning censings, the manipulation of the blood of the bullock sprinkled on the mercy-seat in the holy of holies and on the altar "to make atonement for the holy place, and because of the uncleanness of the children of Israel." The casting of lots over the victims, if it was practised, is not mentioned, but the transference of the iniquities of the people was effected by the priest laying his hands on the head of the live goat as he confessed all their sins over it to bear them away to a solitary land. The carcasses of the bullock and the goat offered as the sin-offering were taken without the camp to be destroyed by fire, the man performing this task being required to engage in a thorough ablution of himself and of his clothes to remove the defilement before re-entering the community. Finally, (29–34a) a note was added explaining that the Day of Atonement was to be regarded as a "high sabbath," and set apart as a fast to enable the people to "afflict their souls," and to do "no manner of work."

In this very primitive ceremonial the original idea of evil as a substantive pollution removable by the sprinkling of blood, censings and lustrations, together with a sin-carrier in the form of an animal, was prominent. The blood made atonement "by reason of the *nephesh*," or soul-substance, contained in it, liberating it as a life-giving agent and wiping away, or covering up, sin. Moreover, it conferred "holiness" on everything it touched as sanctifying power by virtue of its atoning efficacy. Similarly, the smoke of the incense and the holy water were endowed with the same potency, while the "scapegoat," like the bird in the purification of the leper, was a vehicle for the removal of the pollution transferred to it.

Yet in post-exilic Israel it was Yahweh who alone could release from sin, and his first demand was the offering of a clean heart and a broken spirit, in which sacrifice did not necessarily play an essential part. Only an all-righteous and merciful God could forgive sin and pardon iniquity, and He had no need of the blood of bulls and goats and the ashes of a heifer, inasmuch as He stood over and above the ritual order, however integral the priestly oblation may have been in the religious organization of the community. It was generally supposed that the daily sacrifice expiated unintentional breaches of the Law—the evening oblation removed those committed during the day, and the morning holocausts those of the night—while the Day of Atonement piacular *ex opera operato* removed sins committed with a "high hand," but always on the condition that the offering was accompanied by repentance.

Behind this conception of sin and expiation lay the covenant relationship of Yahweh and Israel. This required an appropriate act of repentance and ceremonial amendment to effect expiation when there had been any departure from the prescribed rule of life, conduct and worship, whether in the sphere of ethics, theology or ritual, made either intentionally or accidentally. The entire action moved on the spiritual plane since it was directed Godwards, and it was sacrificial inasmuch as it presupposed a relationship between a living God and His people established and maintained by the worship at the altar. Sin as the violation of the divine law was an affront to the holiness of God and resulted in an estrangement between the creature and his Creator; the cutting off of the soul from the source of its life. Therefore, any breach committed wittingly or unwittingly had this effect, without respect of its nature and character, or the intentions of the sinner. Animals and inanimate objects like the sanctuary and its vessels, partook of this "uncleanness" and so required the same purification as human beings who ministered at the altar.

This sacredness, in short, was as synonymous as in non-moral holiness and demanded a sin-offering by way of appeasement to restore the covenant relationship and secure release from harmful supernatural influences. But the fact that on the Day of Atonement the goat was laden with *all* the sins of the nation (i.e. ethical as well as ceremonial), and that the Rabbinic doctrine maintained that the rite was efficacious only when it was performed with sincerity of heart and true repentance, suggests that it was more than an act of ritual expiation. The book of Leviticus is a *rituale* rather than a manual of devotion like the Psalms, and in such a work it is the things to be done, set forth in terms of liturgical rubrics, rather than their ethical significance, that are described. Nevertheless, in the Mishna the Day itself was represented as expiating sin, the objective efficacy attributed to the rites being dependent on the use made of them by God Himself. As

His duly appointed divine instruments and dramatic symbols of forgiveness, to neglect them would be equivalent to spurning the atonement offered by the penitent sinner through them. Therefore, the Day was set apart as a Sabbath of great sanctity on which work of every description was absolutely forbidden and a strict fast enjoined. To enable those who could not take part in the observances in the temple at Jerusalem to share in their efficacy, the penitential aspects of the ritual performed by the high-priest in the holy of holies were reproduced in the form of confessions of sin, and in the prayer for forgiveness in the synagogue liturgy. In this way greater emphasis was given to the purification of the heart, and with the destruction of the temple in A.D. 70, the ceremonial expiation necessarily ceased, leaving the symbolic synagogue service as a devout spiritual exercise set against the background of the earlier sacrificial priestly expiation and the piaculum.

The prophetic movement had prepared the way for an ethical conception of repentance independent of ceremonial atonement, but the loss of the scapegoat ritual was keenly felt in Rabbinical circles because it was so intimately related to the need for the expiation of sin, regulated by the belief in the covenant relationship between Yahweh and Israel. It was not that an angry God had to be propitiated by gifts and offerings. That notion had been dispelled by Jeremiah and the eighth-century prophets. Evil, however, remained as a taint that had to be "covered" or "wiped out" if the divine fellowship of the theocracy was to be maintained. With the cessation of the temple and its sacrificial system repentance was left the sole condition of remission of sins, as neither the manipulation of the blood of the victim nor the offices of a scapegoat was available.

The Scapegoat King
Jacob Bronowski

The Scapegoat

The word "scapegoat" is an invention of Tindale's bible; it is not clear that the Old Testament word which it purports to translate is anything but a name. It was the name of one of a pair of sacrificial goats to which the community transferred its sins and so got rid of them. This custom was world-wide; the Jews were unusual only in being content to offer the life of an animal; for in many other places the scapegoat was human. The Athenians kept a reserve of such outcasts, and each spring drew from it one man and one woman and stoned them to death. On the Niger, the two victims were (and may still be) bought with the fines of those who had sinned; on this scale, grave sinners such as thieves and witches paid in 1858 about £2 apiece towards the cost of the human sacrifice. In Siam, the prostitute who was singled out to carry the sins of the community was not killed, but thrown on a dunghill beyond the walls and ever afterwards forbidden the city.

Many of these ceremonies are specific about the victim's sex, and in some of them sex is central to the sacrifice. The Asiatic Greeks began the murder of their human scapegoat to the sound of flutes, by beating him on his genitals with branches of the wild fig. Was this to expiate the universal sin of sex? Or was it to make their trees fertile? The Mexicans each year beheaded a girl at puberty so that her blood might be sprinkled in the temple of the goddess of maize. The

George Braziller, Inc.—from *The Face of Violence* by Jacob Bronowski; reprinted with the permission of the publisher. Copyright © 1955 by George Braziller, Inc.

Whitsun Mummers went dressed in leaves to their mock killing. In all this we catch in part a ritual in which the death of man makes nature fertile. Yet what is being conjured is not all fertility, but the fertility of tended crops: the fig, the maize, the corngod. Nature is being propitiated in order that she may connive at man's first and gravest communal imposition on her, which is the practice of agriculture. The dying man dies for all farming men, and carries all their sins; and the chief of these is the sin of farming itself. The sin is civilization; the scapegoat is less a sinner than a tribute paid to nature. When the Greeks of Asia Minor played the fatal flute tune and bared the victim's sex, their dreadful gestures were a symbol of the perpetual tension between the culture of society and its lush base of animal nature.

The Sin of Authority

In this fight against natural chaos, the guilt of society is that it is a society. The guilt is order, and the guilty are those whose authority imposes order. If the scapegoat is to shoulder this sin, then it is a farce to have him a child or a broken-down prostitute. Only the man of authority can expiate the sin of order. Either he must die himself, or what should be his death must indeed sink to farce.

This is the root from which springs and proliferates the wonderful folklore of doomed kings. Sometimes the king must prepare to die, probably at the hands of his sons, when a frenzy seizes his people; in this mood the people of Sumatra would chant for the death of their king. Sometimes, as in Bengal, the king may be attacked at any time, but may defend himself. Or he may be attacked only after a fixed reign, though even then his defence may be as bloody and ceremonial as at Calicut on the Malabar Coast; there the attacker had to fight his way through 40,000 guards, and never reached the king alive.

These are variants of a classical pattern, which is the ritual death of the king after a fixed reign. Before the seventeenth century, the king of Calicut did not surround himself with guards, but when he had reigned twelve years he held a great feast at the end of which "he saluted his guests, and went on the scaffold, and very decently cut his own throat in the view of the assembly." The ritual was the same in Quilacare in Southern India, where after the feast the king publicly sliced off pieces of his flesh until he had only enough strength hurriedly to cut his throat. I am struck by an echo of this in the story of Oedipus who, though he had seemed to escape the waiting sphinx, ended by putting out his eyes in the act of abdication. And indeed the sin of hubris, which to the Greeks was the tragedy of all kingship, is the pitting of authority against the imperturbable flesh of nature.

There are three strands which run from this theme, of the king who gives order to a state and dies for it. One is the farce at which I have already glanced, in which the king's place is taken by a mock king. When the mock king reigns, he naturally makes a mock of order: this is the second strand, the reign of licence in the saturnalia. The third strand is the terrible pleasure of the city at the death of the king, real or in farce.

The Mock King

If the king is himself to avoid the fate of the scapegoat, then he must make the scapegoat a king. He may really find a royal substitute by killing his heir. There is a Swedish tradition that kings reigned and survived only for nine years; but king Aun killed one of his sons in his place every nine years, until he had killed nine sons. He would have killed the tenth had not the Swedes prevented him and so forced him to die.

More usually the king finds a commoner to play his part. The princes elsewhere in Malabar gave their despotic power outright to a native substitute for five years, and at the end of that time cut off his head and threw it to the populace; whoever caught it succeeded to the post.

Of all such proxy kings and gods, the most famous is the handsome young man whom the Mexicans sacrificed each year at the feast of Toxcatl. He was taught to behave altogether like an Aztec gentleman, and "when this bejewelled exquisite lounged through the streets playing on his flute, puffing at a cigar, and smelling at a nosegay, the people whom he met threw themselves on the earth before him with sighs and tears, taking up the dust in their hands and putting it in their mouths in token of the deepest humiliation and subjection."

Towards the end of his year's reign or godhead he was given four noble wives, and the real king stayed out of sight and ceded the court to him. In the last ritual, the mock king was killed by having his heart torn out and held up to the sun.

Like others, this may be a ritual in which the true king escapes death only by giving up his kingship for a time almost whole. More commonly, the proxy king plays his office as a farce, and in doing so turns all order upside down.

The Fool as King

When once the city can pay for the hubris of civilization, not with the true king's life, but with a false king, it becomes natural to crown for this sad office a sad creature whom no one will mourn. Even the Aztecs chose for their elegant proxy, not one of their own community, but a captive. So all over the world we meet these caricatures of royalty, the boys and the idiots, the dwarfs and the slaves. The gaudy fool at court is such a symbol, whom revengeful nature shall mistake and accept for the king. The depth below depth of irony in *King Lear* flows up from this source, when the king and his fool shelter together from the storm of nature in the hovel of a fake idiot.

Yet these poor half-wit sacrifices must be kings; they must command, be absolute, and hold a state. The divine chaotic anger will not be hoodwinked; unless the fool has all the powers of the king, his death will not pay for the king's life. The Babylonians took a prisoner from the death-cells and made him absolute king, to whom even the royal harem was opened, to turn the social order upside down, for five days. The fool must be allowed a despot's will; and since he is so soon to die, what form shall his will take but a desperate licence?

So the mock king's reign becomes the reign of licence. By one of those spectacular inversions which, in social as in personal psychology, mirror the duality of the human mind, the man who is to die for the unnatural sin of order must be allowed to be king of disorder; and the city happily basks in his short misrule.

The best known of these violent reigns is the Roman saturnalia. Restraint and law were broken; masters waited on slaves; a mock king was chosen and dressed royally; and having pleased his vilest whims, at the end of a week or a month he cut his throat on the altar of Saturn. This is the ancient ritual as it was still practised by Roman soldiers when they garrisoned the Danube. To this day in Bohemia, when the king of the Whitsun revelry is caught, he is scourged with rods and the executioner asks the crowd "Shall I behead this king?" The crowd cries "Behead him!" and there is a mock execution.

The Crown of Thorns

Pontius Pilate also asked "What shall I do then with Jesus?" And the crowd, who had mocked Jesus as king of the Jews and crowned him with thorns, made the ritual answer "Let him be crucified!" Therefore Frazer, from whom my examples are drawn, enquires: Was Jesus king of the saturnalia (or of a Jewish counterpart) in the year of his death?

The question is not rhetorical; long after this, in 303 A.D., a Christian soldier who refused to play the lecherous doomed king in a Roman saturnalia was martyred. And the question suddenly lifts us out of the penny dreadfuls of ceremonial into history. The man who is mocked is a proxy thrown not only to remote nature. He is thrown to human nature; the sphinx that tears is in the crowd.

For the saturnalia was not a slightly improper ceremonial gravely stepped out by a team of gentlemen Morris-dancers. From the Gold Coast to India, among Tibetans and South Sea Islanders and Iroquois, the saturnalia was a real feast of lust. For an instant in the year, crime and violence became a glory; men long cowed by hierarchy worshipped again their own chaotic will; and they mocked happily at the murder of a king. It is reported of the Hos of North East India that they are an unusually reserved and decorous people in family life, but during their saturnalia sons and daughters revile their parents in gross language. This revolt against authority is the heart of the saturnalia everywhere.

There is in this a hidden shift in the tension between authority and natural anarchy. Society is built in the face of natural forces, and for this sin of pride the head of state must pay with his life. When the society pays not in real coin but in counterfeit, the false king remains a symbol of law, and those who watch his public death take pleasure in the humbling of authority. Yet he has been king only of misrule; as a scapegoat, the sins which he carries off are surely the sins of licence, rather than of pride. But the human mind is suppler and more brutal than such pedestrian logic. It pictures, it repeats the sin in the sacrifice. The crucified man is both the symbol and the mock of authority, and if he has been king at an orgy, this proves that the king himself has animal feet. The crowd that cries "Behead him!" in Bohemia, whether at an ancient May mummery or a modern purge, is there to see authority degraded; and part of the process is to show that the man in authority was after all only a poor human creature from the first.

Death as a Spectacle

A film of the Dreyfus case or of some famous surrender dwells with poker-faced pomp on the long ritual of humiliation: the stripping of insignia, the handing over or breaking of swords, and everything which symbolizes that those who were once powerful are now spat upon. This is the spectacle for which the sphinx prowls the roofs. There have been psychologists who have held that laughter has no other source than the fall of the dignified. Every spectacle has an element of this: Mr. Punch and the circus clown, and the hero of Greek tragedy and the dying gladiator alike give to those who watch their defeat a stab of shameful pleasure in the collapse of human dignity.

Let me quote a modern sociologist, Gunnar Myrdal:

> Any rumour of a scandal around a person in public life, however unjust or incredible, any degradation of a high endeavour, is eagerly imbibed by the public. As most people are educated and as they are living in the constant experience of frustration, they seek lust in indulging in what is shabby, weak and insufficient in their neighbours. The masochistic character of this urge is revealed in the fact that it is specifically directed against their own leaders and their own innermost ideals.

Behind the professional language, the insight is trenchant. These are the feelings on which the Sunday papers and the sexy comic strips batten. They delight above all in a long public trial, in which the victim is pushed day by day from the temple to the ditch, as the Mexicans used to roll him down the altar steps. The trials of Oscar Wilde and of Alger Hiss and Radek are plain instances.

In the most spectacular of these trials, there is a special horror in the victim's self-abasement. He accuses himself: he testifies that his authority was always an abuse. Zinoviev and Petkov, Clementis and Slansky and who next, beat their breasts in an endless procession like the conjured kings in *Macbeth*. More, the dramatic prosecutor at one trial accuses himself as dramatically at the next; so Yagoda in Russia and Kostov in Bulgaria went to their deaths reviling themselves. And if the juror asks, how could these masters of misrule deceive me so long? his silent answer is that all rule is misrule.

To recant, to be abject and yet to suffer was the sequence at the inquisition against heresy and the trials for witchcraft. Now in the fall of the great, the crowd has the same gleam of a darker vision, when the man burning at the stake collapses to an animal. The Nazis liked to please and to threaten their mob with this glimpse of the tortured man. They took pleasure in making animals of the torturer and the victim together, until the victim was willing to buy his life at the price of becoming an executioner. This was how the Ghetto of Warsaw was decimated and how the concentration camps were run. What men in revolt against their manhood can make of man was told at the trial of Joseph Wiener in May, 1948, at Malines in Belgium. Wiener, after long suffering in Austrian camps, had been brought by the Germans to the camp at Breendonck in Belgium during the war. By that time he was quite mad, and was treated by the German guards as their private clown. He was put in charge of the camp pigs. Hungry prisoners tried to steal garbage from his pigs, and Wiener informed against the men. This was the crime for which he now stood before the court at Malines. The court tried to reason with him, for Wiener had once been Professor of International Law at the University of Vienna. When he heard the court, the crazed man had among his mutterings one lucid moment. He spoke a sentence of four words: "Nemo repente fuit turpissimus." The quotation is from Juvenal: The depths of depravity are not reached in one step.

The Scapegoat Psychology

Erich Neumann

. . . THIS GUILT-FEELING based on the existence of the shadow is discharged from the system in the same way by both the individual and the collective—that is to say, by the phenomenon of the *projection of the shadow*. The shadow, which is in conflict with the acknowledged values, cannot be accepted as a negative part of one's own psyche and is therefore projected—that is, it is transferred to the outside world and experienced as an outside object. It is combated, punished, and exterminated as "the alien out there" instead of being dealt with as "one's own inner problem."

The way in which the old ethic provides for the elimination of these feelings of guilt and the discharge of the excluded negative forces is in fact one of the gravest perils confronting mankind. What we have in mind here is that classic psychological expedient—the institution of a scapegoat. This technique for attempting a solution of the problem is to be found wherever human society exists.[1] It is, however, best known as a ritual in Judaism. Here the purification of the collective was carried out by solemnly heaping all impurity and evil upon the head of the scapegoat, which was then sent away into exile in the wilderness—to Azazel.[2]

The unconscious psychic conflicts of groups and masses

[1] Cf. *The Golden Bough*, by J. G. Frazer.
[2] Lev. 16:8 (R.S.V.)—(*Trans*).

find their most spectacular outlets in epidemic eruptions such as wars and revolutions, in which the unconscious forces which have accumulated in the collective get the upper hand and "make history." The *scapegoat psychology* is in fact an example of an early, though still inadequate, attempt to deal with these unconscious conflicts. This psychology shapes the inner life of nations just as much as it does their international relationships. Often the outbreak of mass epidemics and the scapegoat psychology are interconnected psychological reactions which stem from a single unconscious conflict. From the point of view of the final outcome, it is a matter of comparative indifference whether the conflict in question was not yet ripe for consciousness or whether it was one which had been previously repressed.

On the primitive level, where the consciousness of the individuals who make up the collective is still relatively weak, progress in the direction of the values necessary to society can be achieved in no other way than by the external projection of the shadow. At this stage, evil can only be made conscious by being solemnly paraded before the eyes of the populace and then ceremonially destroyed. The effect of purification is achieved precisely by the process of making evil conscious through making it visible and by liberating the unconscious from this content through projection. On this level, therefore, evil, though not recognised by the individual as his own, is nevertheless recognised as evil. To put it more accurately, evil is recognised as belonging to the collective structure of one's own tribe and is eliminated in a collective manner—for example by the High Priest transferring the sins of the people to the scapegoat as a vicarious sacrifice.

A purification of this kind will retain its psychological validity so long as the collective still feels identified with the vicarious sacrifice and is genuinely moved by it—so long, that is, as the immolation of the victim has not been debased to the status of a mere spectacle.

At this stage, the scapegoat psychology is still dominated by ethics at their most primitive level—that is, by group responsibility and group identity. It is true that in Judaism at a later date the individual is also involved as such in the purification by the confession of his sins and is in this way made aware of the existence of his shadow side. Even at that stage, however, the confession is not individual, but is born out of the spirit of collective responsibility, since each individual castigates himself for the sins of the collective and proclaims, "*We* have sinned, we have betrayed," etc.

For primitive man—and the mass man in every nation reacts, as we know, like a primitive man—evil cannot be acknowledged as "his own evil" at all, since consciousness is still too weakly developed to be able to deal with the resulting conflict. It is for this reason that evil is invariably experienced by mass man as something alien, and the victims of shadow projection are therefore, always and everywhere, the aliens.

Inside a nation, the aliens who provide the objects for this projection are the minorities; if these are of a different racial or ethnological complexion or, better still, of a different colour, their suitability for this purpose is particularly obvious. This psychological problem of the minorities is to be found with religious, national, racial and social variations; it is, however, symptomatic, in every case, of a split in the structure of the collective psyche. The role of the alien which was played in former times by prisoners of war or shipwrecked mariners is now being played by the Chinese, the Negroes, and the Jews. The same principle governs the treatment of religious minorities in all religions; and the Fascist plays the same part in a Communist society as the Communist in a Fascist society.

In the economy of the psyche, the outcast role of the alien is immensely important as an object for the projection of the shadow. The shadow—that part of our personality which is "alien" to the ego, our own unconscious counter-position, which is subversive of our conscious attitude and security— can be exteriorised and subsequently destroyed. The fight against heretics, political opponents and national enemies is actually the fight against our own religious doubts, the insecurity of our own political position, and the one-sidedness of our own national viewpoint.

It will continue to be necessary for the collective to liberate itself by exploiting the psychology of the scapegoat so long as there are unconscious feelings of guilt which arise, as a splitting phenomenon, from the formation of the shadow. It is our subliminal awareness that we are actually not good enough for the ideal values which have been set before us that results in the formation of the shadow; at the same time, however, it also leads to an unconscious feeling of guilt and to inner insecurity, since the shadow confutes the ego's pipe-dream that it is identical with the ideal values.

It follows that any kind of situation which is calculated to inspire us with confidence that our life is really in harmony with these values will be sought after and exploited. But the simplest way of achieving this object is to exterminate the shadow in the figure of the scapegoat.

The second class of people who play the part of victims in the scapegoat psychology are the "ethically inferior"—that is to say, those persons who fail to live up to the absolute values of the collective and who are also incapable of achieving ethical adaptation by the formation of a "façade personality." The ethically inferior (who include psychopaths and other pathological and atavistic persons, and in effect all those who belong psychologically to an earlier period in the evolution of mankind) are branded, punished and executed by the law and its officers. That at all events is what happens when it is not possible for this class of people to be made use of by the collective. In wartime, on the other hand, they are eagerly exploited.

This class, too, is treated as alien and exterminated as a foreign body, since that is the most spectacular way of bringing home to the collective its own otherness and difference from evil. The solemnity with which the extermination of evil is carried out by the collective is derived from the original collective significance which the sacrifice of the scapegoat actually possessed on the primitive level. The representatives of Church and State take part in the execution of judgement on the unfortunate victims of the scapegoat psychology in the fullest pride of a "good conscience"; and the relief felt by both individual and collective at the elimination of the "evil out there" is palpable in every case.

That these two classes of scapegoat victims are interchangeable—that not only is the evil man experienced as alien but that the alien, in his turn, is experienced as evil—is one of the basic facts of human psychology. It is a leitmotif which can be traced uninterruptedly from the psychology of primitives right down to the policy towards aliens of contemporary, so-called civilised states.

There is yet a third class of persons who are singled out to be victims by the scapegoat psychology—though they stand in the sharpest possible contrast to the class of the morally inferior which we have just described. This third class of victims consists of personalities who are actually superior—for example, leaders and men of genius. Many social customs provide illustrations of the primitive tendency to make a ritual, vicarious sacrifice of the best and most outstanding personality and to exploit him as a scapegoat for the expiation of the sins of one's own collective. This is probably the connecting link between the totemistic vestiges which Freud misunderstood as "patricide," the ritual murder of the king in the earliest days of human history and the doctrine of the sacrificial death of the suffering god.

There are two interconnected motifs here. The representative capacity of the outstanding personality also qualifies him to serve as a representative sacrifice on behalf of the collective before the face of "the Powers." At the same time, however, from the collective's point of view, the outstanding personality is regarded once again as an alien element. The occupants of marginal positions—whether they are inferior personalities who fall below the collective average or superior personalities who have the temerity to rise above it—are sacrificed by the masses, whose basic indolence makes them unwilling to budge from their own position at the centre.

Normally, the history of the so-called civilised nations is also characterised by the sacrifice of certain outstanding individuals, though these are in fact the concentrated fulcra of power by whose action history itself is carried forwards. Socrates, Jesus and Galileo were alike members of this unending series. All nations and all periods of time have contributed to this scapegoat sacrifice of the outstanding, even if the ritual is nowadays no longer conscious but unconscious—a somewhat doubtful piece of progress.

Whether this reaction is the revenge taken by the collective for the exacting and in fact excessive cultural demands made on it by the outstanding personality is a question which we cannot examine here. It is, however, essential to realise that the unconscious shadow element from which the collective is attempting to liberate itself with the aid of the scapegoat psychology has its fling once again in the very cruelty which accompanies the sacrifice of the scapegoat—though the collective remains unconscious of this relationship. True to the basic principle of the scapegoat psychology, the conscious mind believes itself to be identical with the higher values and commits the most appalling atrocities in the sublime self-assurance of an "absolutely clear conscience." All wars (and in particular, all wars of religion), all class wars and all party conflicts provide examples of this coexistence between a good conscience in the conscious mind and a breakthrough of the shadow on the level of action.

We must distinguish here between two classes of persons— the suppressors of the shadow side, who combine an ascetic and heroic attitude to life with a conscious feeling of guilt and with suffering, and the repressors, in whom both the feelings of guilt and the suffering caused by them remain unconscious.

In both classes we find, as a consequence of the denial of the negative, an unconscious reinforcement of the negative in practice to the point of sadism and a bestial lust for destruction. The difference between them is simply this: in the ascetic class, the sadism is nearer to consciousness and assumes a rationalised and systematic form, whereas in the repressive class, the masses, it is of the wildest emotionality and overwhelms consciousness.

Puritanism and the Inquisition, the legalistic Judaism of the Pharisees and the parade-ground discipline of the Prussian mentality are all subject to the same psychological law. The severity of the ascetic attitude is compensated by an aggressive sadism which finds its outlet in the institutions controlled by the leading ascetics.

A group which is psychologically split by being consciously identified with ethical values and at the same time unconscious of its shadow will display, in addition to unconscious feelings of guilt, a psychological sense of insecurity which is a compensation for the self-righteousness of its conscious attitude. Repression will have to be continually on the defensive against a dawning apperception of the shadow side, since the unconscious reinforcement of the shadow will make it increasingly difficult for the ego and the conscious mind not to become aware of its existence at some point in the process.

The inner split caused by this apperception of the shadow will then lead to an unconscious feeling of inferiority and to reactions of the kind discovered by Alfred Adler. The feeling of inferiority will be over-compensated by a tendency to exaggerated self-vindication and will culminate in a reinforcement of the repression. The projection of the shadow will now become systematised, and the final result will be the paranoid reactions of individuals and whole nations, whose own repressed aggressive tendencies reappear in the shape of fear of persecution at the hands of other people and of the world at large. Slogans such as the policy of encirclement, the conspiracy of the Elders of Zion, the white, black or yellow peril, the drive for world domination of capitalism or Bolshevism, etc., and all paranoid systems of this kind serve only one purpose—to repress the aggression and the shadow side of their originators.

Within the collective, this type of self-righteousness found expression in traditional methods of education and penal justice. Here too we meet the compromise of the scapegoat psychology, which under the pretext of ethical conduct allows its own shadow to have its fling by inflicting punishment, torture or deterrence. Appalling scope for the operations of the archetypal shadow is in fact provided, in varying degrees, by such institutional expressions of the ethical collective as executions, sentences of hard labour, prisons and penal establishments of every kind, probation—and even school and family life. All law which is based on punishment, that is to say, not on the knowledge that the collective itself is a party to the guilt of every evil-doer, is nothing but lynch law, under another name.

The institutional form of the scapegoat psychology is used by the task-masters of the old ethic (that is, by the ruling ascetics) primarily as an instrument of culture and civilisation; its emotional side, on the other hand, plays a far more significant and indeed catastrophic role in human history. The institutions of the scapegoat psychology no longer possess their original orgiastic character, which made it possible for them in former times to redeem the collective from its shadow problem by such devices as the holding of a ritual execution in the presence of the whole tribe. In these circumstances, there is an urgent and redoubled need for the collective to liberate itself from the aggressive drives which have accumulated within its bosom by some form of violent and explosive discharge; in this way, at least some transient relief can be obtained from the tension caused by these dammed-up energies. The resultant outbursts, which partake of the character of mass epidemics, wreak their fury on the scapegoat classes in the collective. At the same time, however, that basic phenomenon of the scapegoat psychology which we have described as the projection of the shadow also plays a decisive part in the international disputes between collectives which are known as wars.

No war can be waged unless the enemy can be converted into the carrier of a shadow projection; and the lust and joy of warlike conflict, without which no human being can be induced actually to fight in a war, is derived from the satisfaction of the unconscious shadow side. Wars are the correlative of the old ethic, and warfare is the visible expression of the breakthrough of the unconscious shadow side of the collective.

We find the same psychological constellation at work here as in the case of the individual. Any nation which is possessed by the inflation of a good conscience "knows" itself to be identical with the highest values of humanity; in fact, it identifies itself with these values and prays with a good conscience to "its God," as the undiluted quintessence of the light side, who is of course in duty bound to award it the victory. But this inflation by the good conscience is not in the slightest degree disturbed by the acting out of a bestial shadow.[3]

This split between the world of ethical values in the conscious mind and a value-negating, anti-ethical world in the unconscious which has to be suppressed or repressed generates guilt feelings in the human psyche and accumulations of blocked energies in the unconscious. Naturally, these are now hostile to the conscious attitude, and when they finally burst their dams they are capable of transforming the course of human history into an unprecedented orgy of destruction.

The old ethic must be held responsible not only for the

---

[3] Today, it is true, certain differences may already be discernible between the nations; the total bestial unconsciousness of repression may in fact coexist with a somewhat greater degree of awareness, which recognises the negative element in destruction as negative and accepts it with a new kind of moral responsibility.

denial of the shadow side but also for the creation of the resultant split, the healing of which is now of crucial importance for the future of humanity. The further progress of mankind will in fact depend, to no small degree, on whether it proves possible to prevent the occurrence of this splitting process in the collective psyche.

Issues for Discussion

The following questions can serve as a check on the accuracy and comprehension of the individual's reading, alerting him to central points he may have overlooked or insufficiently understood. In addition, they may aid both students and instructors in comparing, relating, contrasting, and drawing conclusions from the important and illuminating aspects of the material. The questions are intended to be suggestive only; each should generate additional issues for discussion and writing assignments that are here left largely implicit.

1. What is the principle or explanation of vicarious suffering upon which the savage operates?

2. Frazer equates suffering with "a low level of social and intellectual culture." Does this seem a historically valid equation? What evidence would you point to that it is not? Do you think this view of Frazer's is meant ironically? If so, what is the point of this irony?

3. Why is the scapegoat expelled? In most cases when does this occur? Does it differ as to times of the year in different cultures? What reasons can you think of that would explain these differences?

4. What are the different forms taken by the scapegoat? What explanations do you see for their variety? Why do you think more than one kind of scapegoat is used in certain ceremonies and cultures?

5. What is the cultural function of the scapegoat ritual? Is this different from its psychological role? Are they related?

6. What are the major modes of scapegoat ritual? That is, what sorts of practices are observed?

7. What part does chance play in selecting the scapegoat? What other means are used? What is the significance of physical appearance and wealth as factors in the selection?

8. Does Frazer think that scapegoat rituals were originally occasional or periodic? Why does he think they follow this pattern of development?

9. What kinds of response by society precede or follow the scapegoat ritual proper?

10. Can a general ritual pattern of the scapegoat be formulated? What flaws do you see in this method? In this connection you might wish to consult Joseph Campbell's *The Hero with a Thousand Faces*.

11. What do you think the main stages in such a pattern would be?

12. What are the reasons for making divine as well as ordinary creatures scapegoats?

13. Do we find scapegoat rituals occurring in civilized nations of the past? Of the present? What differences are there in the respective ritual forms and in their place in society?

14. What was the original reason for the sacrifice of the dying god? Why was he transformed into a scapegoat? What flaws do you find in Frazer's theory of this transformation? Does he recognize any himself? What do they consist of?

15. What parallels strike you between human scapegoats and Christ's crucifixion? What significance can be attributed to them? What possible explanations for the parallels might be offered? Do the explanations have radically differing implications?

16. How do the acts of atonement differ for the individual and the nation? Give Biblical examples of the difference.

17. Chart the ritual patterns of atonement discussed by Frazer and James. Note their specific differences.

18. What differences does James suggest exist between Leviticus and the Psalms? How does the significance of the Psalms complement that of Leviticus? How does this differ from the primitive and classical attitudes and emphases?

19. Does the sex of the human scapegoats figure in the ritual? In what ways? Give examples drawn from your reading. What significance do you see in this?

20. Why is a man of authority selected as a scapegoat? How does the selection of such persons as scapegoats differ in modern times from those of ancient days?

21. Bronowski emphasizes the scapegoat figure as society's response to the problem of authority. What are the three elements he distinguishes that stem from the Greek concern with *hubris* as the tragedy of kingship?

22. What purpose is served by the mock king as scapegoat? What examples of this does Bronowski discuss?

23. When is the fool made a ritual king? What specific form does his reign take? What historical examples illustrate this figure?

24. Does the Crucifixion involve a mock king or a fool as king? What part does the crown of thorns play in the ritual? What connections does Frazer note between the Crucifixion and ancient Jewish rituals? How emphatic is he about this? Does the case seem valid to you?

25. Frazer describes the ritual "Carrying out of Death" as the expulsion of the accumulated evils of the old year. What significance do you see in the use of such an abstraction or personification as a scapegoat image?

26. Bronowski regards the modern inclination to treat death-as-a-spectacle as a form of violence. What specific examples does he provide? What connections do these situations have with Frazer's discussion of the Carrying out of Death?

PART TWO

The Scapegoat
in Literature

Euripides

Aeschylus, Sophocles, and Euripides were the three great authors of classical Greek tragedy. Euripides (*c.* 485–406 B.C.) was the latest, though he died a year before Sophocles. Although little is known about his life, it is clear that he provoked the civil authorities by the views expressed in his plays, for he went into exile in support of his intellectual positions. This action is perhaps the most important aspect of Euripides's life apart from his playwriting. It indicates the central characteristic of his role in his age. As a member of the Sophist movement, he was a relentless questioner of the accepted ideas and opinions of his time, especially those bearing on ethics and theology. This is significant because, according to the mores of that period, Greek citizens were duty-bound to support the established religious cults. To fail to do so or to endeavor to change them markedly was regarded as impious and treated as a legal offense. Some sophists were actually accused of atheism, which for Greeks was a more serious matter and at the same time a less sweeping one than it is today. Atheism was regarded as a threat not only to religious reality but also to political stability. The term itself, however, implied no more than an extended rational doubt as to whether particular deities were actually gods or not.

Since more plays by Euripides (almost twenty in all) survive than by Aeschylus and Sophocles put together, we are able to see a greater range of technique and theme or subject matter. With regard to construction, Euripides veers from one extreme to the other. His plays range from a taut, controlled artistry that rivals Sophocles, to the most casually organized sequence of scenes. In this and several other ways, he testifies to the irksomeness of the traditional dramatic conventions and to his desire for modes more viable for the age. One of *the most important signs of this impatience is his treatment of the chorus, which from earliest times had been a distinctive feature of Greek tragedy, occupying a central dramatic position as it does in Aeschylus. With Euripides, the chorus became less important, providing eloquent lyrics between dramatic episodes, forming a backdrop of concerned spectators, and inadvertently clogging the flow of action. Yet not all of Euripides's dramatic innovations are negative by any means. His use of extended rhetorical debates between opposing major characters reveals his concern for the dramatic possibilities of thought. It also indicates his profound curiosity about the human mind, its responses to the strongest of emotional impulses, and its capacity to rationalize and therefore persuasively disguise these impulses. He also shows considerable skill in shaping protracted and intricate speeches by messengers explaining events not witnessed on stage. In this, he was coping with the Greek theater's lack of a curtain and backdrops, which today make for quick set changes and realistic staging.*

Although some of the dramatic conventions of Greek tragedy have been touched on, there are others of almost equal or greater significance. Perhaps the most important of these, especially as a problem for Euripides, was the fact that, so far as we can tell, tragedy originated with a religious festival—the festival of Dionysus. It is likely that in pre-Greek days myths about the gods were acted out by human participants. Though evidence of such origins is scanty and uncertain, legends and myths of an ancient order are clearly embedded in the plots and actions of Greek tragedies. Thus, for Euripides ambivalence was built into his role as a playwright. He could not accept the religious and mythical world with the veneration Aeschylus afforded it. At the same time, he was aware of the profound mysteries of human nature and the physical universe. He knew they contained forces both at odds with and unconquerable by rationality. Nowhere is his solution to the challenge inherent in the traditions of Greek tragedy more clearly or dramatically rendered than in
The Bacchae.

Extended treatments of the origins, conventions, and staging of Greek drama are: A. E. Haigh and A. W. Pickard-Cambridge,
The Attic Theater *(1907); R. C. Flickinger,* The Greek Theater

and Its Drama *(1936); M. Bieber,* The History of the Greek and Roman Theater *(1939); A. W. Pickard-Cambridge,* Dithyramb, Tragedy and Comedy, *2nd ed. (1962); and P. D. Arnott,* An Introduction to the Greek Theater *(1959). General considerations of Euripides most of which also deal specifically with* The Bacchae *are: Gilbert Murray,* Euripides and His Age *(1913); G. Norwood,* Greek Tragedy *(1928) and* Essays on Euripidean Drama *(1954); H. D. F. Kitto,* Greek Tragedy: A Literary Study *(1939); G. M. A. Grube,* The Drama of Euripides *(1941); G. Verrall,* The Bacchants of Euripides *(1910); D. J. Conacher,* Euripidean Drama *(1967); T. B. L. Webster,* The Tragedies of Euripides *(1967); L. H. G. Greenwood,* Aspects of Euripidean Tragedy *(1953); T. G. Rosenmeyer,* The Masks of Tragedy *(1963); R. P. Winnington-Ingram,* Euripides and Dionysus *(1948); and R. Y. Hathorn,* Tragedy, Myth and Mystery *(1962).*

The Bacchae

Euripides

Translated by Philip Vellacott

CHARACTERS

DIONYSUS
CHORUS *of Oriental women, devotees of Dionysus*
TEIRESIAS, *a blind Seer*
CADMUS, *founder of Thebes, and formerly king*
PENTHEUS, *his grandson, now king of Thebes*
A GUARD *attending Pentheus*
A HERDSMAN
A MESSENGER
AGAUË, *daughter of Cadmus and mother of Pentheus*

Scene: Before the palace of Pentheus in Thebes. At one side of the stage is the monument of Semele; above it burns a low flame, and around it are the remains of ruined and blackened masonry.

DIONYSUS *enters on stage right. He has a crown of ivy, a thyrsus in his hand, and a fawnskin draped over his body. He has long flowing hair and a youthful, almost feminine beauty.*

DIONYSUS: I am Dionysus, son of Zeus. My mother was Semele, daughter of Cadmus; I was delivered from her womb by

Euripides: *The Bacchae*, from *The Bacchae and Other Plays* translated by Philip Vellacott. Copyright © Philip Vellacott, 1954. Reprinted by permission of Penguin Books, Ltd., Harmondsworth.

the fire of a lightning-flash. To-day I have laid aside the appearance of a god, and have come disguised as a mortal man to this city of Thebes, where flow the two rivers, Dirce and Ismenus. Here by the palace I see the monument recording my mother's death by lightning; here are the smouldering ruins of her house, which bear the still living flame of Zeus's fire—the undying token of Hera's cruelty to my mother. Cadmus does well to keep this ground untrodden, a precinct consecrated to his daughter; and I now have decked it round with sprays of young vine-leaves.

From the fields of Lydia and Phrygia, fertile in gold, I came to the sun-beaten Persian plains, the walled towns of Bactria, harsh Media, wealthy Arabia, and the whole of that Asian sea-board where Greeks and Orientals live side by side in crowded magnificent cities; and before reaching this, the first city of Hellas I have seen, I had already, in all those regions of the East, danced my dance and established my ritual, to make my godhead manifest to mortal men.

And the reason why Thebes is the first place in Hellas where, at my command, women have raised the Bacchic shout, put on the fawnskin cloak, and taken my weapon in their hands, the thyrsus[1] wreathed with ivy—the reason is this: my mother's sisters said—what they should have been the last to say—that I, Dionysus, was not the progeny of Zeus; but that Semele, being with child by some mortal, at her father's suggestion ascribed to Zeus the loss of her virginity; and they loudly insisted that this lie about the fatherhood of her child was the sin for which Zeus had struck her dead.

Therefore I have plagued these same sisters with madness, and driven them all frantic out of doors; now their home is the mountains, and their wits are gone. And I made them carry the emblems of my mysteries; and the whole female population of Thebes, every woman there was in the town, I drove raving from their homes; now they have joined the

---

[1] Thyrsus: a light stick of reed or fennel, with fresh strands of ivy twined round it. It was carried by every devotee of Dionysus; and the action of the play illustrates the supernatural power that was held to reside in it.

daughters of Cadmus, and there they are, sitting roofless on the rocks under the silver fir-trees. Thebes must learn, unwilling though she is, that my Bacchic revels are something beyond her present knowledge and understanding; and I must vindicate the honour of my mother Semele, by manifesting myself before the human race as the god whom she bore to Zeus.

Now Cadmus has handed over his kingly honours and his throne to his daughter's son Pentheus. And this Pentheus is a fighter against God—he defies me, excludes me from libations, never names me in prayer. Therefore I will demonstrate to him, and to all Thebes, that I am a god.

When I have set all in order here, I will pass on to some other place, and manifest myself. Meanwhile, if the Theban city in anger tries to bring the Bacchae home from the mountains by force, I will join that army of women possessed and lead them to battle. And this is why I have changed my divine form to human, and appear in the likeness of a man.

Come, my holy band of revellers, women I have brought from lands of the East, from the slopes of Tmolus, bastion of Lydia, to be with me and share my travels! Raise the music of your Phrygian home, the timbrels invented by Rhea the Great Mother and by me; surround the palace of Pentheus and strike up such a peal of sound as shall make Thebes turn to look! I will go to the glens of Cithaeron where my Bacchae are, and join their dances.

DIONYSUS *goes out towards the mountain; the* CHORUS *enter where* DIONYSUS *entered, from the road by which they have travelled.*

CHORUS:

> From far-off lands of Asia,   [*Strophe 1*
> From Tmolus the holy mountain,
> We run with the god of laughter;
> Labour is joy and weariness is sweet,
> And our song resounds to Bacchus!

> Beware of the interloper!   [*Antistrophe 1*
> Indoors or out, who listens?
> Let every lip be holy;

Stand well aloof, be silent, while we sing
The appointed hymn to Bacchus!

Blest is the happy man   [*Strophe 2*
Who knows the mysteries the gods ordain,
And sanctifies his life,
Joins soul with soul in mystic unity,
And, by due ritual made pure,
Enters the ecstasy of mountain solitudes;
Who observes the mystic rites
Made lawful by Cybele the Great Mother;
Who crowns his head with ivy,
And shakes aloft his wand in worship of Dionysus.

On, on! Run, dance, delirious, possessed!
Dionysus comes to his own;
Bring from the Phrygian hills to the broad streets of Hellas
The god, child of a god,
Spirit of revel and rapture, Dionysus!

Once, on the womb that held him   [*Antistrophe 2*
The fire-bolt flew from the hand of Zeus;
And pains of child-birth bound his mother fast,
And she cast him forth untimely,
And under the lightning's lash relinquished life;
And Zeus the son of Cronos
Ensconced him instantly in a secret womb
Chambered within his thigh,
And with golden pins closed him from Hera's sight.

So, when the Fates had made him ripe for birth,
Zeus bore the bull-horned god
And wreathed his head with wreaths of writhing snakes;
Which is why the Maenads catch
Wild snakes, nurse them and twine them round their hair.

O Thebes, old nurse that cradled Semele,   [*Strophe 3*
Be ivy-garlanded, burst into flower
With wreaths of lush bright-berried bryony,
Bring sprays of fir, green branches torn from oaks,
Fill soul and flesh with Bacchus' mystic power;

Fringe and bedeck your dappled fawnskin cloaks
With woolly tufts and locks of purest white.
There's a brute wildness in the fennel-wands—
Reverence it well. Soon the whole land will dance
    When the god with ecstatic shout
    Leads his companies out
    To the mountain's mounting height
    Swarming with riotous bands
    Of Theban women leaving
    Their spinning and their weaving
    Stung with the maddening trance
      Of Dionysus!

O secret chamber the Curetes knew!   [*Antistrophe 3*
O holy cavern in the Cretan glade
Where Zeus was cradled, where for our delight
The triple-crested Corybantes drew
Tight the round drum-skin, till its wild beat made
Rapturous rhythm to the breathing sweetness
Of Phrygian flutes! Then divine Rhea found
The drum could give her Bacchic airs completeness;
    From her, the Mother of all,
    The crazy Satyrs soon,
    In their dancing festival
    When the second year comes round,
    Seized on the timbrel's tune
    To play the leading part
    In feasts that delight the heart
      Of Dionysus.

O what delight is in the mountains!   [*Epode*
There the celebrant,[2] wrapped in his sacred fawnskin,
Flings himself on the ground surrendered,
While the swift-footed company streams on;
There he hunts for blood, and rapturously
Eats the raw flesh of the slaughtered goat,

---

[2] The celebrant: Dionysus and the Chorus comprise the typical group
of Bacchic worshippers, a male leader with a devoted band of women
and girls. The leader *flings himself on the ground* in the climax of ecstasy,
when the power of the god enters into him and he becomes possessed.

Hurrying on to the Phrygian or Lydian mountain heights.
Possessed, ecstatic, he leads their happy cries;
The earth flows with milk, flows with wine,
Flows with nectar of bees;
The air is thick with a scent of Syrian myrrh.
The celebrant runs entranced, whirling the torch
That blazes red from the fennel-wand in his grasp,
And with shouts he rouses the scattered bands,
Sets their feet dancing,
As he shakes his delicate locks to the wild wind.
And amidst the frenzy of song he shouts like thunder:
'On, on! Run, dance, delirious, possessed!
You, the beauty and grace of golden Tmolus,
Sing to the rattle of thunderous drums,
Sing for joy,
Praise Dionysus, god of joy!
Shout like Phrygians, sing out the tunes you know,
While the sacred pure-toned flute
Vibrates the air with holy merriment,
In time with the pulse of the feet that flock
To the mountains, to the mountains!'
And, like a foal with its mother at pasture,
Runs and leaps for joy every daughter of Bacchus.

Enter TEIRESIAS. *Though blind, he makes his way unaided to the door, and knocks.*

TEIRESIAS: Who keeps the gate? [*A servant is heard answering from inside.*] Call out Cadmus, the son of Agenor, who came from Sidonia to build these walls of Thebes. Go, someone, tell him Teiresias is looking for him. He knows why I have come—the agreement I made with him—old as I am, and he older still—to get myself a Bacchic wand, put on the fawnskin cloak, and wear a garland of young ivy-shoots.

Enter CADMUS.

CADMUS: O my dear friend, I knew your voice, although I was indoors, as soon as I heard it—the wise voice of a wise man. Look, I am ready, I have everything the god prescribes. Dionysus is my own daughter's son; and now he has shown himself to the world as a god, it is right that I should do all I can to exalt him. Where should we go to dance, and take our stand with the rest, tossing our old grey beards? You must guide me in this, Teiresias—you're nearly as old as I am, and you understand such matters. No, it won't be too much for me; I can beat time with my thyrsus night and day! It's a happy thing to forget one's age.

TEIRESIAS: Then you feel just as I do. I am young too; I'll make an attempt at the dance.

CADMUS: You don't think we should make our way to the mountains in a carriage?

TEIRESIAS: No, no, that would not show the same respect for the god.

CADMUS: I'll be your guide then—two old men together.

TEIRESIAS: The god will guide us there, and without weariness.

CADMUS: Shall we be the only men in Thebes who dance to Bacchus?

TEIRESIAS: We are the only men right-minded; the rest are perverse.

CADMUS: We are wasting time. Now, take my hand.

TEIRESIAS: There; hold firmly, with a good grip.

CADMUS: Mortals must not make light of the gods—*I* would never do so.

TEIRESIAS: We entertain no theories or speculations in divine matters. The beliefs we have received from our ancestors— beliefs as old as time—cannot be destroyed by any argument, nor by any ingenuity the mind can invent. No doubt I shall be criticized for wearing an ivy-wreath and setting off for the dance; they will say I have no sense of what befits my age. They will be wrong: the god has drawn no distinction between young and old, which should dance and which should not. He wishes to receive honour alike from all; he will not have his worship made a matter of nice calculation.

CADMUS: Teiresias, since you are blind I must be your prophet. I see Pentheus the son of Echion, to whom I have resigned my rule in Thebes, hurrying towards the palace. He looks thoroughly upset! What is he going to tell us?

Enter PENTHEUS. *He addresses the audience, without at first noticing* CADMUS *and* TEIRESIAS, *who stand at the opposite side of the stage.*

PENTHEUS: I've been away from Thebes, as it happens; but I've heard the news—this extraordinary scandal in the city.

Our women, I discover, have abandoned their homes on some pretence of Bacchic worship, and go gadding about in the woods on the mountain side, dancing in honour of this upstart god Dionysus, whoever he may be. They tell me, in the midst of each group of revellers stands a bowl full of wine; and the women go creeping off this way and that to lonely places and there give themselves to lecherous men, under the excuse that they are Maenad priestesses; though in their ritual Aphrodite comes before Bacchus.

Well, those that I've caught, my guards are keeping safe; we've tied their hands, and lodged them at State expense. Those still at large on the mountain I am going to hunt out; and that includes my own mother Agauë, and her sisters Ino and Autonoe. Once I have them secure in iron chains I shall soon put a stop to this outrageous Bacchism.

I understand too that some Oriental magician or conjurer has arrived from Lydia, a fellow with golden hair flowing in scented ringlets, the flush of wine in his face and the charm of Aphrodite in his eyes; and that he entices our young girls with his Bacchic mysteries, and spends day and night in their company. Only let me get that fellow inside my walls—I'll cut his head from his shoulders; that will finish his thyrsus-waving and hair-tossing. *He* is the one—this foreigner—who has spread stories about Dionysus, that he is a god, that he was sewn up in Zeus's thigh. The truth about Dionysus is that he's dead, burnt to a cinder by lightning along with his mother, because she lied about Zeus—said that Zeus had lain with her. But whoever this man may be, does not his insufferable behaviour merit the worst of punishments, hanging?

He turns to go, and sees CADMUS *and* TEIRESIAS.

Why, look! Another miracle! Here's the prophet Teiresias, and my mother's father, playing the Bacchant, in dappled fawnskin and carrying fennel-wands! Well, there's a sight for laughter! [*But he is raging, not laughing.*] Sir, I am ashamed to see two men of your age with so little sense of decency. Come, you are my grandfather: throw away your garland, get rid of that thyrsus. *You* persuaded him into this, Teiresias. No doubt you hope that, when you have introduced this new god to the people, you will be his appointed seer, you will collect the fees for sacrifices. Your grey hairs are your protection; otherwise you should sit with all these crazy females in prison, for encouraging such pernicious performances.

As for women, my opinion is this: when the sparkle of sweet wine appears at their feasts, no good can be expected from their ceremonies.

CHORUS: What profanity! Sir, do you not revere the gods, or Cadmus, who sowed the seed of the earth-born men? Echion your father was one of them—will you shame your own blood?

TEIRESIAS: When a clever man has a plausible theme to argue, to be eloquent is no great feat. But though you seem, by your glib tongue, to be intelligent, yet your words are foolish. Power and eloquence in a headstrong man can only lead to folly; and such a man is a danger to the state.

This new divinity whom you ridicule—no words of mine could adequately express the ascendancy he is destined to achieve through the length and breadth of Hellas. There are two powers, young man, which are supreme in human affairs: first, the goddess Demeter; she is the Earth—call her by what name you will; and she supplies mankind with solid food. Second, Dionysus the son of Semele; the blessing he provides is the counterpart to the blessing of bread; he discovered and bestowed on men the service of drink, the juice that streams from the vine-clusters; men have but to take their fill of wine, and the sufferings of an unhappy race are banished, each day's troubles are forgotten in sleep— indeed this is our only cure for the weariness of life. Dionysus, himself a god, is poured out in offering to the gods; so that through him mankind receives blessing.

Now for the legend that he was sewn up in Zeus's thigh— do you mock at it? Then I will explain to you the truth that lies in the legend. When Zeus snatched the infant Dionysus away from the fire of the lightning, and brought him to Olympus as a god, Hera wanted to cast him out of heaven; so, to prevent her, Zeus—as you would expect—devised a plan. He broke off a piece of the sky that envelops the earth, made it into the likeness of a child, and gave it to Hera as a pledge, to soothe her jealousy. He entrusted the true Dionysus to others to bring up. Now the ancient word for a *pledge*[3] is very similar to our word 'thigh'; and so in time the word was mistaken, and men said Dionysus was saved by Zeus's *thigh*, instead of by Zeus's *pledge*, because a pledge was given to Hera in his likeness.

And this god is a prophet; for the Bacchic ecstasy and frenzy contain a strong element of prophecy. When Dionysus enters in power into a human body, he endows the possessed person with power to foretell the future. He also in some degree shares the function of Ares, god of war. It has happened that an army, equipped and stationed for battle, has fled in panic before a spear has been raised. This too is a madness sent by Dionysus.

Ay, and the day will come when you shall see him on the very rocks of Delphi, amidst flaring torches bounding over the twin-peaked ridge, hurling and brandishing his Bacchic staff, honoured by all Hellas.

Come, Pentheus, listen to me. You rely on force; but it is not force that governs human affairs. If you think otherwise—beware of mistaking your perverse opinion for wisdom. Welcome Dionysus to Thebes; pour libations to him, garland your head and celebrate his rites. Dionysus will not compel women to control their lusts. Self-control in all things depends on our own natures. This is a fact you should consider; for a chaste-minded woman will come to no harm in the rites of Bacchus. And think of this too: when crowds stand at the city gates, and the people glorify the name of Pentheus, you are filled with pleasure; so, I think, Dionysus is glad to receive honour.

So then I, and Cadmus, whom you mock, will wear the ivy-wreath and join in the dancing—we are both old men, but this is our duty; and no words of yours shall persuade me to fight against the gods. For your mind is most pitifully diseased; and there is no medicine that can heal you. Yet . . . there is one remedy[4] for your madness.

---

[3] The ancient word for a pledge: the translation necessarily expands the original. *Homeros* means 'pledge', and *meros* 'thigh'.

[4] There is one remedy: the prophet hints at Pentheus' approaching death.

CHORUS: What you have said, Teiresias, means no dishonour to Phoebus, whose prophet you are; and shows your wisdom in honouring Dionysus as a great god.

CADMUS: My son, Teiresias has advised you well. Do not venture outside the customary pieties; stay with us. Just now your wits are scattered; you think you are talking sense, but it is not sense at all. And even if you are right, and this god is not a god, at least let him have your word of acknowledgment; lie for a good purpose, so that Semele may be honoured as mother of a god, and I and our whole family may gain in dignity. Remember Actaeon—his tragic end; he boasted, out in these valleys, that he was a better hunter than Artemis, and was torn to pieces and devoured by the very hounds he had bred. Don't invite the same fate! Come, let me put this ivy-wreath on your head. Join us in worshipping Dionysus.

PENTHEUS: Keep your hands off! Go to your Bacchic rites; and don't wipe off your crazy folly on me! But I will punish this man who has taught you your lunacy. Go, one of you, immediately to the place of augury where Teiresias practises, smash it with crowbars, knock down the walls, turn everything upside down, fling out his holy fripperies to the winds. That will sting him more than anything else. The rest of you, comb the city and find this effeminate foreigner, who plagues our women with this strange disease and turns them into whores. If you catch him, bring him here in chains, and I'll have him stoned to death. He shall be sorry he ever came revelling in Thebes.

Exit PENTHEUS.

TEIRESIAS: Foolhardy man, you don't know what you are saying. You were out of your mind before; now you are raving mad.

Come, Cadmus; let us go and pray both for this man, brutish as he is, and for Thebes, and entreat Dionysus to be forbearing. Come, take your thyrsus and follow. Try to support me—there, we will help each other. It would be a pity for us both to fall; but never mind that. We must pay our service to Dionysus the son of Zeus.

CADMUS: the name *Pentheus* means *grief*. Let us hope he is not going to bring grief on your house. I am not speaking by

inspiration; I judge by his conduct. The things he has said
reveal the depth of his folly.

Exeunt Teiresias *and* Cadmus.

CHORUS:

Holiness, Queen of heaven,   [*Strophe 1*
Holiness, golden-winged ranging the earth,
Do you hear his blasphemy?
Pentheus dares—do you hear?—to revile the god of joy,
The son of Semele, who when the gay-crowned feast is set
Is named among gods the chief;
Whose gifts are joy and union of soul in dancing,
Joy in music of flutes,
Joy when sparkling wine at feasts of the gods
Soothes the sore regret,
Banishes every grief,
When the reveller rests, enfolded deep
In the cool shade of ivy-shoots,
On wine's soft pillow of sleep.

The brash, unbridled tongue,   [*Antistrophe 1*
The lawless folly of fools, will end in pain.
But the life of wise content
Is blest with quietness, escapes the storm
And keeps its house secure.
Though blessed gods dwell in the distant skies,
They watch the ways of men.
To know much is not to be wise.
Pride more than mortal hastens life to its end;
And they who in pride pretend
Beyond man's limit, will lose what lay
Close to their hand and sure.
I count it madness, and know no cure can mend
The evil man and his evil way.

O to set foot on Aphrodite's island,   [*Strophe 2*
On Cyprus, haunted by the Loves, who enchant
Brief life with sweetness; or in that strange land
Whose fertile river carves a hundred channels
To enrich her rainless sand;

Or where the sacred pastures of Olympus slant
Down to Pieria, where the Muses dwell—
Take me, O Bromius, take me and inspire
Laughter and worship! There our holy spell
And ecstasy are welcome; there the gentle band
Of Graces have their home, and sweet Desire.

Dionysus, son of Zeus, delights in banquets;   [*Antistrophe 2*
And his dear love is Peace, giver of wealth,
Saviour of young men's lives—a goddess rare!
In wine, his gift that charms all griefs away,
Alike both rich and poor may have their part.
His enemy is the man who has no care
To pass his years in happiness and health,
His days in quiet and his nights in joy,
Watchful to keep aloof both mind and heart
From men whose pride claims more than mortals may.
The life that wins the poor man's common voice,
His creed, his practice—this shall be my choice.

Some of the guards whom PENTHEUS *sent to arrest*
DIONYSUS *now enter with their prisoner.* PENTHEUS *enters*
from the palace.

GUARD: Well, sir, we went after this lion you told us to hunt,
and we have been successful. But—we found the lion was
tame! He made no attempt to escape, but freely held out his
hands to be bound. He didn't even turn pale, but kept the
fresh colour you see in his face now, smiling, and telling us
to tie him up and run him in; waited for me, in fact—gave
us no trouble at all. Naturally I felt a bit awkward. 'You'll
excuse me, sir,' I said, 'I don't want to arrest you, but it's
the king's orders.'

And there's another thing, sir. Those women you rounded
up and put in fetters and in prison, those religious maniacs
—why, they're all gone, let loose to the glens; and there they
are, dancing and calling on Bacchus. The fetters simply fell
from their limbs, the bolts flew back without the touch of
any mortal hand, and let the doors open. Master, this man
has come to our city of Thebes with a load of miracles.
What is going to happen next is your concern, not mine.

PENTHEUS: Untie his hands.[5] [*The guard does so.*] He is in the trap, and he's not nimble enough to escape me now.

Well, my man: you have a not unhandsome figure—for attracting women, which is your object in coming to Thebes. Those long curls of yours show that you're no wrestler—cascading close over your cheeks, most seductively. Your complexion, too, shows a carefully-preserved whiteness; you keep out of the sun and walk in the shade, to use your lovely face for courting Aphrodite. . . . Ah, well; tell me first what country you were born in.

DIONYSUS: That is easily told without boasting. Doubtless you have heard of the flowery mountain, Tmolus.

PENTHEUS: Yes, the range that curves round the city of Sardis.

DIONYSUS: That was my home; I am a Lydian.

PENTHEUS: And why do you bring these rituals to Hellas?

DIONYSUS: Dionysus the son of Zeus instructed me.

PENTHEUS: Is there a Lydian Zeus, then, who begets new gods?

DIONYSUS: No; I speak of your Zeus, who made Semele his bride here in Thebes.

PENTHEUS: And when Dionysus took possession of you, did he appear in a dream by night, or visible before your eyes?

DIONYSUS: I saw him face to face; and he entrusted to me these mysteries.

PENTHEUS: What form do these mysteries of yours take?

DIONYSUS: That cannot be told to the uninitiated.

PENTHEUS: What do the worshippers gain from it?

DIONYSUS: That is not lawful for you to hear—yet it is worth hearing.

PENTHEUS: A clever answer, baited to rouse my curiosity.

DIONYSUS: Curiosity will be useless; the rites of the god abhor an impious man.

PENTHEUS: If you say you saw Dionysus clearly—what was his appearance?

DIONYSUS: It was what he wished it to be. I had no say in that.

PENTHEUS: Another clever evasion, telling nothing.

DIONYSUS: *A wise speech sleeps in a foolish ear.*

---

[5] Untie his hands: the text is uncertain. A very slight alteration gives a completely different meaning: 'You are more mad than he is'—addressed to the guard and his fellows.

PENTHEUS: Is this the first place where you have introduced Dionysus?

DIONYSUS: No; every Eastern land dances these mysteries.

PENTHEUS: I believe it. Oriental standards are altogether inferior to ours.

DIONYSUS: In this point they are superior. But their customs are different.

PENTHEUS: Do you celebrate your mysteries by night or by day?

DIONYSUS: Chiefly by night. Darkness induces religious awe.

PENTHEUS: For women darkness is treacherous and impure.

DIONYSUS: Impurity can be practised by daylight too.

PENTHEUS: It is time you were punished for your foul, slippery tongue.

DIONYSUS: And you for your crass impieties.

PENTHEUS: How bold his Bacchic inspiration makes him! He knows how to argue too.

DIONYSUS: Tell me my sentence. What punishment are you going to inflict?

PENTHEUS: First I'll cut off your scented silky hair.

DIONYSUS: My hair I keep for the god; it is sacred to him.

PENTHEUS: Next, hand over that thyrsus.

DIONYSUS: Take it from me yourself. I carry it for Dionysus, whose it is.

PENTHEUS: And I shall keep you safe in prison.

DIONYSUS: The god himself will set me free whenever I wish.

PENTHEUS: Set you free? When you stand among those frenzied women and pray to him—no doubt!

DIONYSUS: He is here, close by me, and sees what is being done to me.

PENTHEUS: Oh, indeed? Where? To my eyes he is quite invisible.

DIONYSUS: Here at my side. You, being a blasphemer, cannot see him.

PENTHEUS [to the guards]: Get hold of him. He is laughing at me and the whole city.

DIONYSUS [to the guards]: I warn you not to bind me. . . . [To PENTHEUS.] I am sane, you are mad.

PENTHEUS [to DIONYSUS]: My orders overrule yours. [To the guards.] Bind him, I tell you.

DIONYSUS: You do not know what life you live, or what you do, or who you are.

PENTHEUS: Who I am? Pentheus, son of Echion and Agauë.

DIONYSUS: *Pentheus* means 'sorrow.' The name fits you well.

PENTHEUS: Take him away. Imprison him over there in the stables; he'll have all the darkness he wants.—You can dance in there! As for these women you've brought to aid and abet you, I shall either send them to the slave market, or retain them in my own household to work at the looms; that will keep their hands from drumming on tambourines!

DIONYSUS: I will go. Nothing can happen to me that is not my destiny. But Dionysus, who you say is dead, will pursue you and take his revenge for this sacrilege. You are putting *him* in prison, when you lay hands on me.

Guards take DIONYSUS *away to the stables; Pentheus follows.*

CHORUS:

> Dirce, sweet and holy maid,   [*Strophe*
> Acheloüs' Theban daughter,
> Once the child of Zeus was made
> Welcome in your welling water,
> When the lord of earth and sky
> Snatched him from the undying flame,
> Laid him safe within his thigh,
> Calling loud the infant's name:
> 'Twice-born Dithyrambus! Come,
> Enter here your father's womb;
> Bacchic child, I now proclaim
> This in Thebes shall be your name.'

Now, divine Dirce, when my head is crowned
And my feet dance in Bacchus' revelry—
Now you reject me from your holy ground.
Why should you fear me? By the purple fruit
That glows in glory on Dionysus' tree,
His dread name yet shall haunt your memory!

> O what anger lies beneath   [*Antistrophe*
> Pentheus' voice and sullen face—
> Offspring of the dragon's teeth,
> And Echion's earth-born race,

Brute with bloody jaws agape,
God-defying, gross and grim,
Slander of his human shape!
Soon he'll chain us limb to limb—
Bacchus' servants! Yes, and more:
Even now our comrade lies
Deep on his dark prison floor.
Dionysus! do your eyes
See us? O son of Zeus, the oppressor's rod
Falls on your worshippers; come, mighty god,
Brandish your golden thyrsus and descend
From great Olympus; touch this murderous man,
And bring his violence to a sudden end!

Where are you, Dionysus? Leading your dancing   [*Epode*
    bands
Over the mountain slopes, past many a wild beast's lair,
Or upon rocky crags, with the thyrsus in their hands?
Or in the wooded coverts, maybe, of Olympus, where
Orpheus once gathered the trees and mountain beasts,
Gathered them with his lyre, and sang an enchanting air.
Happy vale of Pieria! Bacchus delights in you;
He will cross the flood and foam of the Axius river, and
    there
He will bring his whirling Maenads, with dancing and with
    feasts,—
Cross the father of waters, Lydias, generous giver
Of wealth and luck, they say, to the land he wanders
    through,
Whose famous horses graze by the rich and lovely river.

*Suddenly a shout is heard from inside the building—the
voice of* DIONYSUS.

DIONYSUS:
    Io, Io! Do you know my voice, do you hear?
    Worshippers of Bacchus! Io, Io!
CHORUS: Who is that? Where is he? The voice of Dionysus
    calling to us!
DIONYSUS: Io, Io! Hear me again: I am the son of Semele, the
    son of Zeus!

CHORUS:

> Io, Io, our lord, our lord!
> Come, then, come to our company, lord of joy!

DIONYSUS: O dreadful earthquake, shake the floor of the world!

CHORUS [*with a scream of terror*]:

> Pentheus' palace is falling, crumbling in pieces! [*They continue severally.*]
> Dionysus stands in the palace; bow before him!
> We bow before him. See how the roof and pillars
> Plunge to the ground! God from the inner prison
> Will shout the shout of victory.

The flame on Semele's tomb grows and brightens.

DIONYSUS:

> Fan to a blaze the flame the lightning lit;
> Kindle the conflagration of Pentheus' palace!

CHORUS:

> Look, look, look!
> Do you see, do you see the flame of Semele's tomb,
> The flame that remained when she died of the lightning-stroke?

A noise of crashing masonry is heard.

> Down, trembling Maenads! Hurl yourselves to the ground!
> Your god is wrecking the palace, roof to floor;
> He heard our cry—he is coming, the son of Zeus!

The doors open and DIONYSUS *appears.*

DIONYSUS: Women of Asia, why are you cowering terrified on the ground? You heard Bacchus himself shattering Pentheus' palace; come, stand up! Stop this trembling! Courage!

CHORUS: Oh, what a joy to hear your Bacchic shout! You have saved us. We were deserted and alone: how happy we are to see you!

DIONYSUS: Were you plunged in despair, when I was sent inside to be thrown into Pentheus' dark dungeon?

CHORUS: How could we help it? Who was there to protect us, if you were taken? But tell us how you escaped from the clutches of this wicked man.

DIONYSUS: I alone with effortless ease delivered myself.

CHORUS: But did he not bind your arms with knotted ropes?

DIONYSUS: Ha, ha! There I made a mockery of him. He thought he was binding me; but he fed himself on delusion —he neither took hold of me nor even touched me. Near the stall where he took me to shut me in, he found a bull; and he was tying his rope round the bull's knees and hooves, panting with rage, dripping sweat, and biting his lips; while I sat quietly by and watched him. And it was then that Bacchus came and shook the building and made the flame on his mother's tomb flare up. When Pentheus saw this, he imagined the place was on fire, and went rushing this way and that, calling to the servants to bring water, till the whole household was in commotion—all for nothing.

Then he thought I had escaped. He left throwing water, snatched up his murderous sword and darted into the palace. Thereupon Dionysus—or so it seemed to me; I tell what I thought—made a phantom figure appear in the palace courtyard; and Pentheus flew at it, and kept stabbing at the sunny air, imagining he was killing *me*.

But the god had further humiliation in store for him: he laid the stable-buildings in ruins on the ground—there they lie, a heap of rubble, to break his heart as he looks at my prison. Now he is helpless with exhaustion. He has dropped his sword. He, a mortal man, dared to take arms against a god. I walked quietly out of the palace, and here I am. Pentheus does not disturb me. But I hear his heavy tread indoors; I think he will be out here in a moment. What will he say after this? For all his rage, he shall not ruffle me. The wise man preserves a smooth-tempered self-control.

Enter PENTHEUS.

PENTHEUS: This is outrageous. That foreigner was locked up and in chains a little while ago; now he has escaped me. [*He sees* DIONYSUS *and gives an excited shout.*] That's the man! What's going on? How did you get out? How dare you show yourself here before my very doors?

DIONYSUS: Stay where you are. You are angry. Now control yourself.

PENTHEUS: You were bound and locked in: how did you escape?

DIONYSUS: Did you not hear me say that I should be set free by—

PENTHEUS: By whom? Everything you say is strange.

DIONYSUS: By him who plants for mortals the rich-clustered vine.

PENTHEUS: The god who makes men fools and women mad.[6]

DIONYSUS: A splendid insult, that, to Dionysus!

PENTHEUS [to attendant guards]: Close the gates all round— every gate in the city wall.

DIONYSUS: And why? Cannot gods pass even over walls?

PENTHEUS: Oh, you know everything—except the things you ought to know.

DIONYSUS: The things one ought to know most of all, those things I know.

But first listen to what this man has to tell you; he comes from the mountains with news.—I will stay here; I promise not to run away.

Enter a HERDSMAN.

HERDSMAN: Pentheus, ruler of Thebes! I come from Cithaeron, where the ground is never free from dazzling shafts of snow.

PENTHEUS: And what urgent news do you bring me?

HERDSMAN: I have seen the holy Bacchae, who in madness went streaming bare-limbed out of the city gates. I have come with the intention of telling you, my lord, and the city, of their strange and terrible doings—things past all wonder. But I would like to know first if I may speak freely of what is going on there, or if I should trim my words. I am afraid of your hastiness, my lord, your hot temper; you are too much like a king.

PENTHEUS: Say all that you have to say; fear nothing from me. The more terrible your story about the Bacchae, the more certainly will I execute justice upon this man, the instigator of their wickedness.

HERDSMAN: Just when the sun's rays first beamed out to warm the earth, I was pasturing my cattle and working up towards the high ground; when I saw three groups of women

---

[6] The god who makes . . . : this is conjecturally supplied in place of a missing line.

who had been dancing together. The leader of one group was Autonoe; your mother Agauë was at the head of the second, and Ino of the third. They were all sleeping, stretched out and quiet. Some rested on beds of pine-needles, some had pillows of oak-leaves; they lay just as they had thrown themselves down on the ground,—but with modesty in their posture; they were not drunk with wine, as you told us, or with music of flutes; nor was there any love-making there in the loveliness of the woods.

As soon as your mother Agauë heard the lowing of the horned cattle, she stood up among the Bacchae and called loudly to them to rouse themselves from sleep. And they threw off the strong sleep from their eyes and leapt to their feet. They were a sight to marvel at for modesty and come-liness—women old and young, and girls still unmarried. First they let down their hair over their shoulders; those whose fawnskins had come loose from their fastenings tied them up; and they girdled the dappled fur with snakes which licked their cheeks. And some would have in their arms a young gazelle, or wild wolf-cubs, and give them their own white milk—those who had infants at home recently born, so that their breasts were still full. And they wreathed their heads with garlands of ivy and oak and flowering bryony.

And one of them took her thyrsus and struck it on the rock; and from the rock there gushed a spring of limpid water; another struck her wand down into the earth, and there the god made a fountain of wine spring up; and any who wanted milk had only to scratch the earth with the tip of her fingers, and there was the white stream flowing for her to drink; and from the ivy-bound thyrsus a sweet ooze of honey dripped. Oh! if you had been there and seen all this, you would have entreated with prayers this god whom you now accuse.

Well, we herdsmen and shepherds gathered and stood talking together, and arguing about these strange and extraordinary doings. And one fellow, a gadder up to town, and a good speaker, addressed the rest of us. 'You who live on the holy mountain heights,' he said, 'how if we should hunt down the king's mother, Agauë, bring her away from these orgies, and do the king a service?' We thought it was a good suggestion; so we hid ourselves among the leafy bushes and waited our chance.

When the set time came, the women began brandishing their wands and preparing to dance, calling in unison on the son of Zeus, 'Iacchus! Bromius!' And the whole mountain, and the wild beasts too, became a part of their joyful dance—there was nothing that was not roused to leap and run.

Now Agauë as she ran happened to pass close to me; so I sprang out of the ambush where we lay hidden, meaning to capture her. But she cried out, 'Oh, my swift hounds, we are being hunted by these men. Come, then, and follow; arm yourselves with the thyrsus, and follow me!'

So we fled, and escaped being torn in pieces by these possessed women. But our cattle were feeding there on the fresh grass; and the Bacchae attacked them, with their bare hands. You could see Agauë take up a bellowing young heifer with full udders, and hold it by the legs with her two arms stretched wide. Others were tearing our cows limb from limb, and you could see perhaps some ribs or a cleft hoof being tossed high and low; and pieces of bloody flesh hung dripping on the pine-branches. And bulls, which one moment were savagely looking along their horns, the next were thrown bodily to the ground, dragged down by the soft hands of girls—thousands of them; and they stripped the flesh off their bodies faster than you could wink your royal eyes.

Then, like birds, skimming the ground as they ran, they scoured the plain which stretches by the river Asopus and produces a rich harvest for Thebes; and like an enemy army they bore down on the villages of Hysiae and Erythrae, which lie on the low slopes of Cithaeron, and ransacked them. They snatched up children out of the houses; all the plunder they laid on their shoulders stayed safely there without any fastening; nothing fell to the dark earth, not bronze or iron even; they carried fire on their heads, and their hair was not burnt.

The villagers, of course, were furious at being plundered by the Bacchae, and they resisted with weapons; and then, my lord, was an astonishing sight to behold. The spears cast by the villagers drew no blood; but the women, hurling the thyrsus like a spear, dealt wounds; those women turned the men to flight. There was the power of a god in that.

Then they went back to the place they had started from, to those fountains the god had made flow for them. And they washed off the blood, and the snakes licked the stains clean from their cheeks.

So, master, whoever this god may be, receive him in our city. He has great power in many ways; but especially, as I hear, it was he who gave men the gift of the vine as a cure for sorrow. And if there were no more wine, why, there's an end of love, and of every other pleasure in life.

CHORUS: I hesitate to speak freely before the king; yet I will say it: there is no greater god than Dionysus.

PENTHEUS: This outrageous Bacchism advances on us like a spreading fire, disgracing us before all Hellas. We must waste no time. [*To the* HERDSMAN.] Go at once to the Electran gate; tell all my men who bear shields, heavy or light, all who ride fast horses or twang the bowstring, to meet me there in readiness for an assault on the Bacchae. This is past all bearing, if we are to let women so defy us.

DIONYSUS: You refuse, Pentheus, to listen to what I say or to alter your behaviour. Yet, in spite of all I have suffered at your hands, I warn you to stay where you are and not to take arms against a god. Dionysus will not stand quietly by and see you drive his Bacchae from their mountain rites.

PENTHEUS: I want no instruction from you. You have escaped from your fetters—be content; or I will punish you again.

DIONYSUS: You are a mortal, he is a god. If I were you I would control my rage and sacrifice to him, rather than kick against the pricks.

PENTHEUS: Sacrifice! I will indeed—an offering of women's blood, slaughtered as they deserve in the glens of Cithaeron.

DIONYSUS: You will all be put to flight. It would be disgraceful for the wands of Bacchic women to rout your brazen shields.

PENTHEUS: This foreigner is an impossible man to deal with; in prison or out, he will not hold his tongue.

DIONYSUS: My friend! A happy settlement may still be found.

PENTHEUS: How? By making me a slave to my own slaves?

DIONYSUS: I will bring those women here, without use of weapons.

PENTHEUS: Heaven help us, you are plotting some trick.

DIONYSUS: A trick? If I use my power to save you?

PENTHEUS: This is something you have arranged with the women, so that the revelling may continue.

DIONYSUS: This is something, certainly, that I have arranged —not with them, but with the god.

PENTHEUS: That is enough from you.—Bring out my armour, there!

DIONYSUS [*with an authoritative shout*]: Wait! [*Then, quietly.*] Would you like to *see* those women, sitting together, there in the mountains?

PENTHEUS: Yes, indeed; I would give a large sum of gold to see them.

From now on DIONYSUS *gradually establishes a complete ascendancy over* PENTHEUS.

DIONYSUS: And what has betrayed you into this great eagerness?

PENTHEUS: I am not eager to see them drunk; that would be a painful sight.

DIONYSUS: Yet you would be glad to see a sight that would pain you?

PENTHEUS: I would, yes; if I could sit quietly under the pinetrees and watch.

DIONYSUS: However secretly you go they will track you down.

PENTHEUS: You are quite right. I will go openly.

DIONYSUS: Shall I show you the way, then? You will venture on this?

PENTHEUS: Lead me there at once; I am impatient.

DIONYSUS: Then, first dress yourself in a fine linen gown.

PENTHEUS: Why a linen gown? Must I change my sex?

DIONYSUS: They will kill you if you are seen there dressed as a man.

PENTHEUS: You are quite right; you think of everything!

DIONYSUS: It was Dionysus who inspired me with that thought.

PENTHEUS: How can your suggestion best be carried out?

DIONYSUS: I will come indoors with you and dress you.

PENTHEUS: Dress me? Not in woman's clothes? I would be ashamed.

DIONYSUS: You have lost your enthusiasm for watching the Maenads.

PENTHEUS: What kind of dress do you say you will put on me?

DIONYSUS: I will cover your head with long, flowing hair.

PENTHEUS: And after that? What will my costume look like?

DIONYSUS: A robe falling to your feet; and a snood on your head.

PENTHEUS: Anything else?

DIONYSUS: A thyrsus in your hand, and a dappled fawnskin round you.

PENTHEUS: I could never wear woman's clothes.

DIONYSUS: If you join battle with the Bacchae there will be bloodshed.

PENTHEUS: You are right; I must first go to spy on them.

DIONYSUS: That is wiser than inviting violence by using it.

PENTHEUS: And how shall I get through the streets of Thebes without being seen?

DIONYSUS: We will go by lonely ways; I will guide you.

PENTHEUS: I must not be laughed at by the Bacchae—anything rather than that. Now I will go in, and decide how best to act.

DIONYSUS: You may. My own preparations are all made.

PENTHEUS: I will go, then; and I will either visit the mountains armed—or else I will follow your advice.

Exit PENTHEUS.

DIONYSUS: Women, this man is walking into the net. He will visit the Bacchae; and there he shall be punished with death.

Dionysus (for you are not far away), all is now in your hands. Let us be revenged on him! And—first assail him with fantastic madness and drive him out of his mind; for while he is sane he will never consent to put on a woman's clothes; but once he has broken from the rein of reason he will put them on. I long to set Thebes laughing at him, as I lead him dressed like a woman through the streets; to humble him from the arrogance with which he threatened me at first.

Now I will go, to array Pentheus in the dress which he will take down with him to the world of the dead, slaughtered by his own mother's hands. And he shall know the son of Zeus, Dionysus; who, though most gentle to mankind, can prove a god of terror irresistible.

DIONYSUS *follows* PENTHEUS *into the palace.*

CHORUS:

O for long nights of worship, gay   [*Strophe*
With the pale gleam of dancing feet,
With head tossed high to the dewy air—
Pleasure mysterious and sweet!
O for the joy of a fawn at play
In the fragrant meadow's green delight,
Who has leapt out free from the woven snare,
Away from the terror of chase and flight,
And the huntsman's shout, and the straining pack,
And skims the sand by the river's brim
With the speed of wind in each aching limb,
To the blessed lonely forest where
The soil's unmarked by a human track,
And leaves hang thick and the shades are dim.

What prayer should we call wise?   [*Refrain*
What gift of Heaven should man
Count a more noble prize,
A prayer more prudent, than
To stretch a conquering arm
Over the fallen crest
Of those who wished us harm?
And what is noble every heart loves best.

Slow, yet unfailing, move the Powers   [*Antistrophe*
Of heaven with the moving hours.
When mind runs mad, dishonours God,
And worships self and senseless pride,
Then Law eternal wields the rod.
Still Heaven hunts down the impious man,
Though divine subtlety may hide
Time's creeping foot. No mortal ought
To challenge Time—to overbear
Custom in act, or age in thought.
All men, at little cost, may share
The blessing of a pious creed;
Truths more than mortal, which began
In the beginning, and belong

To very nature—these indeed
Reign in our world, are fixed and strong.

What prayer should we call wise?   [*Refrain*
What gift of heaven should man
Count a more noble prize,
A prayer more prudent, than
To stretch a conquering arm
Over the fallen crest
Of those who wished us harm?
And what is noble every heart loves best.

Blest is the man who cheats the stormy sea   [*Epode*
And safely moors beside the sheltering quay;
So, blest is he who triumphs over trial.
One man, by various means, in wealth or strength
Outdoes his neighbour; hope in a thousand hearts
Colours a thousand different dreams; at length
Some find a dear fulfilment, some denial.
    But this I say,
    That he who best
    Enjoys each passing day
    Is truly blest.

Enter DIONYSUS. *He turns to call* PENTHEUS.

DIONYSUS: Come, perverse man, greedy for sights you should
    not see, impatient for deeds you should not do—Pentheus!
    Come out of the palace and show yourself to me, wearing
    the garb of a frenzied Bacchic woman, ready to spy on your
    mother and all her company!

Enter PENTHEUS *dressed as a Bacchic devotee. He is dazed,
and entirely subservient to* DIONYSUS.

Ah! You look exactly like one of Cadmus' daughters.
PENTHEUS: Why—I seem to see two suns; I see a double
    Thebes, and the city wall with its seven gates—double! I
    see you leading me forward—you are like a bull, you have
    horns growing on your head. Tell me, were you an animal a
    little while ago? You have certainly become a bull.
DIONYSUS: The god did not favour us before; now he is with
    us, and we have made our peace with him. Now you see as
    you ought to see.

PENTHEUS: Well, how do I look? Do you think I stand like Ino or like my mother Agauë?

DIONYSUS: I think you are their very image. Wait—this curl of hair is out of place, not as I arranged it under your snood.

PENTHEUS: I must have shaken it loose indoors, tossing my head up and down like a Bacchic reveller.

DIONYSUS: Come, it is for me to look after you; I will set it straight. Now, lift your head.

PENTHEUS: There, *you* put it right. I depend entirely on you.

DIONYSUS: And your girdle is loose; and the folds of your gown are not hanging straight to your ankles.

PENTHEUS: I agree, they are not—at least, here by the right foot. But on the other side the gown hangs well to the heel.

DIONYSUS: I think you will reckon me the chief of your friends, when you see the Bacchae and find to your surprise how well they are behaving—will you not?

But PENTHEUS *is not listening.*

PENTHEUS: Ought I to hold my thyrsus in this hand or in the right, to look more like a Bacchanal?

DIONYSUS: Hold it in your right hand, and raise it at the same time as you raise your right foot. [PENTHEUS *attempts it.*] I am glad you are so—changed in mind.

PENTHEUS: Do you think I could lift up on my shoulders the glens of Cithaeron, with all the women revelling there?

DIONYSUS: You could, if you wished. Before, your mind was diseased; now, it is as it should be.

PENTHEUS: Shall we take crowbars? Or shall I simply set my shoulder, or my arm, against the mountain peaks, and tear them up with my hands?

DIONYSUS: No, you must not destroy the homes of the Nymphs, and the haunts where Pan sits piping.

PENTHEUS: You are right. Women are not to be subdued by brute force. I will hide among the pine-trees.

DIONYSUS: Hide? Yes! You shall find the right hiding-place to hide you—coming like a crafty spy to watch the Maenads!

PENTHEUS: Yes, I can picture them—like birds in the thickets, wrapped in the sweet snare of love.

DIONYSUS: That is the very thing you are going to look for; and perhaps you will catch them—if you are not first caught yourself.

PENTHEUS: Now lead me through the central streets of Thebes.

There is no one dares to do this—I am the only *man* among
them.

DIONYSUS: You alone suffer for the whole city—you alone; and
the struggle that awaits you is your destined ordeal. Come;
I will see you safely there; another shall bring you home.

PENTHEUS: You mean my mother?

DIONYSUS: A sight for all to see.

PENTHEUS: It is for that I am going.

DIONYSUS: You will be carried home—

PENTHEUS: What splendour that will be!

DIONYSUS: —in your mother's arms.

PENTHEUS: Why, you make a weakling of me!

DIONYSUS: That is—one way of putting it.

PENTHEUS: Yet it is what I deserve.

Exit PENTHEUS.

DIONYSUS: Pentheus, you are a man to make men fear; and
fearful will be your end—an end that shall raise your fame
to the height of heaven. Stretch out your hands, Agauë, and
you her sisters, daughters of Cadmus! I am bringing the
young man to his battle; and I and Dionysus shall be victors.
[*Then he adds quietly*] What more shall happen, the event
will show.

Exit DIONYSUS.

CHORUS:
Hounds of Madness, fly to the mountain, fly   [*Strophe*
Where Cadmus' daughters are dancing in ecstasy!
Madden them like a frenzied herd stampeding,
Against the madman hiding in woman's clothes
To spy on the Maenad's rapture!
First his mother shall see him craning his neck
Down from a rounded rock or a withered trunk,
And shout to the Maenads, 'Who is the man, you Bacchae,
Who has come to the mountain, come to the mountain
     spying
On the swift wild mountain-dances of Cadmus' daughters?
Which of you is his mother?
No, that lad never lay in a woman's womb;
A lioness gave him suck, or a Libyan Gorgon!'

Justice, now be revealed! Now let your sword
Thrust—through and through—to sever the throat
Of the godless, lawless, shameless son of Echion,
Who sprang from the womb of Earth!

See! With contempt of right, with a reckless   [*Antistrophe*
    rage
To combat your and your mother's mysteries, Bacchus,
With maniac fury out he goes, stark mad,
For a trial of strength against *your* invincible arm!
The sober and humble heart
That accords the gods their due without carp or cavil,
And knows that his days are as dust, shall live untouched.
I have no wish to grudge the wise their wisdom;
But the joys *I* seek are greater, outshine all others,
And lead our life to goodness and loveliness:
The joy of the holy heart
That night and day is bent to honour the gods
And disown all custom that breaks the bounds of right.

Justice, now be revealed! Now let your sword
Thrust—through and through—to sever the throat
Of the godless, lawless, shameless son of Echion,
Who sprang from the womb of Earth!

*Then with growing excitement, shouting in unison, and
dancing to the rhythm of their words.*

>   Come, Dionysus!   [*Epode*
>   Come, and appear to us!
>   Come like a bull or a
>   Hundred-headed serpent,
>   Come like a lion snorting
>   Flame from your nostrils!
>   Swoop down, Bacchus, on the
>   Hunter of the Bacchae;
>   Smile at him and snare him;
>   Then let the stampeding
>   Herd of the Maenads
>   Throw him and throttle him,
>   Catch, trip, trample him to death!

Enter a MESSENGER.

MESSENGER: O house once glorious throughout Hellas, house of the old Sidonian king who sowed in this soil the dragon's earth-born crop! How I weep for you! I am a slave; but a good slave feels the blow that strikes his master.

CHORUS: What has happened? Have you news from the mountains?

MESSENGER: Pentheus, the son of Echion, is dead.

CHORUS: Dionysus, god of rapture! Your power is revealed!

MESSENGER: What? What did you say? Do you even exult at the cruel end that has overtaken my master?

CHORUS: I am no Greek; I sing for joy in a foreign tune. Now I've no need to cower in terror of prison.

MESSENGER: Do you suppose Thebes has no men left to take command?

CHORUS: Dionysus commands *me; not* Thebes, but Dionysus.

MESSENGER: Allowance must be made for you; yet, when irreparable wrong has been done, it is shameful to rejoice.

CHORUS: Tell me what happened; tell me, how did he die—this tyrant pursuing his tyranny?

MESSENGER: When we had left the houses of Thebes behind, and crossed the river Asopus, we began climbing the foothills of Cithaeron, Pentheus and I—I was attending my master—, and that foreigner who was showing us the way to what we were to see.

Well, first we sat down in a grassy glade; we kept our footsteps and our talk as quiet as possible, so as to see without being seen. We were in a valley full of streams, with cliffs on either side; and there, under the close shade of pine-trees, the Maenads were sitting, their hands busy at their happy tasks. Some of them were twining with fresh leaves a thyrsus that had lost its ivy; others, like foals let loose from the painted yokes, were singing holy songs[7] to each other in turn.

But the ill-fated Pentheus did not see these women; and

---

[7] Were singing holy songs: the Greek word is *Bacchic* songs. In English this adjective is too often associated with the 'profane' drinking of wine, whereas in this play it always has a religious or at least a ritualistic meaning. In translation I have been deliberately inconsistent, using both *Bacchic* and *holy* for the sake of keeping both ideas operative.

he said, 'From where we are standing, my friend, I cannot clearly make out these pretended worshippers, these Maenads; if I climbed a towering pine-tree on the cliff-side I could have a proper view of their shameful behaviour.'

And then—I saw that foreigner do an amazing thing. He took hold of the topmost skiey branch of a pine and dragged it down, down, down to the dark earth. It was bent in a circle as a bow is bent, as the curve of a wheel, drawn with peg and line, bends the running rim to its own shape;[8] so the foreigner took that mountain-pine in his hands and bent it to the ground—a thing no mortal man could do. Then he set Pentheus on the top branches, and began letting the tree spring upright, slipping it steadily through his grip, and taking care not to unseat him; and the pine-trunk straightened itself and soared into the soaring sky with the King sitting astride; so that he was more plainly visible to the women than they were to him.

And he was just coming into view on his lofty perch,— the foreigner was nowhere to be seen—when a voice—I suppose it was Dionysus—pealed out from heaven: 'Women! I bring you the man who made a mockery of you, and of me, and of my holy rites. Now punish him.' And in the very moment the voice spoke, a flash of unearthly fire stretched between the sky and the ground.

The whole air fell silent. The wooded glade held every leaf silent. You could hear no cry of any beast. The women had not caught distinctly what the voice said; they stood up and gazed around. Then came a second word of command. As soon as Cadmus' daughters recognized the clear bidding of Bacchus, they darted forward with the speed of doves on the wing, and all the Bacchae after them. Up the valley, along by the stream, over the rocks they went leaping on, possessed with the very breath of the god. When they saw the king sitting in the tree, first they climbed the cliff where it rose up like a battlement, and with all their strength pelted him with pieces of rock, or aimed pine-

---

[8] As the curve of a wheel . . . : a difficult passage, of which no satisfactory translation can be made. An emended text gives: 'As a bow by which an untrue wheel, chiselled on a lathe, is swiftly rotated.' This would refer to the use of a bent pole or tree as a source of power.

branches at him like javelins. Some were hurling the thyrsus at their pitiable target; but the shots fell short—the
height was too great for all their efforts; while the wretched
man sat there trapped and helpless.

At last, with a force like lightning, they tore down
branches of oak, and used these as levers, trying to tear out
the tree's roots. All their struggles were useless. Then
Agauë spoke to them: 'Come, you Maenads, stand round the
tree and grip it. We must catch this climbing beast, or he
will reveal the secret dances of Dionysus.' A thousand hands
grasped the tree; and they tore it from the earth. Then
from his high perch plunging and crashing to the ground
came Pentheus, with one incessant scream as he understood what end was near.

First his mother, as priestess, began the ritual of death,
and fell upon him. He tore off the headband from his hair,
that his wretched mother might recognize him and not kill
him. 'Mother!' he cried, touching her cheek, 'it is I, your
son, Pentheus, whom you bore to Echion. O mother, have
mercy on me; I have sinned, but I am your son: do not
kill me!'

Agauë was foaming at the mouth, her eyes were rolling
wildly. She was not in her right mind; she was under the
power of Dionysus; and she would not listen to him. She
gripped his right arm between wrist and elbow; she set her
foot against his ribs; and she tore his arm off by the shoulder. It was no strength of hers that did it; the god was in
her fingers and made it easy. Ino was at him on the other
side, tearing at his flesh; and now Autonoe joined them, and
the whole pack of raving women. There was a single continuous yell—Pentheus shrieking as long as life was left in
him, the women howling in triumph. One of them was carrying an arm, another had a foot with the shoe still on it;
the ribs were stripped—clawed clean. Every hand was thick
red with blood; and they were tossing and catching, to and
fro, like a ball, the flesh of Pentheus.

His body lies scattered, some under hard rocks, some in
the deep green woods; it will not be easy to find. His poor
head—his mother is holding it; she has fixed it on the point
of her thyrsus, and carries it openly over the mountain-side,

leaving her sisters dancing with the Maenads. And she is coming here to the palace, exulting in her fearful and horrible prey, shouting to Bacchus as her fellow-hunter, calling him her partner in the kill, her comrade in victory. But Bacchus gives her tears for her reward.

I am going; I want to be far away from this horror before Agauë comes.

The noblest thing a man can have is a humble and quiet heart that reveres the gods. I think that is also the wisest thing for a man to possess, if he will but use it.

Exit.

CHORUS:
Let us dance a dance to Bacchus, shout and sing
For the fall of Pentheus, heir of the dragon's seed,
Who hid his beard in a woman's gown,
And sealed his death with the holy sign
Of ivy wreathing a fennel-reed,
When bull led man to the ritual slaughter-ring.
Frenzied daughters of Cadmus, what renown
Your victory wins you—such a song
As groans must stifle, tears must drown!
Emblem of conquest, brave and fine!—
A mother's hand, defiled
With blood and dripping red
Caresses the torn head
Of her own murdered child!

But look! I see Pentheus' mother, Agauë, running towards the palace, with eyes wildly rolling. Welcome the worshipping company of Dionysus!

AGAUË *appears, frenzied and panting, with* PENTHEUS' *head held in her hand. The rest of her band of devotees, whom the* CHORUS *saw approaching with her, do not enter; but a few are seen standing by the entrance, where they wait until the end of the play.*

AGAUË: Women of Asia! Worshippers of Bacchus!

AGAUË *tries to show them* PENTHEUS' *head; they shrink from it.*

CHORUS: Why do you urge me? Oh!
AGAUË: I am bringing home from the mountains
A vine-branch freshly cut,
For the gods have blessed our hunting.
CHORUS: We see it . . . and welcome you in fellowship.
AGAUË: I caught him without a trap,
A lion-cub, young and wild.
Look, you may see him: there!
CHORUS: Where was it?
AGAUË: On Cithaeron;
The wild and empty mountain—
CHORUS: Cithaeron!
AGAUË: . . . spilt his life-blood.
CHORUS: Who shot him?
AGAUË: I was first;
All the women are singing,
'Honour to great Agauë!'
CHORUS: And then—who next?
AGAUË: Why, Cadmus' . . .
CHORUS: What—Cadmus?
AGAUË: Yes, his daughters—
But after me, after me—
Laid their hands to the kill.
To-day was a splendid hunt!
Come now, join in the feast!
CHORUS: What, wretched woman? *Feast?*
AGAUË [*tenderly stroking the head as she holds it*]:
This calf is young: how thickly
The new-grown hair goes crisping
Up to his delicate crest!
CHORUS: Indeed, his long hair makes him
Look like some wild creature.
AGAUË: The god is a skilled hunter;
And he poised his hunting women,
And hurled them at the quarry.
CHORUS: True, our god is a hunter.
AGAUË: Do you praise me?
CHORUS: Yes, we praise you.

AGAUË: So will the sons of Cadmus . . .

CHORUS: And Pentheus too, Agauë?[9]

AGAUË: Yes, he will praise his mother
For the lion-cub she killed.

CHORUS: Oh, fearful!

AGAUË: Ay, fearful!

CHORUS: You are happy?

AGAUË: I am enraptured;
Great in the eyes of the world,[10]
Great are the deeds I've done,
And the hunt that I hunted there!

CHORUS: Then, poor Agauë, show this triumphant spoil of yours that you've carried home—show it to the people of Thebes.

AGAUË: Come, then, all you Thebans who live in this lofty and lovely city, come and see the beast we have caught and killed—we, Cadmus' daughters; caught not with nets or thonged Thessalian javelins, but with our own white arms and fingers. After this, should huntsmen boast, who buy their paltry tools from the armourer? We with our bare hands caught this quarry, then tore it limb from limb.

Where is my father? Let him come here! And my son Pentheus, where is he? Let him get a strong ladder, and take this head, and climb up and nail it to the top of the palace wall, this lion that I hunted and brought home!

Enter CADMUS *with attendants bearing the body of* PEN-
THEUS.

CADMUS: Come, men. Bring your sad burden that was Pentheus; bring him to his home. I found the fragments of his

---

[9] And Pentheus too, Agauë?: the Chorus are physically shocked by the sight of Agauë and her prey; but their attitude does not change to pity. Agauë has been (in their view, justly) punished for her blasphemy against Dionysus, by being tricked into performing the usual Bacchic rite of slaughter, not upon the usual victim, a beast, but upon a man, and that her own son. She is now an abhorred and polluted creature, unfit for the company of the 'pure' Bacchae. Hence, though they welcome the punishment of Pentheus, their tone towards Agauë is one not of admiration but of contempt. This line in particular indicates the complete absence of pity.

[10] Great in the eyes of the world: another hint of the 'manifestation' of the nature of the god.

body scattered in a thousand places, no two together, about the glens of Cithaeron, or hidden in thick woods; and with weary search I gathered them, and have brought them here.

I had already returned with old Teiresias from the Bacchic dance, and was inside the walls of the city, when news was brought me of my daughters' terrible deed. I turned straight back to the mountain; and here I bring my son, killed by the Maenads. I saw Autonoe, who bore Acteon to Aristaeus, and her sister Ino, there among the copses, still in their unhappy frenzy; but I understand that Agauë came raving towards the palace—it is true, there she is! Oh, what a terrible sight!

AGAUË: Father! You may boast as loudly as you will, that no man living is so blest in his daughters; I mean all three, but myself especially. I have left weaving at the loom for greater things—for hunting wild beasts with my bare hands. See here what I carry in my arms; this is the prize I won; I have brought it to hang on your palace wall. Take it, Father; hold it. Be proud of my hunting, and call your friends to a banquet; let them all envy and congratulate you, for the splendour of my deed.

CADMUS: O anguish unmeasured, intolerable! O pitiful hands —your splendid deed is murder! What victim is this you would lay at the gods' feet, calling Thebes, and me, to a banquet? Your suffering is worst, but mine is next. Dionysus, god of joy, has been just, but too cruel. He was born of my blood, and he has destroyed my house.

AGAUË: How ill-humoured old age makes a man! How he scowls at me! I wish that my son were a great hunter, like his mother, pursuing wild beasts with all the young men of Thebes; but he can only fight against gods. Father, you must reason with him. Let someone call him here before me, to see my good fortune.

CADMUS: Oh, my daughters! If you come to understand what you have done, how terrible your suffering will be! But if you remain always as you are now, though you could not be called happy, at least you will not know your own misery.

AGAUË: Misery? What is wrong? Where is my cause for misery?

CADMUS: First, turn your eyes this way—look at the sky.

AGAUË: I am looking. Why do you tell me to look at it?

CADMUS: Is it still the same, or does it seem to you to have changed?

AGAUË: It is brighter than before—more luminous.

CADMUS: And this madness you suffered from—is it still with you?

AGAUË: I do not know what you mean. But I feel a change in my mind; my thoughts are somehow clearer.

CADMUS: Can you now hear and answer clearly?

AGAUË: Yes . . . I have forgotten what we said just now, Father.

CADMUS: When you were married, whose house did you come to?

AGAUË: You gave me to Echion, who was said to have been sown in the ground.

CADMUS: Then, Echion had a son born to him—who was he?

AGAUË: Pentheus—my son and his father's.

CADMUS: Yes: and whose head is that you hold in your arms?

AGAUË: A lion's—or so the women said who hunted it.

CADMUS: Now look straight at it; it is not much trouble to look.

AGAUË *looks at the head in silence; then cries out.*

AGAUË: Oh! What am I looking at? What am I holding?

CADMUS: Look at it steadily, and understand more clearly.

AGAUË: I see—O gods, what horror! What torture!

CADMUS: Does this seem to you like a lion?

AGAUË: No, it is Pentheus' head I hold in my accursed hand.

CADMUS: Tears have been shed for him already—before you knew it was he.

AGAUË: Who killed him? How did he come into my hands?

CADMUS: O bitter truth, revealed in a cruel hour!

AGAUË: Tell me—my heart is bursting—I must know the rest.

CADMUS: You killed him—you and your sisters.

AGAUË: Where was it done? At home? Or where else?

CADMUS: Where Actaeon was torn by hounds.

AGAUË: Cithaeron? What evil fate brought Pentheus there?

CADMUS: He went in scorn of Dionysus and your frenzied worship.

AGAUË: But how was it we were all there?

CADMUS: You were mad; the whole city was possessed by Dionysus.

AGAUË: Now I understand: Dionysus has destroyed us.

CADMUS: He was insulted and abused. You did not acknowledge his godhead.

AGAUË: Where is the dear body of my son, Father?

CADMUS: It is here. I searched long for it, and brought it.

AGAUË: Is it decently composed, limb to limb?

CADMUS: [11] Not yet; we came here as quickly as possible.

AGAUË: I will do it myself, if I may be allowed to touch him.

CADMUS: You will be allowed; your guilt is not greater than his.

AGAUË: But what part had Pentheus in my madness?

CADMUS: He was like you in not reverencing Dionysus. Therefore the god has joined all in one destruction, you and your sisters, and Pentheus, to strike down my house and me. I have no son; and now I see the child of your womb, my unhappy daughter, cut off by a shameful and horrible death. Pentheus, dear boy, my daughter's child, this house looked to you as its head; you were its bond of strength; and Thebes feared you. No man would slight your old grandfather if he saw you near; you would give him his deserts. Now I, Cadmus the Great, who sowed in the ground the seed of the Theban race, and reaped a glorious harvest, shall live, a dishonoured exile, far from my home.

O dearest son—yes, even in death you shall be held most dear to me—never again will you touch my beard, and call me Grandfather, and put your arm round me and say, 'Who has wronged you, or insulted you? Who is unkind to you or vexes you? Tell me, Grandfather, that I may punish him.' . . . Never again. Now there is only misery for me, suffering for you, tears for your mother, torment for all our family.

If there be any man who derides the unseen world, let him consider the death of Pentheus, and acknowledge the gods.[12]

CHORUS: Cadmus, I grieve for you. Your grandson suffered justly, but you most cruelly.

AGAUË: Father, you see how one terrible hour has shattered my whole life,[13] and turned my pride to shame, my hap-

[11] Not yet; we came here . . . : this and the following two lines are missing in the text, and here conjecturally supplied.

[12] . . . and acknowledge the gods: the climax of the play's irony.

[13] . . . has shattered my whole life: after these words there is a long gap in the MS. From quotations found in ancient writers editors have collected a considerable number of fragments probably belonging to this

piness to horror. Now I long only to compose my son's body for burial, and lament for him; and then to go away and die. But I do not know if this is lawful; my hands are filthy with a pollution of their own making. When I have spilt the blood that is my own, torn the flesh that grew in my own womb, how can I, without offence to the gods, clasp him to my breast, or chant his ritual dirge? Yet I beg you, if you think it not blasphemous, let me touch my son, and say farewell to that dear body which I loved, and destroyed unknowing. It is right that you should pity, for you suffer too, although you have not sinned.

CADMUS: My daughter, you and I and our whole house are crushed and broken by the anger of Dionysus. It is not for me to keep you from your son. Only I would warn you to steel your heart against a sight that must be fearful to any eyes, but most of all to a mother's. [*To his attendants*] Lay your burden here before her, and remove the covering, that Agauë may see her son.

The coffin is laid on the ground before AGAUË, *who kneels beside it.*

AGAUË: O dearest child, how unnatural are these tears, that should have fallen from your eyes upon my dead face. Now I shall die with none to weep for me. I am justly punished; for in pride I blasphemed the god Dionysus, and did not understand the things I ought to have understood. You too are punished for the same sin; and I cannot tell whether your fate or mine is the more terrible. But since you have suffered with me, you will forgive me both for what I did, not knowing what I did, and for what I do now, touching you with unholy hands—at once your cruellest enemy and your dearest lover.

Now I place your limbs as they should lie; I kiss the flesh that my own body fed, my own care reared to manhood.

---

gap; and the lines here printed are pieced together from these, in a form something like that we may expect Euripides to have used. The MS text begins again with the words, *You shall change your form to a serpent*, on p. 100.

The puzzling prophecy that follows thereafter raises too many questions to be dealt with here; see the excellent note on this passage in Professor Dodds's edition.

Come, father, help me; lay his poor head here; as far as we can, make all exact and seemly.

O dearest face, O young fresh cheek; O kingly eyes, your light now darkened! O my son! See, with this veil I now cover your head, your torn and bloodstained limbs.

Now take him up and carry him to burial—a king lured to a shameful death by the anger of a god.

DIONYSUS *appears above the wall of the palace.*

CHORUS: But look! What is this? It is he, our lord Dionysus himself, no longer disguised as mortal, but in the glory of his godhead!

DIONYSUS: Behold me, a god great and powerful, Dionysus, immortal son of Zeus and Semele!

I come to the City of Seven Gates, to Thebes, whose men and women mocked me, denied my divinity, and refused to receive my holy rites. Now they see clearly the result of impious folly. The royal house is overthrown; the city's streets are full of guilty fear, as every Theban repents too late for his blindness and blasphemy. First and chief in sin was this man Pentheus, who not only rejected my just claims, but put me in fetters and insulted me. Therefore death came to him in the most shameful way of all, at the hands of his own mother. This fate he has justly suffered; for no god can see his worship scorned, and hear his name profaned, and not pursue vengeance to the utmost limit; that mortal men may know that the gods are greater than they.

Now listen further, while I reveal what is destined for the people of Thebes. The day will come when they will be driven from their city to wander East and West over the earth; for Zeus will not suffer a godless city to remain.

Agauë and her sisters must leave Thebes this very day; their exile will prove a full and just penance for the foul pollution they have incurred in this bloodshed. Never again shall they see their native land; for it is an offence to piety that hands so defiled should remain to take part in the city's sacrifices.

Now, Cadmus, I will tell you what suffering you yourself are destined to fulfil. You shall change your form to a serpent; and your wife Harmonia, whom you, though mortal,

received from her divine father Ares, shall likewise change
to a beast of the earth, and become a snake. Thus says the
oracle of Zeus: You, at the head of a barbaric army, shall
with your wife drive a pair of oxen yoked to a wagon; with
your innumerable host you shall destroy many cities; but
when they plunder the temple of Apollo's oracle, their reward shall be sorrow at their home-coming. But you yourself and Harmonia shall be saved by Ares, who shall bestow
on you immortal life among the blessed ones.

I, who tell you this, am Dionysus, son of no mortal father,
but of Zeus. If you all had chosen wisdom, when you would
not, you would have found the son of Zeus your friend, and
you would now be happy.

CADMUS: Dionysus, have mercy on us; we have sinned.

DIONYSUS: You recognize me too late; when you should have
known me, you did not.

CADMUS: All this we have realized; but your vengeance is too
heavy.

DIONYSUS: I am a god; and you insulted me.

CADMUS: Gods should not be like men, keeping anger for ever.

DIONYSUS: Zeus my father ordained this from the beginning.

AGAUË: All hope is gone, father. Our sentence is passed: we
are exiles.

DIONYSUS: Why then put off what is inevitable?

Exit DIONYSUS.

CADMUS: O my daughter, what utter misery and horror has
overtaken us all—you, and your sisters, and me your unhappy father. In my old age I must leave my home and travel
to strange lands. Further than that, it is foretold that I shall
lead a mixed barbarian horde against Hellas. Both I and my
wife, Harmonia, child of Ares, must take the brute form of
serpents, and thus I am to lead her, at the head of an armed
force, to desecrate the altars and tombs of the Hellenes. And
I am to find no respite from suffering; I may not even cross
the deep-flowing stream of Acheron to find peace in death.

AGAUË: And I shall live in exile, separated from you, father.

CADMUS: Poor child! Why do you throw your arms round me,
cherishing my white hair as a swan cares for its old and helpless ones?

AGAUË: Where am I to turn, driven from my home and country?

CADMUS: I do not know, child; your father is little help to you.

AGAUË:

    Farewell, my home; farewell the land I know.

    Exiled, accursed and wretched, now I go

    Forth from this door where first I came a bride.

CADMUS:

    Go, daughter; find some secret place to hide

    Your shame and sorrow.

AGAUË: Father, I weep for you.

CADMUS: I for your suffering, and your sisters' too.

AGAUË:

    There is strange tyranny in the god who sent

    Against your house this cruel punishment.

CADMUS:

    Not strange: our citizens despised his claim,

    And you, and they, put him to open shame.

AGAUË: Father, farewell.

CADMUS: Poor child! I cannot tell

    How you can *fare well;* yet I say, Farewell.

AGAUË:

    I go to lead my sisters by the hand

    To share my wretchedness in a foreign land.

She turns to the Theban women who have been waiting at the edge of the stage.

    Come, see me forth.

                    Gods, lead me to some place

    Where loath'd Cithaeron may not see my face,

    Nor I Cithaeron. I have had my fill

    Of mountain-ecstasy; now take who will

    My holy ivy-wreath, my thyrsus-rod,

    All that reminds me how I served this god!

Exit, followed by CADMUS.

CHORUS:

    Gods manifest themselves in many forms,

    Bring many matters to surprising ends;

    The things we thought would happen do not happen;

    The unexpected God makes possible:

    And that is what has happened here to-day.

Exeunt.

Euripides' "Bacchae" and the Ritual Pattern of Tragedy

Gilbert Murray

What is a Greek Tragedy? Euripides' Early Plays up to 438 B.C.: "Alcestis" and "Telephus"

To the public of the present day a play is merely an entertainment, and it was the same to the Elizabethans. Shakespeare can say to his audience "Our true intent is all for your delight," and we feel no particular shock in reading the words. The companies were just noblemen's servants; and it was natural enough that if Lord Leicester's players did not amuse Lord Leicester's guests, they should be sent away and others hired. If they too proved dull, the patron could drop the play altogether and call for tumblers and dancing dogs.

To a playwright of the twelfth century, who worked out in the church or in front of it his presentation of the great drama of the Gospel, such an attitude would have seemed debased and cynical. However poor the monkish players or playwright might be, surely that which they were presenting was in itself enough to fill the mind of a spectator. To them, as the great medievalist, Gaston Paris, puts it, "the universe was a vast stage, on which was played an eternal drama, full of tears and joy, its actors divided between heaven, earth and hell; a drama whose end is foreseen, whose changes of fortune are directed by the hand of God, yet whose every scene is rich and thrilling."

From *Euripides and His Age* by Gilbert Murray. Reprinted by permission of George Allen & Unwin Ltd.

The spectator was admitted to the councils of the Trinity; he saw the legions of darkness mingling themselves with the lives of humanity, tempting and troubling, and the saints and angels at their work of protection or intercession; he saw with his own eyes the kiss of Judas, the scourging and crucifixion, the descent into Hell, the resurrection and ascension; and, lastly, the dragging down to red and bloody torment of the infinite multitudes of the unorthodox or the wicked. Imagine what passed in the minds of those who witnessed in full faith such a spectacle! (*Poésie du Moyen Age I*, Essay I.)

Now, in spite of a thousand differences of social organization and religious dogma, the atmosphere of primitive Greek tragedy must have been most strangely similar to this. It is not only that, like the medieval plays, Greek tragedy was religious; that it was developed out of a definite ritual; not even that the most marked links of historical continuity can be traced between the death-and-resurrection ritual of certain Pagan "saviours" and those of the medieval drama. It is that the ritual on which tragedy was based embodied the most fundamental Greek conceptions of life and fate, of law and sin and punishment.

When we say that tragedy originated in a dance, ritual or magical, intended to represent the death of the vegetation this year and its coming return in triumph next year, the above remarks may seem hard to justify. But we must remember several things. First, a dance was in ancient times essentially religious, not a mere capering with the feet but an attempt to express with every limb and sinew of the body those emotions for which words, especially the words of simple and unlettered men, are inadequate. . . . Again, vegetation is to us an abstract common noun; to the ancient it was a personal being, not "it" but "He." His death was as our own deaths, and His re-birth a thing to be anxiously sought with prayers and dances. For if He were not re-born, what would happen? Famine, and wholesale death by famine, was a familiar thought, a regularly returning terror, in these primitive agricultural villages. Nay, more, why must the cycle of summer and winter roll as it does? Why must "He" die and men die? Some of the oldest Greek philosophers have no doubt about the answer: there has been "Hubris" or "Adikia," Pride or Injustice, and the result thereof must needs be death. Every year He waxes too strong and commits "Hubris," and such sin has its proper punishment. "The sun shall not transgress his measures," says Heraclitus; "if he does he shall be pursued by Furies, till justice be re-fulfilled." It is the law of all existing things. "They all pay retribution for injustice, one to another, according to the Ordinance of Time" (*Heraclitus*, fr. 94, *Anaximander*, fr. 9). And the history of each year's bloom was an example of this refluent balance. The Year Daemon—Vegetation Spirit or Corn God or whatever we call him—waxes proud and is slain by his enemy, who becomes thereby a murderer and must in turn perish at the hands of the expected avenger, who is at the same time the Wronged One re-risen. The ritual of this Vegetation Spirit is extraordinarily widespread in all quarters of the globe, and may best be studied in Frazer's *The Golden Bough*, especially in the part entitled, "*The Dying God.*" Dionysus, the daemon of tragedy, is one of these Dying Gods, like Attis, Adonis, Osiris.

The Dionysiac ritual which lay at the back of tragedy, may be conjectured in its full form to have had six regular stages: (1) an Agôn or Contest, in which the Daemon fights against his enemy, who—since it is really this year fighting last year—is apt to be almost identical with himself; (2) a Pathos, or disaster, which very commonly takes the shape of a "Sparagmos," or Tearing in pieces; the body of the Corn God being scattered in innumerable seeds over the earth; sometimes of some other sacrificial death; (3) a Messenger, who brings the news; (4) a Lamentation, very often mixed with a Song of Rejoicing, since the death of the Old King is also the accession of the new; (5) the Discovery or Recognition of the hidden or dismembered god; and (6) his Epiphany or Resurrection in glory.[1]

This ritual of Dionysus, being made into a drama and falling into the hands of a remarkable set of creative artists, developed into what we know as Greek tragedy. The creative passion of the artist gradually conquered the emotion of the mere worshipper.

Exactly the same development took place in medieval drama,

---

[1] The above is the present writer's re-statement, published in Jane Harrison's *Themis*, pp. 341 ff., of the orthodox view of the origin of tragedy. See also Cornford, *From Religion to Philosophy*, first few chapters. The chief non-Dionysiac theory is Sir William Ridgeway's, which derives tragedy directly from the funeral cult of individual heroes: *Origin of Tragedy*, Cambridge, 1910.

or rather it was taking place when new secular influences broke in and destroyed it. The liturgical plays first enacted the main story of the New Testament; then they emphasized particular parts—there is a beautiful play, for instance, on the Massacre of the Innocents; then they developed imaginatively scenes that are implied but not mentioned in the Gospel, such as the experiences of the Magdalen when she lived "in joy," her dealings with cosmetic-sellers and the like; then, ranging right outside the Gospel histories, they dealt with the lives of St. Nicholas, St. Antony or any person who provided a good legend and had some claim to an atmosphere of sanctity.

In the same way Greek tragedy extended its range first to embrace the histories of other Heroes or Daemons—the difference is slight—who were essentially like Dionysus: Pentheus, Lycurgus, Hippolytus, Actaeon and especially, I should be inclined to add, Orestes. Then it took in any heroes to whose memory some ritual was attached. For the play is, with the rarest and most doubtful exceptions, essentially the enactment of a ritual, or rather of what the Greeks called an *aition*—that is, a supposed historical event which is the origin or "cause" of the ritual. Thus the death of Hippolytus is the "aition" of the lamentation rite performed at the grave of Hippolytus; the death of Aias is the "aition" of the festival called Aianteia; the death of Medea's children, the "aition" of a certain ritual at Corinth; the story of Prometheus the "aition" of a certain Fire-festival in Athens. The tragedy, as ritual, enacts its own legendary origin.

There is then a further extension of the theme, to include a very few events in recent history. But we must observe that only those events were chosen which were felt to have about them some heroic grandeur or mystery; I think we may even say, only those events which, like the Battle of Salamis or the Fall of Miletus, had been made the subject of some religious celebration.

However that may be, the general temper of tragedy moved strongly away from the monotony of fixed ritual. The subjects thus grew richer and more varied; the mode of representation loftier and more artistic. What had begun as almost pure ritual ended by being almost pure drama. By the time Euripides began to write, the master tragedian Aeschylus had already lifted Greek drama to its highest level: whole generations have read his plays without even suspecting the ritual form that lies behind them. Aeschylus had also made the whole performance much longer and more impressive: he composed three continuous tragedies forming a single whole and followed by the strange performance called a Satyr-play. The wild element of revelry which was proper to Dionysus worship, with its bearded dancing half-animal satyrs, had been kept severely away from the stage during the three tragedies and must burst in to have its fling when they were finished. The other tragedians do not seem to have written in trilogies, and Euripides at any rate moved gradually away from satyr-plays. In their stead he put a curious sort of prosatyric tragedy, a play in the tragic convention and free from the satyric coarseness, but containing at least one half-comic figure and preserving some fantastic quality of atmosphere.

On the Great Festival of Dionysus each year—and sometimes on other festivals—this ritual of tragedy was solemnly performed in the theatre of the god. Like most Greek festivals the performance took the form of a competition. The ground of this custom was, I suspect, religious. It was desired to get a spirit of "Nikê," or victory, into the celebration, and you could only get this by means of a contest. The Archon, or magistrate, in charge of the festival selected three poets to compete, and three rich men to be their "Chorêgoi," that is, to provide all the expenses of the performance. The poet was then said to have "obtained a chorus," and his work now was to "teach the chorus." At the end of the festival a body of five judges, somewhat elaborately and curiously chosen, awarded a first, second and third prize. Even the last competitor must have a kind of "victory"; any mention of "failure" at such a time would be ill-omened. . . .

A reader of the *Bacchae* who looks back at the ritual sequence described above (p. 105 f.) will be startled to find how close this drama, apparently so wild and imaginative, has kept to the ancient rite. The regular year-sequence is just clothed in sufficient myth to make it a story. The daemon must have his enemy who is his Double; then we must have the Contest, the Tearing Asunder, the Messenger, the Lamentation mixed with Joy-cries, the Discovery of the scattered members—and by a sort of doubling the Discovery of the true God—and the Epiphany of the Daemon in glory. All are there in the *Bacchae*.

The god Dionysus, accompanied by his Wild Women, comes to his own land and is rejected by his kinsman, King Pentheus, and by the women of the royal house. The god sends his divine madness on the women. The wise Elders of the tribe warn the king; but Pentheus first binds and imprisons the god; then yielding gradually to the divine power, agrees to go disguised in woman's garb to watch the secret worship of the Maenads on Mt. Kithairon. He goes, is discovered by the Maenads and torn in fragments. His mother, Agave, returns in triumph dancing with her son's head, which, in her madness, she takes for a lion's. There is Lamentation mixed with mad Rejoicing. The scattered body is recovered; Agave is restored to her right mind and to misery; the god appears in majesty and pronounces doom on all who have rejected him. The mortals go forth to their dooms, still faithful, still loving one another. The ghastly and triumphant god ascends into heaven. The whole scheme of the play is given by the ancient ritual. It is the original subject of Attic tragedy treated once more, as doubtless it had already been treated by all or almost all the other tragedians.

But we can go further. We have enough fragments and quotations from the Aeschylean plays on this subject—especially the Lycurgus trilogy—to see that all kinds of small details which seemed like invention, and rather fantastic invention, on the part of Euripides, are taken straight from Aeschylus or the ritual or both. The timbrels, the fawnskin, the ivy, the sacred pine, the god taking the forms of Bull and Lion and Snake; the dances on the mountain at dawn; the Old Men who are by the power of the god made young again; the god represented as beardless and like a woman; the god imprisoned and escaping; the earthquake that wrecks Pentheus' palace; the victim Pentheus disguised as a woman; all these and more can be shown to be in the ritual and nearly all are in the extant fragments of Aeschylus. Even variants of the story which have been used by previous poets have somehow a place found for them. There was, for instance, a variant which made Pentheus lead an army against the Wild Women; in the *Bacchae* this plan is not used, but Pentheus is made to think of it and say he will perhaps follow it, and Dionysus is made to say what will happen if he does. . . . There never was a great play so steeped in tradition as the *Bacchae*.

The *Iphigenîa* was all invention, construction, brilliant psychology; it was a play of new plot and new characters. The *Bacchae* takes an old fixed plot, and fixed formal characters: Dionysus, Pentheus, Cadmus, Teiresias, they are characters that hardly need proper names. One might just as well call them— The God, the Young King, the Old King, the Prophet; and as for Agave, our MSS. do as a rule simply call her "Woman." The *Iphigenîa* is full of informalities, broken metres, interruptions. Its Chorus hardly matters to the plot and has little to sing. The *Bacchae* is the most formal Greek play known to us; its Chorus is its very soul and its lyric songs are as long as they are magnificent. For the curious thing is that in this extreme of formality and faithfulness to archaic tradition Euripides has found both his greatest originality and his most perfect freedom.

He is re-telling an old story; but he is not merely doing that. In the *Bacchae* almost every reader feels that there is something more than a story. There is a meaning, or there is at least a riddle. And we must try in some degree to understand it. Now, in order to keep our heads cool, it is first necessary to remember clearly two things. The *Bacchae* is not free invention; it is tradition. And it is not free personal expression, it is drama. The poet cannot simply and without a veil state his own views; he can only let his own personality shine through the dim curtain in front of which his puppets act their traditional parts and utter their appropriate sentiments. Thus it is doubly elusive. And therein no doubt lay its charm to the poet. He had a vehicle into which he could pour many of those "vaguer faiths and aspirations which a man feels haunting him and calling to him, but which he cannot state in plain language or uphold with a full acceptance of responsibility." But our difficulties are even greater than this. The personal meaning of a drama of this sort is not only elusive; it is almost certain to be inconsistent with itself or at least incomplete. For one only feels its presence strongly when in some way it clashes with the smooth flow of the story. . . .

Nathaniel Hawthorne

An important factor in the development of American literature is brilliantly and fully exemplified by the writings of Nathaniel Hawthorne (1804–1864). In virtually all of his short stories and novels, Hawthorne analyzed with subtle but remorseless logic the nature and effects of Puritanism in the American experience. Largely through the medium of historical, moral, and psychological allegories, he probed the major themes of human guilt and its concealment, the corrosive nature of pride, whether intellectual, moral, or spiritual, the tensions between emotion and reason, and the influence of the past on the present. Hawthorne made these concerns his own so effectively that they have significantly shaped the interests of American writers since his day, as with Herman Melville, Henry James, and William Faulkner.

In many ways, Hawthorne's focus on the American Puritan sensibility came easily to him. He was born in Salem, Massachusetts, of a family whose ancestors included a judge at the celebrated Salem witchcraft trials of the late seventeenth century. When Hawthorne was four, his father died abroad of a tropical disease incurred in the course of his profession as a sea-captain. The effect on his mother was pronounced, but there is some uncertainty as to its form or duration. At any rate, she did manifest a certain passion for solitude together with a measure of eccentricity. These tendencies were transmitted to Hawthorne himself, though not to the degree scholars once thought. His own inclination to be withdrawn was as much due to artistic interests as to heredity or maternal influence. Reflective, sensitive, and imaginative, Hawthorne spent much of his childhood and adolescence reading widely in the poetry and romances of English literature. This literary education was completed formally when he graduated from

Bowdoin College, Maine, in 1825. On his return to Salem he begin his career as an author with a number of stories and a novel, Fanshawe (*1828*), *which was both loosely autobiographical and poor in quality. Many of these stories, including some of his most famous ones, were assembled in* Twice-Told Tales (*1837*).

About 1836 he began a more commercial and social life by doing editorial and writing assignments for Samuel G. Goodrich, a prominent Boston publisher of educational and juvenile books. From 1839 to 1841 he also worked in the Boston Custom House, which brought him into even closer contact with the business world and current affairs. Around the same period he spent time living at Brook Farm, a cooperative community advocating a Transcendentalist philosophy dedicated to the development of man's cultural capacities. This experience was much later utilized rather ironically in The Blithedale Romance (*1852*). *Despite his ultimate lack of sympathy for Transcendentalism, Hawthorne married a convinced exponent of it and they settled happily at Concord, the home of the movement. There he pursued his literary career as well as serving as Surveyor for the municipality of Salem from 1846 to 1849. In 1846 he published* Mosses from an Old Manse, *a collection of his tales of guilt and punishment. Many of these form a natural prelude to his masterpiece* The Scarlet Letter (*1850*), *which is his most profound rendering of the varieties of victimization man is capable of producing.*

In the 1850's his experience broadened and his literary productivity increased. The remainder of his work appeared during this decade, except for a volume of essays, a romance The Marble Faun (*1860*), *and several posthumous fragments of novels and excerpts from his notebooks. These were also the years when he made the acquaintance of Herman Melville, his only contemporary peer in America as a writer of prose fiction. In addition, he served as American consul in Liverpool, England (1853–1857), and lived for two additional years in Italy. In 1860 he returned to Concord and resumed his writing career, though hampered by a slowing of imaginative energies.*

Hawthorne speaks with particular relevance to the American sensibility. Not only does he see man in the New World as a creature informed by a religious consciousness of sin and guilt, but he also regards that fact ambiguously and ironically by dwelling on the loss of innocence in a manner that hovers between seeing the action as either inevitable or accidental, as tragic fall or as mature progression. The tension between the real and the ideal is constant and is exquisitely balanced. This more than anything is responsible for his use of allegory and symbolism as well as of the romance genre, all of which function in an open-ended manner that draws the reader into ever-widening circles of imaginative speculation. The tragic complexity of his work lies in a brooding sense of the mystery of existence and the inescapable yet vital duality of human nature. Balancing this brooding is his compassionate ironic vision, which enables him to reconcile all anguish and frustration in a serenity of clear aesthetic design. The Scarlet Letter is the great illustration of this, but equally representative are stories like "Young Goodman Brown," "Ethan Brand," "Rappaccini's Daughter," and "My Kinsman, Major Molineux."

The critical literature on Hawthorne is immense, varied, and of several distinct phases. The best biography is Randall Stewart's Nathaniel Hawthorne: A Biography *(1948). The same author's edition of* The American Notebooks *(1932) provides a lucid orientation to Hawthorne's character types and recurrent themes. H. W. Schneider's* The Puritan Mind *(1930) sets Hawthorne in relation to the Puritan aspect of his American heritage, while F. O. Matthiessen's* American Renaissance *(1941) illuminates Hawthorne's relationship to his milieu. Helpful criticism of "My Kinsman, Major Molineux" may be found in: H. Waggoner,* Hawthorne, A Critical Study *(1955); S. Lesser,* Fiction and the Unconscious *(1957); Q. D. Leavis, "Hawthorne as Poet,"* Sewanee Review, *59 (Spring and Summer, 1951); and R. H. Fogle,* Hawthorne's Fiction: The Light and the Dark, *rev. ed. (1964).*

My Kinsman,
Major Molineux

Nathaniel Hawthorne

AFTER THE KINGS OF GREAT BRITAIN had assumed the right of appointing the colonial governors, the measures of the latter seldom met with the ready and general approbation which had been paid to those of their predecessors, under the original charters. The people looked with most jealous scrutiny to the exercise of power which did not emanate from themselves, and they usually rewarded their rulers with slender gratitude for the compliances by which, in softening their instructions from beyond the sea, they had incurred the reprehension of those who gave them. The annals of Massachusetts Bay will inform us, that of six governors in the space of about forty years from the surrender of the old charter, under James II., two were imprisoned by a popular insurrection; a third, as Hutchinson inclines to believe, was driven from the province by the whizzing of a musket-ball; a fourth, in the opinion of the same historian, was hastened to his grave by continual bickerings with the House of Representatives; and the remaining two, as well as their successors, till the Revolution, were favored with few and brief intervals of peaceful sway. The inferior members of the court party, in times of high political excitement, led scarcely a more desirable life. These remarks may serve as a preface to the following adventures, which chanced upon a summer night, not far from a hundred years ago. The reader, in order to avoid a long and dry detail of colonial affairs, is requested to dispense with an account of the train of circumstances that had caused much temporary inflammation of the popular mind.

It was near nine o'clock of a moonlight evening, when a boat crossed the ferry with a single passenger, who had obtained his conveyance at that unusual hour by the promise of an extra fare. While he stood on the landing-place, searching in either pocket for the means of fulfilling his agreement, the ferryman lifted a lantern, by the aid of which, and the newly risen moon, he took a very accurate survey of the stranger's figure. He was a youth of barely eighteen years, evidently country-bred, and now, as it should seem, upon his first visit to town. He was clad in a coarse gray coat, well worn, but in excellent repair; his under garments were durably constructed of leather, and fitted tight to a pair of seviceable and well-shaped limbs; his stockings of blue yarn were the incontrovertible work of a mother or a sister; and on his head was a three-cornered hat, which in its better days had perhaps sheltered the graver brow of the lad's father. Under his left arm was a heavy cudgel formed of an oak sapling, and retaining a part of the hardened root; and his equipment was completed by a wallet, not so abundantly stocked as to incommode the vigorous shoulders on which it hung. Brown, curly hair, well-shaped features, and bright, cheerful eyes were nature's gifts, and worth all that art could have done for his adornment.

The youth, one of whose names was Robin, finally drew from his pocket the half of a little province bill of five shillings, which, in the depreciation in that sort of currency, did but satisfy the ferryman's demand, with the surplus of a sexangular piece of parchment, valued at three pence. He then walked forward into the town, with as light a step as if his day's journey had not already exceeded thirty miles, and with as eager an eye as if he were entering London city, instead of the little metropolis of a New England colony. Before Robin had proceeded far, however, it occurred to him that he knew not whither to direct his steps; so he paused, and looked up and down the narrow street, scrutinizing the small and mean wooden buildings that were scattered on either side.

"This low hovel cannot be my kinsman's dwelling," thought he, "nor yonder old house, where the moonlight enters at the broken casement; and truly I see none hereabouts that might be worthy of him. It would have been wise to inquire my way of the ferryman, and doubtless he would have gone with me, and earned a shilling from the Major for his pains. But the next man I meet will do as well."

He resumed his walk, and was glad to perceive that the street now became wider, and the houses more respectable in their appearance. He soon discerned a figure moving on moderately in advance, and hastened his steps to overtake it. As Robin drew nigh, he saw that the passenger was a man in years, with a full periwig of gray hair, a wide-skirted coat of dark cloth, and silk stockings rolled above his knees. He carried a long and polished cane, which he struck down perpendicularly before him at every step; and at regular intervals he uttered two successive hems, of a peculiarly solemn and sepulchral intonation. Having made these observations, Robin laid hold of the skirt of the old man's coat, just when the light from the open door and windows of a barber's shop fell upon both their figures.

"Good evening to you, honored sir," said he, making a low bow, and still retaining his hold of the skirt. "I pray you tell me whereabouts is the dwelling of my kinsman, Major Molineux."

The youth's question was uttered very loudly; and one of the barbers, whose razor was descending on a well-soaped chin, and another who was dressing a Ramillies wig, left their occupations, and came to the door. The citizen, in the mean time, turned a long-favored countenance upon Robin, and answered him in a tone of excessive anger and annoyance. His two sepulchral hems, however, broke into the very centre of his rebuke, with most singular effect, like a thought of the cold grave obtruding among wrathful passions.

"Let go my garment, fellow! I tell you, I know not the man you speak of. What! I have authority, I have—hem, hem—authority; and if this be the respect you show for your betters, your feet shall be brought acquainted with the stocks by daylight, tomorrow morning!"

Robin released the old man's skirt, and hastened away, pursued by an ill-mannered roar of laughter from the barber's shop. He was at first considerably surprised by the result of his question, but, being a shrewd youth, soon thought himself able to account for the mystery.

"This is some country representative," was his conclusion, "who has never seen the inside of my kinsman's door, and lacks the breeding to answer a stranger civilly. The man is old, or verily—I might be tempted to turn back and smite him on the nose. Ah, Robin, Robin! even the barber's boys laugh at you for choosing such a guide! You will be wiser in time, friend Robin."

He now became entangled in a succession of crooked and narrow streets, which crossed each other, and meandered at no great distance from the water-side. The smell of tar was obvious to his nostrils, the masts of vessels pierced the moonlight above the tops of the buildings, and the numerous signs, which Robin paused to read, informed him that he was near the centre of business. But the streets were empty, the shops were closed, and lights were visible only in the second stories of a few dwelling-houses. At length, on the corner of a narrow lane, through which he was passing, he beheld the broad countenance of a British hero swinging before the door of an inn, whence proceeded the voices of many guests. The casement of one of the lower windows was thrown back, and a very thin curtain permitted Robin to distinguish a party at supper, round a well-furnished table. The fragrance of the good cheer steamed forth into the outer air, and the youth could not fail to recollect that the last remnant of his travelling stock of provision had yielded to his morning appetite, and that noon had found and left him dinnerless.

"Oh, that a parchment three-penny might give me a right to sit down at yonder table!" said Robin, with a sigh. "But the Major will make me welcome to the best of his victuals; so I will even step boldly in, and inquire my way to his dwelling."

He entered the tavern, and was guided by the murmur of voices and the fumes of tobacco to the public-room. It was a long and low apartment, with oaken walls, grown dark in the continual smoke, and a floor which was thickly sanded, but of no immaculate purity. A number of persons—the larger part of whom appeared to be mariners, or in some way connected with the sea—occupied the wooden benches, or leather-bottomed chairs, conversing on various matters, and occasionally lending their attention to some topic of general interest. Three or four little groups were draining as many bowls of punch, which the West India trade had long since made a familiar drink in the colony. Others, who had the appearance of men who lived by regular and laborious handicraft, preferred the insulated bliss of an unshared potation, and became more taciturn under its influence. Nearly all, in short, evinced a predilection for the Good Creature in some of its various shapes, for this is a vice to which, as Fast Day sermons of a hundred years ago will testify, we have a long hereditary claim. The only guests to whom Robin's sympathies inclined him were two or three sheepish countrymen, who were using the inn somewhat after the fashion of a Turkish caravansary; they had gotten themselves into the darkest corner of the room, and heedless of the Nicotian atmosphere, were supping on the bread of their own ovens, and the bacon cured in their own chimney-smoke. But though Robin felt a sort of brotherhood with these strangers, his eyes were attracted from them to a person who stood near the door, holding whispered conversation with a group of ill-dressed associates. His features were separately striking almost to grotesqueness, and the whole face left a deep impression on the memory. The forehead bulged out into a double prominence, with a vale between; the nose came boldly forth in an irregular curve, and its bridge was of more than a finger's breadth; the eyebrows were deep and shaggy, and the eyes glowed beneath them like fire in a cave.

While Robin deliberated of whom to inquire respecting his kinsman's dwelling, he was accosted by the innkeeper, a little man in a stained white apron, who had come to pay his professional welcome to the stranger. Being in the second generation from a French Protestant, he seemed to have inherited the courtesy of his parent nation; but no variety of circumstances was ever known to change his voice from the one shrill note in which he now addressed Robin.

"From the country, I presume, sir?" said he, with a profound bow. "Beg leave to congratulate you on your arrival, and trust you intend a long stay with us. Fine town here, sir, beautiful buildings, and much that may interest a stranger. May I hope for the honor of your commands in respect to supper?"

"The man sees a family likeness! the rogue has guessed that I am related to the Major!" thought Robin, who had hitherto experienced little superfluous civility.

All eyes were now turned on the country lad, standing at the door, in his worn three-cornered hat, gray coat, leather breeches, and blue yarn stockings, leaning on an oaken cudgel, and bearing a wallet on his back.

Robin replied to the courteous innkeeper, with such an assumption of confidence as befitted the Major's relative. "My honest friend," he said, "I shall make it a point to patronize your house on some occasion, when"—here he could not help lowering his voice—"when I may have more than a parchment three-pence in my pocket. My present business," continued he, speaking with lofty confidence, "is merely to inquire my way to the dwelling of my kinsman, Major Molineux."

There was a sudden and general movement in the room, which Robin interpreted as expressing the eagerness of each individual to become his guide. But the innkeeper turned his eyes to a written paper on the wall, which he read, or seemed to read, with occasional recurrences to the young man's figure.

"What have we here?" said he, breaking his speech into little dry fragments. " 'Left the house of the subscriber, bounden servant, Hezekiah Mudge,—had on, when he went away, gray coat, leather breeches, master's third-best hat. One pound currency reward to whosoever shall lodge him in any jail of the province.' Better trudge, boy; better trudge!"

Robin had begun to draw his hand towards the lighter end of the oak cudgel, but a strange hostility in every countenance induced him to relinquish his purpose of breaking the courteous innkeeper's head. As he turned to leave the room, he encountered a sneering glance from the bold-featured personage whom he had before noticed; and no sooner was he beyond the door, than he heard a general laugh, in which the innkeeper's voice might be distinguished, like the dropping of small stones into a kettle.

"Now, is it not strange," thought Robin, with his usual shrewdness,—"is it not strange that the confession of an empty pocket should outweigh the name of my kinsman, Major Molineux? Oh, if I had one of those grinning rascals in the woods, where I and my oak sapling grew up together, I would teach him that my arm is heavy though my purse be light!"

On turning the corner of the narrow lane, Robin found himself in a spacious street, with an unbroken line of lofty houses on each side, and a steepled building at the upper end, whence the ringing of a bell announced the hour of nine. The light of the moon, and the lamps from the numerous shop-windows, discovered people promenading on the pavement, and amongst them Robin hoped to recognize his hitherto in-scrutable relative. The result of his former inquiries made him unwilling to hazard another, in a scene of such publicity, and he determined to walk slowly and silently up the street, thrust-ing his face close to that of every elderly gentleman, in search of the Major's lineaments. In his progress, Robin encountered many gay and gallant figures. Embroidered garments of showy colors, enormous periwigs, gold-laced hats, and silver-hilted swords glided past him and dazzled his optics. Travelled youths, imitators of the European fine gentlemen of the period, trod jauntily along, half dancing to the fashionable tunes which they hummed, and making poor Robin ashamed of his quiet and natural gait. At length, after many pauses to examine the gorgeous display of goods in the shop-windows, and after suffering some rebukes for the impertinence of his scrutiny into people's faces, the Major's kinsman found him-self near the steepled building, still unsuccessful in his search. As yet, however, he had seen only one side of the thronged street; so Robin crossed, and continued the same sort of inquisition down the opposite pavement, with stronger hopes than the philosopher seeking an honest man, but with no better fortune. He had arrived about midway towards the lower end, from which his course began, when he overheard the approach of some one who struck down a cane on the flag-stones at every step, uttering, at regular intervals, two sepulchral hems.

"Mercy on us!" quoth Robin, recognizing the sound.

Turning a corner, which chanced to be close at his right hand, he hastened to pursue his researches in some other part of the town. His patience now was wearing low, and he seemed to feel more fatigue from his rambles since he crossed the ferry, than from his journey of several days on the other side. Hunger also pleaded loudly within him, and Robin began to balance the propriety of demanding, violently, and with lifted cudgel, the necessary guidance from the first solitary passen-ger whom he should meet. While a resolution to this effect was gaining strength, he entered a street of mean appearance, on either side of which a row of ill-built houses was straggling towards the harbor. The moonlight fell upon no passenger along the whole extent, but in the third domicile which Robin passed there was a half-opened door, and his keen glance detected a woman's garment within.

"My luck may be better here," said he to himself.

Accordingly, he approached the door, and beheld it shut closer as he did so; yet an open space remained, sufficing for the fair occupant to observe the stranger, without a corresponding display on her part. All that Robin could discern was a strip of scarlet petticoat, and the occasional sparkle of an eye, as if the moonbeams were trembling on some bright thing.

"Pretty mistress," for I may call her so with a good conscience, thought the shrewd youth, since I know nothing to the contrary,—"my sweet pretty mistress, will you be kind enough to tell me whereabouts I must seek the dwelling of my kinsman, Major Molineux?"

Robin's voice was plaintive and winning, and the female, seeing nothing to be shunned in the handsome country youth, thrust open the door, and came forth into the moonlight. She was a dainty little figure, with a white neck, round arms, and a slender waist, at the extremity of which her scarlet petticoat jutted out over a hoop, as if she were standing in a balloon. Moreover, her face was oval and pretty, her hair dark beneath the little cap, and her bright eyes possessed a sly freedom, which triumphed over those of Robin.

"Major Molineux dwells here," said this fair woman.

Now, her voice was the sweetest Robin had heard that night, the airy counterpart of a stream of melted silver; yet he could not help doubting whether that sweet voice spoke Gospel truth. He looked up and down the mean street, and then surveyed the house before which they stood. It was a small, dark edifice of two stories, the second of which projected over the lower floor, and the front apartment had the aspect of a shop for petty commodities.

"Now, truly, I am in luck," replied Robin, cunningly, "and so indeed is my kinsman, the Major, in having so pretty a housekeeper. But I prithee trouble him to step to the door; I will deliver him a message from his friends in the country, and then go back to my lodgings at the inn."

"Nay, the Major has been abed this hour or more," said the lady of the scarlet petticoat; "and it would be to little purpose to disturb him to-night, seeing his evening draught was of the strongest. But he is a kind-hearted man, and it would be as much as my life's worth to let a kinsman of his turn away from the door. You are the good old gentleman's very picture, and I could swear that was his rainy-weather hat. Also he has garments very much resembling those leather small-clothes. But come in, I pray, for I bid you hearty welcome in his name."

So saying, the fair and hospitable dame took our hero by the hand; and the touch was light, and the force was gentleness, and though Robin read in her eyes what he did not hear in her words, yet the slender-waisted woman in the scarlet petticoat proved stronger than the athletic country youth. She had drawn his half-willing footsteps nearly to the threshold, when the opening of a door in the neighborhood startled the Major's housekeeper, and, leaving the Major's kinsman, she vanished speedily into her own domicile. A heavy yawn preceded the appearance of a man, who, like the Moonshine of Pyramus and Thisbe, carried a lantern, needlessly aiding his sister luminary in the heavens. As he walked sleepily up the street, he turned his broad, dull face on Robin, and displayed a long staff, spiked at the end.

"Home, vagabond, home!" said the watchman, in accents that seemed to fall asleep as soon as they were uttered. "Home, or we'll set you in the stocks by peep of day!"

"This is the second hint of the kind," thought Robin. "I wish they would end my difficulties, by setting me there to-night."

Nevertheless, the youth felt an instinctive antipathy towards the guardian of midnight order, which at first prevented him from asking his usual question. But just when the man was about to vanish behind the corner, Robin resolved not to lose the opportunity, and shouted lustily after him,—

"I say, friend! will you guide me to the house of my kinsman, Major Molineux?"

The watchman made no reply, but turned the corner and was gone; yet Robin seemed to hear the sound of drowsy laughter stealing along the solitary street. At that moment, also, a pleasant titter saluted him from the open window above his head; he looked up, and caught the sparkle of a saucy eye; a round arm beckoned to him, and next he heard light footsteps descending the staircase within. But Robin, being of the household of a New England clergyman, was a good youth, as well as a shrewd one; so he resisted temptation, and fled away.

He now roamed desperately, and at random, through the town, almost ready to believe that a spell was on him, like that by which a wizard of his country had once kept three pursuers wandering, a whole winter night, within twenty paces of the cottage which they sought. The streets lay before him, strange and desolate, and the lights were extinguished in almost every house. Twice, however, little parties of men, among whom Robin distinguished individuals in outlandish attire, came hurrying along; but, though on both occasions they paused to address him, such intercourse did not at all enlighten his perplexity. They did but utter a few words in some language of which Robin knew nothing, and perceiving his inability to answer, bestowed a curse upon him in plain English and hastened away. Finally, the lad determined to knock at the door of every mansion that might appear worthy to be occupied by his kinsman, trusting that perseverance would overcome the fatality that had hitherto thwarted him. Firm in this resolve, he was passing beneath the walls of a church, which formed the corner of two streets, when, as he turned into the shade of its steeple, he encountered a bulky stranger, muffled in a cloak. The man was proceeding with the speed of earnest business, but Robin planted himself full before him, holding the oak cudgel with both hands across his body as a bar to further passage.

"Halt, honest man, and answer me a question," said he, very resolutely. "Tell me, this instant, whereabouts is the dwelling of my kinsman, Major Molineux!"

"Keep your tongue between your teeth, fool, and let me pass!" said a deep, gruff voice, which Robin partly remembered. "Let me pass, I say, or I'll strike you to the earth!"

"No, no, neighbor!" cried Robin, flourishing his cudgel, and then thrusting its larger end close to the man's muffled face. "No, no, I'm not the fool you take me for, nor do you pass till I have an answer to my question. Whereabouts is the dwelling of my kinsman, Major Molineux?"

The stranger, instead of attempting to force his passage, stepped back into the moonlight, unmuffled his face, and stared full into that of Robin.

"Watch here an hour, and Major Molineux will pass by," said he.

Robin gazed with dismay and astonishment on the unprecedented physiognomy of the speaker. The forehead with its double prominence, the broad hooked nose, the shaggy eyebrows, and fiery eyes were those which he had noticed at the inn, but the man's complexion had undergone a singular, or, more properly, a twofold change. One side of the face blazed an intense red, while the other was black as midnight, the division line being in the broad bridge of the nose; and a mouth which seemed to extend from ear to ear was black or red, in contrast to the color of the cheek. The effect was as if two individual devils, a fiend of fire and a fiend of darkness, had united themselves to form this infernal visage. The stranger grinned in Robin's face, muffled his parti-colored features, and was out of sight in a moment.

"Strange things we travellers see!" ejaculated Robin.

He seated himself, however, upon the steps of the church-door, resolving to wait the appointed time for his kinsman. A few moments were consumed in philosophical speculations upon the species of man who had just left him; but having settled this point shrewdly, rationally, and satisfactorily, he was compelled to look elsewhere for his amusement. And first he threw his eyes along the street. It was of more respectable appearance than most of those into which he had wandered; and the moon, creating, like the imaginative power, a beautiful strangeness in familiar objects, gave something of romance to a scene that might not have possessed it in the light of day. The irregular and often quaint architecture of the houses, some of whose roofs were broken into numerous little peaks, while others ascended, steep and narrow, into a single point, and others again were square; the pure snow-white of some of their complexions, the aged darkness of others, and the thousand sparklings, reflected from bright substances in the walls of many; these matters engaged Robin's attention for a while, and then began to grow wearisome. Next he endeavored to define the forms of distant objects, starting away, with almost ghostly indistinctness, just as his eye appeared to grasp them; and finally he took a minute survey of an edifice which stood on the opposite side of the street, directly in front of the church-door, where he was stationed. It was a large, square mansion, distinguished from its neighbors by a balcony, which rested on tall pillars, and by an elaborate Gothic window, communicating therewith.

"Perhaps this is the very house I have been seeking," thought Robin.

Then he strove to speed away the time, by listening to a murmur which swept continually along the street, yet was scarcely audible, except to an unaccustomed ear like his; it was a low, dull, dreamy sound, compounded of many noises, each of which was at too great a distance to be separately heard. Robin marvelled at this snore of a sleeping town, and marvelled more whenever its continuity was broken by now and then a distant shout, apparently loud where it originated. But altogether it was a sleep-inspiring sound, and, to shake off its drowsy influence, Robin arose, and climbed a window-frame, that he might view the interior of the church. There the moonbeams came trembling in, and fell down upon the deserted pews, and extended along the quiet aisles. A fainter yet more awful radiance was hovering around the pulpit, and one solitary ray had dared to rest upon the open page of the great Bible. Had nature, in that deep hour, become a worshipper in the house which man had builded? Or was that heavenly light the visible sanctity of the place,—visible because no earthly and impure feet were within the walls? The scene made Robin's heart shiver with a sensation of loneliness stronger than he had ever felt in the remotest depths of his native woods; so he turned away and sat down again before the door. There were graves around the church, and now an uneasy thought obtruded into Robin's breast. What if the object of his search, which had been so often and so strangely thwarted, were all the time mouldering in his shroud? What if his kinsman should glide through yonder gate, and nod and smile to him in dimly passing by?

"Oh that any breathing thing were here with me!" said Robin.

Recalling his thoughts from this uncomfortable track, he sent them over forest, hill, and stream, and attempted to imagine how that evening of ambiguity and weariness had been spent by his father's household. He pictured them assembled at the door, beneath the tree, the great old tree,

which had been spared for its huge twisted trunk and venerable shade, when a thousand leafy brethren fell. There, at the
going down of the summer sun, it was his father's custom to
perform domestic worship, that the neighbors might come and
join with him like brothers of the family, and that the way-
faring man might pause to drink at that fountain, and keep his
heart pure by freshening the memory of home. Robin distinguished the seat of every individual of the little audience;
he saw the good man in the midst, holding the Scriptures in
the golden light that fell from the western clouds; he beheld
him close the book and all rise up to pray. He heard the old
thanksgiving for daily mercies, the old supplications for their
continuance, to which he had so often listened in weariness,
but which were now among his dear remembrances. He per-
ceived the slight inequality of his father's voice when he came
to speak of the absent one; he noted how his mother turned
her face to the broad and knotted trunk; how his elder
brother scorned, because the beard was rough upon his upper
lip, to permit his features to be moved; how the younger sister
drew down a low hanging branch before her eyes; and how the
little one of all, whose sports had hitherto broken the de-
corum of the scene, understood the prayer for her playmate,
and burst into clamorous grief. Then he saw them go in at the
door; and when Robin would have entered also, the latch
tinkled into its place, and he was excluded from his home.

"Am I here, or there?" cried Robin, starting; for all at once,
when his thoughts had become visible and audible in a dream,
the long, wide, solitary street shone out before him.

He aroused himself, and endeavored to fix his attention
steadily upon the large edifice which he had surveyed before.
But still his mind kept vibrating between fancy and reality;
by turns, the pillars of the balcony lengthened into the tall,
bare stems of pines, dwindled down to human figures, settled
again into their true shape and size, and then commenced a
new succession of changes. For a single moment, when he
deemed himself awake, he could have sworn that a visage—
one which he seemed to remember, yet could not absolutely
name as his kinsman's—was looking towards him from the
Gothic window. A deeper sleep wrestled with and nearly over-
came him, but fled at the sound of footsteps along the opposite
pavement. Robin rubbed his eyes, discerned a man passing at

the foot of the balcony, and addressed him in a loud, peevish, and lamentable cry.

"Hallo, friend! must I wait here all night for my kinsman, Major Molineux?"

The sleeping echoes awoke, and answered the voice; and the passenger, barely able to discern a figure sitting in the oblique shade of the steeple, traversed the street to obtain a nearer view. He was himself a gentleman in his prime, of open, intelligent, cheerful, and altogether prepossessing countenance. Perceiving a country youth, apparently homeless and without friends, he accosted him in a tone of real kindness, which had become strange to Robin's ears.

"Well, my good lad, who are you sitting here?" inquired he. "Can I be of service to you in any way?"

"I am afraid not, sir," replied Robin, despondingly; "yet I shall take it kindly, if you'll answer me a single question. I've been searching, half the night, for one Major Molineux; now, sir, is there really such a person in these parts, or am I dreaming?"

"Major Molineux! The name is not altogether strange to me," said the gentleman, smiling. "Have you any objection to telling me the nature of your business with him?"

Then Robin briefly related that his father was a clergyman, settled on a small salary, at a long distance back in the country, and that he and Major Molineux were brothers' children. The Major, having inherited riches, and acquired civil and military rank, had visited his cousin, in great pomp, a year or two before; had manifested much interest in Robin and an elder brother, and, being childless himself, had thrown out hints respecting the future establishment of one of them in life. The elder brother was destined to succeed to the farm which his father cultivated in the interval of sacred duties; it was therefore determined that Robin should profit by his kinsman's generous intentions, especially as he seemed to be rather the favorite, and was thought to possess other necessary endowments.

"For I have the name of being a shrewd youth," observed Robin, in this part of his story.

"I doubt not you deserve it," replied his new friend, good-naturedly; "but pray proceed."

"Well, sir, being nearly eighteen years old, and well grown, as you see," continued Robin, drawing himself up to his full height, "I thought it high time to begin the world. So my mother and sister put me in handsome trim, and my father gave me half the remnant of his last year's salary, and five days ago I started for this place, to pay the Major a visit. But, would you believe it, sir! I crossed the ferry a little after dark, and have yet found nobody that would show me the way to his dwelling; only, an hour or two since, I was told to wait here, and Major Molineux would pass by."

"Can you describe the man who told you this?" inquired the gentleman.

"Oh, he was a very ill-favored fellow, sir," replied Robin, "with two great bumps on his forehead, a hook nose, fiery eyes; and, what struck me as the strangest, his face was of two different colors. Do you happen to know such a man, sir?"

"Not intimately," answered the stranger, "but I chanced to meet him a little time previous to your stopping me. I believe you may trust his word, and that the Major will very shortly pass through this street. In the mean time, as I have a singular curiosity to witness your meeting, I will sit down here upon the steps and bear you company."

He seated himself accordingly, and soon engaged his companion in animated discourse. It was but of brief continuance, however, for a noise of shouting, which had long been remotely audible, drew so much nearer that Robin inquired its cause.

"What may be the meaning of this uproar?" asked he. "Truly, if your town be always as noisy, I shall find little sleep while I am an inhabitant."

"Why, indeed, friend Robin, there do appear to be three or four riotous fellows abroad to-night," replied the gentleman. "You must not expect all the stillness of your native woods here in our streets. But the watch will shortly be at the heels of these lads and"—

"Ay, and set them in the stocks by peep of day," interrupted Robin, recollecting his own encounter with the drowsy lantern-bearer. "But, dear sir, if I may trust my ears, an army of watchmen would never make head against such a multitude of rioters. There were at least a thousand voices went up to make that one shout."

"May not a man have several voices, Robin, as well as two complexions?" said his friend.

"Perhaps a man may; but Heaven forbid that a woman

should!" responded the shrewd youth, thinking of the seduc-
tive tones of the Major's housekeeper.

The sounds of a trumpet in some neighboring street now
became so evident and continual, that Robin's curiosity was
strongly excited. In addition to the shouts, he heard frequent
bursts from many instruments of discord, and a wild and
confused laughter filled up the intervals. Robin rose from the
steps, and looked wistfully towards a point whither people
seemed to be hastening.

"Surely some prodigious merry-making is going on," exclaimed he. "I have laughed very little since I left home, sir,
and should be sorry to lose an opportunity. Shall we step
round the corner by that darkish house, and take our share of
the fun?"

"Sit down again, sit down, good Robin," replied the gentleman, laying his hand on the skirt of the gray coat. "You forget
that we must wait here for your kinsman; and there is reason
to believe that he will pass by, in the course of a very few
moments."

The near approach of the uproar had now disturbed the
neighborhood; windows flew open on all sides; and many
heads, in the attire of the pillow, and confused by sleep suddenly broken, were protruded to the gaze of whoever had
leisure to observe them. Eager voices hailed each other from
house to house, all demanding the explanation, which not a
soul could give. Half-dressed men hurried towards the unknown commotion, stumbling as they went over the stone
steps that thrust themselves into the narrow foot-walk. The
shouts, the laughter, and the tuneless bray, the antipodes of
music, came onwards with increasing din, till scattered individuals, and then denser bodies, began to appear round a
corner at the distance of a hundred yards.

"Will you recognize your kinsman, if he passes in this
crowd?" inquired the gentleman.

"Indeed, I can't warrant it, sir; but I'll take my stand here,
and keep a bright lookout," answered Robin, descending to the
outer edge of the pavement.

A mighty stream of people now emptied into the street, and
came rolling slowly towards the church. A single horseman
wheeled the corner in the midst of them, and close behind him
came a band of fearful wind-instruments, sending forth a

fresher discord now that no intervening buildings kept it from the ear. Then a redder light disturbed the moonbeams, and a dense multitude of torches shone along the street, concealing, by their glare, whatever object they illuminated. The single horseman, clad in a military dress, and bearing a drawn sword, rode onward as the leader, and, by his fierce and variegated countenance, appeared like war personified; the red of one cheek was an emblem of fire and sword; the blackness of the other betokened the mourning that attends them. In his train were wild figures in the Indian dress, and many fantastic shapes without a model, giving the whole march a visionary air, as if a dream had broken forth from some feverish brain, and were sweeping visibly through the midnight streets. A mass of people, inactive, except as applauding spectators, hemmed the procession in; and several women ran along the sidewalk, piercing the confusion of heavier sounds with their shrill voices of mirth or terror.

"The double-faced fellow has his eye upon me," muttered Robin, with an indefinite but an uncomfortable idea that he was himself to bear a part in the pageantry.

The leader turned himself in the saddle, and fixed his glance full upon the country youth, as the steed went slowly by. When Robin had freed his eyes from those fiery ones, the musicians were passing before him, and the torches were close at hand; but the unsteady brightness of the latter formed a veil which he could not penetrate. The rattling of wheels over the stones sometimes found its way to his ear, and confused traces of a human form appeared at intervals, and then melted into the vivid light. A moment more, and the leader thundered a command to halt: the trumpets vomited a horrid breath, and then held their peace; the shouts and laughter of the people died away, and there remained only a universal hum, allied to silence. Right before Robin's eyes was an uncovered cart. There the torches blazed the brightest, there the moon shone out like day, and there, in tar-and-feathery dignity, sat his kinsman, Major Molineux!

He was an elderly man, of large and majestic person, and strong, square features, betokening a steady soul; but steady as it was, his enemies had found means to shake it. His face was pale as death, and far more ghastly; the broad forehead was contracted in his agony, so that his eye-brows formed one grizzled line; his eyes were red and wild, and the foam hung white upon his quivering lip. His whole frame was agitated by a quick and continual tremor, which his pride strove to quell, even in those circumstances of overwhelming humiliation. But perhaps the bitterest pang of all was when his eyes met those of Robin; for he evidently knew him on the instant, as the youth stood witnessing the foul disgrace of a head grown gray in honor. They stared at each other in silence, and Robin's knees shook, and his hair bristled, with a mixture of pity and terror. Soon, however, a bewildering excitement began to seize upon his mind; the preceding adventures of the night, the unexpected appearance of the crowd, the torches, the confused din and the hush that followed, the spectre of his kinsman reviled by that great multitude,—all this, and, more than all, a perception of tremendous ridicule in the whole scene, affected him with a sort of mental inebriety. At that moment a voice of sluggish merriment saluted Robin's ears; he turned instinctively, and just behind the corner of the church stood the lantern-bearer, rubbing his eyes, and drowsily enjoying the lad's amazement. Then he heard a peal of laughter like the ringing of silvery bells; a woman twitched his arm, a saucy eye met his, and he saw the lady of the scarlet petticoat. A sharp, dry cachinnation appealed to his memory, and, standing on tiptoe in the crowd, with his white apron over his head, he beheld the courteous little innkeeper. And lastly, there sailed over the heads of the multitude a great, broad laugh, broken in the midst by two sepulchral hems; thus, "Haw, haw, haw,— hem, hem,—haw, haw, haw, haw!"

The sound proceeded from the balcony of the opposite edifice, and thither Robin turned his eyes. In front of the Gothic window stood the old citizen wrapped in a wide gown, his gray periwig exchanged for a nightcap, which was thrust back from his forehead, and his silk stockings hanging about his legs. He supported himself on his polished cane in a fit of convulsive merriment, which manifested itself on his solemn old features like a funny inscription on a tombstone. Then Robin seemed to hear the voices of the barbers, of the guests of the inn, and of all who had made sport of him that night. The contagion was spreading among the multitude, when all at once, it seized upon Robin, and he sent forth a shout of laughter that echoed through the street,—every man shook his sides, every man emptied his lungs, but Robin's shout was the loudest there. The cloud-spirits peeped from their silvery islands, as the congregated mirth went roaring up the sky! The Man in the Moon heard the far bellow. "Oho," quoth he, "the old earth is frolicsome to-night!"

When there was a momentary calm in that tempestuous sea of sound, the leader gave the sign, the procession resumed its march. On they went, like fiends that throng in mockery around some dead potentate, mighty no more, but majestic still in his agony. On they went, in counterfeited pomp, in senseless uproar, in frenzied merriment, trampling all on an old man's heart. On swept the tumult, and left a silent street behind.

"Well, Robin, are you dreaming?" inquired the gentleman, laying his hand on the youth's shoulder.

Robin started, and withdrew his arm from the stone post to which he had instinctively clung, as the living stream rolled by him. His cheek was somewhat pale, and his eye not quite as lively as in the earlier part of the evening.

"Will you be kind enough to show me the way to the ferry?" said he, after a moment's pause.

"You have, then, adopted a new subject of inquiry?" observed his companion, with a smile.

"Why, yes, sir," replied Robin, rather dryly. "Thanks to you, and to my other friends, I have at last met my kinsman, and he will scarce desire to see my face again. I begin to grow weary of a town life, sir. Will you show me the way to the ferry?"

"No, my good friend Robin,—not to-night, at least," said the gentleman. "Some few days hence, if you wish it, I will speed you on your journey. Or, if you prefer to remain with us, perhaps, as you are a shrewd youth, you may rise in the world without the help of your kinsman, Major Molineux."

Yankee Bumpkin and Scapegoat King

Daniel Hoffman

"IN YOUTH, men are apt to write more wisely than they really know or feel; and the remainder of life may be not idly spent in realizing and convincing themselves of the wisdom which they uttered long ago." This reflection occurred to Hawthorne as he gathered his fugitive writings of two decades for *The Snow-Image, and Other Twice-Told Tales*. The very last of these, whether so placed as a capstone or an afterthought, proves to be his earliest full success and one of the most durable and contemporary fictions of his entire career. "My Kinsman, Major Molineux" is unusual among Hawthorne's writings in its overt treatment of the most important political and cultural problem of the American republic: self-determination and its consequences. The tale is striking, too, in its bold and direct appropriation from folk traditions and popular culture of the representative traits of the New England character. Hawthorne would use these humorously in "Mr. Higginbotham's Catastrophe," ironically in portraying Holgrave in *The House of the Seven Gables,* and descriptively in his war-time account of President Lincoln. But now, in 1832, he anticipates by a quarter-century Melville's use of similar materials and themes in "Benito Cereno" and *The Confidence-Man* to attack the popular doctrines of optimism and self-reliance which those traditions themselves exemplify. In "My Kinsman, Major Molineux" these folk themes are

placed in dramatic opposition to an eighteenth-century Colonial reenactment of the ancient ritual of the deposition of
the Scapegoat King. This ritual occurs in the story as the fulfillment of the hero's quest for his influential kinsman; its
function, in terms of his own development, is to provide a
ceremony of initiation. What is revealed to him is self-knowl-
edge far deeper than his callow folk-character had hitherto
anticipated.

In Hawthorne's tale, a youth named Robin, now eighteen
and thinking it "high time to begin the world," sets out from
his father's farm on his "first visit to town." There, with the
help of Major Molineux, his father's cousin, he expects to make
his fortune. Thus Robin is on the threshold of metamorphosis,
like young Ben Franklin walking up Market Street with a loaf
of bread under his arm. Committed to upward mobility, he
is as yet dependent upon benevolent, paternalistic authority.
As he becomes "entangled in a succession of crooked and
narrow streets" his quest for his kinsman brings him only
bafflement and mocking laughter from every quarter: from a
ridiculously solemn old man, from a barber, an innkeeper, a
demoniac fiery-eyed patron at the inn, a trollop in a scarlet
petticoat, a watchman. Parties of men approach, speak to him
in gibberish, and when he cannot answer curse him in plain
English. In desperation Robin accosts a muffled burly stranger
with his cudgel and demands to be directed to his kinsman.
Instead of forcing his passage the man says, "Watch here an
hour, and Major Molineux will pass by." With a start Robin
recognizes the demoniac of the inn. "One side of the face
blazed an intense red, while the other was black as midnight
. . . as if two individual devils, a fiend of fire and a fiend of
darkness, had united themselves to form this infernal visage."
Now, waiting by moonlight on the church steps, Robin thinks
of the home he has left. In a reverie he sees his father giving
the family blessings: "Then he saw them go in at the door; and
when Robin would have entered also, the latch tinkled into
place, and he was excluded from his home." He dreams—or
wakes—to see his kinsman's face regarding him from a nearby
window. Waking in truth, he asks a passing stranger whether
he must wait all night for Major Molineux. The stranger, a
mature, prepossessing man, "perceiving a country youth, apparently homeless and without friends . . . accosted him in

a tone of real kindness." When Robin tells his mission the gentleman replies, "I have a singular curiosity to witness your meeting," and sits beside him. Soon sounds of a Saturnalia approach, then a wild procession headed by the double-faced man, who watches Robin the while, swirls past by torch-light, drawing a cart. "There, in tar-and-feathery dignity, sat his kinsman, Major Molineux!"

> He was an elderly man, of large and majestic person, and strong, square features, betokening a steady soul; but steady as it was, his enemies had found means to shake it. . . . But perhaps the bitterest pang of all was when his eyes met those of Robin; for he evidently knew him on the instant, as the youth stood witnessing the foul disgrace of head grown gray in honor. They stared at each other in silence, and Robin's knees shook, and his hair bristled, with a mixture of pity and terror.

Then, one by one, the laughing mockers of his night-long adventure add their derisive voices to the din. "The contagion . . . all at once seized upon Robin . . . Robin's shout was the loudest there." At the leader's signal, "On they went, like fiends that throng in mockery around some dead potentate, mighty no more, but majestic still in his agony . . . and left a silent street behind." Robin's companion lays a hand on his shoulder. "Well, Robin, are you dreaming?" Robin, "his eye not quite as lively as in the earlier part of the evening," replies by asking to be shown the way to the ferry. "I grow weary of town life, sir." But this friendly stranger declines to oblige him, suggesting that "If you prefer to remain with us, perhaps, as you are a shrewd youth, you may rise in the world without the help of your kinsman, Major Molineux."

From even this crude précis of the plot it is hard to take seriously Parrington's strictures against Hawthorne as a mere romancer of the murky past who avoided dealing with the problems and issues of Jacksonian democracy. One of the two chief interpretations of "My Kinsman, Major Molineux," that of Q. D. Leavis,[1] suggests how deeply involved Hawthorne was with the basic problems of American self-realization. She sees

---

[1] "Hawthorne as Poet" [Part I], *Sewanee Review*, LIX (Spring, 1951), 198–205.

this tale as "a symbolic action which . . . takes the form of something between a pageant and a ritual drama, disguised in the emotional logic of a dream." She suggests that the tale be subtitled "America Comes of Age," and reads it as an historic parable in which Robin "represents the young America" who has come to town, "that is, the contemporary scene where the historic future will be decided." The opening paragraphs of the tale establish that popular insurrections and violent deaths of the governors were characteristic of the history of the colonies.

A quite different reading is suggested by Hyatt H. Waggoner and elaborated by Roy R. Male.[2] Waggoner emphasizes the dreamlike manipulation of incident, sound, and color in the tale, and reads its primary meaning as a revelation of an Oedipal conflict. The tale reveals "man's image of himself as the destroyer of the father—because he has wished the destruction—a destroyer bathed in guilt yet somehow justified. . . . Passing through the stages of initial identification with the father image, rejection, and shame, Robin at last emerges with the help of the stranger into maturity." Male's elaboration of this Freudian reading suggests "that visions of the father figure may commonly be split into two or more images." The pompous old man and the watchman then "are shapes of what Robin is attempting to leave behind." Other figures are "various forms of the cultured kinsman he is seeking."

> Thus as he verges upon maturity the young man's yearnings for freedom from authority and for a worldly patrimony take on exaggerated proportions. The dual aspect of this psychic conflict can be seen in the 'infernal visage' of the 'double-faced fellow,' whose complexions are split. . . . The grotesque fusion of the two forms is a distorted father image in which youthful misrepresentation of both the real father and the real uncle are combined.

Robin's real father appears in his dream of home, and again as the kindly stranger who stays by his side during the imaged destruction of Major Molineux. The kinsman, of course, is the most potent father-image in the story.

---

[2] Waggoner, *Hawthorne, A Critical Study* (Cambridge, 1955), pp. 47–53; Male, *Hawthorne's Tragic Vision* (Austin, Tex., 1957), pp. 48–53.

The truth of the tale includes both these theories and more. Hawthorne's most successful fictions may be described by a phrase from one of his least effective stories: "I can never separate the idea from the symbol in which it manifests itself."[3] In his best tales, simple arrangements of objects, persons, or actions are the symbols, but these are so economically chosen as to represent complex constellations of ideas. Certainly the pattern of action in "My Kinsman, Major Molineux" is at the same time a journey, a search, an initiation. Robin is indeed a representative American, first as witness, then as participant, in a cultural-political experience of archetypal significance to our national identity. He is also a representative young man who must come to terms with his feelings about his father, about the past, about authority, in order to pass from adolescence into maturity.

In psychological terms, Male is probably right that all the men in the story are displacements or substitutions for the father, in his several aspects: as authority (to be feared, courted, or ridiculed), and as paternity (to be loved, escaped from, and depended upon). But there are other implications necessary to a full involvement with the tale. Major Molineux is not only the Father as Authority, he is also the Past which must be rejected. Specifically, he represents British rule—in political terms he is the representative of the Crown. If psychologically the Major displaces Robin's father, politically and culturally he actually displaces the King. As authority figure, whether patristic or regal, he represents Order, Tradition, Stability. But as the Father-King in a cart whose "tar-and-feathery dignity" inspire the tragic emotions of pity and terror, Major Molineux takes on yet further dimensions. He is the Sacrificed King, the Royal Scapegoat, the "dead potentate . . . majestic still in his agony" around whom the townsfolk "throng in mockery." Frazer analyzes the Scapegoat King as a ritual role invested with two functions, the expulsion of evil and the sacrificial death of the divine ruler whose declining potency is renewed in his young successor. One can hardly suggest that this modern anthropological theory was available to Hawthorne in 1832, but from his tale we can infer his intuitive understanding of the primitive ritual which he used

[3] "The Antique Ring," *Works*, XII, 67.

metaphorically in describing the downfall of Major Molineux. The rebellion in the tale, although dated vaguely around 1730, is clearly a "type" of the American Revolution. This was indeed the supercession of an old order by a new, from which ensued a revitalization of the energies of American society. Hawthorne remarks that the colonists had frequently attacked the person of their royal governors, however suppliant to their demands the governors, as individuals, had been. In this there is the inference that in tarring and feathering Major Molineux the conspirators are symbolically ridding the colony of a symbol of the chief evil that prepossessed their consciousness as a culture. Further warrant for inferring Major Molineux to represent a Scapegoat King is suggested by one of the identities of his antagonist, the man with the double visage.

This character may be, as Male proposes, a double father-image combining "youthful misrepresentation of both the real father and the real uncle." Yet we must also take him more literally than this; or, if we take him in metaphors, let the metaphors be Hawthorne's own. He is described as both "a fiend of fire and a fiend of darkness," and, when he rides on horseback at the head of the ceremonial procession, "his fierce and variegated countenance appeared like war personified; the red of one cheek was an emblem of fire and sword; the blackness of the other betokened the mourning that attends them." He is War, Death, and Destruction, and again he is the Devil, with "his train [of] wild figures in Indian dress," his "infernal visage," and his eyes that glowed "like fire in a cave." He is well chosen to play the part of Riot, of Disorder, of the Lord of Misrule, in the pageant it is Robin's destiny to behold. He is in charge of the procession of "fiends" and of their lurid rites, the "counterfeited pomp," the "senseless uproar" in which the tumultuous multitude lead Major Molineux to his humiliation.

And Robin joins this yelling mob! His mocking laughter is the loudest there! Not even the shame, the agony of his kinsman, not even his own emotions of pity and terror, can hold him from making their "frenzied merriment" his own. There are buffetings of passion, there are possibilities of evil and of guilt, which Robin's callow rationalism cannot fathom. Setting out merely to make his way in the world, he has wandered unknowingly toward an appointed rendezvous, a ceremony which seems to have been prepared specifically for his benefit. It is his initiation.

But an initiation into what? The sensitive suggestions of Mrs. Leavis, Waggoner, and Male may be supplemented by a closer scrutiny of Robin himself. When we have seen who he is and what he represents up to the moment of his initiation, we can better understand the significance of that ritual for him.

Seven times in this tale Robin is characterized as "a shrewd youth." Like his antecedent bumpkins in popular tradition— Brother Jonathan, the peddlers of folk anecdote, Jack Downing, Sam Slick—he is nothing if not shrewd. But Robin is shrewd only by his own report. "I'm not the fool you take me for," he warns the double-faced demon, yet that is exactly what he is. Although mystified at every turn, denied the common civilities by those he meets, taunted and mocked by strangers at the mention of his kinsman's name, he never once loses confidence in his own shrewdness. Rebuffed by the pompous old man and the innkeeper, fleeing the temptations of the prostitute, his response to their jeering laughter is thrice again to account himself "a shrewd youth." Even in his last encounter with the stranger who proves to be kindly, Robin is still depending on his motherwit to carry him through all situations. "For I have the name of being a shrewd youth," Robin tells his older friend. "I doubt not that you deserve it," the friend replies. Yet at the beginning of his night of misadventure Robin had stepped jauntily off the ferry without realizing that he had no idea where he was going. "It would have been wise to inquire my way of the ferryman," he muses, "But the next man I meet will do as well." This, however, is not at all the case. Everyone he meets is, unknown to him, involved in the conspiracy to overthrow his kinsman the royal governor. When Robin cannot give their password, parties of conspirators curse him in plain language. When he obstinately inquires for the Major the people in the inn and the barbershop hoot at him. When he tries the door of the pretty little prostitute she tells him that she knows his kinsman well. "But Robin, being of the household of a New England clergyman, was a good youth, as well as a shrewd one; so he resisted temptation, and fled away." He cannot yet face the knowledge that Major Molineux, his kinsman (and father), has had carnal knowledge of a woman, just as Young Goodman Brown will be dismayed to learn that his father had followed the Devil to the witches' carnal Sabbath before him.

It is characteristic of Robin that he always accepts the most simplistic rationalizations of the most baffling and ominous experiences. One would think him affrighted by the demoniac double-faced man he accosts before the church. We recognize this portentous apparition as ringleader of the uprising, but Robin merely muses, "Strange things we travellers see!" and sits down to await the Major. "A few moments were consumed in philosophical speculations upon the species of man who had just left him; but having settled this point shrewdly, rationally, and satisfactorily, he was compelled to look elsewhere for his amusement"! Now the moonlight plays over the commonplace scene "like the imaginative power," and Robin cannot define the forms of distant objects which turn ghostly and indistinct "just as his eye appeared to grasp them." His dream of home is more real than the actual things he is now among, and when he wakes "his mind kept vibrating between fancy and reality" as shapes lengthen and dwindle before him. Despite all these physical sensations of confusion and the constant evidence of his noncomprehension of what is happening, Robin trusts to his "name of being a shrewd youth." This is Yankee self-reliance with a vengeance! His "bright, cheerful eyes were nature's gifts," and he would seem to think he needs no others. Robin, the shrewd youth from the backwoods, proves to be the Great American Boob, the naïf whose odyssey leads him, all uncomprehending, into the dark center of experience.

When the tale opens, Robin has just made a crossing of the water and entered the city. He has left behind him the security as well as the simplicity of his rural birthplace—in his reverie before the church his country home seemed an Arcadian bower of "venerable shade" and "golden light." But in his dream of returning home the door closes before him. Like Wakefield, Robin has left his home and cannot return. It is true that, as opposed to Wakefield's perverse impulse, he had good reasons (Robin is a younger son and won't inherit the farm), but nonetheless by leaving his appointed place and station to participate in the fluidity of egalitarian city life he too has made himself an exile. Just how egalitarian that city life will prove Robin must learn with dismay. The change to which he has committed himself is not only one of place and status but involves also the breaking of human ties, as every act of independence does to some degree. Much as Robin resembles the folk characters of Yankee yarn and jokelore, the difference—and it is tremendous—is that such characters had no human ties to break.

Robin's journey toward independence is magnified a thousandfold by the throes of the town itself on the evening of his arrival. In their quest for self-determination the urban conspirators of the town are far in advance of the country-bred youth whom they mock. Until the very end of the tale Robin still counts on his kinsman's preferment; the independence he seeks is therefore qualified, not absolute. The townsfolk no longer accept the limited independence granted by royal governors, even those who "in softening their instructions from beyond the sea . . . incurred the reprehension" of the Crown. They have cast their die for total disseverance of their bonds. Hawthorne's imagery puts them in league with the Devil to do so.

Thus an ironic tension underlies all of Robin's misadventures. Those who deride him are really his mentors, and he, invoking the patronage of their enemy his kinsman, is actually their ally, since both they and he are seeking independence. After his dismay at beholding his kinsman's degradation, Robin's sudden shout of laughter may seem to the reader inexplicable. So it is, from a point of view as rational and "shrewd" as his own. But the emotional logic that produced his outburst is inescapable. It is an emotional not a rational logic, for in that instant, with neither premeditation nor understanding, Robin has cast off the remaining dependence of his immaturity.

Then, at the Devil's behest, the frenzied procession moves on, leaving Robin behind in the silent street. What has he learned from his initiation?

His lessons must be inferred from the tale, for when it ends Robin is still in a state of shock. "I begin to grow weary of town life," he says. He wants to go home. But, as his dream has already told him, he has no home now. He must stay. What he might muse on is his new knowledge of the demonic depths from which the impulse of self-determination leaped up in the torchlight. He might give "a few moments" in "philosophical speculations" upon the Saturnalian passions which

shook him as he, like the populace, dethroned Order and rejected Tradition while under the aegis of the Lord of Misrule.
In their act of revolt they have all thrown down the old king
of Stability and crowned the new prince of War and Destruction.

To judge from the effect upon Robin of his experiences
hitherto, there is little chance of his learning much from these
reflections. Although devoted to the dogma of Yankee self-
reliance, he had learned nothing from anything that had
touched him. We are, however, told that his faith in himself
is rather shaken, for "nature's gift," his "bright, cheerful eyes,"
are now "not quite as lively as in the earlier part of the
evening."

One source of hope for Robin is the continued interest of
the gentleman who had befriended him. This nameless figure,
as we have seen, represents the viable influence of his father
upon his soul: the manly guidance of a non-possessive, non-
inhibiting paternal love. The tale ends with the steadying
voice of this personage, whose interested detachment from
the pillorying of Major Molineux hints that he has seen all
this before. In his experience he knows that this ritual, like
all *rites de passage*, is ever again repeated for the benefit of
each initiate. Even his irony at the end is indulgent without
being patronizing, for he suggests that Robin will have to
make up his own mind, "as you are a shrewd youth," whether
to stay in town and "perhaps . . . rise in the world without
the help of your kinsman, Major Molineux," even though he
surely knows that Robin cannot return to his pastoral home.
This means that Robin now is free of the past, and has the
power of self-determination. But this power comes to him
inextricable from the terrifying and tragic emotions that have
involved him.

And what of the Colony? Is it truly free, or has it exchanged
the rule of a benevolent governor for the tyranny of riot and
chaos? On the political level Hawthorne's fable is less reassur-
ing than on the personal. There is no double of Major
Molineux who represents in the realm of power what Robin's
friend stands for as an aspect of the parent. Yet so closely has
Hawthorne intertwined the cultural with the psychological
implications in this tale that we cannot help taking Robin's
friend as representing also the viable aspects of Major

Molineux. What his patient and tolerant advice to Robin suggests, then, is that this ordeal has been performed before by society as well as by the self. The implication is that the forces of Order and Stability do in the end prove stronger than those of Destruction and Misrule which dethrone them. Harrowing though these disruptive forces be, in Hawthorne's vision of American history they do serve the end of re-establishing a stable order based on institutions more just than those overthrown. (This was in fact the case, as the fire-brained Committees of Correspondence were superseded, after the reign of War and Death, by the framers of the Constitution and the *Federalist Papers*.[4]) Still another indication that the reign of Riot will be but brief lies in the carnival atmosphere which suggests that Major Molineux's successor, the two-faced man, is the Lord of Misrule. His reign is but a mock reign, a temporary season of emotional debauch necessary to the purification and rebirth of society. At its conclusion Order is imposed again upon the rampaging passions of the Saturnalia. On this succession the continuity of culture itself depends. In "My Kinsman," then, there is a qualified, half-skeptical hope that when the town wakes up from its collective nightmare, tradition will be re-established in accordance with the new dispensation of absolute liberty which the Devil's league had won in the darkness.

But as in the case of Robin's personal fate, the consequences of these public actions are not affirmed, not even proposed. All consequences are but inferences from this fable. Our inferences must be guided by the probabilities which the characterization of Robin in terms of the traditional figure of the Yankee naïf suggests. There is no clearer statement in our literature than "My Kinsman, Major Molineux" of the psychological and cultural burdens of personal freedom and of national independence. Hawthorne's Robin allows us no undue confidence in the degree of understanding with which the American character will bear them.

[4] If the spirit of revolt is in this tale a Devil, he appears elsewhere in Hawthorne as "The Gray Champion," the regicide Goffe who signed King Charles's death warrant. "His hour is one of darkness, and adversity, and peril. But should domestic tyranny oppress us . . . still may the Gray Champion come, for he is the type of New England's hereditary spirit." There, as in "Legends of the Province House" and "Endicott and the Red Cross," rebellion is the divine right of an oppressed people.

D. H. Lawrence

Some authors, such as James Joyce, seem to exist solely in and through their works. Others exert as great an influence by their personality and commanding presence as they do by their writing. It is to this latter group that D. H. Lawrence (1885–1930) belongs. The keynote of his personal existence was the struggle for an authenticity that was organic to his individuality. This search led him to journey restlessly through many countries, to write passionately of the need for man's emotional revitalization, and to clash with most of the forces and ideas in the modern world that threatened to thwart his personal identity. He combined a Nietzschean vehemence and torrential energy with a characteristically English attachment to the simple beauties of nature and human life.

Lawrence was born in Eastwood, Nottinghamshire, and spent most of his years until young manhood in and around mining towns of the English Midlands. His father was a coal miner, while his mother taught school. The hardships and ugliness of these early years remained with Lawrence all his life. Nevertheless, he also found much that was important to him in this period, especially his closeknit family life. Particularly close to him was his mother, who encouraged his sensitivity and interest in culture. Lawrence movingly explores the depth of this attachment as well as the conflicts it engendered in Sons and Lovers (1913), which is his artistic attempt to come to terms with her death. At seventeen, after working briefly, he became seriously ill. Following this, he attended Nottingham University College and became a school teacher, a role that he held only a few years. His first poems were published in 1909 and his first novel in 1911. The next year he met Frieda Weekley-Richthofen, the wife of a professor, and they eloped to the Continent, where they lived intermittently until her divorce. During this time Lawrence was writing much poetry and fiction, as well as making the *acquaintance of John Middleton Murry, Katherine Mansfield, and Bertrand Russell. With Russell, he began a joint enterprise of lecturing in opposition to World War I. At this point Lawrence also had his first encounters with British legal censorship when his novel* The Rainbow *(1915) was suppressed as obscene, a judgment that today can, at best, only be regarded as puzzling.*

In 1919 Lawrence left England for Italy, where he continued to write novels, travel books, and essays on literature, history, education, and psychology. From Italy he embarked on journeys which took him to Ceylon, Australia, and finally the western United States and Mexico. The most notable products of these years were the novels Kangaroo *(1923) and* The Plumed Serpent *(1925) and a book of poems,* Birds, Beasts and Flowers *(1923). The middle and late twenties were, for Lawrence, marked by recurrent illnesses, quarrels with friends and acquaintances, and restless journeys back and forth from America to England and Europe. After a particularly severe illness in Mexico, he settled in Italy where he continued to write and to develop rather intensively his life-long interest in painting. In 1928 he published his last novel,* Lady Chatterley's Lover. *It aroused enormous controversy, including charges of pornography that have only been overcome in recent years. The following year his collection of poems* Pansies *was seized by British government officials in manuscript copy, and a number of his paintings were temporarily confiscated by London police. His poor health finally turned into full-fledged tuberculosis, from which he died in the south of France in 1930.*

As a writer, Lawrence was particularly concerned with the sexual nature of man and the world. He sought in his fiction and poetry to explore the full scope of the phenomenon and to indicate both its importance in human nature and its manifold forms. For him, it was not to be reduced to physical behavior since it was intimately connected with the emotions and indeed man's whole manner of conceiving himself and his relation to persons and the world around him. At the same time, he was intensely aware of the forces that threatened to warp the individual's sexual responses and experiences. To these, he was an intransigent opponent, for he saw these forces, whether social, intellectual, or religious, as deathly. They shriveled the individual's sensitivity, imaginative perceptiveness, and capacity for honest expression and enjoy-ment of life. Thus, in many of his works he dramatizes the stultifying and obsession-producing nature of both provincial and cosmopolitan modern life. Many of his characters escape abortively into intellectualism, thrill-seeking, political and religious manias, and emotional atrophy. Against them he poses individuals who by arduous effort and anguish finally win through to a life that is a full realization of their personal identity. The trials they face and the punishments inflicted on them by their society testify to Lawrence's sense of the pervasive nature of the victim-victimizer syndrome in human affairs.

The critical literature on Lawrence has grown enormously since his death, particularly in recent years. Biographical studies that are especially valuable are Richard Aldington, D. H. Lawrence: Portrait of a Genius But . . . *(1950); Harry* T. Moore, The Life and Works of D. H. Lawrence *(1951); and* E. Nehls, ed., D. H. Lawrence: A Composite Biography, *3 vols.* *(1957–59). A convenient bibliography of Lawrence criticism is* Modern Fiction Studies, 5 *(Spring, 1959). Criticism of "Eng-land, My England" in the context of Lawrence's works and ideas may be found in G. Hough,* The Dark Sun: A Study of D. H. Lawrence *(1956); F. R. Leavis,* D. H. Lawrence: Novelist *(1955); E. W. Tedlock, Jr.,* D. H. Lawrence: Artist and Rebel *(1963); G. H. Ford,* Double Measure: A Study of the Novels and Stories of D. H. Lawrence *(1965); J. Moynihan,* The Deed of Life *(1963); K. Widmer,* The Art of Perversity *(1962).*

England, My England

D. H. Lawrence

HE WAS WORKING on the edge of the common, beyond the small brook that ran in the dip at the bottom of the garden, carrying the garden path in continuation from the plank bridge on to the common. He had cut the rough turf and bracken, leaving the grey, dryish soil bare. But he was worried because he could not get the path straight, there was a pleat between his brows. He had set up his sticks, and taken the sights between the big pine trees, but for some reason everything seemed wrong. He looked again, straining his keen blue eyes, that had a touch of the Viking in them, through the shadowy pine trees as through a doorway, at the green-grassed garden-path rising from the shadow of alders by the log bridge up to the sunlit flowers. Tall white and purple columbines, and the butt-end of the old Hampshire cottage that crouched near the earth amid flowers, blossoming in the bit of shaggy wildness round about.

There was a sound of children's voices calling and talking: high, childish, girlish voices, slightly didactic and tinged with domineering: "If you don't come quick, nurse, I shall run out there to where there are snakes." And nobody had the sangfroid to reply: "Run then, little fool." It was always, "No, darling. Very well, darling. In a moment, darling. Darling, you *must* be patient."

His heart was hard with disillusion: a continual gnawing and resistance. But he worked on. What was there to do but submit!

The sunlight blazed down upon the earth, there was a vivid-ness of flamy vegetation, of fierce seclusion amid the savage peace of the commons. Strange how the savage England lingers in patches: as here, amid these shaggy gorse commons, and marshy, snake-infested places near the foot of the south downs. The spirit of place lingering on primeval, as when the Saxons came, so long ago.

Ah, how he had loved it! The green garden path, the tufts of flowers, purple and white columbines, and great oriental red poppies with their black chaps and mulleins tall and yellow: this flamy garden which had been a garden for a thousand years, scooped out in the little hollow among the snake-infested commons. He had made it flame with flowers, in a sun cup under its hedges and trees. So old, so old a place! And yet he had re-created it.

The timbered cottage with its sloping, cloak-like roof was old and forgotten. It belonged to the old England of hamlets and yeomen. Lost all alone on the edge of the common, at the end of a wide, grassy, briar-entangled lane shaded with oak, it had never known the world of to-day. Not till Egbert came with his bride. And he had come to fill it with flowers.

The house was ancient and very uncomfortable. But he did not want to alter it. Ah, marvellous to sit there in the wide, black, time-old chimney, at night when the wind roared over-head, and the wood which he had chopped himself sputtered on the hearth! Himself on one side the angle, and Winifred on the other.

Ah, how he had wanted her: Winifred! She was young and beautiful and strong with life, like a flame in sunshine. She moved with a slow grace of energy like a blossoming, red-flowered bush in motion. She, too, seemed to come out of the old England, ruddy, strong, with a certain crude, passionate quiescence and a hawthorn robustness. And he, he was tall and slim and agile, like an English archer with his long supple legs and fine movements. Her hair was nut-brown and all in en-ergic curls and tendrils. Her eyes were nut-brown, too, like a robin's for brightness. And he was white-skinned with fine, silky hair that had darkened from fair, and a slightly arched nose of an old country family. They were a beautiful couple.

The house was Winifred's. Her father was a man of energy, too. He had come from the north poor. Now he was moderately rich. He had bought this fair stretch of inexpensive land, down in Hampshire. Not far from the tiny church of the almost extinct hamlet stood his own house, a commodious old farm-house standing back from the road across a bare grassed yard. On one side of this quadrangle was the long, long barn or shed which he had made into a cottage for his youngest daughter Priscilla. One saw little blue-and-white check curtains at the long windows, and inside, overhead, the grand old timbers of the high-pitched shed. This was Prissy's house. Fifty yards away was the pretty little new cottage which he had built for his daughter Magdalen, with the vegetable garden stretching away to the oak copse. And then away beyond the lawns and rose-trees of the house-garden went the track across a shaggy, wild grass space, towards the ridge of tall black pines that grew on a dyke-bank, through the pines and above the sloping little bog, under the wide, desolate oak trees, till there was Winifred's cottage crouching unexpectedly in front, so much alone, and so primitive.

It was Winifred's own house, and the gardens and the bit of common and the boggy slope were hers: her tiny domain. She had married just at the time when her father had bought the estate, about ten years before the war, so she had been able to come to Egbert with this for a marriage portion. And who was more delighted, he or she, it would be hard to say. She was only twenty at the time, and he was only twenty-one. He had about a hundred and fifty pounds a year of his own—and nothing else but his very considerable personal attractions. He had no profession: he earned nothing. But he talked of litera-ture and music, he had a passion for old folk-music, collecting folk-songs and folk-dances, studying the Morris-dance and the old customs. Of course, in time he would make money in these ways.

Meanwhile youth and health and passion and promise. Winifred's father was always generous: but still, he was a man from the north with a hard head and a hard skin too, having received a good many knocks. At home he kept the hard head out of sight, and played at poetry and romance with his lit-erary wife and his sturdy, passionate girls. He was a man of courage, not given to complaining, bearing his burdens by himself. No, he did not let the world intrude far into his home. He had a delicate, sensitive wife whose poetry won some fame in the narrow world of letters. He himself, with his tough old barbarian fighting spirit, had an almost child-like delight in verse, in sweet poetry, and in the delightful game of a cultured home. His blood was strong even to coarseness. But that only made the home more vigorous, more robust and Christmassy. There was always a touch of Christmas about him, now he was well off. If there was poetry after dinner, there were also chocolates, and nuts, and good little out-of-the-way things to be munching.

Well then, into this family came Egbert. He was made of quite a different paste. The girls and the father were strong-limbed, thick-blooded people, true English, as holly-trees and hawthorn are English. Their culture was grafted on to them, as one might perhaps graft a common pink rose on to a thorn-stem. It flowered oddly enough, but it did not alter their blood.

And Egbert was a born rose. The age-long breeding had left him with a delightful spontaneous passion. He was not clever, nor even "literary." No, but the intonation of his voice, and the movement of his supple, handsome body, and the fine texture of his flesh and his hair, the slight arch of his nose, the quickness of his blue eyes would easily take the place of poetry. Winifred loved him, loved him, this southerner, as a higher being. A *higher* being, mind you. Not a deeper. And as for him, he loved her in passion with every fibre of him. She was the very warm stuff of life to him.

Wonderful then, those days at Crockham Cottage, the first days, all alone save for the woman who came to work in the mornings. Marvellous days, when she had all his tall, supple, fine-fleshed youth to herself, for herself, and he had her like a ruddy fire into which he could cast himself for rejuvenation. Ah, that it might never end, this passion, this marriage! The flame of their two bodies burnt again into that old cottage, that was haunted already by so much bygone, physical desire. You could not be in the dark room for an hour without the influences coming over you. The hot blood-desire of bygone yeomen, there in this old den where they had lusted and bred for so many generations. The silent house, dark, with thick, timbered walls and the big black chimney-place, and the sense of secrecy. Dark, with low, little windows, sunk into the earth. Dark, like a lair where strong beasts had lurked and mated, lonely at night and lonely by day, left to themselves and their own intensity for so many generations. It seemed to cast a spell on the two young people. They became different. There was a curious secret glow about them, a certain slumbering flame hard to understand, that enveloped them both. They too felt that they did not belong to the London world any more. Crockham had changed their blood: the sense of the snakes that lived and slept even in their own garden, in the sun, so that he, going forward with the spade, would see a curious coiled brownish pile on the black soil, which suddenly would start up, hiss, and dazzle rapidly away, hissing. One day Winifred heard the strangest scream from the flower-bed under the low window of the living room: ah, the strangest scream, like the very soul of the dark past crying aloud. She ran out, and saw a long brown snake on the flower-bed, and in its flat mouth the one hind leg of a frog was striving to escape, and screaming its strange, tiny, bellowing scream. She looked at the snake, and from its sullen flat head it looked at her, obstinately. She gave a cry, and it released the frog and slid angrily away.

That was Crockham. The spear of modern invention had not passed through it, and it lay there secret, primitive, savage as when the Saxons first came. And Egbert and she were caught there, caught out of the world.

He was not idle, nor was she. There were plenty of things to be done, the house to be put into final repair after the workmen had gone, cushions and curtains to sew, the paths to make, the water to fetch and attend to, and then the slope of the deep-soiled, neglected garden to level, to terrace with little terraces and paths, and to fill with flowers. He worked away, in his shirt-sleeves, worked all day intermittently doing this thing and the other. And she, quiet and rich in herself, seeing him stooping and labouring away by himself, would come to help him, to be near him. He of course was an amateur—a born amateur. He worked so hard, and did so little, and nothing he ever did would hold together for long. If he terraced the garden, he held up the earth with a couple of long narrow planks that soon began to bend with the pressure from behind, and would not need many years to rot through and break and let the soil slither all down again in a heap towards the stream-bed. But there you are. He had not been brought up to come to grips with anything, and he thought it would do.

Nay, he did not think there was anything else except little temporary contrivances possible, he who had such a passion for his old enduring cottage, and for the old enduring things of the bygone England. Curious that the sense of permanency in the past had such a hold over him, whilst in the present he was all amateurish and sketchy.

Winifred could not criticize him. Town-bred, everything seemed to her splendid, and the very digging and shovelling itself seemed romantic. But neither Egbert nor she yet realized the difference between work and romance.

Godfrey Marshall, her father, was at first perfectly pleased with the ménage down at Crockham Cottage. He thought Egbert was wonderful, the many things he accomplished, and he was gratified by the glow of physical passion between the two young people. To the man who in London still worked hard to keep steady his modest fortune, the thought of this young couple digging away and loving one another down at Crockham Cottage, buried deep among the commons and marshes, near the pale-showing bulk of the downs, was like a chapter of living romance. And they drew the sustenance for their fire of passion from him, from the old man. It was he who fed their flame. He triumphed secretly in the thought. And it was to her father that Winifred still turned, as the one source of all surety and life and support. She loved Egbert with passion. But behind her was the power of her father. It was the power of her father she referred to, whenever she needed to refer. It never occurred to her to refer to Egbert, if she were in difficulty or doubt. No, in all the *serious* matters she depended on her father.

For Egbert had no intention of coming to grips with life. He had no ambition whatsoever. He came from a decent family, from a pleasant country home, from delightful surroundings. He should, of course, have had a profession. He should have studied law or entered business in some way. But no—that fatal three pounds a week would keep him from starving as long as he lived, and he did not want to give himself into bondage. It was not that he was idle. He was always doing something, in his amateurish way. But he had no desire to give himself to the world, and still less had he any desire to fight his way in the world. No, no, the world wasn't worth it. He wanted to ignore it, to go his own way apart, like a casual pilgrim down the forsaken side-tracks. He loved his wife, his cottage and garden. He would make his life there, as a sort of epicurean hermit. He loved the past, the old music and dances and customs of old England. He would try and live in the spirit of these, not in the spirit of the world of business.

But often Winifred's father called her to London: for he loved to have his children round him. So Egbert and she must have a tiny flat in town, and the young couple must transfer themselves from time to time from the country to the city. In town Egbert had plenty of friends, of the same ineffectual sort as himself, tampering with the arts, literature, painting, sculpture, music. He was not bored.

Three pounds a week, however, would not pay for all this. Winifred's father paid. He liked paying. He made her only a very small allowance, but he often gave her ten pounds—or gave Egbert ten pounds. So they both looked on the old man as the mainstay. Egbert didn't mind being patronized and paid for. Only when he felt the family was a little *too* condescending, on account of money, he began to get huffy.

Then of course children came: a lovely little blonde daughter with a head of thistle-down. Everybody adored the child. It was the first exquisite blonde thing that had come into the family, a little mite with the white, slim, beautiful limbs of its father, and as it grew up the dancing, dainty movement of a wild little daisy-spirit. No wonder the Marshalls all loved the child: they called her Joyce. They themselves had their own grace, but it was slow, rather heavy. They had every one of them strong, heavy limbs and darkish skins, and they were short in stature. And now they had for one of their own this light little cowslip child. She was like a little poem in herself.

But nevertheless, she brought a new difficulty. Winifred must have a nurse for her. Yes, yes, there must be a nurse. It was the family decree. Who was to pay for the nurse? The grandfather—seeing the father himself earned no money. Yes, the grandfather would pay, as he had paid all the lying-in expenses. There came a slight sense of money-strain. Egbert was living on his father-in-law.

After the child was born, it was never quite the same between him and Winifred. The difference was at first hardly perceptible. But it was there. In the first place Winifred had a new centre of interest. She was not going to adore her child.

But she had what the modern mother so often has in the place of spontaneous love: a profound sense of duty towards her child. Winifred appreciated her darling little girl, and felt a deep sense of duty towards her. Strange, that this sense of duty should go deeper than the love for her husband. But so it was. And so it often is. The responsibility of motherhood was the prime responsibility in Winifred's heart: the responsibility of wifehood came a long way second.

Her child seemed to link her up again in a circuit with her own family. Her father and mother, herself, and her child, that was the human trinity for her. Her husband——? Yes, she loved him still. But that was like play. She had an almost barbaric sense of duty and of family. Till she married, her first human duty had been towards her father: he was the pillar, the source of life, the everlasting support. Now another link was added to the chain of duty: her father, herself, and her child.

Egbert was out of it. Without anything happening, he was gradually, unconsciously excluded from the circle. His wife still loved him, physically. But, but—he was *almost* the unnecessary party in the affair. He could not complain of Winifred. She still did her duty towards him. She still had a physical passion for him, that physical passion on which he had put all his life and soul. But—but——

It was for a long while an ever-recurring *but*. And then, after the second child, another blonde, winsome touching little thing, not so proud and flame-like as Joyce—after Annabel came, then Egbert began truly to realize how it was. His wife still loved him. But—and now the but had grown enormous— her physical love for him was of secondary importance to her. It became ever less important. After all, she had had it, this physical passion, for two years now. It was not this that one lived from. No, no—something sterner, realer.

She began to resent her own passion for Egbert—just a little she began to despise it. For after all there he was, he was charming, he was lovable, he was terribly desirable. But—but —oh, the awful looming cloud of that *but!*—he did not stand firm in the landscape of her life like a tower of strength, like a great pillar of significance. No, he was like a cat one has about the house, which will one day disappear and leave no trace. He was like a flower in the garden, trembling in the wind of life, and then gone, leaving nothing to show. As an adjunct, as an accessory, he was perfect. Many a woman would have adored to have him about her all her life, the most beautiful and desirable of all her possessions. But Winifred belonged to another school.

The years went by, and instead of coming to grips with life, he relaxed more. He was of a subtle, sensitive, passionate nature. But he simply *would* not give himself to what Winifred called life, *Work*. No, he would not go into the world and work for money. No, he just would not. If Winifred liked to live beyond their small income—well, it was her look-out.

And Winifred did not really want him to go out into the world to work for money. Money became, alas, a word like a firebrand between them, setting them both aflame with anger. But that is because we must talk in symbols. Winifred did not really care about money. She did not care whether he earned or did not earn anything. Only she knew she was dependent on her father for three-fourths of the money spent for herself and her children, that she let that be the *casus belli*, the drawn weapon between herself and Egbert.

What did she want—what did she want? Her mother once said to her, with that characteristic touch of irony: "Well, dear, if it is your fate to consider the lilies, that toil not, neither do they spin, that is one destiny among many others, and perhaps not so unpleasant as most. Why do you take it amiss, my child?"

The mother was subtler than her children, they very rarely knew how to answer her. So Winifred was only more confused. It was not a question of lilies. At least, if it were a question of lilies, then her children were the little blossoms. They at least *grew*. Doesn't Jesus say: "Consider the lilies *how they grow*." Good then, she had her growing babies. But as for that other tall, handsome flower of a father of theirs, he was full grown already, so she did not want to spend her life considering him in the flower of his days.

No, it was not that he didn't earn money. It was not that he was idle. He was *not* idle. He was always doing something, always working away, down at Crockham, doing little jobs. But, oh dear, the little jobs—the garden paths—the gorgeous flowers—the chairs to mend, old chairs to mend!

It was that he stood for nothing. If he had done something unsuccessfully, and *lost* what money they had! If he had but striven with something. Nay, even if he had been wicked, a waster, she would have been more free. She would have had something to resist, at least. A waster stands for something, really. He says: "No, I will not aid and abet society in this business of increase and hanging together, I will upset the apple-cart as much as I can, in my small way." Or else he says: "No, I will *not* bother about others. If I have lusts, they are my own, and I prefer them to other people's virtues." So, a waster, a scamp, takes a sort of stand. He exposes himself to opposition and final castigation: at any rate in story-books.

But Egbert! What are you to do with a man like Egbert? He had no vices. He was really kind, nay generous. And he was not weak. If he had been weak Winifred could have been kind to him. But he did not even give her that consolation. He was not weak, and he did not want her consolation or her kindness. No, thank you. He was of a fine passionate temper, and of a rarer steel than she. He knew it, and she knew it. Hence she was only the more baffled and maddened, poor thing. He, the higher, the finer, in his way the stronger, played with his garden, and his old folk-songs and Morris-dances, just played, and let her support the pillars of the future on her own heart.

And he began to get bitter, and a wicked look began to come on his face. He did not give in to her; not he. There were seven devils inside his long, slim, white body. He was healthy, full of restrained life. Yes, even he himself had to lock up his own vivid life inside himself, now she would not take it from him. Or rather, now that she only took it occasionally. For she had to yield at times. She loved him so, she desired him so, he was so exquisite to her, the fine creature that he was, finer than herself. Yes, with a groan she had to give in to her own unquenched passion for him. And he came to her then—ah, terrible, ah, wonderful, sometimes she wondered how either of them could live after the terror of the passion that swept between them. It was to her as if pure lightning, flash after flash, went through every fibre of her, till extinction came.

But it is the fate of human beings to live on. And it is the fate of clouds that seem nothing but bits of vapour slowly to pile up, to pile up and fill the heavens and blacken the sun entirely.

So it was. The love came back, the lightning of passion flashed tremendously between them. And there was blue sky and gorgeousness for a little while. And then, as inevitably, as inevitably, slowly the clouds began to edge up again above the horizon, slowly, slowly to lurk about the heavens, throwing an occasional cold and hateful shadow: slowly, slowly to congregate, to fill the empyrean space.

And as the years passed, the lightning cleared the sky more and more rarely, less and less the blue showed. Gradually the grey lid sank down upon them, as if it would be permanent.

Why didn't Egbert do something, then? Why didn't he come to grips with life? Why wasn't he like Winifred's father, a pillar of society, even if a slender, exquisite column? Why didn't he go into harness of some sort? Why didn't he take *some* direction?

Well, you can bring an ass to the water, but you cannot make him drink. The world was the water and Egbert was the ass. And he wasn't having any. He couldn't: he just couldn't. Since necessity did not force him to work for his bread and butter, he would not work for work's sake. You can't make the columbine flowers nod in January, nor make the cuckoo sing in England at Christmas. Why? It isn't his season. He doesn't want to. Nay, he *can't* want to.

And there it was with Egbert. He couldn't link up with the world's work, because the basic desire was absent from him. Nay, at the bottom of him he had an even stronger desire: to hold aloof. To hold aloof. To do nobody any damage. But to hold aloof. It was not his season.

Perhaps he should not have married and had children. But you can't stop the waters flowing.

Which held true for Winifred, too. She was not made to endure aloof. Her family tree was a robust vegetation that had to be stirring and believing. In one direction or another her life *had* to go. In her own home she had known nothing of this diffidence which she found in Egbert, and which she could not understand, and which threw her into such dismay. What was she to do, what was she to do, in face of this terrible diffidence?

It was all so different in her own home. Her father may have had his own misgivings, but he kept them to himself. Perhaps he had no very profound belief in this world of ours, this society which we have elaborated with so much effort, only to find ourselves elaborated to death at last. But Godfrey Marshall was of tough, rough fibre, not without a vein of healthy cunning through it all. It was for him a question of winning through, and leaving the rest to heaven. Without having many illusions to grace him, he still *did* believe in heaven. In a dark and unquestioning way, he had a sort of faith: an acrid faith like the sap of some not-to-be-exterminated tree. Just a blind acrid faith as sap is blind and acrid, and yet pushes on in growth and in faith. Perhaps he was unscrupulous, but only as a striving tree is unscrupulous, pushing its single way in a jungle of others.

In the end, it is only this robust, sap-like faith which keeps man going. He may live on for many generations inside the shelter of the social establishment which he has erected for himself, as pear-trees and currant bushes would go on bearing fruit for many seasons, inside a walled garden, even if the race of man were suddenly exterminated. But bit by bit the wall-fruit-trees would gradually pull down the very walls that sustained them. Bit by bit every establishment collapses, unless it is renewed or restored by living hands, all the while.

Egbert could not bring himself to any more of this restoring or renewing business. He was not aware of the fact: but awareness doesn't help much, anyhow. He just couldn't. He had the stoic and epicurean quality of his old, fine breeding. His father-in-law, however, though he was not one bit more of a fool than Egbert, realized that since we are here we may as well live. And so he applied himself to his own tiny section of the social work, and to doing the best for his family, and to leaving the rest to the ultimate will of heaven. A certain robustness of blood made him able to go on. But sometimes even from him spurted a sudden gall of bitterness against the world and its make-up. And yet—he had his own will-to-succeed, and this carried him through. He refused to ask himself what the success would amount to. It amounted to the estate down in Hampshire, and his children lacking for nothing, and himself of some importance in the world: and *basta!* —Basta! Basta!

Nevertheless do not let us imagine that he was a common pusher. He was not. He knew as well as Egbert what disillusion meant. Perhaps in his soul he had the same estimation of success. But he had a certain acrid courage, and a certain will-to-power. In his own small circle he would emanate power, the single power of his own blind self. With all his spoiling of his children, he was still the father of the old English type. He was too wise to make laws and to domineer in the abstract. But he had kept, and all honour to him, a certain primitive dominion over the souls of his children, the old, almost magic prestige of paternity. There it was, still burning in him, the old smoky torch of paternal godhead.

And in the sacred glare of this torch his children had been brought up. He had given the girls every liberty, at last. But he had never really let them go beyond his power. And they, venturing out into the hard white light of our fatherless world, learned to see with the eyes of the world. They learned to criticize their father, even, from some effulgence of worldly white light, to see him as inferior. But this was all very well in the head. The moment they forgot their tricks of criticism, the old red glow of his authority came over them again. He was not to be quenched.

Let the psycho-analyst talk about father complex. It is just a word invented. Here was a man who had kept alive the old red flame of fatherhood, fatherhood that had even the right to sacrifice the child to God, like Isaac. Fatherhood that had life-and-death authority over the children: a great natural power. And till his children could be brought under some other great authority as girls; or could arrive at manhood and become themselves centres of the same power, continuing the same male mystery as men; until such time, willy-nilly, Godfrey Marshall would keep his children.

It had seemed as if he might lose Winifred. Winifred had *adored* her husband, and looked up to him as to something wonderful. Perhaps she had expected in him another great authority, a male authority greater, finer than her father's. For having once known the glow of male power, she would not easily turn to the cold white light of feminine independence. She would hunger, hunger all her life for the warmth and shelter of true male strength.

And hunger she might, for Egbert's power lay in the abnegation of power. He was himself the living negative of power. Even of responsibility. For the negation of power at last means the negation of responsibility. As far as these things went, he would confine himself to himself. He would try to confine his own *influence* even to himself. He would try, as far as possible,

to abstain from influencing his children by assuming any responsibility for them. "A little child shall lead them——" His
child should lead, then. He would try not to make it go in any
direction whatever. He would abstain from influencing it.
Liberty!—

Poor Winifred was like a fish out of water in this liberty,
gasping for the denser element which should contain her. Till
her child came. And then she knew that she must be responsible for it, that she must have authority over it.

But here Egbert, silently and negatively, stepped in. Silently,
negatively, but fatally he neutralized her authority over her
children.

There was a third little girl born. And after this Winifred
wanted no more children. Her soul was turning to salt.

So she had charge of the children, they were her responsibility. The money for them had come from her father. She
would do her very best for them, and have command over their
life and death. But no! Egbert would not take the responsibility. He would not even provide the money. But he would
not let her have her way. Her dark, silent, passionate authority he would not allow. It was a battle between them, the
battle between liberty and the old blood-power. And of course
he won. The little girls loved him and adored him. "Daddy!
Daddy!" They could do as they liked with him. Their mother
would have ruled them. She would have ruled them passionately, with indulgence, with the old dark magic of parental
authority, something looming and unquestioned and, after all,
divine: if we believe in divine authority. The Marshalls did,
being Catholic.

And Egbert, he turned her old dark, Catholic blood-authority
into a sort of tyranny. He would not leave her her children. He
stole them from her, and yet without assuming responsibility
for them. He stole them from her, in emotion and spirit, and
left her only to command their behaviour. A thankless lot for a
mother. And her children adored him, adored him, little knowing the empty bitterness they were preparing for themselves
when they too grew up to have husbands: husbands such as
Egbert, adorable and null.

Joyce, the eldest, was still his favourite. She was now a
quicksilver little thing of six years old. Barbara, the youngest,
was a toddler of two years. They spent most of their time down

at Crockham, because he wanted to be there. And even Winifred loved the place really. But now, in her frustrated and
blinded state, it was full of menace for her children. The
adders, the poison-berries, the brook, the marsh, the water
that might not be pure—one thing and another. From mother
and nurse it was a guerilla gunfire of commands, and blithe,
quicksilver disobedience from the three blonde, never-still
little girls. Behind the girls was the father, against mother and
nurse. And so it was.

"If you don't come quick, nurse, I shall run out there to
where there are snakes."

"Joyce, you *must* be patient. I'm just changing Annabel."

There you are. There it was: always the same. Working away
on the common across the brook he heard it. And he worked
on, just the same.

Suddenly he heard a shriek, and he flung the spade from
him and started for the bridge, looking up like a startled deer.
Ah, there was Winifred—Joyce had hurt herself. He went on
up the garden.

"What is it?"

The child was still screaming—now it was—"Daddy! Daddy!
Oh—oh, Daddy!" And the mother was saying:

"Don't be frightened, darling. Let mother look."

But the child only cried:

"Oh, Daddy, Daddy, Daddy!"

She was terrified by the sight of the blood running from her
own knee. Winifred crouched down, with her child of six in
her lap, to examine the knee. Egbert bent over also.

"Don't make such a noise, Joyce," he said irritably. "How
did she do it?"

"She fell on that sickle thing which you left lying about after
cutting the grass," said Winifred, looking into his face with
bitter accusation as he bent near.

He had taken his handkerchief and tied it round the knee.
Then he lifted the still sobbing child in his arms, and carried
her into the house and upstairs to her bed. In his arms she
became quiet. But his heart was burning with pain and with
guilt. He had left the sickle there lying on the edge of the grass,
and so his first-born child whom he loved so dearly had come
to hurt. But then it was an accident—it was an accident. Why
should he feel guilty? It would probably be nothing, better in

two or three days. Why take it to heart, why worry? He put it aside.

The child lay on the bed in her little summer frock, her face very white now after the shock. Nurse had come carrying the youngest child: and little Annabel stood holding her skirt. Winifred, terribly serious and wooden-seeming, was bending over the knee, from which she had taken his blood-soaked handkerchief. Egbert bent forward, too, keeping more sangfroid in his face than in his heart. Winifred went all of a lump of seriousness, so he had to keep some reserve. The child moaned and whimpered.

The knee was still bleeding profusely—it was a deep cut right in the joint.

"You'd better go for the doctor, Egbert," said Winifred bitterly.

"Oh, no! Oh, no!" cried Joyce in a panic.

"Joyce, my darling, don't cry!" said Winifred, suddenly catching the little girl to her breast in a strange tragic anguish, the *Mater Dolorata*. Even the child was frightened into silence. Egbert looked at the tragic figure of his wife with the child at her breast, and turned away. Only Annabel started suddenly to cry: "Joycey, Joycey, don't have your leg bleeding!"

Egbert rode four miles to the village for the doctor. He could not help feeling that Winifred was laying it on rather. Surely the knee itself wasn't hurt! Surely not. It was only a surface cut.

The doctor was out. Egbert left the message and came cycling swiftly home, his heart pinched with anxiety. He dropped sweating off his bicycle and went into the house, looking rather small, like a man who is at fault. Winifred was upstairs sitting by Joyce, who was looking pale and important in bed, and was eating some tapioca pudding. The pale, small, scared face of his child went to Egbert's heart.

"Doctor Wing was out. He'll be here about half-past two," said Egbert.

"I don't want him to come," whimpered Joyce.

"Joyce, dear, you must be patient and quiet," said Winifred. "He won't hurt you. But he will tell us what to do to make your knee better quickly. That is why he must come."

Winifred always explained carefully to her little girls: and it always took the words off their lips for the moment.

"Does it bleed yet?" said Egbert.

Winifred moved the bedclothes carefully aside.

"I think not," she said.

Egbert stooped also to look.

"No, it doesn't," he said. Then he stood up with a relieved look on his face. He turned to the child.

"Eat your pudding, Joyce," he said. "It won't be anything. You've only got to keep still for a few days."

"You haven't had your dinner, have you, Daddy?"

"Not yet."

"Nurse will give it to you," said Winifred.

"You'll be all right, Joyce," he said, smiling to the child and pushing the blonde hair aside off her brow. She smiled back winsomely into his face.

He went downstairs and ate his meal alone. Nurse served him. She liked waiting on him. All women liked him and liked to do things for him.

The doctor came—a fat country practitioner, pleasant and kind.

"What, little girl, been tumbling down, have you? There's a thing to be doing, for a smart little lady like you! What! And cutting your knee! Tut-tut-tut! That *wasn't* clever of you, now was it? Never mind, never mind, soon be better. Let us look at it. Won't hurt you. Not the least in life. Bring a bowl with a little warm water, nurse. Soon have it all right again, soon have it all right."

Joyce smiled at him with a pale smile of faint superiority. This was *not* the way in which she was used to being talked to.

He bent down, carefully looking at the little, thin, wounded knee of the child. Egbert bent over him.

"Oh, dear, oh, dear! Quite a deep little cut. Nasty little cut. Nasty little cut. But, never mind. Never mind, little lady. We'll soon have it better. Soon have it better, little lady. What's your name?"

"My name is Joyce," said the child distinctly.

"Oh, really!" he replied. "Oh, really! Well, that's a fine name too, in my opinion. Joyce, eh?—And how old might Miss Joyce be? Can she tell me that?"

"I'm six," said the child, slightly amused and very condescending.

"Six! There now. Add up and count as far as six, can you? Well, that's a clever little girl, a clever little girl. And if she has to drink a spoonful of medicine, she won't make a murmur, I'll be bound. Not like *some* little girls. What? Eh?"

"I take it if mother wishes me to," said Joyce.

"Ah, there now! That's the style! That's what I like to hear from a little lady in bed because she's cut her knee. That's the style——"

The comfortable and prolix doctor dressed and bandaged the knee and recommended bed and a light diet for the little lady. He thought a week or a fortnight would put it right. No bones or ligatures damaged—fortunately. Only a flesh cut. He would come again in a day or two.

So Joyce was reassured and stayed in bed and had all her toys up. Her father often played with her. The doctor came the third day. He was fairly pleased with the knee. It was healing. It was healing—yes—yes. Let the child continue in bed. He came again after a day or two. Winifred was a trifle uneasy. The wound seemed to be healing on the top, but it hurt the child too much. It didn't look quite right. She said so to Egbert.

"Egbert, I'm sure Joyce's knee isn't healing properly."

"I think it is," he said. "I think it's all right."

"I'd rather Doctor Wing came again—I don't feel satisfied."

"Aren't you trying to imagine it worse than it really is?"

"You would say so, of course. But I shall write a post card to Doctor Wing now."

The doctor came next day. He examined the knee. Yes, there was inflammation. Yes, there *might* be a little septic poisoning —there might. There might. Was the child feverish?

So a fortnight passed by, and the child *was* feverish, and the knee was more inflamed and grew worse and was painful, painful. She cried in the night, and her mother had to sit up with her. Egbert still insisted it was nothing, really—it would pass. But in his heart he was anxious.

Winifred wrote again to her father. On Saturday the elderly man appeared. And no sooner did Winifred see the thick, rather short figure in its grey suit than a great yearning came over her.

"Father, I'm not satisfied with Joyce. I'm not satisfied with Doctor Wing."

"Well, Winnie, dear, if you're not satisfied we must have further advice, that is all."

The sturdy, powerful, elderly man went upstairs, his voice

sounding rather grating through the house, as if it cut upon the tense atmosphere.

"How are you, Joyce, darling?" he said to the child. "Does your knee hurt you? Does it hurt you, dear?"

"It does sometimes." The child was shy of him, cold towards him.

"Well, dear, I'm sorry for that. I hope you try to bear it, and not trouble mother too much."

There was no answer. He looked at the knee. It was red and stiff.

"Of course," he said, "I think we must have another doctor's opinion. And if we're going to have it, we had better have it at once. Egbert, do you think you might cycle in to Bingham for Doctor Wayne? I found him *very* satisfactory for Winnie's mother."

"I can go if you think it necessary," said Egbert.

"Certainly I think it necessary. Even if there *is* nothing, we can have peace of mind. Certainly I think it necessary. I should like Doctor Wayne to come this evening if possible."

So Egbert set off on his bicycle through the wind, like a boy sent on an errand, leaving his father-in-law a pillar of assurance, with Winifred.

Doctor Wayne came, and looked grave. Yes, the knee was certainly taking the wrong way. The child might be lame for life.

Up went the fire of fear and anger in every heart. Doctor Wayne came again the next day for a proper examination. And, yes, the knee had really taken bad ways. It should be X-rayed. It was very important.

Godfrey Marshall walked up and down the lane with the doctor, beside the standing motor-car: up and down, up and down in one of those consultations of which he had had so many in his life.

As a result he came indoors to Winifred.

"Well, Winnie, dear, the best thing to do is to take Joyce up to London, to a nursing home where she can have proper treatment. Of course this knee has been allowed to go wrong. And apparently there is a risk that the child may even lose her leg. What do you think, dear? You agree to our taking her up to town and putting her under the best care?"

"Oh, father, you *know* I would do anything on earth for her."

"I know you would, Winnie darling. The pity is that there has been this unfortunate delay already. I can't think what Doctor Wing was doing. Apparently the child is in danger of losing her leg. Well then, if you will have everything ready, we will take her up to town to-morrow. I will order the large car from Denley's to be here at ten. Egbert, will you take a telegram at once to Doctor Jackson? It is a small nursing home for children and for surgical cases, not far from Baker Street. I'm sure Joyce will be all right there."

"Oh, father, can't I nurse her myself?"

"Well, darling, if she is to have proper treatment, she had best be in a home. The X-ray treatment, and the electric treatment, and whatever is necessary."

"It will cost a great deal——" said Winifred.

"We can't think of cost, if the child's leg is in danger—or even her life. No use speaking of cost," said the elder man impatiently.

And so it was. Poor Joyce, stretched out on a bed in the big closed motor-car—the mother sitting by her head, the grandfather in his short grey beard and a bowler hat, sitting by her feet, thick, and implacable in his responsibility—they rolled slowly away from Crockham, and from Egbert who stood there bareheaded and a little ignominious, left behind. He was to shut up the house and bring the rest of the family back to town, by train, the next day.

Followed a dark and bitter time. The poor child. The poor, poor child, how she suffered, an agony and a long crucifixion in that nursing home. It was a bitter six weeks which changed the soul of Winifred for ever. As she sat by the bed of her poor, tortured little child, tortured with the agony of the knee, and the still worse agony of these diabolic, but perhaps necessary modern treatments, she felt her heart killed and going cold in her breast. Her little Joyce, her frail, brave, wonderful, little Joyce, frail and small and pale as a white flower! Ah, how had she, Winifred, dared to be so wicked, so wicked, so careless, so sensual.

"Let my heart die! Let my woman's heart of flesh die! Saviour, let my heart die. And save my child. Let my heart die from the world and from the flesh. Oh, destroy my heart that is so wayward. Let my heart of pride die. Let my heart die."

She prayed beside the bed of her child. And like the Mother

with the seven swords in her breast, slowly her heart of pride and passion died in her breast, bleeding away. Slowly it died, bleeding away, and she turned to the Church for comfort, to Jesus, to the Mother of God, but most of all, to that great and enduring institution, the Roman Catholic Church. She withdrew into the shadow of the Church. She was a mother with three children. But in her soul she died, her heart of pride and passion and desire bled to death, her soul belonged to her Church, her body belonged to her duty as a mother.

Her duty as a wife did not enter. As a wife she had no sense of duty: only a certain bitterness towards the man with whom she had known such sensuality and distraction. She was purely the *Mater Dolorata*. To the man she was closed as a tomb.

Egbert came to see his child. But Winifred seemed to be always seated there, like the tomb of his manhood and his fatherhood. Poor Winifred: she was still young, still strong and ruddy and beautiful like a ruddy hard flower of the field. Strange—her ruddy, healthy face, so sombre, and her strong, heavy, full-blooded body, so still. She, a nun! Never. And yet the gates of her heart and soul had shut in his face with a slow, resonant clang, shutting him out for ever. There was no need for her to go into a convent. Her will had done it.

And between this young mother and this young father lay the crippled child, like a bit of pale silk floss on the pillow, and a little white pain-quenched face. He could not bear it. He just could not bear it. He turned aside. There was nothing to do but to turn aside. He turned aside, and went hither and thither, desultory. He was still attractive and desirable. But there was a little frown between his brow as if he had been cleft there with a hatchet: cleft right in, for ever, and that was the stigma.

The child's leg was saved: but the knee was locked stiff. The fear now was lest the lower leg should wither, or cease to grow. There must be long-continued massage and treatment, daily treatment, even when the child left the nursing home. And the whole of the expense was borne by the grandfather.

Egbert now had no real home. Winifred with the children and nurse was tied to the little flat in London. He could not live there: he could not contain himself. The cottage was shut-up—or lent to friends. He went down sometimes to work in his garden and keep the place in order. Then with the empty house around him at night, all the empty rooms, he felt his heart go wicked. The sense of frustration and futility, like some slow, torpid snake, slowly bit right through his heart. Futility, futility, futility: the horrible marsh-poison went through his veins and killed him.

As he worked in the garden in the silence of day he would listen for a sound. No sound. No sound of Winifred from the dark inside of the cottage: no sound of children's voices from the air, from the common, from the near distance. No sound, nothing but the old dark marsh-venomous atmosphere of the place. So he worked spasmodically through the day, and at night made a fire and cooked some food alone.

He was alone. He himself cleaned the cottage and made his bed. But his mending he did not do. His shirts were slit on the shoulders, when he had been working, and the white flesh showed through. He would feel the air and the spots of rain on his exposed flesh. And he would look again across the common, where the dark, tufted gorse was dying to seed, and the bits of cat-heather were coming pink in tufts, like a sprinkling of sacrificial blood.

His heart went back to the savage old spirit of the place: the desire for old gods, old, lost passions, the passion of the cold-blooded, darting snakes that hissed and shot away from him, the mystery of blood-sacrifices, all the lost, intense sensations of the primeval people of the place, whose passions seethed in the air still, from those long days before the Romans came. The seethe of a lost, dark passion in the air. The presence of unseen snakes.

A queer, baffled, half-wicked look came on his face. He could not stay long at the cottage. Suddenly he must swing on to his bicycle and go—anywhere. Anywhere, away from the place. He would stay a few days with his mother in the old home. His mother adored him and grieved as a mother would. But the little, baffled, half-wicked smile curled on his face, and he swung away from his mother's solicitude as from everything else.

Always moving on—from place to place, friend to friend: and always swinging away from sympathy. As soon as sympathy, like a soft hand, was reached out to touch him, away he swerved, instinctively, as a harmless snake swerves and swerves and swerves away from an outstretched hand. Away he must go. And periodically he went back to Winifred.

He was terrible to her now, like a temptation. She had devoted herself to her children and her Church. Joyce was once
more on her feet; but, alas! lame, with iron supports to her
leg, and a little crutch. It was strange how she had grown into
a long, pallid, wild little thing. Strange that the pain had not
made her soft and docile, but had brought out a wild, almost
mænad temper in the child. She was seven, and long and white
and thin, but by no means subdued. Her blonde hair was
darkening. She still had long sufferings to face, and, in her own
childish consciousness, the stigma of her lameness to bear.

And she bore it. An almost mænad courage seemed to possess
her, as if she were a long, thin, young weapon of life. She
acknowledged all her mother's care. She would stand by her
mother for ever. But some of her father's fine-tempered desperation flashed in her.

When Egbert saw his little girl limping horribly—not only
limping but lurching horribly in crippled, childish way, his
heart again hardened with chagrin, like steel that is tempered
again. There was a tacit understanding between him and his
little girl: not what we would call love, but a weapon-like
kinship. There was a tiny touch of irony in his manner towards her, contrasting sharply with Winifred's heavy, un-
leavened solicitude and care. The child flickered back to him
with an answering little smile of irony and recklessness: an
odd flippancy which made Winifred only the more sombre and
earnest.

The Marshalls took endless thought and trouble for the
child, searching out every means to save her limb and her ac-
tive freedom. They spared no effort and no money, they spared
no strength of will. With all their slow, heavy power of will
they willed that Joyce should save her liberty of movement,
should win back her wild, free grace. Even if it took a long
time to recover, it should be recovered.

So the situation stood. And Joyce submitted, week after
week, month after month, to the tyranny and pain of the treatment. She acknowledged the honourable effort on her behalf.
But her flamy reckless spirit was her father's. It was he who
had all the glamour for her. He and she were like members of
some forbidden secret society who know one another but may
not recognize one another. Knowledge they had in common,
the same secret of life, the father and the child. But the child

stayed in the camp of her mother, honourably, and the father wandered outside like Ishmael, only coming sometimes to sit in the home for an hour or two, an evening or two beside the camp fire, like Ishmael, in a curious silence and tension, with the mocking answer of the desert speaking out of his silence, and annulling the whole convention of the domestic home.

His presence was almost an anguish to Winifred. She prayed against it. That little cleft between his brow, that flickering, wicked little smile that seemed to haunt his face, and above all, the triumphant loneliness, the Ishmael quality. And then the erectness of his supple body, like a symbol. The very way he stood, so quiet, so insidious, like an erect, supple symbol of life, the living body, confronting her downcast soul, was torture to her. He was like a supple living idol moving before her eyes, and she felt if she watched him she was damned.

And he came and made himself at home in her little home. When he was there, moving in his own quiet way, she felt as if the whole great law of sacrifice, by which she had elected to live, were annulled. He annulled by his very presence the laws of her life. And what did he substitute? Ah, against that question she hardened herself in recoil.

It was awful to her to have to have him about—moving about in his shirt-sleeves, speaking in his tenor, throaty voice to the children. Annabel simply adored him, and he teased the little girl. The baby, Barbara, was not sure of him. She had been born a stranger to him. But even the nurse, when she saw his white shoulder of flesh through the slits of his torn shirt, thought it a shame.

Winifred felt it was only another weapon of his against her.

"You have other shirts—why do you wear that old one that is all torn, Egbert?" she said.

"I may as well wear it out," he said subtly.

He knew she would not offer to mend it for him. She *could* not. And no, she would not. Had she not her own gods to honour? And could she betray them, submitting to his Baal and Ashtaroth? And it was terrible to her, his unsheathed presence, that seemed to annul her and her faith, like another revelation. Like a gleaming idol evoked against her, a vivid life-idol that might triumph.

He came and he went—and she persisted. And then the great war broke out. He was a man who could not go to the dogs. He could not dissipate himself. He was pure-bred in his English-ness, and even when he would have liked to be vicious, he could not.

So when the war broke out his whole instinct was against it: against war. He had not the faintest desire to overcome any foreigners or to help in their death. He had no conception of Imperial England, and Rule Britannia was just a joke to him. He was a pure-blooded Englishman, perfect in his race, and when he was truly himself he could no more have been aggres-sive on the score of his Englishness than a rose can be ag-gressive on the score of its rosiness.

No, he had no desire to defy Germany and to exalt England. The distinction between German and English was not for him the distinction between good and bad. It was the distinction between blue water-flowers and red or white bush-blossoms: just difference. The difference between the wild boar and the wild bear. And a man was good or bad according to his nature, not according to his nationality.

Egbert was well-bred, and this was part of his natural under-standing. It was merely unnatural to him to hate a nation *en bloc*. Certain individuals he disliked, and others he liked, and the mass he knew nothing about. Certain deeds he disliked, certain deeds seemed natural to him, and about most deeds he had no particular feeling.

He had, however, the one deepest pure-bred instinct. He recoiled inevitably from having his feelings dictated to him by the mass feeling. His feelings were his own, his understanding was his own, and he would never go back on either, willingly. Shall a man become inferior to his own true knowledge and self, just because the mob expects it of him?

What Egbert felt subtly and without question, his father-in-law felt also in a rough, more combative way. Different as the two men were, they were two real Englishmen, and their in-stincts were almost the same.

And Godfrey Marshall had the world to reckon with. There was German military aggression, and the English non-military idea of liberty and the "conquests of peace"—meaning in-dustrialism. Even if the choice between militarism and indus-trialism were a choice of evils, the elderly man asserted his choice of the latter, perforce. He whose soul was quick with the instinct of power.

Egbert just refused to reckon with the world. He just refused even to decide between German militarism and British
industrialism. He chose neither. As for atrocities, he despised
the people who committed them, as inferior criminal types.
There was nothing national about crime.

And yet, war! War! Just war! Not right or wrong, but just
war itself. Should he join? Should he give himself over to war?
The question was in his mind for some weeks. Not because he
thought England was right and Germany wrong. Probably
Germany was wrong, but he refused to make a choice. Not
because he felt inspired. No. But just—war.

The deterrent was, the giving himself over into the power of
other men, and into the power of the mob-spirit of a democratic army. Should he give himself over? Should he make
over his own life and body to the control of something which
he *knew* was inferior, in spirit, to his own self? Should he
commit himself into the power of an inferior control? Should
he? Should he betray himself?

He was going to put himself into the power of his inferiors,
and he knew it. He was going to subjugate himself. He was
going to be ordered about by petty *canaille* of non-commis-
sioned officers—and even commissioned officers. He who was
born and bred free. Should he do it?

He went to his wife, to speak to her.

"Shall I join up, Winifred?"

She was silent. Her instinct also was dead against it. And
yet a certain profound resentment made her answer:

"You have three children dependent on you. I don't know
whether you have thought of that."

It was still only the third month of the war, and the old
pre-war ideas were still alive.

"Of course. But it won't make much difference to them. I
shall be earning a shilling a day, at least."

"You'd better speak to father, I think," she replied heavily.

Egbert went to his father-in-law. The elderly man's heart
was full of resentment.

"I should say," he said rather sourly, "it is the best thing you
could do."

Egbert went and joined up immediately, as a private soldier.
He was drafted into the light artillery.

Winifred now had a new duty towards him: the duty of a

wife towards a husband who is himself performing his duty towards the world. She loved him still. She would always love him, as far as earthly love went. But it was duty she now lived by. When he came back to her in khaki, a soldier, she submitted to him as a wife. It was her duty. But to his passion she could never again fully submit. Something prevented her, for ever: even her own deepest choice.

He went back again to camp. It did not suit him to be a modern soldier. In the thick, gritty, hideous khaki his subtle physique was extinguished as if he had been killed. In the ugly intimacy of the camp his thorough-bred sensibilities were just degraded. But he had chosen, so he accepted. An ugly little look came on to his face, of a man who has accepted his own degradation.

In the early spring Winifred went down to Crockham to be there when primroses were out, and the tassels hanging on the hazel-bushes. She felt something like a reconciliation towards Egbert, now he was a prisoner in camp most of his days. Joyce was wild with delight at seeing the garden and the common again, after the eight or nine months of London and misery. She was still lame. She still had the irons up her leg. But she lurched about with a wild, crippled agility.

Egbert came for a week-end, in his gritty, thick, sandpaper khaki and puttees and the hideous cap. Nay, he looked terrible. And on his face a slightly impure look, a little sore on his lip, as if he had eaten too much or drunk too much or let his blood become a little unclean. He was almost uglily healthy, with the camp life. It did not suit him.

Winifred waited for him in a little passion of duty and sacrifice, willing to serve the soldier, if not the man. It only made him feel a little more ugly inside. The week-end was torment to him: the memory of the camp, the knowledge of the life he led there; even the sight of his own legs in that abhorrent khaki. He felt as if the hideous cloth went into his blood and made it gritty and dirty. Then Winifred so ready to serve the *soldier*, when she repudiated the man. And this made the grit worse between his teeth. And the children running around playing and calling in the rather mincing fashion of children who have nurses and governesses and literature in the family. And Joyce so lame! It had all become unreal to him, after the camp. It only set his soul on edge. He left at dawn on the Monday morning, glad to get back to the realness and vulgarity of the camp.

Winifred would never meet him again at the cottage—only in London, where the world was with them. But sometimes he came alone to Crockham, perhaps when friends were staying there. And then he would work awhile in his garden. This summer still it would flame with blue anchusas and big red poppies, the mulleins would sway their soft, downy erections in the air: he loved mulleins: and the honeysuckle would stream out scent like memory, when the owl was whooing. Then he sat by the fire with the friends and with Winifred's sisters, and they sang the folk-songs. He put on thin civilian clothes and his charm and his beauty and the supple dominancy of his body glowed out again. But Winifred was not there.

At the end of the summer he went to Flanders, into action. He seemed already to have gone out of life, beyond the pale of life. He hardly remembered his life any more, being like a man who is going to take a jump from a height, and is only looking to where he must land.

He was twice slightly wounded, in two months. But not enough to put him off duty for more than a day or two. They were retiring again, holding the enemy back. He was in the rear—three machine-guns. The country was all pleasant, war had not yet trampled it. Only the air seemed shattered, and the land awaiting death. It was a small, unimportant action in which he was engaged.

The guns were stationed on a little bushy hillock just outside a village. But occasionally, it was difficult to say from which direction came the sharp crackle of rifle-fire, and beyond, the far-off thud of cannon. The afternoon was wintry and cold.

A lieutenant stood on a little iron platform at the top of the ladders, taking the sights and giving the aim, calling in a high, tense, mechanical voice. Out of the sky came the sharp cry of the directions, then the warning numbers, then "Fire!" The shot went, the piston of the gun sprang back, there was a sharp explosion, and a very faint film of smoke in the air. Then the other two guns fired, and there was a lull. The officer was uncertain of the enemy's position. The thick clump of horse-chestnut trees below was without change. Only in the far distance the sound of heavy firing continued, so far off as to give a sense of peace.

The gorse bushes on either hand were dark, but a few sparks of flowers showed yellow. He noticed them almost unconsciously as he waited, in the lull. He was in his shirt-sleeves, and the air came chill on his arms. Again his shirt was slit on the shoulders, and the flesh showed through. He was dirty and unkempt. But his face was quiet. So many things go out of consciousness before we come to the end of consciousness.

Before him, below, was the highroad, running between high banks of grass and gorse. He saw the whitish, muddy tracks and deep scores in the road, where the part of the regiment had retired. Now all was still. Sounds that came, came from the outside. The place where he stood was still silent, chill, serene: the white church among the trees beyond seemed like a thought only.

He moved into a lightning-like mechanical response at the sharp cry from the officer overhead. Mechanism, the pure mechanical action of obedience at the guns. Pure mechanical action at the guns. It left the soul unburdened, brooding in dark nakedness. In the end, the soul is alone, brooding on the face of the uncreated flux, as a bird on a dark sea.

Nothing could be seen but the road, and a crucifix knocked slanting and the dark, autumnal fields and woods. There appeared three horsemen on a little eminence, very small, on the crest of a ploughed field. They were our own men. Of the enemy, nothing.

The lull continued. Then suddenly came sharp orders, and a new direction of the guns, and an intense, exciting activity. Yet at the centre the soul remained dark and aloof, alone.

But even so, it was the soul that heard the new sound: the new, deep "papp!" of a gun that seemed to touch right upon the soul. He kept up the rapid activity at the machine-gun, sweating. But in his soul was the echo of the new, deep sound, deeper than life.

And in confirmation came the awful faint whistling of a shell, advancing almost suddenly into a piercing, tearing shriek that would tear through the membrane of life. He heard it in his ears, but he heard it also in his soul, in tension. There was relief when the thing had swung by and struck, away beyond.

He heard the hoarseness of its explosion, and the voice of the soldier calling to the horses. But he did not turn round to look. He only noticed a twig of holly with red berries fall like a gift on to the road below.

Not this time, not this time. Whither thou goest I will go. Did he say it to the shell, or to whom? Whither thou goest I will go. Then, the faint whistling of another shell dawned, and his blood became small and still to receive it. It drew nearer, like some horrible blast of wind; his blood lost consciousness. But in the second of suspension he saw the heavy shell swoop to earth, into the rocky bushes on the right, and earth and stones poured up into the sky. It was as if he heard no sound. The earth and stones and fragments of bush fell to earth again, and there was the same unchanging peace. The Germans had got the aim.

Would they move now? Would they retire? Yes. The officer was giving the last lightning-rapid orders to fire before withdrawing. A shell passed unnoticed in the rapidity of action. And then, into the silence, into the suspense where the soul brooded, finally crashed a noise and a darkness and a moment's flaming agony and horror. Ah, he had seen the dark bird flying towards him, flying home this time. In one instant life and eternity went up in a conflagration of agony, then there was a weight of darkness.

When faintly something began to struggle in the darkness, a consciousness of himself, he was aware of a great load and a clanging sound. To have known the moment of death! And to be forced, before dying, to review it. So, fate, even in death.

There was a resounding of pain. It seemed to sound from the outside of his consciousness: like a loud bell clanging very near. Yet he knew it was himself. He must associate himself with it. After a lapse and a new effort, he identified a pain in his head, a large pain that clanged and resounded. So far he could identify himself with himself. Then there was a lapse.

After a time he seemed to wake up again, and waking, to know that he was at the front, and that he was killed. He did not open his eyes. Light was not yet his. The clanging pain in his head rang out the rest of his consciousness. So he lapsed away from consciousness, in unutterable sick abandon of life.

Bit by bit, like a doom, came the necessity to know. He was hit in the head. It was only a vague surmise at first. But in the swinging of the pendulum of pain, swinging ever nearer and nearer, to touch him into an agony of consciousness and a consciousness of agony, gradually the knowledge emerged—he must be hit in the head—hit on the left brow; if so, there would be blood—was there blood?—could he feel blood in his left eye? Then the clanging seemed to burst the membrane of his brain, like death-madness.

Was there blood on his face? Was hot blood flowing? Or was it dry blood congealing down his cheek? It took him hours even to ask the question: time being no more than an agony in darkness, without measurement.

A long time after he had opened his eyes he realized he was seeing something—something, something, but the effort to recall what was too great. No, no; no recall!

Were they the stars in the dark sky? Was it possible it was stars in the dark sky? Stars? The world? Ah, no, he could not know it! Stars and the world were gone for him, he closed his eyes. No stars, no sky, no world. No, no! The thick darkness of blood alone. It should be one great lapse into the thick darkness of blood in agony.

Death, oh, death! The world all blood, and the blood all writhing with death. The soul like the tiniest little light out on a dark sea, the sea of blood. And the light guttering, beating, pulsing in a windless storm, wishing it could go out, yet unable.

There had been life. There had been Winifred and his children. But the frail death-agony effort to catch at straws of memory, straws of life from the past, brought on too great a nausea. No, no! No Winifred, no children. No world, no people. Better the agony of dissolution ahead than the nausea of the effort backwards. Better the terrible work should go forward, the dissolving into the black sea of death, in the extremity of dissolution, than that there should be any reaching back towards life. To forget! To forget! Utterly, utterly to forget, in the great forgetting of death. To break the core and the unit of life, and to lapse out on the great darkness. Only that. To break the clue, and mingle and commingle with the one darkness, without afterwards or forwards. Let the black sea of death itself solve the problem of futurity. Let the will of man break and give up.

What was that? A light! A terrible light! Was it figures? Was it legs of a horse colossal—colossal above him: huge, huge?

The Germans heard a slight noise, and started. Then, in the glare of a light-bomb, by the side of the heap of earth thrown up by the shell, they saw the dead face.

Myth and Ritual in "England, My England"

John B. Vickery

IN "ENGLAND, MY ENGLAND" the gradual transformation
of the passionate idyll of Egbert's and Winifred's marriage
into a savage combat that culminates with World War I and
Egbert's death is Lawrence's version of the myth of the dying
god and the rites of expulsion that accompany the scapegoat.
He takes great pains at the beginning of the story to stress the
ancient, primitive character both of the scene and of the
protagonists. Crockham, where the newlyweds settled, "belonged to the old England of hamlets and yeomen" and "it lay
there secret, primitive, savage as when the Saxons first came."
It is one of those places where "the savage England lingers in
patches." Into this bygone world come Winifred and Egbert to
reflect its sense of the past: "She, too, seemed to come out of
the old England, ruddy, strong, with a certain crude, passionate quiescence and a hawthorn robustness. And he, he was
tall and slim and agile, like an English archer with his long
supple legs and fine movements." Egbert enhances this affinity
by having "a passion for old folk-music, collecting folk-songs
and folk-dances, studying the Morris-dance and the old customs."

The connection with the past demonstrated in the setting,
the appearance, and the interests of the characters culminates
in their marital behavior. Though the desire is their own, it is
intensified by and derives from their immediate physical setting: "The flame of their two bodies burnt again into that old

Modern Fiction Studies, © 1959 by Purdue Research Foundation, Lafay-
ette, Indiana.

cottage, that was haunted already by so much bygone, physical desire. You could not be in the dark room for an hour without the influences coming over you. The hot blood-desire of bygone yeomen, there in this old den where they had lusted and bred for so many generations." In celebrating so triumphantly what Arnold van Gennep calls the fecundation rites of marriage, the couple not only fuse modern individuals with the medieval world of the yeoman but also suggest the truly primitive character of that world. One of the central rites of ancient times that persisted into more recent ages among the European peasantry is the mimetic observance by human beings of the Sacred Marriage of the god and goddess. It is just such an imitative rite that Egbert and Winifred are unconsciously involved in, as Lawrence intimates by juxtaposing the images of their union and the flourishing vegetation and garden which Egbert is said to have "re-created." Further support for this is found in Winifred's being regarded as "a ruddy fire into which he could cast himself for rejuvenation" since *The Golden Bough* emphasizes the procreative and purificatory powers of fire and its employment in conjunction with the Sacred Marriage ritual.

Lawrence, however, is writing a story of savage irony and despairing anguish, and hence he focuses not on the joyous celebration of renewed life that normally follows the ritual marriage but on the expulsion and death of the protagonist. This is ironically prepared for in the midst of the ritual of erotic ecstasy by the intrusion of the author's mock invocation "Ah, that it might never end, this passion, this marriage!" That it will end is certain not only because Egbert and Winifred prove to be incompatible personalities but also because they are unconsciously miming the ritual existence of the fertility deity who suffers a cyclic rejection and demise. And in the same scene an image of the impersonal yet necessary cruelty inherent in the mythic world is revealed in the snake's endeavor to swallow a frog who is uttering "the strangest scream, like the very soul of the dark past crying aloud." Nor is it accident that this ritual of self-preservation should have been witnessed by Winifred, who is to take the lead in Egbert's expulsion from the marriage, the family, and life itself.

In connection with the growing alienation that develops

between Egbert and Winifred it is important to notice that
the strain between them is not derived from the contrast of
Egbert's indolent dilettantism to her passion for responsibility
and duty nor even from his habit of sponging off her father.
These are, at the most, contributory factors. The genuine
source of their estrangement lies in a virtually inevitable
change in the structure of their world. Instructive here is van
Gennep's point, made in *Les Rites de Passage,* that the life of
the individual passes through certain successive stages and
that this is achieved through the intermediary of ceremonies
calculated to make the transition a safe one. These *rites de
passage* are threefold, consisting of those which van Gennep
calls *"séparation, marge, et agrégation."* The crucial change in
the world of the two characters comes when they enter the
state of parenthood. Here is the beginning of the ritual of
separation, of detachment from the old world and the old life.
Winifred finds in her child "a new center of interest" so that
"without anything happening, he was gradually, unconsciously
excluded from the circle." Then, following their second child,
she begins to resent and despise that physical love which has
already become of secondary importance to her in the role of
dutiful and responsible mother. To provide a conscious justi-
fication for this attitude, she turns to the issue of money and
his failure to earn a living. Having thus articulated her sense
of critical detachment from her husband, she at length formu-
lates what it is that really separates them: "It was that he
stood for nothing."

With this we come to the central antithesis in the story,
that between her husband and her father. The basic desire of
the former is "to hold aloof. It was not his season." The latter,
on the other hand, plunges into the struggle of existence with
"an acrid faith like the sap of some not-to-be-exterminated
tree. Just a blind acrid faith as sap is blind and acrid, and
yet pushes on in growth and in faith." The "stoic and epicurean" husband confronts the hardy vegetative father and
succumbs, in the last analysis, because he lacks the father's
"will-to-power, . . . the single power of his own blind self."
Their struggle, however, is not direct but operates through and
in the person of Winifred. For her, the basic familial unit is
comprised of her parents, herself, and her child; in it she finds

the core of life, "the human trinity for her." She does so because her father has maintained "a certain primitive dominion over the souls of his children, the old, almost magic prestige of paternity. There it was, still burning in him, the old smoky torch of parental godhead. . . . Fatherhood that had life-and-death authority over the children." The only thing that could have supplanted her father would have been Winifred's finding in her husband a greater male power and authority. But since Egbert does not possess this power, Lawrence ironically inverts the mythical formula which calls for the young ruler or deity to succeed the old one. Egbert rejects the possibility of his own divinity as a human being replete with power and becomes in contrast to the father a *tabu*-figure, "the living negative of power." And what he taboos by his very presence is Winifred's attempt to exercise "her dark, silent, passionate authority," "the old blood-power," "the old dark magic of parental authority." To this end he uses his own form of magic and witchcraft not only to transform her parental authority into "a sort of tyranny" but also to steal the children (the image is Lawrence's) from her. His magic is that which most completely captures children, namely, the exercise of complete license in behavior: "They could do as they liked with him."

Out of the two men's indirect struggle for the role of father has come the ritual of separation celebrated by Winifred in her increasing sexual reticence and by Egbert in his denial of her parental authority coupled with his own rejection of responsibility. This, however, is but the first stage in the rites of passage, that of detachment from the old life. It is followed by what van Gennep calls the *"rite de marge,"* the behavior that marks the interim stage between the old and the new modes of life. In *England, My England* this is reflected in the incident of the first-born child's being lamed as a result of falling on a sickle left in the grass by Egbert. With this the antithesis between Winifred's passion for duty and authority (a worship of hierarchy) and Egbert's rejection of responsibility and power (a belief in liberty and self-determination) is projected into the visible and external world so forcefully that husband and wife are seen to be completely separated, to be living in different worlds. In the weeks that follow the accident, both are moving toward their new and distinct modes of existence. As a period of physical, emotional, and spiritual transition it is "a dark and bitter time" for all.

Yet this incident and its repercussions are not significant solely as a rite of transition from marriage to legal separation. For in the early part of the story Egbert has been identified as a representative and worshipper of phallic potency who like the primitive divine king rules only so long as he can demonstrate his power as a fertility figure. When Winifred denies him this, she makes him "lock up his own vivid life inside himself" and thereby reduces him to virtual impotence. Both Egbert and the divine king react in the same way: through a sacrifice of the first-born, man may continue to live as he has, to retain a wife as well as a throne, to prolong a marriage as well as a reign. Clearly, such a rite could not be deliberately embarked upon by a member of the civilized world for whom it would be a monstrously evil act. But as Lawrence seems to indicate, it would be quite possible to desire this in the subconscious where the primitive and savage impulses of man linger even yet. Thus, the contemporary consciousness registers this longing for sacrifice literally as "a wicked look" and metaphorically as Egbert's having "seven devils inside his long, slim, white body."

Similarly, Egbert himself, immediately after the accident, seeks to assuage his deep sense of guilt by insisting on the accidental character of the event. What is at the core of this guilt, however, is not his own superficial carelessness but rather his profound and abiding responsibility. In times of great calamity, *The Golden Bough* tells us, it was customary to sacrifice the first-born. And for Egbert there could be no greater calamity than losing Winifred, for, as has been suggested, it is through her that his spirit of fertility is released and his rejuvenation effected. By indirectly attempting to sacrifice the child, Egbert is seeking to acquire a new lease on life, to atone for his sins (especially the denial of parental authority's divinity), and to demonstrate that he, like Winifred's father, "had kept alive the old red flame of fatherhood, the fatherhood that had even the right to sacrifice the child to God, like Isaac." That Egbert is using the child as a substitute for himself is further suggested by the weapon's being a sickle, the instrument employed in harvest rituals to sacrifice the fertility deity. Even more striking is the fact that, according to Frazer, "the corn-spirit is conceived as a child who is separated from its mother by the stroke of the sickle."

It is part, however, of Lawrence's ironic intention that this effort at prolonging a state of existence regarded as fruitful and idyllic should be thwarted. He is concerned not with the revival but with the death of human society and its protagonists. This is borne out by the sacrifice of the child, which as a ritual of transition proves to be "an agony and a long crucifixion." The irony appears in that the sacrifice is not complete, the child does not die, and so the father cannot restore the marriage to its sacred status. A further irony follows from the fact that the ultimate ritual sacrifice is made by Egbert as a result of his being the scapegoat in the accident. It is with his assumption of this role that the final stage of the *"rite du passage"* is reached. Following the marginal, transitional observance there is the absorption into a new world and a new mode of life. For Winifred the child's injury completely ends her passionate attachment to Egbert. The existence into which she is drawn is that of institutional religion, the Roman Catholic Church. Here she finds an alternative to the life of passion, sensuality, and distraction she has known with Egbert.

It is from this that Egbert's own ritual of absorption or assimilation follows. When Winifred becomes "purely the *Mater Dolorata*," he finds that for him "she was closed as a tomb, . . . the tomb of his manhood and his fatherhood," an image which both adumbrates his fate and reveals the degree of her responsibility. Like the primitive scapegoat, he finds that he is shut out forever from the community he has known, compelled "to turn aside," to wander "hither and thither, desultory," possessed of "no real home." Even clearer evidence of his assumption of the role of ritual outcast from society is the hatchet-like cleft in his brow developed since the accident which he bears as his Cain-like "stigma." It is this together with his relation to her and her family that gives him for Winifred "the Ishmael quality." But the scapegoat is not simply the creature who wanders in lonely isolation until overtaken by death. It is also representative of the divinity whose death is preordained as an elaborate ritual of sacrifice. Egbert's divinity is revealed by his appearing to Winifred's now nun-like soul as "an erect, supple symbol of life, the living body" and to her Christianized eyes as "Baal and Ashtaroth," "a supple living idol" that "if she watched him she was damned."

To her he appears godlike, but to himself he is the object of sacrifice. Thus, in the landscape bits of vegetation seem to him "like a sprinkling of sacrificial blood." And from this his imagination comes to be dominated by "the savage old spirit of the place: the desire for old gods, old, lost passions, the passion of the cold-blooded, darting snakes that hissed and shot away from him, the mystery of blood-sacrifices, all the lost, intense sensations of the primeval people of the place, whose passions seethed in the air still, from those long days before the Romans came."

The opportunity for the blood-sacrifice of the scapegoat is provided by the war into which he is projected by his wife and father-in-law. With his enlistment the various rites associated with the scapegoat are performed. The customary inversion of the social hierarchy is reflected in Egbert's awareness that joining the army meant "he was going to put himself into the power of his inferiors. . . . He was going to subjugate himself." Similarly, Winifred's being "so ready to serve the *soldier*, when she repudiated the man" (Lawrence's italics) mirrors the scapegoat's being permitted sexual intercourse with a woman usually forbidden him. And finally, Egbert's being wounded twice before his death approximates the custom of beating and wounding the scapegoat before putting him to death. By these rites he is confirmed in his role; now he is not simply expelled from his family, he has "gone out of life, beyond the pale of life." Nor is it without significance that Lawrence should present Egbert under the image of "a man who is going to take a jump from a height," for the scapegoat commonly met his fate by being hurled from a cliff. Out of these rites comes a feeling of participation in an inescapable experience that sustains him through even his death agonies and permits him to will the completion of the scapegoat ritual by which the myth of the dying god is enacted.

William Faulkner

William Faulkner (1897–1962) has moved from critical ob-
scurity to world eminence. Though his novels began appearing
in the 1920's, it was only with Malcolm Cowley's edition of the
Viking Portable Faulkner *in 1946 that serious public attention*
came to be focused on his work. Since that time he has gained
recognition as one of the preeminent novelists in the history
of American literature, surpassed perhaps only by Henry
James. He and his works have seized the imagination of
readers not only in America but also in Europe and Asia. His
voice speaks with peculiar intensity and authenticity of the
complexities and agonies inherent in the human condition. In
France especially he has exercised an enormous influence both
through Maurice Coindreau's translations of his works and the
critical admiration of such important figures as Jean-Paul
Sartre, Albert Camus, and André Malraux.

Faulkner was born in a small town in Mississippi, a region
that most of his fiction explores with a loving but thoroughly
unsentimental care. His schooling was sporadic and his goals
uncertain during his early years. World War I led him, how-
ever, to enlist in the Canadian Air Force and to see service in
France. On his return after the Armistice, he attended the
University of Mississippi in a desultory fashion for a couple
of years but never graduated. In subsequent years he was
befriended by Sherwood Anderson in New Orleans, visited
Europe, and worked briefly in New York. Anderson helped
him get his first novel published, but only with his return to
Mississippi and his beginning to explore through fiction the
life of his region did his work take on its distinctive thematic
and technical features. With the appearance of The Sound and
the Fury *(1929) and* As I Lay Dying *(1930), his claim to a major*
place in American literature was inaugurated. In later years
it was consolidated and expanded with the appearance of

Light in August (*1932*), Absalom, Absalom! (*1936*), The Hamlet (*1940*), *and* Go Down, Moses (*1942*).

Throughout his career, Faulkner exhibited a continuing interest in certain overriding themes as well as in technical experimentation. The latter includes subtle and varied uses of the stream-of-consciousness technique, multiple narrators and discordant points of view, doubling of plots, mixing of genres (as 'in Requiem for a Nun), *and shifting levels of style ranging from the labrynthine to the colloquial. His enduring preoccupations are with the ironies in man's modes of apprehending experience and with the individual's struggle to assert his own intrinsic moral nature. In exploring the different ways of apprehending experience, Faulkner creates the elaborate and daring treatments of perception, language, and time, of truth, legend, and fact, that make up such works as* The Sound and the Fury, As I Lay Dying, *and* Absalom, Absalom! *The moral concerns of Faulkner center on the individual's efforts to achieve a viable relationship with his society, its mores, traditions, and beliefs. As a Southern writer, Faulkner finds this theme most graphically, though not exclusively, exemplified in the tangled history of the relationship between the black and white races and individuals in his native region. Preeminent in this respect is* Light in August *for its moving drama of one man's quest for personal and racial identity. In many ways this novel elaborates upon the central actions of "Dry September." In different ways, the same is substantially true of* Absalom, Absalom!, Go Down, Moses, Intruder in the Dust, Requiem for a Nun, *and stories like "Red Leaves," "That Evening Sun," and "Pantaloon in Black."*

At present no full-scale biography of Faulkner exists, though several are projected. In their absence, information on Faulkner's life can best be gleaned from the relevant portions of Edmond L. Volpe's A Reader's Guide to William Faulkner (*1964*), *Michael Millgate's* The Achievement of William Faulkner (*1965*), *and Robert Coughlan's* The Private World of William Faulkner (*1954*). *In recent years there has been a dramatic upsurge of critical interest in Faulkner. Useful bibliographical aids to the criticism of Faulkner are F. J. Hoffman & Olga W. Vickery, eds.,* William Faulkner: Three Decades of Criticism (*1960*); *and* Modern Fiction Studies, *13*

(*Spring, 1967*). *A general approach to Faulkner's short stories in relation to the rest of his work can be found in the last chapter of Olga Vickery's* The Novels of William Faulkner (*1964*). *In addition to the essay included here, other treatments of "Dry September" are William B.* Bache, "Moral Awareness in 'Dry September,' " Faulkner Studies, *3* (*Winter, 1954*), *53–57; Glenn O.* Carey, "Social Criticism in Faulkner's 'Dry September,' " English Record, *15* (*December, 1964*) *27–30; Arthur L.* Ford, "Dust and Dreams: A Study of Faulkner's 'Dry September,' " College English, *24* (*December, 1962*), *219–20; Daniel Weiss, "William Faulkner and the Runaway Slave,"* Northwest Review, *6* (*Summer, 1963*), *71–79; Ralph H. Wolfe and Edgar F. Daniels, "Beneath the Dust of 'Dry September,' "* Studies in Short Fiction, *1* (*Winter, 1964*), *158–59.*

Dry September

William Faulkner

THROUGH THE BLOODY SEPTEMBER TWILIGHT, after-
math of sixty-two rainless days, it had gone like a fire in dry
grass—the rumor, the story, whatever it was. Something about
Miss Minnie Cooper and a Negro. Attacked, insulted, frightened: none of them, gathered in the barber shop on that
Saturday evening where the ceiling fan stirred, without freshening it, the vitiated air, sending back upon them, in recurrent
surges of stale pomade and lotion, their own stale breath and
odors, knew exactly what had happened.

"Except it wasn't Will Mayes," a barber said. He was a man
of middle age; a thin, sand-colored man with a mild face, who
was shaving a client. "I know Will Mayes. He's a good nigger.
And I know Miss Minnie Cooper, too."

"What do you know about her?" a second barber said.

"Who is she?" the client said. "A young girl?"

"No," the barber said. "She's about forty, I reckon. She
aint married. That's why I dont believe—"

"Believe, hell!" a hulking youth in a sweat-stained silk shirt
said. "Wont you take a white woman's word before a nigger's?"

"I dont believe Will Mayes did it," the barber said. "I know
Will Mayes."

"Maybe you know who did it, then. Maybe you already got
him out of town, you damn niggerlover."

"I dont believe anybody did anything. I dont believe anything happened. I leave it to you fellows if them ladies that get old without getting married dont have notions that a man cant—"

"Then you are a hell of a white man," the client said. He moved under the cloth. The youth had sprung to his feet.

"You dont?" he said. "Do you accuse a white woman of lying?"

The barber held the razor poised above the half-risen client. He did not look around.

"It's this durn weather," another said. "It's enough to make a man do anything. Even to her."

Nobody laughed. The barber said in his mild, stubborn tone: "I aint accusing nobody of nothing. I just know and you fellows know how a woman that never—"

"You damn niggerlover!" the youth said.

"Shut up, Butch," another said. "We'll get the facts in plenty of time to act."

"Who is? Who's getting them?" the youth said. "Facts, hell! I—"

"You're a fine white man," the client said. "Aint you?" In his frothy beard he looked like a desert rat in the moving pictures. "You tell them, Jack," he said to the youth. "If there aint any white men in this town, you can count on me, even if I aint only a drummer and a stranger."

"That's right, boys," the barber said. "Find out the truth first. I know Will Mayes."

"Well, by God!" the youth shouted. "To think that a white man in this town—"

"Shut up, Butch," the second speaker said. "We got plenty of time."

The client sat up. He looked at the speaker. "Do you claim that anything excuses a nigger attacking a white woman? Do you mean to tell me you are a white man and you'll stand for it? You better go back North where you came from. The South dont want your kind here."

"North what?" the second said. "I was born and raised in this town."

"Well, by God!" the youth said. He looked about with a strained, baffled gaze, as if he was trying to remember what it was he wanted to say or to do. He drew his sleeve across his sweating face. "Damn if I'm going to let a white woman—"

"You tell them, Jack," the drummer said. "By God, if they—"

The screen door crashed open. A man stood in the floor, his feet apart and his heavy-set body poised easily. His white shirt was open at the throat; he wore a felt hat. His hot, bold glance swept the group. His name was McLendon. He had commanded troops at the front in France and had been decorated for valor.

"Well," he said, "are you going to sit there and let a black son rape a white woman on the streets of Jefferson?"

Butch sprang up again. The silk of his shirt clung flat to his heavy shoulders. At each armpit was a dark halfmoon. "That's what I been telling them! That's what I—"

"Did it really happen?" a third said. "This aint the first man scare she ever had, like Hawkshaw says. Wasn't there something about a man on the kitchen roof, watching her undress, about a year ago?"

"What?" the client said. "What's that?" The barber had been slowly forcing him back into the chair; he arrested himself reclining, his head lifted, the barber still pressing him down.

McLendon whirled on the third speaker. "Happen? What the hell difference does it make? Are you going to let the black sons get away with it until one really does it?"

"That's what I'm telling them!" Butch shouted. He cursed, long and steady, pointless.

"Here, here," a fourth said. "Not so loud. Dont talk so loud."

"Sure," McLendon said; "no talking necessary at all. I've done my talking. Who's with me?" He poised on the balls of his feet, roving his gaze.

The barber held the drummer's face down, the razor poised. "Find out the facts first, boys. I know Willy Mayes. It wasn't him. Let's get the sheriff and do this thing right."

McLendon whirled upon him his furious, rigid face. The barber did not look away. They looked like men of different races. The other barbers had ceased also above their prone clients. "You mean to tell me," McLendon said, "that you'd take a nigger's word before a white woman's? Why, you damn niggerloving—"

The third speaker rose and grasped McLendon's arm; he

too had been a soldier. "Now, now. Let's figure this thing out. Who knows anything about what really happened?"

"Figure out hell!" McLendon jerked his arm free. "All that're with me get up from there. The ones that aint—" He roved his gaze, dragging his sleeve across his face.

Three men rose. The drummer in the chair sat up. "Here," he said, jerking at the cloth about his neck; "get this rag off me. I'm with him. I dont live here, but by God, if our mothers and wives and sisters—" He smeared the cloth over his face and flung it to the floor. McLendon stood in the floor and cursed the others. Another rose and moved toward him. The remainder sat uncomfortable, not looking at one another, then one by one they rose and joined him.

The barber picked the cloth from the floor. He began to fold it neatly. "Boys, dont do that. Will Mayes never done it. I know."

"Come on," McLendon said. He whirled. From his hip pocket protruded the butt of a heavy automatic pistol. They went out. The screen door crashed behind them reverberant in the dead air.

The barber wiped the razor carefully and swiftly, and put it away, and ran to the rear, and took his hat from the wall. "I'll be back as soon as I can," he said to the other barbers. "I cant let—" He went out, running. The two other barbers followed him to the door and caught it on the rebound, leaning out and looking up the street after him. The air was flat and dead. It had a metallic taste at the base of the tongue.

"What can he do?" the first said. The second one was saying "Jees Christ, Jees Christ" under his breath. "I'd just as lief be Will Mayes as Hawk, if he gets McLendon riled."

"Jees Christ, Jees Christ," the second whispered.

"You reckon he really done it to her?" the first said.

She was thirty-eight or thirty-nine. She lived in a small frame house with her invalid mother and a thin, sallow, unflagging aunt, where each morning between ten and eleven she would appear on the porch in a lace-trimmed boudoir cap, to sit swinging in the porch swing until noon. After dinner she lay down for a while, until the afternoon began to cool. Then, in one of the three or four new voile dresses which she had each summer, she would go downtown to spend the afternoon in the stores with the other ladies, where they would handle the goods and haggle over the prices in cold, immediate voices, without any intention of buying.

She was of comfortable people—not the best in Jefferson, but good people enough—and she was still on the slender side of ordinary looking, with a bright, faintly haggard manner and dress. When she was young she had had a slender, nervous body and a sort of hard vivacity which had enabled her for a time to ride upon the crest of the town's social life as exemplified by the high school party and church social period of her contemporaries while still children enough to be un-classconscious.

She was the last to realize that she was losing ground; that those among whom she had been a little brighter and louder flame than any other were beginning to learn the pleasure of snobbery—male—and retaliation—female. That was when her face began to wear that bright, haggard look. She still carried it to parties on shadowy porticoes and summer lawns, like a mask or a flag, with that bafflement of furious repudiation of truth in her eyes. One evening at a party she heard a boy and two girls, all schoolmates, talking. She never accepted another invitation.

She watched the girls with whom she had grown up as they married and got homes and children, but no man ever called on her steadily until the children of the other girls had been calling her "aunty" for several years, the while their mothers told them in bright voices about how popular Aunt Minnie had been as a girl. Then the town began to see her driving on Sunday afternoons with the cashier in the bank. He was a widower of about forty—a high-colored man, smelling always faintly of the barber shop or of whisky. He owned the first automobile in town, a red runabout; Minnie had the first motoring bonnet and veil the town ever saw. Then the town began to say: "Poor Minnie." "But she is old enough to take care of herself," others said. That was when she began to ask her old schoolmates that their children call her "cousin" instead of "aunty."

It was twelve years now since she had been relegated into adultery by public opinion, and eight years since the cashier had gone to a Memphis bank, returning for one day each Christmas, which he spent at an annual bachelors' party at a hunting club on the river. From behind their curtains the neighbors would see the party pass, and during the over-the-way Christmas day visiting they would tell her about him, about how well he looked, and how they heard that he was prospering in the city, watching with bright, secret eyes her haggard, bright face. Usually by that hour there would be the scent of whisky on her breath. It was supplied her by a youth, a clerk at the soda fountain: "Sure; I buy it for the old gal. I reckon she's entitled to a little fun."

Her mother kept to her room altogether now; the gaunt aunt ran the house. Against that background Minnie's bright dresses, her idle and empty days, had a quality of furious unreality. She went out in the evenings only with women now, neighbors, to the moving pictures. Each afternoon she dressed in one of the new dresses and went downtown alone, where her young "cousins" were already strolling in the late afternoons with their delicate, silken heads and thin, awkward arms and conscious hips, clinging to one another or shrieking and giggling with paired boys in the soda fountain when she passed and went on along the serried store fronts, in the doors of which the sitting and lounging men did not even follow her with their eyes any more.

The barber went swiftly up the street where the sparse lights, insect-swirled, glared in rigid and violent suspension in the lifeless air. The day had died in a pall of dust; above the darkened square, shrouded by the spent dust, the sky was as clear as the inside of a brass bell. Below the east was a rumor of the twice-waxed moon.

When he overtook them McLendon and three others were getting into a car parked in an alley. McLendon stooped his thick head, peering out beneath the top. "Changed your mind, did you?" he said. "Damn good thing; by God, tomorrow when this town hears about how you talked tonight—"

"Now, now," the other ex-soldier said. "Hawkshaw's all right. Come on, Hawk; jump in."

"Will Mayes never done it, boys," the barber said. "If anybody done it. Why, you all know well as I do there aint any town where they got better niggers than us. And you know how a lady will kind of think things about men when there aint any reason to, and Miss Minnie anyway—"

"Sure, sure," the soldier said. "We're just going to talk to him a little; that's all."

"Talk hell!" Butch said. "When we're through with the—"

"Shut up, for God's sake!" the soldier said. "Do you want everybody in town—"

"Tell them, by God!" McLendon said. "Tell every one of the sons that'll let a white woman—"

"Let's go; let's go: here's the other car." The second car slid squealing out of a cloud of dust at the alley mouth. McLendon started his car and took the lead. Dust lay like fog in the street. The street lights hung nimbused as in water. They drove on out of town.

A rutted lane turned at right angles. Dust hung above it too, and above all the land. The dark bulk of the ice plant, where the Negro Mayes was night watchman, rose against the sky. "Better stop here, hadn't we?" the soldier said. McLendon did not reply. He hurled the car up and slammed to a stop, the headlights glaring on the blank wall.

"Listen here, boys," the barber said; "if he's here, dont that prove he never done it? Dont it? If it was him, he would run. Dont you see he would?" The second car came up and stopped. McLendon got down; Butch sprang down beside him. "Listen, boys," the barber said.

"Cut the lights off!" McLendon said. The breathless dark rushed down. There was no sound in it save their lungs as they sought air in the parched dust in which for two months they had lived; then the diminishing crunch of McLendon's and Butch's feet, and a moment later McLendon's voice:

"Will! . . . Will!"

Below the east the wan hemorrhage of the moon increased. It heaved above the ridge, silvering the air, the dust, so that they seemed to breathe, live, in a bowl of molten lead. There was no sound of nightbird nor insect, no sound save their breathing and a faint ticking of contracting metal about the cars. Where their bodies touched one another they seemed to sweat dryly, for no more moisture came. "Christ!" a voice said; "let's get out of here."

But they didn't move until vague noises began to grow out of the darkness ahead; then they got out and waited tensely in the breathless dark. There was another sound: a blow, a hissing expulsion of breath and McLendon cursing in undertone. They stood a moment longer, then they ran forward. They ran in a stumbling clump, as though they were fleeing something. "Kill him, kill the son," a voice whispered. McLendon flung them back. "Not here," he said. "Get him into the car." "Kill him, kill the black son!" the voice murmured. They dragged the Negro to the car. The barber had waited beside the car. He could feel himself sweating and he knew he was going to be sick at the stomach.

"What is it, captains?" the Negro said. "I aint done nothing. 'Fore God, Mr John." Someone produced handcuffs. They worked busily about the Negro as though he were a post, quiet, intent, getting in one another's way. He submitted to the handcuffs, looking swiftly and constantly from dim face to dim face. "Who's here, captains?" he said, leaning to peer into the faces until they could feel his breath and smell his sweaty reek. He spoke a name or two. "What you all say I done, Mr John?"

McLendon jerked the car door open. "Get in!" he said.

The Negro did not move. "What you all going to do with me, Mr John? I aint done nothing. White folks, captains, I aint done nothing: I swear 'fore God." He called another name.

"Get in!" McLendon said. He struck the Negro. The others expelled their breath in a dry hissing and struck him with random blows and he whirled and cursed them, and swept his manacled hands across their faces and slashed the barber upon the mouth, and the barber struck him also. "Get him in there," McLendon said. They pushed at him. He ceased struggling and got in and sat quietly as the others took their places. He sat between the barber and the soldier, drawing his limbs in so as not to touch them, his eyes going swiftly and constantly from face to face. Butch clung to the running board. The car moved on. The barber nursed his mouth with his handkerchief.

"What's the matter, Hawk?" the soldier said.

"Nothing," the barber said. They regained the highroad and turned away from town. The second car dropped back out of the dust. They went on, gaining speed; the final fringe of houses dropped behind.

"Goddamn, he stinks!" the soldier said.

"We'll fix that," the drummer in front beside McLendon

said. On the running board Butch cursed into the hot rush of air. The barber leaned suddenly forward and touched McLendon's arm.

"Let me out, John," he said.

"Jump out, niggerlover," McLendon said without turning his head. He drove swiftly. Behind them the sourceless lights of the second car glared in the dust. Presently McLendon turned into a narrow road. It was rutted with disuse. It led back to an abandoned brick kiln—a series of reddish mounds and weed- and vine-choked vats without bottom. It had been used for pasture once, until one day the owner missed one of his mules. Although he prodded carefully in the vats with a long pole, he could not even find the bottom of them.

"John," the barber said.

"Jump out, then," McLendon said, hurling the car along the ruts. Beside the barber the Negro spoke:

"Mr Henry."

The barber sat forward. The narrow tunnel of the road rushed up and past. Their motion was like an extinct furnace blast: cooler, but utterly dead. The car bounded from rut to rut.

"Mr Henry," the Negro said.

The barber began to tug furiously at the door. "Look out, there!" the soldier said, but the barber had already kicked the door open and swung onto the running board. The soldier leaned across the Negro and grasped at him, but he had already jumped. The car went on without checking speed.

The impetus hurled him crashing through dust-sheathed weeds, into the ditch. Dust puffed about him, and in a thin, vicious crackling of sapless stems he lay choking and retching until the second car passed and died away. Then he rose and limped on until he reached the highroad and turned toward town, brushing at his clothes with his hands. The moon was higher, riding high and clear of the dust at last, and after a while the town began to glare beneath the dust. He went on, limping. Presently he heard cars and the glow of them grew in the dust behind him and he left the road and crouched again in the weeds until they passed. McLendon's car came last now. There were four people in it and Butch was not on the running board.

They went on; the dust swallowed them; the glare and the

sound died away. The dust of them hung for a while, but soon the eternal dust absorbed it again. The barber climbed back onto the road and limped on toward town.

As she dressed for supper on that Saturday evening, her own flesh felt like fever. Her hands trembled among the hooks and eyes, and her eyes had a feverish look, and her hair swirled crisp and crackling under the comb. While she was still dressing the friends called for her and sat while she donned her sheerest underthings and stockings and a new voile dress. "Do you feel strong enough to go out?" they said, their eyes bright too, with a dark glitter. "When you have had time to get over the shock, you must tell us what happened. What he said and did; everything."

In the leafed darkness, as they walked toward the square, she began to breathe deeply, something like a swimmer preparing to dive, until she ceased trembling, the four of them walking slowly because of the terrible heat and out of solicitude for her. But as they neared the square she began to tremble again, walking with her head up, her hands clenched at her sides, their voices about her murmurous, also with that feverish, glittering quality of their eyes.

They entered the square, she in the center of the group, fragile in her fresh dress. She was trembling worse. She walked slower and slower, as children eat ice cream, her head up and her eyes bright in the haggard banner of her face, passing the hotel and the coatless drummers in chairs along the curb looking around at her: "That's the one: see? The one in pink in the middle." "Is that her? What did they do with the nigger? Did they—?" "Sure. He's all right." "All right, is he?" "Sure. He went on a little trip." Then the drug store, where even the young men lounging in the doorway tipped their hats and followed with their eyes the motion of her hips and legs when she passed.

They went on, passing the lifted hats of the gentlemen, the suddenly ceased voices, deferent, protective. "Do you see?" the friends said. Their voices sounded like long, hovering sighs of hissing exultation. "There's not a Negro on the square. Not one."

They reached the picture show. It was like a miniature fairyland with its lighted lobby and colored lithographs of life caught in its terrible and beautiful mutations. Her lips began to tingle. In the dark, when the picture began, it would be all right; she could hold back the laughing so it would not waste away so fast and so soon. So she hurried on before the turning faces, the undertones of low astonishment, and they took their accustomed places where she could see the aisle against the silver glare and the young men and girls coming in two and two against it.

The lights flicked away; the screen glowed silver, and soon life began to unfold, beautiful and passionate and sad, while still the young men and girls entered, scented and sibilant in the half dark, their paired backs in silhouette delicate and sleek, their slim, quick bodies awkward, divinely young, while beyond them the silver dream accumulated, inevitably on and on. She began to laugh. In trying to suppress it, it made more noise than ever; heads began to turn. Still laughing, her friends raised her and led her out, and she stood at the curb, laughing on a high, sustained note, until the taxi came up and they helped her in.

They removed the pink voile and the sheer underthings and the stockings, and put her to bed, and cracked ice for her temples, and sent for the doctor. He was hard to locate, so they ministered to her with hushed ejaculations, renewing the ice and fanning her. While the ice was fresh and cold she stopped laughing and lay still for a time, moaning only a little. But soon the laughing welled again and her voice rose screaming.

"Shhhhhhhhhhh! Shhhhhhhhhhhhhh!" they said, freshening the icepack, smoothing her hair, examining it for gray; "poor girl!" Then to one another: "Do you suppose anything really happened?" their eyes darkly aglitter, secret and passionate. "Shhhhhhhhhh! Poor girl! Poor Minnie!"

It was midnight when McLendon drove up to his neat new house. It was trim and fresh as a birdcage and almost as small, with its clean, green-and-white paint. He locked the car and mounted the porch and entered. His wife rose from a chair beside the reading lamp. McLendon stopped in the floor and stared at her until she looked down.

"Look at that clock," he said, lifting his arm, pointing. She stood before him, her face lowered, a magazine in her hands. Her face was pale, strained, and weary-looking. "Haven't I told you about sitting up like this, waiting to see when I come in?"

"John," she said. She laid the magazine down. Poised on the balls of his feet, he glared at her with his hot eyes, his sweating face.

"Didn't I tell you?" He went toward her. She looked up then. He caught her shoulder. She stood passive, looking at him.

"Don't John. I couldn't sleep . . . The heat; something. Please, John. You're hurting me."

"Didn't I tell you?" He released her and half struck, half flung her across the chair, and she lay there and watched him quietly as he left the room.

He went on through the house, ripping off his shirt, and on the dark, screened porch at the rear he stood and mopped his head and shoulders with the shirt and flung it away. He took the pistol from his hip and laid it on the table beside the bed, and sat on the bed and removed his shoes, and rose and slipped his trousers off. He was sweating again already, and he stooped and hunted furiously for the shirt. At last he found it and wiped his body again, and, with his body pressed against the dusty screen, he stood panting. There was no movement, no sound, not even an insect. The dark world seemed to lie stricken beneath the cold moon and the lidless stars.

Ritual and Theme in Faulkner's "Dry September"

John B. Vickery

ON THE SURFACE what "Dry September" is about is a false rumor of a Negro assault on a white woman that leads to the lynching of the Negro, the hysterical collapse of the woman, and the increased frustration of the lynch-leader. Likely, most readers would feel that the Negro, Will Mayes, is being treated as a scapegoat. But most would also be thinking of the term "scapegoat" in its limited, contemporary sense wherein it is synonymous with "sucker" or "fall guy." Yet the total significance of the story depends on our recognizing that it is an ironic rendering of the primitive scapegoat ritual, a pattern that encompasses much more than our contemporary outrage at the victimization of an innocent individual. The recurrence of this pattern in several of Faulkner's novels—most notably in *Light in August* and *Intruder in the Dust*—suggests both its centrality and the value of exploring it even on the limited level undertaken here.

The underlying ritual, which focuses the story's themes, is revealed both by the characters and their actions and by the tale's structure. Thus, clearly Will Mayes is a scapegoat in the loose sense of the term: he is slain wantonly and arbitrarily for a deed he did not do. At the same time there are details that suggest he is also the central figure of the ritual. He is regarded as a criminal, is beaten in ritualistic fashion, is taken outside the town by a group of young men, is slain, and is cast into a body of water whose bottomless nature not only conceals the corpse but prevents its return to the community. All of these are, according to such authorities as Sir James Frazer and Jane Harrison, features of primitive and classical rites of the scapegoat.

Also related to the rite is John McLendon, the lynch-leader, who is identified on his first appearance by his most characteristic role: "He had commanded troops at the front in France and had been decorated for valor." Even his opening words are significant, for they indicate that he views the putative crime as an offense against the entire community, as an evil to be purged: " 'Are you going to sit there and let a black son rape a white woman on the streets of Jefferson?' " Both the military nature and the social concern link him to the warrior priests whose task it was to expel the evils threatening the community. McLendon's striking of the Negro constitutes a further link, for traditionally the scapegoat was beaten by the warrior priests who sought to prevent or dispel vegetative infertility such as drought. And though there is nothing priest-like about McLendon, we remember that in *Light in August* Percy Grimm, another warrior (in desire if not in actuality) and leader in the ritual of the scapegoat, is likened to "a young priest."

While Mayes and McLendon exemplify the scapegoat pattern most clearly, Miss Minnie Cooper and Hawkshaw are also related to it. The former is the scapegoat in a minor key and suffers its rites in a more "civilized" form. The rationale for her election to the role is social rather than racial; she is safe from the ordeal only so long as "her contemporaries" are "still children enough to be unclassconscious." And when the time comes, her ritual punishment and expulsion is verbal instead of physical. Thus, "one evening at a party she heard a boy and two girls, all talking. She never accepted another invitation." And later she was "relegated into adultery by public opinion" as a result of "her driving on Sunday afternoons with the cashier in the bank." Hence she is the female counterpart of Will Mayes who also is condemned and made to suffer on the basis of inadequate and irrational judgments. By this doubling process the story further reflects the primitive ritual, for in the latter it was customary to sacrifice two outcasts, a man and a woman, of whom the former was adorned with a black emblem, the latter with a white one.

With Hawkshaw, the barber, the irony inherent in the dramatic situation emerges clearly. In part, this is a result of his being the one major figure not intrinsically a part of the ritual. Throughout the story he stands resolutely opposed to the selection of a scapegoat and the enactment of his bloody ritual. His arguments are of two distinct but related orders: one is based upon faith—not religious but personal and human in nature (" 'I know Will Mayes. He's a good nigger' ")—the other upon logic and ratiocination (" 'She's about forty, I reckon. She ain't married. That's why I don't believe—' "). Experience and rational thought, man's primary means of arriving at the truth, are invoked and flatly contradict the vague, irrational, compulsive reckonings of men like Butch, the traveling salesman, and McLendon who are bent upon performing the ritual they know but do not understand.

Indeed, Hawkshaw is an apostle of rationalism who, like Frazer himself, seeks to expose the superstitious savagery upon which the belief in the necessity and efficacy of a scapegoat is founded. His very name suggests the detective, who insists that the only conceivable method is to " 'find out the facts first.' " To do so, he is convinced, will solve the crime and forestall the pointless ritual of that primitive mind which, according to Frazer, is present even in modern man. The ironic view of the scapegoat ritual provided by Hawkshaw, then, is that of the opponent who is right, who knows that the pattern is fallacious, outmoded, and conducive only to increased frustration and anguish. Its ancient observance was a solemn event marked by a scrupulously hieratic conduct and by a profound understanding of its significance. But the contemporary equivalent is a caricature conceived in ignorance and executed in a frenzy tinged with guilt ("They ran in a stumbling clump, as though they were fleeing something").

The relationship in which the ritual stands to the characters' actions is further pointed up by the story's structure. The five sections each elaborate a particular aspect of the ritual from a dramatically ironic point of view. Section I focuses on the selection of Will Mayes as the scapegoat and on the formal preparations for his expulsion and sacrifice. Originally the choice of the victim was based on all the religious, social, and scientific knowledge possessed by man; a catastrophe affecting existence itself—such as drought or blight—demanded immediate and drastic remedies. The contemporary crisis, on the other hand, involves only society's mores, not its struggle for physical survival. And not only is the occasion intrinsically less significant, but there is even the likelihood that it has not actually taken place. In short, unlike primitive man, who could actually see the disaster he was seeking to remove, "none of them gathered in the barber-shop . . . knew exactly what had happened." This irony through contrast is matched by an irony based on similarity. For by arbitrarily selecting a victim, the twentieth-century mob abandons its rationality for the blind superstition of the primitive mind. This renunciation, this passionate embracing of the illogical and improbable culminates in McLendon's reply to the question " 'Did it really happen?' " He says: " 'What the hell difference does it make? Are you going to let the black sons get away with it until one really does it?' "

While Section I deals with Will Mayes and the present, Section II turns to the past and another scapegoat, Minnie Cooper. This shift of scene and subject produces a thematic parallel-with-a-difference. Minnie, too, has participated in the ritual of the scapegoat as a victim. The difference is that her rite has been extended over approximately twenty years instead of being enacted in a single evening. The thematic significance of this counterpoint lies in its showing that the scapegoat is a permanent figure in the community and in its developing the theme of truth with ironic overtones. The first point raises the question as to whether the society itself may not be in some way responsible for the scapegoat's continued presence. Since this is the very heart of the story, exploration of it will be postponed until other factors upon which it depends have been discussed.

The second point—the theme of truth—is important not only because it dominates the opening sections but also because its relation to the other themes is that of cause to effect. Hawkshaw's insistence that truth is dependent upon fact is contrasted with the view of McLendon and the others who feel that rumor and truth are the same. Miss Minnie, like McLendon, ignores facts and as a result carries a "furious repudiation of truth in her eyes." This refusal to face truth leads to a more permanent aberration embodying the theme of delusion and reality. Ultimately her flouting of truth gives to Miss Minnie "a quality of furious unreality" that is the product of her self-delusion, of "her bright dresses, of her idle and empty days." Ironically enough, this willingness to be deluded links McLendon and Miss Minnie thereby pointing up the falsity of a rite in which both victim and celebrant are duped. Both are frustrated, unstable personalities who react to life with a sense of urgency and loss; their key adjectives are "furious" and "feverish." In contrast, Will Mays and Hawkshaw, who oppose the ritual, are preeminently rational and aware of the equivalence of truth and reality. Their behavior is calm and controlled save during the ritualistic beating and even here their lapse is less an indictment of them than of the frighteningly insidious influence of irrationality.

The first two sections represent the preparation for the ritual. Section III is a vivid but compressed enactment of the expulsion (" 'Not here,' he said, 'Get him into the car' "), the punishment (they "struck him with random blows"), and the slaying. The point of greatest significance here is Hawkshaw's withdrawal from the ritual before the sacrifice. He does so not only because he realizes he cannot bear to witness what for him is a monstrous crime but also because he senses that the participants are entering a kind of living death that is the concomitant of their descent to a hell of their own making: "The narrow tunnel of the road rushed up and past. Their motion was like an extinct furnace blast: cooler, but utterly dead." Here the horror and futility of the rite are fused in the single image of the furnace. The former is conveyed by the completeness of the celebrants' self-destruction ("utterly dead") and the latter by the likening of their action to something useless and exhausted ("an extinct furnace blast"). The contrast between Hawkshaw and the lynchers established by his leaping from the car is further underscored at the very end of the section when Hawkshaw sees the others returning: "They went on; the dust swallowed them; the glare and the sound died away. The dust of them hung for a while, but soon the eternal dust absorbed it again. The barber climbed back onto the road and limped on toward town." In "the eternal dust" there is a reminder that men's mortality and man's immortality can absorb and survive all the fury and violence that the human mind can entertain. Similarly, in climbing back onto the road, Hawkshaw symbolizes the fact that all men travel the same road and that what is important is the direction and the manner in which they travel.

The validity of Hawkshaw's renunciation is borne out by Sections IV and V which deal with the consequences of the ritual's enactment. The former traces out Miss Minnie's response to being once more the center of society's attention. Here again there is both a development of the earlier themes and an ironic view of the scapegoat ritual. With regard to the former, it is clear that her collapse in the theater is the logical sequel to her renunciation of reality described in Section II. Significantly enough, the strain of preserving the fantasy overwhelms her in the movie theater, in the temple of organized delusion whose inclination to fantasy and unreality is suggested by its looking "like a miniature fairyland" in which "the silver dream accumulated, inevitably on and on."

Yet in the reason for her breaking down at exactly this period there is an ironic exposure of the scapegoat ritual and the society which performs it. Crucial in this connection is her attempt to "hold back the laughing so it would not waste away so fast and soon." The laughter is to be carefully rationed because it represents her secret knowledge of the revenge she has inflicted on the community. By her return to the center of the community she has reversed her own role as the scapegoat whose expulsion is permanent and whose return is the greatest of calamities. But her revenge consists of more than simply nullifying her own victimization as the social scapegoat. It also involves the duping of society into performing another ritual with another victim whose unwarranted punishment underscores her own unjustified suffering. And in so doing, her deluded mind reveals with ironic economy and power the irrational beliefs which motivate the ritual of the scapegoat.

If Section IV documents the erroneous, mistaken character of the rite, then just as clearly V presents its basic futility. In it McLendon returns to his house that is "fresh as a bird-cage and almost as small" in which his wife sits in bird-like imprisonment. His entry signals his own entrapment by the frustration inherent in the unwitting perpetration of the scapegoat ritual. His frustration, exhibited by his anger at his wife and his "ripping" of his shirt and flinging it away only to hunt "furiously" for it the next moment, demonstrates the inadequacy of the ritual when performed without understanding. This, however, is not apparent to McLendon; so far as he is concerned the night has been successful—the Negro is dead. Yet he still continues to sweat in the heat so heavily emphasized throughout the story.

It is precisely in the scorching weather "of sixty-two rainless days" that we find both cause and evaluation of that ritual which was designed originally to protect all forms of life— vegetative and cereal as well as human—from drought or disaster. Thus, the facetious remark that " 'It's this durn weather. . . . It's enough to make any man do anything' " takes on added implications. On the immediate psychological level, McLendon's insistence on violence is a subconscious endeavor to blot out his awareness of the heat; it is a kind of meteorologically induced madness. On the more remote mythological level, it constitutes an unconscious appeal to the scapegoat ritual. Lending credence to this notion is the fact that the expulsion rite was frequently practiced in September. In any case, the continued hot weather indicates clearly that whatever McLendon's view of his actions the slaying of Will Mayes does not constitute an efficacious ritual.

Why the slaying is a failure depends partly upon the significance of Will Mayes and partly upon McLendon's ignorance of this significance. Clearly Mayes is chosen as the scapegoat because he is a Negro. Though the story does indict the callous and casual brutality of his treatment, it also interprets it, thereby providing a theme of greater profundity and an attitude that is compounded of more than horror and revulsion. Jefferson, like some cities of classical times, maintains, to use Frazer's words, "a number of degraded and useless beings at public expense" who serve in crises as scapegoats. In its case, however, their selection is dependent not upon fortunes of war but upon pigmentation of the skin. Jefferson too regards its scapegoats as criminals who have violated either some legal or moral injunction. What it and its inhabitants do not realize is that the criminal is only the most recent in a long line of actors to perform the ritual. The line extends back through the king's son and the king himself to the dying and reviving god whose life was intimately bound up with and responsible for that of the community at large.

It is in this unwitting destruction of a man-god whose life is precious to the community that the final irony of the story resides. For as Faulkner has suggested countless times, the continued existence of the white South is to be determined by its attitude toward and treatment of the Negro. In him lies the salvation or the damnation, the flourishing or the extinction of a people. And here the South has slain as hateful what it should reverence and hold in awe. With the death of the god, all existence has been jeopardized so that "the dark world seemed to lie stricken beneath the cold moon and the lidless stars." (Note too the references to the air as "dead" and "lifeless," to the dust as "a pall" in which the day had died and in which the town square was "shrouded," and to the moon as a "hemorrhage.")

This irony founded upon ignorance is made even more harrowing when we remember that the community was supposed to have transferred all its sins to the scapegoat in order to achieve a happy and innocent life, a renewed Golden Age. The Negro is made to bear the white man's guilt: enslavement, brutality, self-delusion, and irrationality are the fault of the Negro not their perpetrator. In effect, this is both a misinterpretation of the nature of the Golden Age and a too literal rendering of its observances. The South equates the Golden Age with the pre-Civil War period instead of with the fabulous reign of Saturn when slavery, war, discord, and greed were unknown. It insists also upon the literal observance of blood sacrifices when in reality they should be performed as the mimetic rites of the Saturnalia, which was associated with the scapegoat ceremony.

From the standpoint of McLendon and his followers there are two reasons why the celebration of the Saturnalia should be forestalled. One is that during it virtually unlimited license was granted to slaves so that, as Frazer remarks, "the distinction between the free and the servile classes was temporarily abolished." To a society shamefacedly dedicated to a sophisticated form of slavery such a practice is inconceivable even as playacting. The second reason is that the festival traditionally involved the sexual union of a man and woman who represent the dying god and the goddess of love. And since Will Mayes, the Negro, is associated with the former, while Minnie Cooper is the latter (albeit manquée), the result would be the unthinkable one of miscegenation. Hence the god must be slain literally as well as figuratively in order to ensure that the union does not occur. Thus, the themes of truth and rumor, delusion and reality receive their broadest and most ironic exemplification, for the community as represented by McLendon both rejects the potency of imaginative truth (by refusing to pretend to free the slaves) and insists upon a delusive reality (by actually killing Will Mayes). At the same time this is more than an exemplification, it is a new theme. Growing out of the rejection of truth and the formulation of a delusion is the theme of the South's failure to see (note the reiterant use of "eyes" as an image of frustration at not understanding) the sociological implications of its behavior which are revealed mythopoeically in the ancient ritual of the scapegoat that it practices implicitly. The destiny of the South can be read in the past which it reveres but does not explore sufficiently to comprehend.

In effect, McLendon, as a representative of the South, by killing Mayes, turns from the idea of total freedom for the whole of mankind that is symbolized by the Saturnalia. And in the unspeakable folly of this decision there dwells the ultimate thematic irony provided by the scapegoat ritual. For one of the most tenaciously held dogmas of McLendon and his like is that of the irrevocable inferiority of the Negro's culture and mentality. And yet, as Frazer observes, the principle of vicarious suffering, which McLendon and Jefferson embrace blindly, is most commonly found in those of a low level of intellectual and social culture. In this, the ironies of contrast, similarity, and ignorance fuse in a vision that is very nearly classical in its tragic intensity and inevitability.

V. S. Pritchett

Some literary figures attain distinction by virtue of towering genius or tortured sensibility or both. Others are noted rather for the aura of fundamental sanity and balance emanating from their works. Such is the case with V. S. Pritchett (1900–), whose essentially English outlook on life and society has been expressed in a variety of literary forms. In many ways he conforms more nearly to the figure of the man of letters than to that of the artist. His fiction is balanced and perhaps in some ways overshadowed by his informal but shrewdly perceptive literary criticism, nonfiction, and journalism.

Mr. Pritchett's firm attachment in his fiction to the everyday world and experiences of English life may possibly be traced to his own formative years. Born in Ipswich, England, he attended several schools but did not go on to a university. Instead, he entered the business world, where he was variously employed as a traveling salesman and clerk. From this he became a writer for a newspaper in France and several other countries. One of these was Spain, where he lived for a few years and about which he has written two books. In the late 1920's he published his first books and since that time has earned his living as an author, journalist, and critic. Married and a family man, Pritchett has nevertheless found the time and opportunity to travel a good deal in a number of countries including America, where he lectured at Princeton University in the mid-1950's. During the late 1940's Mr. Pritchett served for several years as literary editor of the British journal New Statesman and Nation. His weekly column "Books in General" was a widely respected feature of the same journal for a number of years.

Mr. Pritchett has an impressively varied record of literary achievement, having written at least five novels, three volumes each of short stories and literary criticism, and two travel *books on Spain. The settings of his novels are richly diversified, as befits a writer with his interest in travel. He has often been likened to Dickens, for whom he has a profound admiration. This similarity is largely due to Pritchett's strong comic sense, his concern for the common person, and his emphasis on humane values. Novels like* Mr. *Beluncle (1951) are in the mainstream of the traditional English novel, having nothing of the experimental qualities of Joyce or Faulkner. This does not mean, however, that he is indifferent to more universal or symbolic dimensions in fiction, as stories like "The Scapegoat" indicate. Many of his stories—"The Saint," "The Sailor," "The Landlord"—develop the generic significance of central characters in ways which suggest he is continually seeking the lasting and permanent features of human behavior and thought. Other titles allude to the stories' affinities, frequently ironic, with psychological or literary patterns, as in the case of "Oedipus Complex," "A Story of Don Juan," and "The Clerk's Tale." Perhaps because of the deceptively simple surface and undemanding narrative skill of his fiction, Pritchett's work has not received detailed or sustained critical attention.*

The Scapegoat

V. S. Pritchett

THERE WERE LONG TIMES when we were at peace and
when the world left us alone. We could go down Earl Street
and, although we did not like the place and it felt strange to us
and the women stared down from the windows and a child
here and there might call out a name after us, we just walked
on thinking of something else. But we were always more at
ease and more ourselves, even in the quietest times of truce,
when we had turned the corner by the hop-warehouse and had
got back into Terence Street, which was our own. The truth is
that you can't live without enemies, and the best enemies are
the ones nearest home; and though we sometimes went out to
the Green to boo the speakers and some of our lads went after
the Yids or joined a procession up West, that was idleness and
distraction. The people we hated were not a mile away on the
main road where the trams and the buses are and you don't
know one man from the next; no, the people we hated were
round the corner, next door, in Earl Street. They were, we used
to say, a different class of people from ourselves altogether.

I don't know why, but if there was any trouble in the world,
we turned out and attacked them. I don't know either how
these things began. You would know there was trouble coming
when you heard the voices of the children getting shriller and
more excited, until their cries became rhythmic like the pulse
of native war-cries in the forest. We were, indeed, lost in a
jungle of streets. Somehow the children would have sticks,

Reprinted by permission of Alfred A. Knopf, Inc. from *The Sailor, Sense
of Humor, and Other Stories* by V. S. Pritchett. © Copyright, 1956 by
V. S. Pritchett. From *Collected Stories* by V. S. Pritchett by permission
of Chatto and Windus Ltd.

old pieces of board and stones in their hands, and they would be rushing in groups to the hop-warehouse and jeering and then scattering back. A similar thing would be happening in Earl Street. Usually this happened in the warm long evenings of the summer. Then, after the children, the thing got hold of the women and they came down from their windows where they had been watching and scratching their arms, very hot and restless, and would stand at their doorsteps and start shouting at their children. A stone would fly up and then the women would be down in the middle of the street.

It might take a day to work up or it might take longer. You would get the Earl Street girls going down our street talking in loud voices daring us, and our young lads would stand by saying nothing until the girls got to the corner. And then those girls would have to bolt. Towards closing time the Gurneys, the fighting family in Earl Street, would be out and we had our Blackers and then it was a question of who came out of the Freemasons and how he came out. But perhaps nothing would happen and we would just go down Earl Street after dark and merely kick their milk-bottles down the basements.

This has been going on ever since the old people can remember. When the war came we knew everyone in Earl Street was a spy or a Hun or a Conchie. The Great War, for us, was between Earl Street and Terence Street. They had a V.C. and we hadn't, though we had a bunch of other stuff and one man who escaped from the Turks and was in the papers; and, though we did our best, the tea we gave was nothing to the tea they did in Earl Street for their V.C. Where they got the money from was the puzzle. Thirty-two pounds. Some of our women said the Earl Street girls must have been on the streets; and at the Freemasons the men said half of Earl Street were nothing but bloody pensioners. The police came in before we had the question settled. But when the war ended, things changed. Half of our lot was out of work and when we went down Earl Street we would see half of their lot out of work too, and Earl Street did not seem quite so strange to us. One street seemed to blend into the other. This made some of our lot think and they gave their steps an extra clean to show there was a difference between Earl Street and Terence Street after all.

In the years that followed, sometimes we were up on Earl Street, sometimes we were down. We were waiting for some big event. It did not come for a long time and a stranger might have thought that the old frontiers had gone and the reign of universal peace was upon us. It was not. The Jubilee came and we saw our chance. Earl Street had collected thirty-two pounds for its V.C.'s tea-party. We reckoned we would top that for the Jubilee. We would collect forty.

There was a red-haired Jew in our street called Lupinsky. He was a tailor. He was round-shouldered from bending over the table and his eyes were weak from working by gas at night. In the rush season he and his family would be up past midnight working. He was a keen man. He came out in pimples—he was so keen. Lupinsky saw everything before any of us. He saw the Jubilee before the King himself. He had got his house full of bunting and streamers and Union Jacks. "Get in at the early doors," he said. "What'll you have?" he used to say to us when we went to his shop. "Rule Britannia or God Save the King?" "Who's that?" we said. "The King of the Jews?" "Getcha," said Lupinsky, "He's dead. Didn't you hear?" He raked in the money. They had another Jew in Earl Street doing the same. "I say!" called Lupinsky. "I say!"—we used to call him "I-say-what'll-you-have"—"Cohen's sold 120 yards to Earl Street and you've only done 70." So we doubled. "I say," says Lupinsky. "I say. When you going to start collecting? They got ten quid in Earl Street and you haven't started."

And this was true. The trouble was we couldn't agree upon who should collect. We had had a nasty experience with the Club a few years back. And then Lupinsky was hot for doing it himself. He'd got the bunting. He'd seen it coming. He'd even got boxes. He'd thought of everything. We had nothing against Lupinsky, but when we saw him raking in the money on his God Saves and Kiss-me-quicks and his flags of all the nations, we thought he was collecting enough as it was. He might mix up the two collections. "No," we said to Lupinsky. "You're doing your bit, we'll do the rest." "That's O.K.," Lupinsky said. He never bore resentment, he was too keen. "But I hear Earl Street's up to twelve ten." He wasn't upset with us, but he couldn't bear to see us shilly-shallying around while Earl Street walked away with it. "If you don't trust me," he said, "can't you trust yourselves? I don't know what's happened to this street." And he spat from the top of his doorstep into the gutter.

Lupinsky was wrong about us. We trust each other. There is
not a man in Terence Street you cannot trust. In that nasty
business we had with the Club, the man was not a Terence
Street man. We could trust one another. But we were frightened. Forty pounds! We thought. That's a big sum. We didn't
like the handling of it. There wasn't one of us who had seen
forty pounds in his life. The Blackers, a good fighting lot, were
terrified. Albert Smith and his uncle were the most likely, but
they said they were single and didn't like the idea. And we, for
some reason, thought a single man wasn't right for the job.
And the wives, the married ones, though eagerly wanting their
husbands to do it, were so afraid the honour would go to someone else, that they said to give it to a married man was tempting Providence. Lupinsky went down the street almost in tears,
saying Earl Street had touched seventeen ten.

Then suddenly we saw the right man had been staring us in
the face all the time. He was not single and he was not married. He was a widower, made serious by death: Art Edwards.
We chose Art Edwards, and he agreed.

Art Edwards was a man of forty-seven, and the moment he
agreed we were proud of him. He was a grey-haired man, not
very talkative and of middle height, very patient and looked
you straight in the face. He lived with his sister, who looked
after his two children, he had a fruit stall in the main road—
he had been there for twenty years—and every Sunday he used
to go alone with a bunch of flowers for his wife's grave at the
cemetery. The women admired him very much for doing this.
He never changed. His house was the neatest house in our
street and he never seemed to get richer or poorer. He just
went on the same.

He had been a widower a good long time, too, and some
thought he ought to marry again. The women were curious
about him and said you couldn't but respect a man who didn't
take a second, and Art was held up as a model. This didn't
prevent many of them running after him and spreading the
rumour afterwards that his sister was a woman who wouldn't
let a man call his soul his own. But the way Art mourned for
the dead and kept faithful to The First, the ONE AND ONLY, as
the women said, was striking. Some of the men said that being
a model wasn't healthy and that if they had been in Art's
shoes they would muck around on the quiet. They wondered

why the hell he didn't, yet admired him for his restraint. Some of us couldn't have lived with temptation all those years without slipping up.

Art had put a black band on his sleeve when his wife died and had worn it ever since. But when he started collecting for the tea we had the feeling he had put off his mourning and had come alive again. We were pleased about this because, with his modest, retiring ways, we hardly knew him. "It will bring him out," we said. He came round with his little red book and his tin and we said, "What's it now, Art? How we doin'?" Art was slow at adding up, but accurate. He told us. We made a big effort and we touched the ten-pound mark pretty soon.

This woke us up and made us feel good, but Lupinsky came round and said it wasn't any bloody good at all. They'd touched nineteen pounds in Earl Street. So one of the women said they'd help Art. He didn't want this, or his sister didn't. So she joined in, too, to keep the other women off him. They knocked at his door at all hours and stopped him in the street. And when she saw this his sister put on her best hat and coat and went round and stopped their men. The result was everyone was collecting and came round to Art and said:

"Here y'are, Art. One and eight," or

"Here y'are, Art, eight and six."

And two of the Blacker girls had a fight because one said the other wasn't collecting fair but was cheapening herself to get the money. For we touched seventeen and went on to twenty-one.

The night we passed Earl Street some of our girls went out and just walked down Earl Street telling them. They didn't like it. A crowd from Earl Street came round and called "Down with the Yids" outside Lupinsky's. Then Earl Street picked up and passed us again. We went round to Art and planked down more money. Art got out his book and he couldn't write it down fast enough.

"Where do you keep it, Art?" we said.

He showed us a box in the cupboard. It was a fine sight all that money. His sister said:

"Art's picked up a bit in the High Street." We looked at him as if he were a hero. "'Slike business," he said. "You've got to go out for it."

We looked with wonder at him. We had chosen the right

man. It was bringing him out. And he had ideas too. He got some of the kids to go out at night with tins.

We passed Earl Street and they passed us. Then we passed them again. It was ding-dong all the time. Lupinsky flew in and out with the latest like a wasp and stung us to more. Art Edwards, he said, had no life in him. After this, it became madness. People got out their savings.

There was a funny case at Harry Law's. He was a boozer, a big, heavy man, very particular in the house and very religious. Some nights when he was bad he used to beat his wife and we used to look down into their basement window wondering what would be happening inside, for something usually was happening. There were often shouts and curses and screams coming from that room and then times, which made you uncomfortable, when everything was quiet. Harry Law was often out of a job. Mrs Law was a timid woman and everyone was sorry for her. She used to go up to the Freemasons and look through the door at him. She was a thin, round-shouldered woman, always anxious about her husband and sorry that he made a fool of himself, for he got pompous when he was drunk and she hated the way people laughed at him. He used to say she had no ambition and he had dragged her out of the gutter. She said, "*Down* into the gutter, you mean." They used to have guilty arguments like this for hours, each boasting they were better than the other and wondering all the time why they had got into their present situation. Then Harry Law would go to church so as to feel good and find out why, and his wife used to stop at home and think about it too. She would put her arms round him and love him when he came back. And he would be all right for a few days until he got some scheme into his head for making money. When he had the scheme he would go out and get drunk again.

Harry Law wanted to show everyone that he was a man of ideas and ambitions, and better than the rest of us in Terence Street. He used to dress up on Sundays. He used to say he had been better off once and had had a shop. The truth was, as his wife bitterly told everyone, he'd always been the same; up and down all his life. She couldn't bear other people laughing at him, but she used to tear his reputation to bits herself and get great pleasure out of doing it.

It was just at the height of our madness that he came into

the Freemasons and, instead of cadging for drinks, began to order freely. A funny thing had happened, he said. And he said, in his lordly voice, "I want Art Edwards." It turned out that he had been going across the room while his wife was out and had tripped up on something on the floor. There was a bump in the lino. Being a very inquisitive man who never had anything to do, he knelt down and felt the lump. "I thought it was dirt," he said. One of the things he always said about his wife was that she was dirty. He was a very clean man himself. He decided to take up the lino, and underneath he found a lump of money wrapped up in notes. It was his wife's savings.

That was why Harry Law was lording it at the Freemasons. He had hardly given a penny to the Collection, but now, when everyone was present, he was going to make a great gesture and show his greatness. When Art came in, he said, "Here, Art. Have a fiver."

We all stared. Harry Law was leaning against the bar with the notes in the tips of his fingers as if they were dirt, like a duke giving a tip.

At that moment his wife came in.

"That's mine," she screamed. "It's mine."

There was a row and Art wouldn't take the money. Everyone said that a man hadn't the right to take his wife's money. But Harry said, "What!" Wasn't his money as good as anybody's? and we said, "Yes, Harry, but that belongs to your missus." She was crying, and he kept saying, "Go home. I'll teach you to come round here. It is my money. I earned it."

This was awkward. Between her tears, with her hands covering her face, Mrs Law was saying she had saved it. He was always ruining them, so she had to save. Still, if he'd earned it, it was his.

"Take that money," said Harry, dropping it like a lord on the floor. The notes fell down, we all looked at them and no one moved. Mr Bell of the Freemasons got a laugh by saying we were littering up his bar with paper. Then Harry turned his back and we picked it up and were going to give it to Mrs Law, but Harry said in a threatening voice, "That's Art's. For the Collection. I reckon I got Earl Street knocked silly."

That part of the statement was irresistible. While we hesitated, Art said:

"Give it here then. I'll look after it." Lupinsky, who had been sitting there all the time clutching his hands and his eyes starting out of his head with misery at the sight of money lying in the sand, gave a shout.

"That's the boy," he said. "We've got 'em."

We all felt uncomfortable with Harry and we went away in ones and twos and Mrs Law went out still crying. After she went out Art went too, and when we got down the street Art stopped and told Mrs Law he wasn't going to take the money and he made her take it back. She clutched it with both hands and looked at him like a dog with gratitude.

That night half the men in Terence Street wanted to take up their lino and sat up late arguing with their wives; but the madness was still in the air, especially when Earl Street, hearing our news, sent all their kids up West and passed us. There was a fight in the High Street between our kids and the Earl Street kids and one of ours lost her box. But there was nothing in it except stones. They put stones in to make a rattle so that people would think they were doing well. If there had been any money in that box there wouldn't have been a pane of glass in Earl Street left.

"They've passed us," the cry went down our street. In the middle of this Mrs Law came over to Art and gave him back the money. She made him take it.

"Your husband made you," says Art.

"Him," she said scornfully. "He don't know anything about it. I told him you gave it me back and he said, 'A good thing too.' He's feeling sorry for himself. I'll teach him to touch my money, I said. If there's going to be any giving in this house, it's me that's got the money. I'm going to teach my husband a lesson," she said.

This surprised Art, for he had been very sorry for poor Mrs Law, and had shown it. But I've no doubt she was tired of being pitied. That money was all she had. She was going to show us that the Laws had their pride and she wasn't going to let them down. Only *she* was going to give it.

Her eyes shone and were sharp. They were greenish, miserly grey eyes, yet she was not miserly. Now she was proud and not bedraggled with tears and misery, she looked jubilant and cunning. She had been a gay, quick-tongued woman in her time.

"I kept it under the floor. That was wrong of me," she said. "I oughter have put it in the Post Office."

She said she knew her husband was right. It was not right to hide money.

Everyone in Terence Street had supposed Mrs Law to be a poor, timid, beaten soul, and Art had always thought the same, he said; but now he said that she had some spirit. She had opened her heart to him because he had been kind to her and now she said, very proudly, that he should come and have a chat with her husband. She took Art triumphantly to her basement just to show her husband there were other men in the world. Old Harry Law saw this at once—he was always on his dignity—so he just talked largely to Art about the shops he had had, the ups and downs, his financial adventures. Investments, he called them. We had all heard of investments, but none of us had ever had any. If he had his life over again, Harry Law said, he'd invest every penny.

"There's a man," Art said when he went, "who doesn't practise what he preaches." But he respected Harry's preaching, though he despised him a bit. And Harry said, "There's a man who stays the same all his life. Never made a penny, never lost a penny. The only money he's got," said Harry, "isn't his —this collection."

And Harry asked him how much it was. There were some thirty-odd pounds, Art said.

Harry respected him when he heard that and said with a sigh, "Money makes money."

When Art got back, his sister was short with him. "Going after other men's wives," she said. And she lectured him about Mrs Law. It had been such a warm, pleasant, friendly evening over at Harry Law's that Art was hurt about this.

"Him and her," he said, "has got more brains than you think. They've lived, all right. They've had their ups and downs."

"He's a boozer."

"We've all got our faults. He's had his ups and downs."

And that was the phrase that he kept repeating. It fascinated him. He felt generous. It came to him that he had never felt anything for years. He had just gone on standing in the High Street by the stall. He had never taken a holiday. He had never bought himself anything he wanted. He had never done anything. It startled him—but he suddenly did not want his wife who was in the grave. The street had chosen him, singled him out above all others, and there he stood naked, nothing. He was shy about his nonentity. He felt a curious longing for ups and downs.

You will say, "How did we know what Art Edwards thought?" That was the strange thing: we did know. We knew as if he had told us, as if we were inside him. You see, because we had singled him out he was, in a sense, ourselves. We could see him thinking and feeling and doing what we would. He had taken the burden off us. By doing that he had become nearer and more precious to us than any other person.

And there was Terence Street two pounds ahead of Earl Street, drunk with the excitement of it. Art used to get out the money and count it—it was the biggest sum of money he had ever seen—and a sober pride filled him. He had done this. People like Mrs Law had just thrown in all they had. He had put in his bit cautiously, but everyone had scraped and strained and just wildly thrown in the cash. It made him marvel. He marvelled at us, he marvelled—as his hands trembled over the money—that he had been picked out by us to hold it.

We went round once or twice to look at the money too. What a nest egg, what an investment! Over thirty pounds! We said we wished it was ours. We said we wished we could give more, or double it. We all wanted to double it. We looked at it sadly. "If that thirty pounds had been on the winner to-day," some-one said. "Or on the dogs."

We laughed uneasily. And we dreamed. The more we looked at that money the more we thought of things you could do with it—mad things like backing a horse or sensible things like starting a business or having a holiday.

When we got up in Art's kitchen and saw him put the money in the cupboard and lock the door, we nodded our heads sadly. It was like burying the dead.

"It's sad it's got to go," we thought.

And it seemed to us fitting that Art, who had buried the dead and who was a dour man with iron-grey hair and level-looking eyes, should have the grim task of keeping that money, like some sexton. And we were glad to have him doing it, to have him be responsible instead of us. For some of us had to admit we'd go mad at times with temptation tingling in our fingers and hissing like gas in coal in our hearts.

When we left him we felt a kind of sorrow for Art for bearing our burden, for being the custodian of our victory over Earl Street.

It made us all very friendly to Art. The time went by. We used to stop and have a word with him in the street. And Art became friendly too. But he wasn't at the Freemasons much. He went over to Mrs Law's. And Harry Law didn't go on the booze. He stayed at home talking largely to Art. Once or twice Art went out in the evenings with Mr and Mrs Law. Lupinsky used to see them up at the Pictures.

Lupinsky was our reporter of everything, and gradually, expressing no doubt the instinct of the street, he had become our reporter on Art Edwards. We wanted a friendly eye kept on him not because he was valuable but because he was—well, as you would keep an eye on a sick man, say, a man who might have a heart attack or go dizzy in the street. When Lupinsky came back and said, "I see Art Edwards getting on a tram," we used to look up sharply and then, annoyed with ourselves, say, "What of it? What was he doing, having a ride?"

That Jew used to make us tired. And he'd started worrying already about the catering. They'd started arranging about the catering already in Earl Street. "It's a funny thing," we said, "about the Yids. He's only been here fifteen years and you'd think he'd been here for ever. Anyone'd think he'd been born in the street. You'd bloody well think it was Jerusalem."

We had been born there, most of us, and we said:

"It *will* be Jerusalem soon."

But we would have been nowhere without Lupinsky.

And then one morning he came along and said:

"Seen Art?"

"No," we said.

"He's not up in the High Street," said Lupinsky. "And he's not at his house."

"What of it?" we said.

Lupinsky was breathless. All the pimples on his face seemed about to burst. He had the kind of red hair that is coarse and stands up on end and thick arched eyebrows which were raised very high but were now higher for his eyes were starting out of his head. There were always bits of cotton from tailoring on his clothes and he was, as I have said, rather hump-backed from leaning all day over his machine.

"I saw him last night at the station. Nine o'clock. He took a ticket on the North London and hasn't been back."

"Smart baby," we said. But we were thinking of Lupinsky. We didn't believe him and yet we did believe him. "What were you doing up at the station—brother had another fire?" we said. Lupinsky's brother was always having fires.

But it was true. Art hadn't been home that night and his sister was very shifty when we went to see her. We never liked Art's sister and we grinned to think he'd got away from her for a night.

"Art had to go away on business," she said.

Theirs was a tidy house and Art's sister worked hard in it. The window-sills were hearth-stoned. That woman never stopped. She always came to the door with an iron in her hand or a scrubbing-brush or with something she was cleaning or cooking. She was a tall, straight-nosed woman and she had the best teeth I've ever seen, but there was no thickness in her, no give.

She used to say, "I've never had justice done me."

And Art used to sigh and say, "I can never do justice to her."

"What about it now?" said Lupinsky, who was waiting for us.

"Art can go away if he likes," we said. "Why not?"

"Sure, yes, why not?" said Lupinsky. "What you worrying about?"

Later on Lupinsky came and told us Art was still away. His stall was still in the lock-up and he hadn't been down to the market. Lupinsky had a friend who had told him. Then Lupinsky had another friend who said he'd seen Art at Wembley.

"Too many Yids here," said Albert Blacker. "You can't move but you catch one in your clothes. What's up with Wembley?"

We went over to Mrs Law's and called down to her. She was ironing in the light of the window.

"Seen Art Edwards?" we said.

"No," she said. "He hasn't been here for two or three days."

"Oh," we said.

Then Harry Law got up from his chair by the stove and said: "Art gone?"

"We're just looking for him. Thought he might be with you?"

Mrs Law gazed at us and then she looked at her husband. She was one of those women who when anything serious or unexpected happens, when they don't know what to think, when they are bewildered, always turn to their husbands; as if by studying him she would always know the worst about any event in the world and would be prepared. It was like looking up something in a book or gazing into a crystal. And when she had gazed at her husband and thought about him, she said:

"Oh dear." And she put down her iron and her shoulders hunched up. She looked accusingly at her husband and he lowered his eyes. He knew she could read him like that.

We did not think so at the time, but afterwards we said we had the feeling that when Mrs Law looked at her husband in that accusing way, she knew something about Art Edwards that we did not know. It turned out that she did not know. I looked out of the window that night when I went to bed. It was a warm night. I work in a fur-warehouse and the air had the close, dead, laid-out smell of ladies' furs. There was a cold hollow lilac light over the roofs from the arc-lamps in the High Street. At night our street is quiet and often you can hear the moan of a ship's siren from the river like the hoarse voice of someone going away. But the commonest sound is the clinking of shunting trucks on the railway—a sound that is meaningless as if someone who couldn't play the piano had struck the keys anyhow, trying to make a tune. It is a sound which makes you think the city has had an attack of nerves. As I stood there on one leg, undoing my boots, I heard quick footsteps coming along. They were Lupinsky's. Lupinsky was always up late.

"I say. I say," he called up to me. "Art's come back. I just seen him. He came back and let himself in."

That night Art Edwards went into the lock-up in his yard and, attaching his braces to a hook in the roof, he hanged himself. The box in the cupboard was empty. He had gone off to Wembley and lost all the money on the dogs.

We went out into the street in the morning and stood outside the house and stared at the windows. The people from Earl Street came too. All the children came and stared and no one said anything in the street. Albert Blacker went into the yard at the back and Lupinsky was there with the police.

Mrs Law would not leave her house, but stood on her doorstep holding the railing tightly, watching from a distance. Harry Law would not come out. He walked up and down the room and called up to his wife to come down. He could not bear being left alone. She was afraid to leave her house and yet, I thought, wanted to be with Art.

"The bloody twister," we said between our teeth.

"That bloody widower," we said.

"Takes our money and has a night out. Our savings! Our money!"

"The rotten thief."

We muttered like this standing in front of the house. We were sorry for the police who had to touch the body of a man like that.

"You wouldn't trust me," Lupinsky said.

We looked at him. We turned away. We couldn't bear the sight of that man's pimples.

"I'm used to money," Lupinsky said.

I could not repeat all the things we said. I remember clearly the red, white and blue streamers drooping over the street and looking dirty, with "God Save the King" on them. "God Save Art Edwards," said Harry Law, coming up. He was tight.

We thought of the spirit of Art Edwards's sister being humbled. All down the street, at all the windows, the women leaned on their bare arms thinking about this. They cuffed their children and the children cried. There was the low murmur of our voices in the street and then the whining voices of children. Presently a couple of women came down, pushed their way through the crowd and went in to help Art's sister. We gaped at them.

And then Lupinsky, who gave the lead to everything and always knew what we were thinking underneath, said:

"They're jeering at us in Earl Street."

They were. We set our teeth. Kids came round shouting, "Who swiped the money box! Who swiped the money box!" Our kids did nothing for a long time. Then they couldn't stand it. Our kids went for the Earl Street kids. Some of our women came down to pull their kids off and this drew out the Earl Street women. In half an hour Albert Blacker came out of the Freemasons with his sleeves rolled up, just when the Earl Street men were getting together, and then Harry Law came out roaring. Mrs Law ran towards him. But it was too late. A stone went and a window crashed and that brought out the rest of the Blacker family. We got it off our chests that night and we crowded into Earl Street. Half their milk-bottles had gone before the police whistles went.

And then it was clear to us. We knew what to do. Lupinsky headed it. Art Edwards was suddenly our hero. We'd kill the man who said anything against Art Edwards. In our hearts we said, it might have been ourselves. Thirty pounds. We remembered the sight of it! We even listened to Harry Law.

"He was trying to double it at the dogs," he said. "Investing it. Every man has . . ."

His wife pulled his coat and tried to stop him.

"Every man," continued Harry Law, "has his ups and downs."

And to show Earl Street what we were and to show the world what we thought of Art Edwards, we got up the biggest funeral that has ever been seen in our street. He was ourselves, our hero, our god. He had borne our sins. You couldn't see the hearse for flowers. The street was black with people. The sun shone. We'd been round and got every stall-holder, every barrow-man in the neighbourhood. That procession was a mile long when it got going. There was a Jubilee for you, covered in red, white and blue wreaths. Art Edwards our king. It looked like a wedding. The great white trumpets of the lilies rocked thick on the coffin. Earl Street couldn't touch that. And Lupinsky collected the money.

Ritual in the Streets:
A Study of Pritchett's
"The Scapegoat"

J'nan M. Sellery and John B. Vickery

IN V. S. PRITCHETT'S STORY "THE SCAPEGOAT" the archetypal sacrificial victim is displayed in contemporary dress.
The story depicts a community's unconscious search for and
destruction of a modern scapegoat. The word "scapegoat" has
such common usage today that its ritual impact is almost
wholly dissipated. Its primordial power is relatively unknown
and rarely felt. Despite this the modern world still performs
its unconscious versions of the ancient ritual. In writing a
story about this practice, the contemporary British writer
V. S. Pritchett demonstrates both the psychological veracity
of the story and the need of the age for an increased understanding of its own behavior. Pritchett's tale is set in twentieth
century London, but by both the title and incidental details he
conveys an archetypal quality whose full appreciation demands an informed awareness of the primitive ritual pattern
of the scapegoat. The early ritual has a number of general
characteristics which are repeated unconsciously and therefore with greater artistic and psychological reality in the story.

Basically, the scapegoat serves to purify the society of its
sins and ills through the principle of vicarious suffering where-
by the evil is transferred to a person, animal, or object. In
the course of time this purifying of the community became
periodic rather than occasional and sporadic. When it did, it

From Vol. 1, No. 1 of *Psychological Perspectives*, published by The C. G.
Jung Institute of Los Angeles, Inc. Reprinted by permission.

tended to be an annual observance coinciding with an obvious seasonal change which was identified with the beginning of a new year. The custom of the scapegoat was part of ancient religious life which generally was far more closely integrated into the central social life and concerns of the community than is the case in the twentieth century. When the scapegoat figure was human rather than an animal or material object, he was chosen from those regarded as most expendable or imperfect, such as slaves, the ugly or loathsome, or criminals. After his selection he was for a certain period treated royally by the community, having all his pleasures fully indulged. But at the end of this time he was subjected to a varied series of expulsion rites calculated to assure that all the evils and sins of the community were removed through his departure. These rites involved beatings, dancing, noise-making, and finally the putting to death of the scapegoat. Following the expulsion ceremonies, the community enjoyed a period of saturnalian release from the ordinary social restraints during which time scarcely any offense was punished.

When Pritchett comes to adapt this ancient ritual pattern to the modern short story, he chooses to use what Northrop Frye in his epochal *Anatomy of Criticism* has called the principle of displacement. Essentially, by this Frye means that tendency of writers to adapt the pure myth to their own time's notions of verisimilitude and credibility. Clearly, for a twentieth century author to write about Orpheus' descent to hell or the rape of Persephone demands far-reaching changes in the original tale if the story is to plausibly reflect the present day. Pritchett moves the scapegoat myth into the realm of prosaic realism by centering his plot in an English working class urban neighborhood after World War I.

With the prospects of a Royal Jubilee imminent, two traditionally rival streets, Earl Street and Terence Street, set out to collect money for a celebration. Each hopes to surpass the other in funds in order to have a more lavish celebration. Terence Street, however, quickly falls behind because it cannot agree on a suitable treasurer and head fund-raiser. The speaker, whose objective point of view acts as a fine gauge for the reader to experience the emotional power of the scapegoat ritual comes from and sides with Terence Street. The group of people living on Terence Street suspect Lupinsky, an extremely keen and energetic shopkeeper. But this suspicion prevents their choosing him as the treasurer and ultimately as the scapegoat. Therefore, they finally settle on Art Edwards, a devoted widower whose chief characteristic is that "he never seemed to get richer or poorer. He just went on the same."

The street as a whole rallies to the task, the money rapidly accumulates and with it the conviction that "we had chosen the right man." At this point Art's alter ego appears in the person of Harry Law, who is as erratic, unstable, and pretentious as Edwards is the reverse. Gradually, however, Art is drawn to the greater spirit and vigor of Law and his wife. To him, their life with its rhythmical oscillation between extremes comes to be a covert reproach to his own existence in which "he had never done anything" until at length he feels "a curious longing for ups and downs." Then, suddenly Art leaves town secretly, remains away for several days, only to return and hang himself, having lost the entire collection on the dog races at Wembley. After an immediate reaction of vituperative dismay, the street rallies to the challenge to its reputation and imaginative resourcefulness. It honors the death of Art Edwards with the biggest funeral ever seen on the street and proceeds to view him as "ourselves, our hero, our god . . . our king."

The narrative line of the plot clearly conforms to the ancient ritual pattern as something inherent in the experiences recounted in the story. To this end, he makes skillful use of a narrator who is a member of the society, sharing its impulses, feelings, values, and responses. This anonymous narrator unconsciously reveals the full scope of the ritual pattern little by little as he recounts the critical events of the Jubilee festival from his point of view with its naturally limited perspective. He relates the action in the past tense and with a nearly folktale rhetoric of simple sentences. This use of the past tense creates an ambivalence and an anxiety in the reader that are very different from those of the crowd which lived through the experience on the Street. To the reader, knowing the title of the story and having some information about the scapegoat theme, the question uppermost in mind revolves about who is the sacrificial victim and how the sacrifice will occur. The narrator, on the other hand, speaks about the past fact with the objective candor of a judge. Yet he is of the group on

Terence Street that lived out and in effect created the experience.

That Pritchett employs such a narrator reveals, ironically, the scapegoat ritual's concern with purification rather than atonement. The purification, however, does not mean change or growth, just release. Hence as the story ends, the Street is implicitly preparing for another scapegoat and the tone of the narrator's voice shows that too. Even though he is sufficiently detached from the group to be able to share the situation with the reader, he is not affected by it. Rather he is so removed that he is unable to see the impact of the situation at a deeper level and can only journalistically record the scene. Thus the result is that the narrator learns little if anything about the group's motivation or its archetypal patterning despite his being a participant in the events and a member of the society.

Actually the quintessence of the narrator's attitude appears in three remarks. The first is the opening sentence of the story: "There were long times when we were at peace and when the world left us alone." This notion is qualified by the observation: "The truth is that you can't live without enemies, and the best enemies are the ones nearest home." The serenity of Terence Street, and indeed its ultimate identity, is defined with reference to the implicit threat posed by the existence of Earl Street. Whenever the greater world beyond the individual streets makes its presence felt, the streets respond with a purgative ritual of violence calculated to remove their accumulated misfortunes, frustrations, and evils: "I don't know why, but if there was any trouble in the world, we turned out and attacked them." The world's and the nation's problems of peace and war are microcosmically reflected in the streets, which in the modern world assume the role of tribal societies of an ancient and primitive time: "The Great War, for us, was between Earl Street and Terence Street." In this Pritchett is careful to make clear the deliberateness of his intent by stressing both the collective and primitive nature of the response while at the same time displacing it to the child's less brutal world of simulation: "You would know there was trouble coming when you heard the voices of the children getting shriller and more excited, until their cries became rhythmic like the pulse of native war-cries in the forest. We were, indeed, lost in a *jungle* of streets."

This emotional context is undeniably primitive and traditional: "This has been going on ever since the old people can remember." As such, it allows the periodic expression of violence to merge naturally and effortlessly into the development of the scapegoat ritual. The emotional, verbal and physical beatings administered by contemporary tribal warriors —both streets have a "fighting family"—incite the group to desire and accept the scapegoat. As a person, the scapegoat generally is not individualized, for he must appear to be caught up and to live within the ritualistic pattern. Pritchett achieves this effect by having the narrator avoid any penetration of Art Edwards' consciousness. Instead of revealing any direct traces of the protagonist's self-awareness, the narrator deliberately defines Art's understanding through the street's projection of his attitude. He makes this quite explicit when he says:

> You will say, "How did we know what Art Edwards thought?" That was the strange thing: we did know. We knew as if he had told us, as if we were inside him. You see, because we had singled him out he was, in a sense, ourselves. We could see him thinking and feeling and doing what we would. He had taken the burden off us. By doing that he had become nearer and more precious to us than any other person.

Yet it is precisely his difference from the group, indicated by the fact that "he never changed," always wore "a black band on his sleeve," preserved a model fidelity to his dead wife, and possessed "modest, retiring ways," that permits Art (and Lupinsky as well) any identity. Their living among the group but separate from it prepares them for the role of scapegoat.

The necessity of the scapegoat's being in some way distinctive is balanced by the ritual's involving an act of choice as well. The special quality inherent in the victim narrows the number of candidates eligible for the role, but it is the unconscious act of choice which alone actually brings the scapegoat into being. Here, Pritchett elaborates on the communal psychology and controlling motives lying beyond the ancient records and anthropological accounts of the primitive ritual. A book like *The Golden Bough* scrupulously details the various modes of identifying potential scapegoats, but largely avoids the psychological issue of why one person rather than another equally distinctive is chosen. In Pritchett's story, on the other hand, considerable attention is devoted to tracing the society's reasons for selecting as sacrificial victim Art Edwards rather than Lupinsky. It is the latter who is introduced first in the story, as if his distinctiveness were sufficient to warrant his becoming the scapegoat. Lupinsky is not only "a red-haired Jew," he is also physically unattractive and underdeveloped by virtue of his pimples, round shoulders and weak eyes. All of these features are analogous to those described by Frazer as grounds for selecting someone as a ritual victim.

The same is true, ironically enough, of the ostensible reason for the community's not selecting Lupinsky. Past experience with financial collections in the community helps condition the initial response to Lupinsky:

> We had nothing against Lupinsky, but when we saw him raking in the money on his God Saves and Kiss-me-quicks and his flags of all nations, we thought he was collecting enough as it was. He might mix up the two collections.

Ancient societies frequently sought for scapegoats in the criminal class, and it is clear from the above that the community here fears Lupinsky may become a member of it. Thus, what originally would have assured his selection is now grounds for by-passing him. The reasons for this are twofold. In the first place, the role for which a candidate is sought is not initially that of scapegoat but that of fund-collector. Hence the attitude toward criminality must perforce be of a different order. In the second place, it is traditionally a part of the scapegoat ritual that the protagonist be chosen or selected by the community rather than advancing his own candidacy, as Lupinsky does and as Edwards refrains from doing. Taken together, these two points explain on both conscious and unconscious levels why Edwards rather than Lupinsky finds himself selected as the representative of the community.

The interplay of the two potential scapegoat figures is heavily marked in the early part of the story. One function of this is to portray the foregoing differences between the two men. At the same time another is to reveal the measure of the displacement the modern world has effected in the ritual form itself. Both aim at extending the reader's awareness of the social and psychological dynamics governing the narrative

progression. For instance, in the beginning, the reader feels
that Lupinsky may well be the chosen one. He is the one seen
first and his whole orientation is money, the mana of this
ritual. He also possesses a highly valuable insight, which
distinguishes him further even as it renders him incipiently a
danger and a threat to the community: "He was a keen man.
He came out in pimples—he was so keen. Lupinsky saw everything before any of us. He saw the Jubilee before the King
himself." Thus, though he is not chosen to collect for the
Jubilee tea, he is later selected to collect for Art's funeral. In
this, Pritchett manages to suggest why Lupinsky both is and is
not a scapegoat. The choice of Edwards indicates that Lupinsky is not the ritual victim. On the other hand, the story's final
sentence suggests that the street, exemplifying collective mob
behavior, may be preparing the ritual patterns of necessary
future scapegoats. By this means the traditional recurrent
character of ritual is reinforced, for in a marked sense, the
last sentence could easily lead again into the opening statement
of the story. Similarly, the pomp and color of the funeral
ritual lead directly back into the violence of the sudden and
rarely performed ritual that is prepared for in the opening
sentence.

After rejecting Lupinsky for his differences, the community
thinks it chose the first scapegoat figure because of his
similarities:

> Then suddenly we saw the right man had been staring us in
> the face all the time . . . . He was a widower, made serious by
> death: Art Edwards. We chose Art Edwards, and he agreed
> . . . . we were proud of him.

The fact that he has already been touched by death fore-
shadows his enactment of the scapegoat ritual. Equally important is the reason for the community's having sensed that
seriousness so occasioned was desirable in their chosen representative. Just prior to the discovery of Art Edwards as a
viable candidate, the narrator remarks that the group is not
motivated by distrust of one another, for "We could trust one
another. But we were frightened. Forty pounds! We thought.
That's a big sum. We didn't like the handling of it. There
wasn't one of us who had seen forty pounds in his life."
The fact that this fear can be borne only by someone who

has already been exposed to the ultimate terror, anguish and anxiety of death is made explicit later as Art and the community contemplate the accumulating hoard:

> We laughed uneasily. And we dreamed. The more we looked at the money the more we thought of things you could do with it—mad things like backing a horse or sensible things like starting a business or having a holiday.
>
> When we got up in Art's kitchen and saw him put the money in the cupboard and lock the door, we nodded our heads sadly. It was like burying the dead.
>
> "It's sad it's got to go," we thought.
>
> And it seemed to us fitting that Art, who had buried the dead and who was a dour man with iron-grey hair and level-looking eyes, should have the grim task of keeping that money, like some sexton. And we were glad to have him doing it, to have him be responsible instead of us. For some of us had to admit we'd go mad at times with temptation tingling in our fingers and hissing like gas in coal in our hearts.

As guardian, Art is immune to the fear of hidden treasure, but as scapegoat, he is all too susceptible to its temptations. The irony of choice thus takes on a fresh twist or inflection. For by choosing Art, the community has selected incorrectly on the conscious level but correctly on the unconscious plane. Art fails as guardian but succeeds as scapegoat, in contrast to Lupinsky, who would have succeeded as guardian and so perhaps obviated or frustrated the need for a scapegoat.

Interestingly enough, Art's association with death undergoes a profound transformation after his assumption of the guardian-scapegoat role. Hitherto, the community has viewed his fidelity to his dead wife with awe and some hostility. By the women, "Art was held up as a model," while at the same time "some of the men said that being a model wasn't healthy and that if they had been in Art's shoes they would muck around on the quiet." After Art, however, begins to collect for the tea, "we had the feeling he had put off his mourning and had come alive again." Ironically, becoming the unconsciously chosen scapegoat means to move from a living death into a dramatically resurgent life of power and centrality, which in turn is a preparation for a dying life that is self-chosen. And as is typical of scapegoat figures, the group honors his role and takes notice of his achievements:

> We looked with wonder at him. We had chosen the right man.
> It was bringing him out. And he had ideas too. He got some of
> the kids to go out at night with tins.

His quiet and deprecating behavior instills a trust in him on
the part of the community, which gradually replaces its earlier
feeling that "we hardly knew him." As the contest with Earl
Street continues and the temptation of the money intensifies,
the wonder merges with a sense of the pathos of his role,
which in turn generates a compensatory personal regard:

> When we left him we felt a kind of sorrow for Art for bearing
> our burden, for being the custodian of our victory over Earl
> Street.
>   It made us all very friendly to Art. The time went by. We
> used to stop and have a word with him in the street. And Art
> became friendly too.

As we have seen, Pritchett carefully explores the group's
motives in singling out Art Edwards as part of the displacement of the original ritual in the direction of a modern world
engrossed in causation and explanation. In addition he dramatizes the forces that impel Edwards to become more like the
rest of the community and in so doing to design his own destruction and celebration. This dramatization is effected in the
narrative through introducing Harry Law and his wife, who
together function almost as a kind of miniature double plot.
At the height of the contest between the streets, Lupinsky
provokes his community into a state beyond rational bounds
by challenging its leader: "Art Edwards, he said, had no life
in him. After this, it became madness. People got out their
savings." One who does so is Harry Law, a drunken, religious
bully with pretensions of social superiority. A chance discovery
of his wife's savings "just at the height of our madness"
affords him the opportunity of the grandiloquent gesture of a
large donation to the collection. A quarrel between husband
and wife ensues resulting in friction among other couples, but
more importantly, in an increasingly close relationship between Art Edwards and the Laws. Out of their conversations
and visits, Art sees them in a new and attractive light:
"They've lived all right. They've had their ups and downs."
And against his sister's straitened judgment of Harry Law,
Art replies: "We've all got our faults. He's had his ups and

downs." With this Art embarks on a new attitude toward life which carries with it markedly ambiguous consequences:

> And that was the phrase ["ups and downs"] that he kept repeating. It fascinated him. He felt generous. It came to him that he had never felt anything for years. He had just gone on standing in the High Street by the stall. He had never taken a holiday. He had never bought himself anything he wanted. He had never done anything. It startled him—but he suddenly did not want his wife who was in the grave. The street had chosen him, singled him out above all others, and there he stood, naked, nothing. He was shy about his nonentity. He felt a curious longing for ups and downs.

It is Art's desire to be like the Laws and to experience the full reaches of life that leads him to the dog races and the disastrous loss of the collection money. His desire to be fully human, to share in the oscillations of feeling and fortune, is what, in short, impels him to choose to enact his own scapegoat ritual. In an ironic displacement from the original ritual, Pritchett has Art perform his own sacrificial execution. The result is twofold. It points up the full extent to which the ritual has become an unconscious pattern of action in the modern world. Further, it reveals the irony of the community's intuitive sense that he has been chosen by them to remove through enactment their personal sense of sin, evil, and temptation. By his contact with the money and then with the Laws, Art has become defiled or impure, but the community's desire for his ritual expulsion is masked, though incompletely, under the guise of solicitude:

> Lupinsky was our reporter of everything, and gradually, expressing no doubt the instinct of the street, he had become our reporter on Art Edwards. We wanted a friendly eye kept on him not because he was valuable but because he was—well, as you would keep an eye on a sick man, say, a man who might have a heart attack or go dizzy in the street.

With Art's suicide and the disclosure of his failure as a guardian of the collection, the community is free both to purge itself of its alter ego and then to reintegrate it into itself through a ceremonial elevation of the scapegoat. The purging is done through the verbal medium of epithets, and then, under Lupinsky's indication of outside threats to the communal ego ("they're jeering at us in Earl Street"), the group coheres again and goes forth to physical combat with its antagonist. The ritual pattern of hatred, trouble, and violence, announced in the opening paragraph of the story, receives another enactment but this time inaugurated by the separate, special, and infrequent ritual of the scapegoat.

One of the actions present in the primitive scapegoat ritual is the beating or many beatings which precede the victim's expulsion. It is precisely through a variety of beatings that the setting reverberates the central theme of the story and renders it manifest. These ritual beatings and expulsions develop an interlocking pattern of animate and inanimate, of people and things. The inanimate objects which are used for or cause beatings in the story are the streets, the money, the house on Earl Street, as well as minor objects like stones and milk bottles. A numinous quality surrounds these objects, particularly the stones and the money. It is almost as if the object itself creates the beating. For instance, "a stone would fly up and then the women would be down in the middle of the street." Similarly, the substitution in the collection boxes of stones instead of money goads the children on the street into fights. The primitive stone here substitutes for money not only physically but functionally. It serves as a weapon with which to produce the uncontrollable affect that generates the children's battles. Money, an inanimate object, takes on animate life. For the women it attracts the attention of the men, who in turn use it to establish a hierarchy of importance. And both see its being locked up as "like burying the dead."

Beatings exist at nearly all levels of importance in the story. The Blackers are the fighting family on Terence Street. And with a bit of encouragement they can always get a group to beat up the Gurneys who live on Earl Street. In fact, as soon as Terence Street finally recognizes that they have lost the competition because Art has lost their money, "A stone went and a window crashed and that brought out the rest of the Blacker family. We got it off our chests that night and we crowded into Earl Street. Half their milk-bottles had gone before the police whistles went." In addition, Harry Law and his wife beat each other. He regularly assaults her verbally and physically while she responds in a passively aggressive manner by hoarding some of their money. Instead of throwing stones, she saves his money and he trips over it in the room as one would trip on a stone. Thus, again the inanimate money takes on a numinous quality and the people threaten to become caricatures acting out the role assigned.

This possibility is forestalled by the final segment in the scapegoat's ritual arc. With it the ritual of violence is transcended by the elevation of Art from the role of scapegoat to that of dying god whose death is a prelude to a new life most frequently symbolized by a marriage ceremony:

> And to show Earl Street what we were and to show the world what we thought of Art Edwards, we got up the biggest funeral that has ever been seen in our street. He was ourselves, our hero, our god. He had borne our sins. You couldn't see the hearse for flowers. The street was black with people. The sun shone. We'd been round and got every stall-holder, every barrowman in the neighbourhood. The procession was a mile long when it got going. There was a Jubilee for you, covered in red, white and blue wreaths. Art Edwards was our king. It looked like a wedding. The great white trumpets of the lillies rocked thick on the coffin. Earl Street couldn't touch that. And Lupinsky collected the money.

The value, psychological and social, of the scapegoat ritual is thus seen to be what it has always been—a communal means of periodically ridding itself of those elements and powers which left to themselves would destroy the fabric of society. At the same time, Pritchett indicates the intrinsic primitiveness (in the sense of unsophisticated) and barbarism of the ritual by the ironic revelation unconsciously perpetrated by the narrator in suggesting that the aim of the funeral was "to show Earl Street what we were and to show the world what we thought of Art Edwards." For in part what is shown is that the community of Terence Street is prepared to employ the principle of vicarious suffering for its own preservation. So committed is it to this as a necessary part of its existence that it will show its regard for its leaders and guardians by seeing them dead rather than itself facing the full temptations of the human condition. In Pritchett's eyes, both the sacrifice and the celebration are endemic to man as a social being and nowhere more clearly than in the twentieth century.

Shirley Jackson

Occasionally there is a work of literature that bursts on the reading public with devastating effect and ever after becomes virtually synonymous with the name of the author. Such was the case with Shirley Jackson's short story "The Lottery." Immediately upon its appearance in the New Yorker *magazine in 1948 the story touched off a storm of controversy and curiosity about both its meaning and author. The impeccable stylistic control intensified the central shock of the tale's action. All who read it responded in ways that revealed graphically how sensitive a nerve in the modern sensibility had been touched.*

As is so frequently the case with controversial books, the author of "The Lottery" completely belied expectations about her personality. Shirley Jackson (1919–1965) was a warm and very human person who enjoyed the essentials of life as much as the esoteric. After growing up and spending her early years in California, she married Stanley Edgar Hyman, the critic and teacher, in 1940 and settled in Vermont where he taught at Bennington College. There she wrote her books and raised a family, activities to which she was devoted until her death at a regrettably early age.

"The Lottery" was Miss Jackson's most famous work, but it was far from her only one. She wrote six novels and a great many short stories, as well as personal essays largely centering in the activities of her family. The novels and some of the stories develop her abiding concern with the mysteries of human motivation and the incalculable nature of experience, matters in which she made subtle and discriminating use of her wide reading in subjects like magic and witchcraft. Hangsaman (1951), The Road Through the Wall *(1948), and* The Bird's Nest *(1954) all render the macabre reality created by ghosts and living minds interacting with each other. Her*

essays, on the other hand, present the amused tolerant insight of a mature woman engrossed in the delights of the commonplaces of life. The wryness of her observations about her family is amusingly captured in the collection's title Life Among the Savages (*1953*). The range and craftsmanship of her work are well conveyed in the posthumous collections The Magic of Shirley Jackson (*1966*) and Come Along With Me (*1968*) edited by her husband. Unfortunately, despite her skill and reputation her work has not as yet received sustained critical attention, for there are no books or articles devoted exclusively to her appraisal.

The Lottery

Shirley Jackson

THE MORNING OF JUNE 27TH was clear and sunny,
with the fresh warmth of a full-summer day; the flowers were
blossoming profusely and the grass was richly green. The
people of the village began to gather in the square, between
the post office and the bank, around ten o'clock; in some towns
there were so many people that the lottery took two days and
had to be started on June 26th, but in this village, where there
were only about three hundred people, the whole lottery took
less than two hours, so it could begin at ten o'clock in the
morning and still be through in time to allow the villagers to
get home for noon dinner.

The children assembled first, of course. School was recently
over for the summer, and the feeling of liberty sat uneasily on
most of them; they tended to gather together quietly for a
while before they broke into boisterous play, and their talk
was still of the classroom and the teacher, of books and repri-
mands. Bobby Martin had already stuffed his pockets full of
stones, and the other boys soon followed his example, selecting
the smoothest and roundest stones; Bobby and Harry Jones
and Dickie Delacroix—the villagers pronounced this name
"Dellacroy"—eventually made a great pile of stones in one
corner of the square and guarded it against the raids of the
other boys. The girls stood aside, talking among themselves,
looking over their shoulders at the boys, and the very small
children rolled in the dust or clung to the hands of their older
brothers or sisters.

Reprinted with the permission of Farrar, Straus & Giroux, Inc. from *The
Lottery* by Shirley Jackson. Copyright 1948, 1949 by Shirley Jackson. First
published in the *New Yorker*.

Soon the men began to gather, surveying their own children, speaking of planting and rain, tractors and taxes. They stood together, away from the pile of stones in the corner, and their jokes were quiet and they smiled rather than laughed. The women, wearing faded house dresses and sweaters, came shortly after their menfolk. They greeted one another and exchanged bits of gossip as they went to join their husbands. Soon the women, standing by their husbands, began to call to their children, and the children came reluctantly, having to be called four or five times. Bobby Martin ducked under his mother's grasping hand and ran, laughing, back to the pile of stones. His father spoke up sharply, and Bobby came quickly and took his place between his father and his oldest brother.

The lottery was conducted—as were the square dances, the teenage club, the Halloween program—by Mr. Summers, who had time and energy to devote to civic activities. He was a round-faced, jovial man and he ran the coal business, and people were sorry for him, because he had no children and his wife was a scold. When he arrived in the square, carrying the black wooden box, there was a murmur of conversation among the villagers, and he waved and called, "Little late today, folks." The postmaster, Mr. Graves, followed him, carrying a three-legged stool, and the stool was put in the center of the square and Mr. Summers set the black box down on it. The villagers kept their distance, leaving a space between themselves and the stool, and when Mr. Summers said, "Some of you fellows want to give me a hand?" there was a hesitation before two men, Mr. Martin and his oldest son, Baxter, came forward to hold the box steady on the stool while Mr. Summers stirred up the papers inside it.

The original paraphernalia for the lottery had been lost long ago, and the black box now resting on the stool had been put into use even before Old Man Warner, the oldest man in town, was born. Mr. Summers spoke frequently to the villagers about making a new box, but no one liked to upset even as much tradition as was represented by the black box. There was a story that the present box had been made with some pieces of the box that had preceded it, the one that had been constructed when the first people settled down to make a village here. Every year, after the lottery, Mr. Summers began talking again about a new box, but every year the subject was allowed to fade off without anything's being done. The black box grew shabbier each year; by now it was no longer completely black but splintered badly along one side to show the original wood color, and in some places faded or stained.

Mr. Martin and his oldest son, Baxter, held the black box securely on the stool until Mr. Summers had stirred the papers thoroughly with his hand. Because so much of the ritual had been forgotten or discarded, Mr. Summers had been successful in having slips of paper substituted for the chips of wood that had been used for generations. Chips of wood, Mr. Summers had argued, had been all very well when the village was tiny, but now that the population was more than three hundred and likely to keep on growing, it was necessary to use something that would fit more easily into the black box. The night before the lottery, Mr. Summers and Mr. Graves made up the slips of paper and put them in the box, and it was then taken to the safe of Mr. Summers's coal company and locked up until Mr. Summers was ready to take it to the square next morning. The rest of the year, the box was put away, sometimes one place, sometimes another; it had spent one year in Mr. Graves's barn and another year underfoot in the post office, and sometimes it was set on a shelf in the Martin grocery and left there.

There was a great deal of fussing to be done before Mr. Summers declared the lottery open. There were the lists to make up—of heads of families, heads of households in each family, members of each household in each family. There was the proper swearing-in of Mr. Summers by the postmaster, as the official of the lottery; at one time, some people remembered, there had been a recital of some sort, performed by the official of the lottery, a perfunctory, tuneless chant that had been rattled off duly each year; some people believed that the official of the lottery used to stand just so when he said or sang it, others believed that he was supposed to walk among the people, but years and years ago this part of the ritual had been allowed to lapse. There had been, also, a ritual salute, which the official of the lottery had had to use in addressing each person who came up to draw from the box, but this also had changed with time, until now it was felt necessary only for the official to speak to each person approaching. Mr. Summers was very good at all this; in his clean white shirt and blue jeans, with one hand resting carelessly on the black box, he seemed very proper and important as he talked interminably to Mr. Graves and the Martins.

Just as Mr. Summers finally left off talking and turned to the assembled villagers, Mrs. Hutchinson came hurriedly along the path to the square, her sweater thrown over her shoulders, and slid into place in the back of the crowd. "Clean forgot what day it was," she said to Mrs. Delacroix, who stood next to her, and they both laughed softly. "Thought my old man was out back stacking wood," Mrs. Hutchinson went on, "and then I looked out the window and the kids was gone, and then I remembered it was the twenty-seventh and came a-running." She dried her hands on her apron, and Mrs. Delacroix said, "You're in time, though. They're still talking away up there."

Mrs. Hutchinson craned her neck to see through the crowd and found her husband and children standing near the front. She tapped Mrs. Delacroix on the arm as a farewell and began to make her way through the crowd. The people separated good-humoredly to let her through; two or three people said, in voices just loud enough to be heard across the crowd, "Here comes your Missus, Hutchinson," and "Bill, she made it after all." Mrs. Hutchinson reached her husband, and Mr. Summers, who had been waiting, said cheerfully, "Thought we were going to have to get on without you, Tessie." Mrs. Hutchinson said, grinning, "Wouldn't have me leave m'dishes in the sink, now, would you, Joe?" and soft laughter ran through the crowd as the people stirred back into position after Mrs. Hutchinson's arrival.

"Well, now," Mr. Summers said soberly, "guess we better get started, get this over with, so's we can go back to work. Anybody ain't here?"

"Dunbar," several people said. "Dunbar, Dunbar."

Mr. Summers consulted his list. "Clyde Dunbar," he said. "That's right. He's broke his leg, hasn't he? Who's drawing for him?"

"Me, I guess," a woman said, and Mr. Summers turned to look at her. "Wife draws for her husband," Mr. Summers said. "Don't you have a grown boy to do it for you, Janey?" Although Mr. Summers and everyone else in the village knew the answer perfectly well, it was the business of the official of the lottery to ask such questions formally. Mr. Summers waited with an expression of polite interest while Mrs. Dunbar answered.

"Horace's not but sixteen yet," Mrs. Dunbar said regretfully. "Guess I gotta fill in for the old man this year."

"Right," Mr. Summers said. He made a note on the list he was holding. Then he asked, "Watson boy drawing this year?" A tall boy in the crowd raised his hand. "Here," he said. "I'm drawing for m'mother and me." He blinked his eyes nervously and ducked his head as several voices in the crowd said things like "Good fellow, Jack," and "Glad to see your mother's got a man to do it."

"Well," Mr. Summers said, "guess that's everyone. Old Man Warner make it?"

"Here," a voice said, and Mr. Summers nodded.

A sudden hush fell on the crowd as Mr. Summers cleared his throat and looked at the list. "All ready?" he called. "Now, I'll read the names—heads of families first—and the men come up and take a paper out of the box. Keep the paper folded in your hand without looking at it until everyone has had a turn. Everything clear?"

The people had done it so many times that they only half listened to the directions; most of them were quiet, wetting their lips, not looking around. Then Mr. Summers raised one hand high and said, "Adams." A man disengaged himself from the crowd and came forward. "Hi, Steve," Mr. Summers said, and Mr. Adams said, "Hi, Joe." They grinned at one another humorlessly and nervously. Then Mr. Adams reached into the black box and took out a folded paper. He held it firmly by one corner as he turned and went hastily back to his place in the crowd, where he stood a little apart from his family, not looking down at his hand.

"Allen," Mr. Summers said. "Anderson. . . . Bentham."

"Seems like there's no time at all between lotteries any more," Mrs. Delacroix said to Mrs. Graves in the back row. "Seems like we got through with the last one only last week."

"Time sure goes fast," Mrs. Graves said.

"Clark. . . . Delacroix."

"There goes my old man," Mrs. Delacroix said. She held her breath while her husband went forward.

"Dunbar," Mr. Summers said, and Mrs. Dunbar went

steadily to the box while one of the women said, "Go on, Janey," and another said, "There she goes."

"We're next," Mrs. Graves said. She watched while Mr. Graves came around from the side of the box, greeted Mr. Summers gravely, and selected a slip of paper from the box. By now, all through the crowd there were men holding the small folded papers in their large hands, turning them over and over nervously. Mrs. Dunbar and her two sons stood together, Mrs. Dunbar holding the slip of paper.

"Harburt. . . . Hutchinson."

"Get up there, Bill," Mrs. Hutchinson said, and the people near her laughed.

"Jones."

"They do say," Mr. Adams said to Old Man Warner, who stood next to him, "that over in the north village they're talking of giving up the lottery."

Old Man Warner snorted. "Pack of crazy fools," he said. "Listening to the young folks, nothing's good enough for *them*. Next thing you know, they'll be wanting to go back to living in caves, nobody work any more, live *that* way for a while. Used to be a saying about 'Lottery in June, corn be heavy soon.' First thing you know, we'd all be eating stewed chickweed and acorns. There's *always* been a lottery," he added petulantly. "Bad enough to see young Joe Summers up there joking with everybody."

"Some places have already quit lotteries," Mrs. Adams said.

"Nothing but trouble in *that*," Old Man Warner said stoutly. "Pack of young fools."

"Martin." And Bobby Martin watched his father go forward. "Overdyke. . . . Percy."

"I wish they'd hurry," Mrs. Dunbar said to her older son. "I wish they'd hurry."

"They're almost through," her son said.

"You get ready to run tell Dad," Mrs. Dunbar said.

Mr. Summers called his own name and then stepped forward precisely and selected a slip from the box. Then he called, "Warner."

"Seventy-seventh year I been in the lottery," Old Man Warner said as he went through the crowd. "Seventy-seventh time."

"Watson." The tall boy came awkwardly through the crowd.

Someone said, "Don't be nervous, Jack," and Mr. Summers said, "Take your time, son."

"Zanini."

After that, there was a long pause, a breathless pause, until Mr. Summers, holding his slip of paper in the air, said, "All right, fellows." For a minute, no one moved, and then all the slips of paper were opened. Suddenly, all the women began to speak at once, saying, "Who is it?," "Who's got it?," "Is it the Dunbars?," "Is it the Watsons?" Then the voices began to say, "It's Hutchinson. It's Bill," "Bill Hutchinson's got it."

"Go tell your father," Mrs. Dunbar said to her older son.

People began to look around to see the Hutchinsons. Bill Hutchinson was standing quiet, staring down at the paper in his hand. Suddenly, Tessie Hutchinson shouted to Mrs. Summers, "You didn't give him time enough to take any paper he wanted. I saw you. It wasn't fair!"

"Be a good sport, Tessie," Mrs. Delacroix called, and Mrs. Graves said, "All of us took the same chance."

"Shut up, Tessie," Bill Hutchinson said.

"Well, everyone," Mr. Summers said, "that was done pretty fast, and now we've got to be hurrying a little more to get done in time." He consulted his next list. "Bill," he said, "you draw for the Hutchinson family. You got any other households in the Hutchinsons?"

"There's Don and Eva," Mrs. Hutchinson yelled. "Make *them* take their chance!"

"Daughters draw with their husbands' families, Tessie," Mr. Summers said gently. "You know that as well as anyone else."

"It wasn't *fair*," Tessie said.

"I guess not, Joe," Bill Hutchinson said regretfully. "My daughter draws with her husband's family, that's only fair. And I've got no other family except the kids."

"Then, as far as drawing for families is concerned, it's you," Mr. Summers said in explanation, "and as far as drawing for households is concerned, that's you, too. Right?"

"Right," Bill Hutchinson said.

"How many kids, Bill?" Mr. Summers asked formally.

"Three," Bill Hutchinson said. "There's Bill, Jr., and Nancy, and little Dave. And Tessie and me."

"All right, then," Mr. Summers said. "Harry, you got their tickets back?"

Mr. Graves nodded and held up the slips of paper. "Put them in the box, then," Mr. Summers directed. "Take Bill's and put it in."

"I think we ought to start over," Mrs. Hutchinson said, as quietly as she could. "I tell you it wasn't *fair*. You didn't give him time enough to choose. *Every*body saw that."

Mr. Graves had selected the five slips and put them in the box, and he dropped all the papers but those onto the ground, where the breeze caught them and lifted them off.

"Listen, everybody," Mrs. Hutchinson was saying to the people around her.

"Ready, Bill?" Mr. Summers asked, and Bill Hutchinson, with one quick glance around at his wife and children, nodded.

"Remember," Mr. Summers said, "take the slips and keep them folded until each person has taken one. Harry, you help little Dave." Mr. Graves took the hand of the little boy, who came willingly with him up to the box. "Take a paper out of the box, Davy," Mr. Summers said. Davy put his hand into the box and laughed. "Take just *one* paper," Mr. Summers said. "Harry, you hold it for him." Mr. Graves took the child's hand and removed the folded paper from the tight fist and held it while little Dave stood next to him and looked up at him wonderingly.

"Nancy next," Mr. Summers said. Nancy was twelve, and her school friends breathed heavily as she went forward, switching her skirt, and took a slip daintily from the box. "Bill, Jr.," Mr. Summers said, and Billy, his face red and his feet overlarge, nearly knocked the box over as he got a paper out. "Tessie," Mr. Summers said. She hesitated for a minute, looking around defiantly, and then set her lips and went up to the box. She snatched a paper out and held it behind her.

"Bill," Mr. Summers said, and Bill Hutchinson reached into the box and felt around, bringing his hand out at last with the slip of paper in it.

The crowd was quiet. A girl whispered, "I hope it's not Nancy," and the sound of the whisper reached the edges of the crowd.

"It's not the way it used to be," Old Man Warner said clearly. "People ain't the way they used to be."

"All right," Mr. Summers said. "Open the papers. Harry, you open little Dave's."

Mr. Graves opened the slip of paper and there was a general

sigh through the crowd as he held it up and everyone could see that it was blank. Nancy and Bill, Jr., opened theirs at the same time, and both beamed and laughed, turning around to the crowd and holding their slips of paper above their heads.

"Tessie," Mr. Summers said. There was a pause, and then Mr. Summers looked at Bill Hutchinson, and Bill unfolded his paper and showed it. It was blank.

"It's Tessie," Mr. Summers said, and his voice was hushed. "Show us her paper, Bill."

Bill Hutchinson went over to his wife and forced the slip of paper out of her hand. It had a black spot on it, the black spot Mr. Summers had made the night before with the heavy pencil in the coal-company office. Bill Hutchinson held it up, and there was a stir in the crowd.

"All right, folks," Mr. Summers said. "Let's finish quickly."

Although the villagers had forgotten the ritual and lost the original black box, they still remembered to use stones. The pile of stones the boys had made earlier was ready; there were stones on the ground with the blowing scraps of paper that had come out of the box. Mrs. Delacroix selected a stone so large she had to pick it up with both hands and turned to Mrs. Dunbar. "Come on," she said. "Hurry up."

Mrs. Dunbar had small stones in both hands, and she said, gasping for breath, "I can't run at all. You'll have to go ahead and I'll catch up with you."

The children had stones already, and someone gave little Davy Hutchinson a few pebbles.

Tessie Hutchinson was in the center of a cleared space by now, and she held her hands out desperately as the villagers moved in on her. "It isn't fair," she said. A stone hit her on the side of the head.

Old Man Warner was saying, "Come on, come on, every-one." Steve Adams was in the front of the crowd of villagers, with Mrs. Graves beside him.

"It isn't fair, it isn't right," Mrs. Hutchinson screamed, and then they were upon her.

James Baldwin

American literature has long shown a marked concern for violence both personal and public, sexual obsessions, and social ferment. James Baldwin (1924–   ) mirrors these interests as powerfully and individually as any serious writer of the past twenty years. In doing so, he speaks eloquently for the plight of modern man struggling with the necessity of an urban existence. At the same time, he conveys through a variety of moods and forms the precise texture of the black man's experience in America.

Baldwin was born in New York City, where he graduated from De Witt Clinton High School and learned the nature of the ghetto. As a teen-ager he was drawn to the career of a lay preacher, ironically following his stepfather from whom he was alienated in all other respects. Three years later he fled the church and what it represented to him and struck out on his own. Shortly after World War II Baldwin left America for Europe, where he hoped to find a world of greater racial, sexual, and imaginative freedom. He lived abroad for a total of nine years and during that time began to establish himself as a writer of considerable strength and sensitivity. His first novel, Go Tell It on the Mountain (1953), draws on his church experiences in Harlem to present a story of adolescent maturation. His second novel, Giovanni's Room (1956), is radically different in subject and treatment: it deals with love affairs of white homosexuals in Paris in a style of great poignancy and tautness.

Since returning to America Baldwin has continued to grow as an artist and to speak with increasing vigor and candor about the pressing public problems of the day, most notably race relations and civil rights. Some critics have regarded his essays, such as those in Nobody Knows My Name (1961) and The Fire Next Time (1963), as among the very best ever writ-

ten by an American. His fiction, both novels and short stories, and his more recent dramas have become increasingly power-ful. Another Country (*1962*), Blues for Mister Charlie (*1964*), and Tell Me How Long the Train's Been Gone (*1968*) *probe with remorseless honesty and compassion the incredible tangles that people make of human relationships. The dark, mysterious forces of the psyche and society are plumbed by Baldwin. As in his story "Going to Meet the Man," sexual, racial, and social forces intertwine to make individuals enact complicated and scarcely understood rituals of victimization that testify to the persistence and vitality of the scapegoat figure in the modern world.*

Mr. Baldwin's literary career was initially encouraged by Richard Wright, who aided him in securing a Eugene F. Saxton Memorial Trust Award. Since then his writing has been supported and recognized by Rosenwald, Guggenheim, and Partisan Review *Fellowships, among others. Although Baldwin's work has been the subject of a number of magazine articles, in view of the important position he commands in contemporary American literature it is surprising that his writing has received relatively little critical attention. One book by F. J. Eckman,* The Furious Passage of James Baldwin (*1966*), *has been devoted to his career; it contains a helpful critical bibliography. Other bibliographical material appears in Kathleen A. Kindt, "James Baldwin: A Checklist, 1947–62,"* Bulletin of Bibliography, *XXIV* (*1965*), *123–126; Russell G. Fischer, "James Baldwin: A Bibliography, 1947–62,"* Bulletin of Bibliography, *XXIV* (*1965*), *127–130; Fred L. Standley, "James Baldwin: A Checklist, 1963–67,"* Bulletin of Bibliography, *XXV* (*1968*), *135–137, 160.*

Going to Meet the Man

James Baldwin

"WHAT'S THE MATTER?" she asked.

"I don't know," he said, trying to laugh, "I guess I'm tired."

"You've been working too hard," she said. "I keep telling you."

"Well, goddammit, woman," he said, "it's not my fault!" He tried again; he wretchedly failed again. Then he just lay there, silent, angry, and helpless. Excitement filled him just like a toothache, but it refused to enter his flesh. He stroked her breast. This was his wife. He could not ask her to do just a little thing for him, just to help him out, just for a little while, the way he could ask a nigger girl to do it. He lay there, and he sighed. The image of a black girl caused a distant excitement in him, like a far-away light; but, again, the excitement was more like pain; instead of forcing him to act, it made action impossible.

"Go to sleep," she said, gently, "you got a hard day tomorrow."

"Yeah," he said, and rolled over on his side, facing her, one hand still on one breast. "Goddamn the niggers. The black stinking coons. You'd think they'd learn. Wouldn't you think they'd learn? I mean, *wouldn't* you?"

"They going to be out there tomorrow," she said, and took his hand away, "get some sleep."

He lay there, one hand between his legs, staring at the frail sanctuary of his wife. A faint light came from the shutters; the moon was full. Two dogs, far away, were barking at each

other, back and forth, insistently, as though they were agree-
ing to make an appointment. He heard a car coming north on
the road and he half sat up, his hand reaching for his holster,
which was on a chair near the bed, on top of his pants. The
lights hit the shutters and seemed to travel across the room
and then went out. The sound of the car slipped away, he
heard it hit gravel, then heard it no more. Some liver-lipped
students, probably, heading back to that college—but coming
from where? His watch said it was two in the morning. They
could be coming from anywhere, from out of state most likely,
and they would be at the court-house tomorrow. The niggers
were getting ready. Well, they would be ready, too.

He moaned. He wanted to let whatever was in him out; but
it wouldn't come out. Goddamn! he said aloud, and turned
again, on his side, away from Grace, staring at the shutters.
He was a big, healthy man and he had never had any trouble
sleeping. And he wasn't old enough yet to have any trouble
getting it up—he was only forty-two. And he was a good man,
a God-fearing man, he had tried to do his duty all his life, and
he had been a deputy sheriff for several years. Nothing had
ever bothered him before, certainly not getting it up. Sometimes, sure, like any other man, he knew that he wanted a
little more spice than Grace could give him and he would drive
over yonder and pick up a black piece or arrest her, it came
to the same thing, but he couldn't do that now, no more. There
was no telling what might happen once your ass was in the
air. And they were low enough to kill a man then, too, everyone of them, or the girl herself might do it, right while she
was making believe you made her feel so good. The niggers.
What had the good Lord Almighty had in mind when he made
the niggers? Well. They were pretty good at that, all right.
Damn. Damn. Goddamn.

This wasn't helping him to sleep. He turned again, toward
Grace again, and moved close to her warm body. He felt
something he had never felt before. He felt that he would
like to hold her, hold her, hold her, and be buried in her like a
child and never have to get up in the morning again and go
downtown to face those faces, good Christ, they were ugly!
and never have to enter that jail house again and smell that
smell and hear that singing; never again feel that filthy, kinky,
greasy hair under his hand, never again watch those black

breasts leap against the leaping cattle prod, never hear those moans again or watch that blood run down or the fat lips split or the sealed eyes struggle open. They were animals, they were no better than animals, what could be done with people like that? Here they had been in a civilized country for years and they still lived like animals. Their houses were dark, with oil cloth or cardboard in the windows, the smell was enough to make you puke your guts out, and there they sat, a whole tribe, pumping out kids, it looked like, every damn five minutes, and laughing and talking and playing music like they didn't have a care in the world, and he reckoned they didn't, neither, and coming to the door, into the sunlight, just standing there, just looking foolish, not thinking of anything but just getting back to what they were doing, saying, Yes suh, Mr. Jesse. I surely will, Mr. Jesse. Fine weather, Mr. Jesse. Why, I thank you, Mr. Jesse. He had worked for a mail-order house for a while and it had been his job to collect the payments for the stuff they bought. They were too dumb to know that they were being cheated blind, but that was no skin off his ass—he was just supposed to do his job. They would be late—they didn't have the sense to put money aside; but it was easy to scare them, and he never really had any trouble. Hell, they all liked him, the kids used to smile when he came to the door. He gave them candy, sometimes, or chewing gum, and rubbed their rough bullet heads—maybe the candy should have been poisoned. Those kids were grown now. He had had trouble with one of them today.

"There was this nigger today," he said; and stopped; his voice sounded peculiar. He touched Grace. "You awake?" he asked. She mumbled something, impatiently, she was probably telling him to go to sleep. It was all right. He knew that he was not alone.

"What a funny time," he said, "to be thinking about a thing like that—you listening?" She mumbled something again. He rolled over on his back. "This nigger's one of the ringleaders. We had trouble with him before. We must have had him out there at the work farm three or four times. Well, Big Jim C. and some of the boys really had to whip that nigger's ass today." He looked over at Grace; he could not tell whether she was listening or not; and he was afraid to ask again. "They had this line you know, to register"— he laughed, but she did not—"and they wouldn't stay where Big Jim C. wanted them, no, they had to start blocking traffic all around the court house so couldn't nothing or nobody get through, and Big Jim C. told them to disperse and they wouldn't move, they just kept up that singing, and Big Jim C. figured that the others would move if this nigger would move, him being the ringleader, but he wouldn't move and he wouldn't let the others move, so they had to beat him and a couple of the others and they threw them in the wagon—but *I* didn't see this nigger till I got to the jail. They were still singing and I was supposed to make them stop. Well, I couldn't make them stop for me but I knew he could make them stop. He was lying on the ground jerking and moaning, they had threw him in a cell by himself, and blood was coming out his ears from where Big Jim C. and his boys had whipped him. Wouldn't you think they'd learn? I put the prod to him and he jerked some more and he kind of screamed—but he didn't have much voice left. "You make them stop that singing," I said to him, "you hear me? You make them stop that singing." He acted like he didn't hear me and I put it to him again, under his arms, and he just rolled around on the floor and blood started coming from his mouth. He'd pissed his pants already." He paused. His mouth felt dry and his throat was as rough as sandpaper; as he talked, he began to hurt all over with that peculiar excitement which refused to be released. "You all are going to stop your singing, I said to him, and you are going to stop coming down to the court house and disrupting traffic and molesting the people and keeping us from our duties and keeping doctors from getting to sick white women and getting all them Northerners in this town to give our town a bad name—!" As he said this, he kept prodding the boy, sweat pouring from beneath the helmet he had not yet taken off. The boy rolled around in his own dirt and water and blood and tried to scream again as the prod hit his testicles, but the scream did not come out, only a kind of rattle and a moan. He stopped. He was not supposed to kill the nigger. The cell was filled with a terrible odor. The boy was still. "You hear me?" he called. "You had enough?" The singing went on. "You had enough?" His foot leapt out, he had not known it was going to, and caught the boy flush on the jaw. *Jesus*, he thought, *this ain't no nigger, this is a goddamn bull*, and he screamed again, "You had enough? You going to make them stop that singing now?"

But the boy was out. And now he was shaking worse than the boy had been shaking. He was glad no one could see him. At the same time, he felt very close to a very peculiar, particular joy; something deep in him and deep in his memory was stirred, but whatever was in his memory eluded him. He took off his helmet. He walked to the cell door.

"White man," said the boy, from the floor, behind him.

He stopped. For some reason, he grabbed his privates.

"You remember Old Julia?"

The boy said, from the floor, with his mouth full of blood, and one eye, barely open, glaring like the eye of a cat in the dark, "My grandmother's name was Mrs. Julia Blossom. *Mrs.* Julia Blossom. You going to call our women by their right names yet.—And those kids ain't going to stop singing. We going to keep on singing until every one of you miserable white mothers go stark raving out of your minds. Then he closed the one eye; he spat blood; his head fell back against the floor.

He looked down at the boy, whom he had been seeing, off and on, for more than a year, and suddenly remembered him: Old Julia had been one of his mail-order customers, a nice old woman. He had not seen her for years, he supposed that she must be dead.

He had walked into the yard, the boy had been sitting in a swing. He had smiled at the boy, and asked, "Old Julia home?"

The boy looked at him for a long time before he answered. "Don't no Old Julia live here."

"This is her house. I know her. She's lived here for years."

The boy shook his head. "You might know a Old Julia someplace else, white man. But don't nobody by that name live here."

He watched the boy; the boy watched him. The boy certainly wasn't more than ten. *White man.* He didn't have time to be fooling around with some crazy kid. He yelled, "Hey! Old Julia!"

But only silence answered him. The expression on the boy's face did not change. The sun beat down on them both, still and silent; he had the feeling that he had been caught up in a nightmare, a nightmare dreamed by a child; perhaps one of the nightmares he himself had dreamed as a child. It had that feeling—everything familiar, without undergoing any other change, had been subtly and hideously displaced: the trees, the sun, the patches of grass in the yard, the leaning porch and the weary porch steps and the cardboard in the windows and the black hole of the door which looked like the entrance to a cave, and the eyes of the pickaninny, all, all, were charged with malevolence. *White man.* He looked at the boy. "She's gone out?"

The boy said nothing.

"Well," he said, "tell her I passed by and I'll pass by next week." He started to go; he stopped. "You want some chewing gum?"

The boy got down from the swing and started for the house. He said, "I don't want nothing you got, white man." He walked into the house and closed the door behind him.

Now the boy looked as though he were dead. Jesse wanted to go over to him and pick him up and pistol whip him until the boy's head burst open like a melon. He began to tremble with what he believed was rage, sweat, both cold and hot, raced down his body, the singing filled him as though it were a weird, uncontrollable, monstrous howling rumbling up from the depths of his own belly, he felt an icy fear rise in him and raise him up, and he shouted, he howled, "You lucky we *pump* some white blood into you every once in a while—your women! Here's what I got for all the black bitches in the world—!" Then he was, abruptly, almost too weak to stand; to his bewilderment, his horror, beneath his own fingers, he felt himself violently stiffen—with no warning at all; he dropped his hands and he stared at the boy and he left the cell.

"All that singing they do," he said. "All that singing." He could not remember the first time he had heard it; he had been hearing it all his life. It was the sound with which he was most familiar—though it was also the sound of which he had been least conscious—and it had always contained an obscure comfort. They were singing to God. They were singing for mercy and they hoped to go to heaven, and he had even sometimes felt, when looking into the eyes of some of the old women, a few of the very old men, that they were singing for mercy for his soul, too. Of course he had never thought of their heaven or of what God was, or could be, for them; God was the same for everyone, he supposed, and heaven was where good people went—he supposed. He had never thought much about what it meant to be a good person. He tried to be a good person and treat everybody right: it wasn't his fault if the niggers had taken it into their heads to fight against God and go against the rules laid down in the Bible for everyone to read! Any preacher would tell you that. He was only doing his duty: protecting white people from the niggers and the niggers from themselves. And there were still lots of good niggers around—he had to remember that; they weren't all like that boy this afternoon; and the good niggers must be mighty sad to see what was happening to their people. They would thank him when this was over. In that way they had, the best of them, not quite looking him in the eye, in a low voice, with a little smile: We surely thanks you, Mr. Jesse. From the bottom of our hearts, we thanks you. He smiled. They hadn't all gone crazy. This trouble would pass.—He knew that the young people had changed some of the words to the songs. He had scarcely listened to the words before and he did not listen to them now; but he knew that the words were different; he could hear that much. He did not know if the faces were different, he had never, before this trouble began, watched them as they sang, but he certainly did not like what he saw now. They hated him, and this hatred was blacker than their hearts, blacker than their skins, redder than their blood, and harder, by far, than his club. Each day, each night, he felt worn out, aching, with their smell in his nostrils and filling his lungs, as though he were drowning— drowning in niggers; and it was all to be done again when he awoke. It would never end. It would never end. Perhaps this was what the singing had meant all along. They had not been singing black folks into heaven, they had been singing white folks into hell.

Everyone felt this black suspicion in many ways, but no one knew how to express it. Men much older than he, who had been responsible for law and order much longer than he, were now much quieter than they had been, and the tone of their jokes, in a way that he could not quite put his finger on, had changed. These men were his models, they had been friends to his father, and they had taught him what it meant to be a man. He looked to them for courage now. It wasn't that he didn't know that what he was doing was right—he knew that, nobody had to tell him that; it was only that he missed the ease of former years. But they didn't have much time to hang out with each other these days. They tended to stay close to their families every free minute because nobody knew what might happen next. Explosions rocked the night of their tranquil town. Each time each man wondered silently if perhaps this time the dynamite had not fallen into the wrong hands. They thought that they knew where all the guns were; but they could not possibly know every move that was made in that secret place where the darkies lived. From time to time it was suggested that they form a posse and search the home of every nigger, but they hadn't done it yet. For one thing, this might have brought the bastards from the North down on their backs; for another, although the niggers were scattered throughout the town—down in the hollow near the railroad tracks, way west near the mills, up on the hill, the well-off ones, and some out near the college—nothing seemed to happen in one part of town without the niggers immediately knowing it in the other. This meant that they could not take them by surprise. They rarely mentioned it, but they *knew* that some of the niggers had guns. It stood to reason, as they said, since, after all, some of them had been in the Army. There were niggers in the Army right now and God knows they wouldn't have had any trouble stealing this half-assed government blind—the whole world was doing it, look at the European countries and all those countries in Africa. They made jokes about it—bitter jokes; and they cursed the government in Washington, which had betrayed them; but they had not yet formed a posse. Now, if their town had been laid out like some towns in the North, where all the niggers lived together in one locality, they could have gone down and set fire to the houses and brought about peace that way. If the niggers had all lived in one place, they could have kept the fire in one place. But the way this town was laid out, the fire could hardly be controlled. It would spread all over town—and the niggers would probably be helping it to spread. Still, from time to time, they spoke of doing it, anyway; so that now there was a real fear among them that somebody might go crazy and light the match.

They rarely mentioned anything not directly related to the

war that they were fighting, but this had failed to establish between them the unspoken communication of soldiers during a war. Each man, in the thrilling silence which sped outward from their exchanges, their laughter, and their anecdotes, seemed wrestling, in various degrees of darkness, with a secret which he could not articulate to himself, and which, however directly it related to the war, related yet more surely to his privacy and his past. They could no longer be sure, after all, that they had all done the same things. They had never dreamed that their privacy could contain any element of terror, could threaten, that is, to reveal itself, to the scrutiny of a judgment day, while remaining unreadable and inaccessible to themselves; nor had they dreamed that the past, while certainly refusing to be forgotten, could yet so stubbornly refuse to be remembered. They felt themselves mysteriously set at naught, as no longer entering into the real concerns of other people—while here they were, outnumbered, fighting to save the civilized world. They had thought that people would care—people didn't care; not enough, anyway, to help them. It would have been a help, really, or at least a relief, even to have been forced to surrender. Thus they had lost, probably forever, their old and easy connection with each other. They were forced to depend on each other more and, at the same time, to trust each other less. Who could tell when one of them might not betray them all, for money, or for the ease of confession? But no one dared imagine what there might be to confess. They were soldiers fighting a war, but their relationship to each other was that of accomplices in a crime. They all had to keep their mouths shut.

> *I stepped in the river at Jordan.*

Out of the darkness of the room, out of nowhere, the line came flying up at him, with the melody and the beat. He turned wordlessly toward his sleeping wife. *I stepped in the river at Jordan.* Where had he heard that song?

"Grace," he whispered. "You awake?"

She did not answer. If she was awake, she wanted him to sleep. Her breathing was slow and easy, her body slowly rose and fell.

> *I stepped in the river at Jordan.*
> *The water came to my knees.*

He began to sweat. He felt an overwhelming fear, which yet contained a curious and dreadful pleasure.

> *I stepped in the river at Jordan.*
> *The water came to my waist.*

It had been night, as it was now, he was in the car between his mother and his father, sleepy, his head in his mother's lap, sleepy, and yet full of excitement. The singing came from far away, across the dark fields. There were no lights anywhere. They had said good-bye to all the others and turned off on this dark dirt road. They were almost home.

> *I stepped in the river at Jordan,*
> *The water came over my head,*
> *I looked way over to the other side,*
> *He was making up my dying bed!*

"I guess they singing for him," his father said, seeming very weary and subdued now. "Even when they're sad, they sound like they just about to go and tear off a piece." He yawned and leaned across the boy and slapped his wife lightly on the shoulder, allowing his hand to rest there for a moment. "Don't they?"

"Don't talk that way," she said.

"Well, that's what we going to do," he said, "you can make up your mind to that." He started whistling. "You see? When I begin to feel it, I gets kind of musical, too."

> *Oh, Lord! Come on and ease my troubling mind*

He had a black friend, his age, eight, who lived nearby. His name was Otis. They wrestled together in the dirt. Now the thought of Otis made him sick. He began to shiver. His mother put her arm around him.

"He's tired," she said.

"We'll be home soon," said his father. He began to whistle again.

"We didn't see Otis this morning," Jesse said. He did not know why he said this. His voice, in the darkness of the car, sounded small and accusing.

"You haven't seen Otis for a couple of mornings," his mother said.

That was true. But he was only concerned about *this* morning.

"No," said his father, "I reckon Otis's folks was afraid to let him show himself this morning."

"But Otis didn't do nothing!" Now his voice sounded questioning.

"Otis *can't* do nothing," said his father, "he's too little." The car lights picked up their wooden house, which now solemnly approached them, the lights falling around it like yellow dust. Their dog, chained to a tree, began to bark.

"We just want to make sure Otis *don't* do nothing," said his father, and stopped the car. He looked down at Jesse. "And you tell him what your Daddy said, you hear?"

"Yes sir," he said.

His father switched off the lights. The dog moaned and pranced, but they ignored him and went inside. He could not sleep. He lay awake, hearing the night sounds, the dog yawning and moaning outside, the sawing of the crickets, the cry of the owl, dogs barking far away, then no sounds at all, just the heavy, endless buzzing of the night. The darkness pressed on his eyelids like a scratchy blanket. He turned, he turned again. He wanted to call his mother, but he knew his father would not like this. He was terribly afraid. Then he heard his father's voice in the other room, low, with a joke in it; but this did not help him, it frightened him more, he knew what was going to happen. He put his head under the blanket, then pushed his head out again, for fear, staring at the dark window. He heard his mother's moan, his father's sigh; he gritted his teeth. Then their bed began to rock. His father's breathing seemed to fill the world.

That morning, before the sun had gathered all its strength, men and women, some flushed and some pale with excitement, came with news. Jesse's father seemed to know what the news was before the first jalopy stopped in the yard, and he ran out, crying, "They got him, then? They got him?"

The first jalopy held eight people, three men and two women and three children. The children were sitting on the laps of the grown-ups. Jesse knew two of them, the two boys; they shyly and uncomfortably greeted each other. He did not know the girl.

"Yes, they got him," said one of the women, the older one,

who wore a wide hat and a fancy, faded blue dress. "They found him early this morning."

"How far had he got?" Jesse's father asked.

"He hadn't got no further than Harkness," one of the men said. "Look like he got lost up there in all them trees—or maybe he just got so scared he couldn't move." They all laughed.

"Yes, and you know it's near a graveyard, too," said the younger woman, and they laughed again.

"Is that where they got him now?" asked Jesse's father.

By this time there were three cars piled behind the first one, with everyone looking excited and shining, and Jesse noticed that they were carrying food. It was like a Fourth of July picnic.

"Yeah, that's where he is," said one of the men, "declare, Jesse, you going to keep us here all day long, answering your damn fool questions. Come on, we ain't got no time to waste."

"Don't bother putting up no food," cried a woman from one of the other cars, "we got enough. Just come on."

"Why, thank you," said Jesse's father, "we be right along, then."

"I better get a sweater for the boy," said his mother, "in case it turns cold."

Jesse watched his mother's thin legs cross the yard. He knew that she also wanted to comb her hair a little and maybe put on a better dress, the dress she wore to church. His father guessed this, too, for he yelled behind her, "Now don't you go trying to turn yourself into no movie star. You just come on." But he laughed as he said this, and winked at the men; his wife was younger and prettier than most of the other women. He clapped Jesse on the head and started pulling him toward the car. "You all go on," he said, "I'll be right behind you. Jesse, you go tie up that there dog while I get this car started."

The cars sputtered and coughed and shook; the caravan began to move; bright dust filled the air. As soon as he was tied up, the dog began to bark. Jesse's mother came out of the house, carrying a jacket for his father and a sweater for Jesse. She had put a ribbon in her hair and had an old shawl around her shoulders.

"Put these in the car, son," she said, and handed everything to him. She bent down and stroked the dog, looked to see if there was water in his bowl, then went back up the three porch steps and closed the door.

"Come on," said his father, "ain't nothing in there for nobody to steal." He was sitting in the car, which trembled and belched. The last car of the caravan had disappeared but the sound of singing floated behind them.

Jesse got into the car, sitting close to his father, loving the smell of the car, and the trembling, and the bright day, and the sense of going on a great and unexpected journey. His mother got in and closed the door and the car began to move. Not until then did he ask, "Where are we going? Are we going on a picnic?"

He had a feeling that he knew where they were going, but he was not sure.

"That's right," his father said, "we're going on a picnic. You won't ever forget *this* picnic—!"

"Are we," he asked, after a moment, "going to see the bad nigger—the one that knocked down old Miss Standish?"

"Well, I reckon," said his mother, "that we *might* see him."

He started to ask, *Will a lot of niggers be there? Will Otis be there?*—but he did not ask his question, to which, in a strange and uncomfortable way, he already knew the answer. Their friends, in the other cars, stretched up the road as far as he could see; other cars had joined them; there were cars behind them. They were singing. The sun seemed, suddenly very hot, and he was, at once very happy and a little afraid. He did not quite understand what was happening, and he did not know what to ask—he had no one to ask. He had grown accustomed, for the solution of such mysteries, to go to Otis. He felt that Otis knew everything. But he could not ask Otis about this. Anyway, he had not seen Otis for two days; he had not seen a black face anywhere for more than two days; and he now realized, as they began chugging up the long hill which eventually led to Harkness, that there were no black faces on the road this morning, no black people anywhere. From the houses in which they lived, all along the road, no smoke curled, no life stirred—maybe one or two chickens were to be seen, that was all. There was no one at the windows, no one in the yard, no one sitting on the porches, and the doors were closed. He had come this road many a time and seen women washing in the yard (there were no clothes on the clothes-lines) men working in the fields, children playing in the dust; black men passed them on the road other mornings, other days, on foot, or in wagons, sometimes in cars, tipping their hats, smiling, joking, their teeth a solid white against their skin, their eyes as warm as the sun, the blackness of their skin like dull fire against the white of the blue or the grey of their torn clothes. They passed the nigger church—dead-white, desolate, locked up; and the graveyard, where no one knelt or walked, and he saw no flowers. He wanted to ask, *Where are they? Where are they all?* But he did not dare. As the hill grew steeper, the sun grew colder. He looked at his mother and his father. They looked straight ahead, seeming to be listening to the singing which echoed and echoed in this graveyard silence. They were strangers to him now. They were looking at something he could not see. His father's lips had a strange, cruel curve, he wet his lips from time to time, and swallowed. He was terribly aware of his father's tongue, it was as though he had never seen it before. And his father's body suddenly seemed immense, bigger than a mountain. His eyes, which were grey-green, looked yellow in the sunlight; or at least there was a light in them which he had never seen before. His mother patted her hair and adjusted the ribbon, leaning forward to look into the car mirror. "You look all right," said his father, and laughed. "When that nigger looks at you, he's going to swear he throwed his life away for nothing. Wouldn't be surprised if he don't come back to haunt you." And he laughed again.

The singing now slowly began to cease; and he realized that they were nearing their destination. They had reached a straight, narrow, pebbly road, with trees on either side. The sunlight filtered down on them from a great height, as though they were under-water; and the branches of the trees scraped against the cars with a tearing sound. To the right of them, and beneath them, invisible now, lay the town; and to the left, miles of trees which led to the high mountain range which his ancestors had crossed in order to settle in this valley. Now, all was silent, except for the bumping of the tires against the rocky road, the sputtering of motors, and the sound of a crying child. And they seemed to move more slowly. They were beginning to climb again. He watched the cars ahead as they toiled patiently upward, disappearing into the sunlight of the clearing. Presently, he felt their vehicle also rise, heard his father's changed breathing, the sunlight hit his face, the trees moved away from them, and they were there. As their car crossed the clearing, he looked around. There seemed to be millions, there were certainly hundreds of people in the clearing, staring toward something he could not see. There was a fire. He could not see the flames, but he smelled the smoke. Then they were on the other side of the clearing, among the trees again. His father drove off the road and parked the car behind a great many other cars. He looked down at Jesse.

"You all right?" he asked.

"Yes sir," he said.

"Well, come on, then," his father said. He reached over and opened the door on his mother's side. His mother stepped out first. They followed her into the clearing. At first he was aware only of confusion, of his mother and father greeting and being greeted, himself being handled, hugged, and patted, and told how much he had grown. The wind blew the smoke from the fire across the clearing into his eyes and nose. He could not see over the backs of the people in front of him. The sounds of laughing and cursing and wrath—and something else—rolled in waves from the front of the mob to the back. Those in front expressed their delight at what they saw, and this delight rolled backward, wave upon wave, across the clearing, more acrid than the smoke. His father reached down suddenly and sat Jesse on his shoulders.

Now he saw the fire—of twigs and boxes, piled high; flames made pale orange and yellow and thin as a veil under the steadier light of the sun; grey-blue smoke rolled upward and poured over their heads. Beyond the shifting curtain of fire and smoke, he made out first only a length of gleaming chain, attached to a great limb of the tree; then he saw that this chain bound two black hands together at the wrist, dirty yellow palm facing dirty yellow palm. The smoke poured up; the hands dropped out of sight; a cry went up from the crowd. Then the hands slowly came into view again, pulled upward by the chain. This time he saw the kinky, sweating, bloody head—he had never before seen a head with so much hair on it, hair so black and so tangled that it seemed like another jungle. The head was hanging. He saw the forehead, flat and high, with a kind of arrow of hair in the center, like he had, like his father had; they called it a widow's peak; and the mangled eye brows, the wide nose, the closed eyes, and the glinting eye lashes and the hanging lips, all streaming with blood and sweat. His hands were straight above his head. All his weight pulled downward from his hands; and he was a big man, a bigger man than his father, and black as an African jungle Cat, and naked. Jesse pulled upward; his father's hands held him firmly by the ankles. He wanted to say something, he did not know what, but nothing he said could have been heard, for now the crowd roared again as a man stepped forward and put more wood on the fire. The flames leapt up. He thought he heard the hanging man scream, but he was not sure. Sweat was pouring from the hair in his armpits, poured down his sides, over his chest, into his navel and his groin. He was lowered again; he was raised again. Now Jesse knew that he heard him scream. The head went back, the mouth wide open, blood bubbling from the mouth; the veins of the neck jumped out; Jesse clung to his father's neck in terror as the cry rolled over the crowd. The cry of all the people rose to answer the dying man's cry. He wanted death to come quickly. They wanted to make death wait: and it was they who held death, now, on a leash which they lengthened little by little. *What did he do?* Jesse wondered. *What did the man do? What did he do?*—but he could not ask his father. He was seated on his father's shoulders, but his father was far away. There were two older men, friends of his father's, raising and lowering the chain; everyone, indiscriminately, seemed to be responsible for the fire. There was no hair left on the nigger's privates, and the eyes, now, were wide open, as white as the eyes of a clown or a doll. The smoke now carried a terrible odor across the clearing, the odor of something burning which was both sweet and rotten.

He turned his head a little and saw the field of faces. He watched his mother's face. Her eyes were very bright, her mouth was open: she was more beautiful than he had ever seen her, and more strange. He began to feel a joy he had never felt before. He watched the hanging, gleaming body, the most beautiful and terrible object he had ever seen till then. One of his father's friends reached up and in his hands he held a knife: and Jesse wished that he had been that man. It was a long, bright knife and the sun seemed to catch it, to play with it, to caress it—it was brighter than the fire. And a wave of laughter swept the crowd. Jesse felt his father's hands on his ankles slip and tighten. The man with the knife walked toward the crowd, smiling slightly; as though this were a signal, silence fell; he heard his mother cough. Then the man with the knife walked up to the hanging body. He turned and smiled again. Now there was a silence all over the field. The hanging head looked up. It seemed fully conscious now, as though the fire had burned out terror and pain. The man with the knife took the nigger's privates in his hand, one hand, still smiling, as though he were weighing them. In the cradle of the one white hand, the nigger's privates seemed as remote as meat being weighed in the scales; but seemed heavier, too, much heavier, and Jesse felt his scrotum tighten; and huge, huge, much bigger than his father's, flaccid, hairless, the largest thing he had ever seen till then, and the blackest. The white hand stretched them, cradled them, caressed them. Then the dying man's eyes looked straight into Jesse's eyes—it could not have been as long as a second, but it seemed longer than a year. Then Jesse screamed, and the crowd screamed as the knife flashed, first up, then down, cutting the dreadful thing away, and the blood came roaring down. Then the crowd rushed forward, tearing at the body with their hands, with knives, with rocks, with stones, howling and cursing. Jesse's head, of its own weight, fell downward toward his father's head. Someone stepped forward and drenched the body with kerosene. Where the man had been, a great sheet of flame appeared. Jesse's father lowered him to the ground.

"Well, I told you," said his father, "you wasn't never going to forget *this* picnic." His father's face was full of sweat, his eyes were very peaceful. At that moment Jesse loved his father more than he had ever loved him. He felt that his father had carried him through a mighty test, had revealed to him a great secret which would be the key to his life forever.

"I reckon," he said. "I reckon."

Jesse's father took him by the hand and, with his mother a little behind them, talking and laughing with the other women, they walked through the crowd, across the clearing. The black body was on the ground, the chain which had held it was being rolled up by one of his father's friends. Whatever the fire had left undone, the hands and the knives and the stones of the people had accomplished. The head was caved in, one eye was torn out, one ear was hanging. But one had to look carefully to realize this, for it was, now, merely, a black charred object on the black, charred ground. He lay spread-eagled with what had been a wound between what had been his legs.

"They going to leave him here, then?" Jesse whispered.

"Yeah," said his father, "they'll come and get him by and by. I reckon we better get over there and get some of that food before it's all gone."

"I reckon," he muttered now to himself, "I reckon." Grace stirred and touched him on the thigh: the moonlight covered her like glory. Something bubbled up in him, his nature again returned to him. He thought of the boy in the cell; he thought of the man in the fire; he thought of the knife and grabbed himself and stroked himself and a terrible sound, something between a high laugh and a howl, came out of him and dragged his sleeping wife up on one elbow. She stared at him in a moonlight which had now grown cold as ice. He thought of the morning and grabbed her, laughing and crying, crying and laughing, and he whispered, as he stroked her, as he took her, "Come on, sugar, I'm going to do you like a nigger, just like a nigger, come on, sugar, and love me just like you'd love a nigger." He thought of the morning as he labored and she moaned, thought of morning as he labored harder than he ever had before, and before his labors had ended, he heard the first cock crow and the dogs begin to bark, and the sound of tires on the gravel road.

August Strindberg

Late nineteenth century European literature is remarkable for a number of reasons, not the least of which is the number of authors who led tormented, obsessed lives that they reflected in their works. Charles Baudelaire, Arthur Rimbaud, Gerard de Nerval, and a host of others expressed their anguish, frustration, deprivation, and suffering in works that seared even as they shaped the prevailing sensibility of the modern world. It is in this company that August Strindberg (1849–1912) belongs as one of its most notable figures. His plays and novels run the gamut from naturalism to expressionism and relentlessly probe the dark side of man's mind and the twisted ambivalence of human motives.

Strindberg was born in Stockholm to Swedish parents of divergent social classes who were totally indifferent to the welfare of any of their twelve children. His life as a child both at home and in school was a nightmare of fear, poverty, neglect, and religious obsessions. Efforts to support himself and to find a satisfactory life led him into a number of abortive occupations: lay preacher, tutor, university student, drunkard, medical student, painter, journalist, and telegraph operator. He married three times—in 1877, 1891, and 1901— and had six children, each marriage ending in divorce. The dominant reason for this was Strindberg's towering cruelty, which manifested itself in unrelenting and perversely ingenious sadism and masochism. As time went on, his obsessions deepened into paranoia and he experienced mental illness of such seriousness that for certain periods (especially 1895– 1898) he could not be considered sane. During much of his life he lived on the fringes of vagrancy and wandered throughout Europe virtually destitute despite his ever-growing fame as an author. His career was a recital of contradictory interests and attitudes. He was at various times a rationalist and a religious enthusiast, a socialist and a reactionary, a philosophical naturalist and a dabbler in alchemy, the occult, and magic. Throughout it all he clung to his contemptuous hatred of others. At the end of his life, therefore, when the Swedish nation made a national celebration of his birthday, he derided it and rejected the idea of a Nobel Prize. His death was the result of cancer.

With an author so prolific and mercurial as Strindberg it is virtually impossible in a brief space to indicate the range and character of his achievement. Though his greatest fame came perhaps as a dramatist, it was his novel The Red Room *(1879) that first established his reputation. In this first phase of his career he utilized his own experiences to portray the horrors perpetrated on individuals by inhuman social concepts and institutions. He went on to render these experiences most memorably in his great realistic or naturalistic plays of the 1890's such as* The Father, The Stronger, *and most notably* Miss Julie. *Together with Henrik Ibsen, the Norwegian dramatist, Strindberg was responsible for the frightening revelation of the subtleties of torment and repression inflicted by society on the individual and of the latter's determined efforts to achieve personal freedom.*

Later in the decade Strindberg's collapse (the so-called "Inferno Period") marked his transition from realistic to expressionistic techniques, particularly in the theater. Important influences in this phase of his writing were the French novelist Honoré Balzac and the Swedish religious thinker Emmanuel Swedenborg. Both encouraged through their works his interest in alchemy and spiritualist topics. The result was a greater concern with symbolic perspectives and hallucinatory states of mind, which he expressed in the innovative dramas of his last years, such as A Dream Play, Easter, *and* The Ghost Sonata. *To ensure their production he founded his own theater, but after three years abandoned the effort because of financial failure and growing disillusionment with the theater as an artistic medium. Instead he was once again strongly attracted to the novel since, as he observed, "it permits one to explain himself, interpret individuals, see them within, to their foundations." The result was* The Scapegoat, *which he completed in 1906 and which marked the conclusion of his career as a novelist.*

A *convenient and readable account of Strindberg's life is* Elizabeth Sprigge's The Strange Life of August Strindberg (*1940*). *A somewhat fuller and still useful critical biography that relates his works to his life is V. J. McGill's* August Strindberg, The Bedeviled Viking (*1930*). *The most extended criticism in English of* The Scapegoat *itself is in E. O. Johanneson,* The Novels of August Strindberg (*1968*). *Studies that place* The Scapegoat *in relation to the body of his writing are B. M. E. Mortensen and B. W. Downs,* Strindberg: An Introduction to His Life and Works (*1949*) *and the earlier G. A. Campbell,* Strindberg (*1930*).

The Scapegoat

August Strindberg

Translated by Arvid Paulson

To the north of Holaveden, in a hilly mountain region in Sweden, lies a little town far down at the bottom of a valley, shaped like a caldron. The hills surround the town like a ring of walls. Therefore the sun rises later than it should, and descends earlier. However, the wall is not high enough to be oppressive, for it is a safeguard and a protection against the winds, and shuts them out. Thus the weather there is usually calm. The hills are barren, the landscape denuded, but a little brook, edged with alder and reed, flows through the town, so that the inhabitants, whose property faces the little river, can sit in their miniature summerhouses on the jetties and enjoy both flowing water and nature.

In the past the town had been renowned for its health-giving mineral springs; and the pavilion with its memorials to successful cures still stands there, its walls covered with crutches and walking sticks. The water is still as potent as in former days, the apothecary analyzes it regularly every year— but no one takes it, for no one believes any more in its curative power.

Elderly pensioners, widows, and invalids, on the other hand, have discovered the little town without any railroad connection, where they can hide away with their ailments and their pains and prepare themselves for the final journey. Daily they sit on the green benches in the city park, showing no signs of any desire to know one another. Some sit scribbling in the sand with walking sticks or parasols, their noses pointing to the earth, as though they were writing the saga of their lives. Others sit with their eyes lifted toward the sky, looking out over human beings and treetops, as if they had already left this world and were living somewhere beyond this planet. But there are still others who keep indoors and never go out. These sit by the windows, gazing in their reflector mirrors, in which they can see everyone but themselves. These oldsters pore over the newspapers, have social intercourse with one another, and receive visitors. When they read the obituaries they pay close attention to the age of the departed ones. "Heavens, he was eighty, and I am only seventy-two! Well, the truth comes out at last!"

At the big market square are situated the City Tavern, the church, and the Town Hall. The latter houses the rathskeller and the post and telegraph offices; and the police also have their headquarters there. Nearby, the bank is located on the corner of Main Street, next door to the book and stationery shop.

Down by North Street stands a one-story house. It is a very long, broad building, ugly in appearance, with tiny windows and a steep roof. At one end, several steps lead into the public house for the farmers; at the other end are the driveway and entrance gate to the courtyard, in which are stables and outhouses, built for the convenience of the customers from the neighboring farming districts. Through this entranceway the patrons of the public house have to find their way to the basement. This restaurant is second-rate and is frequented by the town's lone clerk of the Magistrate's Court, employees of the post office, teachers and diverse representatives of the middle class who take their meals by the month or get them on credit. The principal attraction of this place, however, exists behind the outhouse building. There lie the garden, the bowling alleys, and the pavilions at the edge of the little river that flows by. In the summertime the place is like a paradise, especially as it boasts a bathhouse at the edge of the brook; while it is not very roomy, it is large enough to accommodate a hungry young man who wishes to rinse off the dust and perspiration before sitting down at table.

The interior of the restaurant does not correspond with its

insignificant exterior. It surpasses it to such a degree that the visitor is truly struck by the neatness and good taste of the decorative arrangements. The main dining room has a distinctive atmosphere in its half-light, displaying long rows of bottles with chains round their necks, antique greenish old rummers and East Indian bowls from the days of the old Swedish East Indian Company, Japanese spice jars, containers, jugs, earthenware, and engraved cups, and goblets of crystal ware with lids. The solid oak counter, with cash drawer and slate, the bracketed candlesticks on the wall, the small side tables, beckoning to two or at most three guests, and standing not too close upon one another—everything favors repose and intimacy. On one side the dining room adjoins the large, expansive glass veranda, on the opposite one the private dining rooms. There are so many of these that three of them have been furnished with pianos, each one of these rooms at a respectable distance from the others. Every such little room has its own distinctive appearance and contributes to its own atmosphere through the color of its curtains, the design of the wallpaper, or through the reproduction of some oil painting hanging in its frame above the sofa. Naturally it is all well smoked and presents the kind of home-like semishabbiness that inclines one to forget the cold, abstract cleanliness.

The establishment was named for the owner and was always called simply Askanius's. In his youth Askanius had traveled the world over as a member of a singing quartet. Endowed with a natural voice, he had sung before the Russian Czar, for the Emperor of Germany, and for a variety of kings. Having saved his money, he finally settled down in his native town, purchased the building, and worked up the restaurant business. He was now considered to be affluent. He was in reality an estimable man, calm, quiet, and sober. He generally gave his orders merely with a glance or a gesture, went about dressed in redingote, seldom drank with his customers, never entered into conversation with anyone except when invited. Most of the time he was seated at the counter, at the end close to the pantry window, through which his wife from time to time would poke her head while the service was in progress. At no time was there any exchange of temperament between them; neither was there, on the other hand, any sign of great friendliness. Everything was done correctly and without coddling or squeamishness. The serving was done by females of uncertain age, no flirtation, no nonsense. The owner was strict but just. When he corrected anyone or anything, it was done without ado. There was a tone of family atmosphere about the establishment, yet the feeling of discipline could be felt in the air, and most of the customers were under obligation to Askanius through credit he had extended to them.

Askanius kept close track of his customers. He knew which of them patronized him only when they were out of funds and would go to the City Café when their pockets were full. Credit was granted merely for the utterance of a single word, but self-assumed credit was abruptly refused. If a customer deserted him for the City Café while his name was still on the slate, he considered it comparable to treason. Yet he would say nothing. He had no desire to compete with the first-class City Café. He never mentioned this restaurant by name; and if anyone tried to get into his good graces by making an uncomplimentary remark about it, he kept quiet, or said something in its favor.

Because of his customers' dependence on him, Askanius had developed a certain attitude of superiority. He tolerated no criticism, whether justified or not. One day, for instance, a German traveling salesman entered the café and ordered a bottle of beer. He was served a bottle and a glass. But he wanted a different type of glass, a *real* glass. None could be found to please him, and when the guest continued to complain, Askanius stepped in. Without any ado, and with an imperial look in his eyes, he whispered to the salesman: "If there is anything wrong with the glass, you may go elsewhere, sir."

Another time a guest complained about the soup. Askanius stepped up to the dissatisfied customer, leaned down over him as if to entrust him with a confidence, and spoke in a whisper: "There is nothing wrong with the soup! I have just had some myself!" The customer never complained again.

Askanius lived with his wife in a small wing in the back of the house. Their three rooms were very handsomely furnished and looked out upon the garden and the little river. There they enjoyed their pleasant moments: the early mornings, the forenoons, and two hours in the afternoon. He would then read out of his beautifully bound books and play the piano. But he never sang. He would show his old lady his medals and diplomas. The medals he prized especially. They meant more than mere orders and such decorations, he declared; any tradesman could get these. And now and then he made a speech about the courts of the Czar and Napoleon III at Versailles.

And Sundays the couple went to church in the forenoon.

Often the old lady asked him when they were going to retire and move to the country.—"When I have all the money I need . . ." he would answer, without giving any further details.

Time and time again the old woman insisted that they close the bar for the farmers because it was noisy and a disturbance; but Askanius voted that down, for the drinking provided his principal income. He looked upon the dining service as a necessary evil. Neither husband nor wife ever visited the disgraceful barroom. It was a sort of blot on their escutcheon, and they shut their eyes to the shame of it and the fact that their gain was illgotten, coming as it did from the booze joint. From time to time there were fights; but Askanius would not go near the place. He merely sent for the police.

As a restaurant man he liked, of course, to see that people ate plenty. But generally he preferred to lose a little rather than to see one of his customers drunk. Once he took it upon himself to enter one of the private dining rooms and give a warning to a gathering of young blades who had imbibed much too freely.—"You should not drink so much," was all he said.—"He is a peculiar one to run a restaurant," was the comment of the youngsters.

That is the way Askanius was. But for all his severity, he was a man of goodwill and charity. He had had a hard time during his childhood and youth; now, when old age was approaching, he patiently looked forward to the time when he could withdraw to the serenity of pastoral life.

One day, at noontime, Askanius was sitting by the counter, grappling with his figures on the slate, daubing and erasing, when an unknown young man in his late twenties or early thirties came in. The stranger had the appearance of being of some sort of foreign birth. One could see he was struggling to hide his embarrassment over his intrusion into a company where all were known to one another. Their curiosity had something of animosity in it, and the stranger was kept waiting behind turned backs, shutting him off from the smörgasbord.

Askanius scrutinized the new customer, observed that his black suit was threadbare and that his footwear were worn at the heels. His face was not one likely to captivate anyone; he had a low forehead, his hair was black and his mustache was curled, and his face had a yellow pallor. It would have been humanly impossible to guess the man's profession.

But the stranger's patience seemed to be superhuman. When he had succeeded in getting hold of a slice of bread at the smörgasbord, he stood and held it in his hand, silently waiting for a chance to advance to the butter, showing not the slightest sign of annoyance. After a long wait one of the attacking kind swiftly retreated a step and trampled on the stranger's foot. Instead of showing anger, he merely smiled a sad smile and gave the offender a few words of comfort: "Why, it's nothing at all!"

The proprietor had followed the scene with keen interest. The stranger did not attract him; yet the sad smile, which affected him just as though the man had been weeping, moved him. Askanius rose, stepped over to the smörgasbord line and, using the technique he had developed to perfection, broke through it without hurt or injury to anyone. Then he took a knife, put some butter on it, and offered it to the hungry one. Overwhelmed by such show of kindliness, the newcomer made a bow, almost too deep a bow, and expressed his thanks.

When the attacking line at last had dwindled, the stranger took his sandwich and his schnapps and went in search of a table, and to scrutinize the menu. This impressed Askanius, and he made the observation that the man was a cultivated gentleman. There was, however, no vacant table. The stranger was about to occupy a chair at one of the tables, but a sharp "The seat is taken" stopped him. The expression on the lonely man's face, as he stood there like an outcast in the center of the room, sandwich in hand, took on such a look of despair that Askanius rose once again and invited the stranger to seat himself at his own private table, directly underneath the clock.

Undoubtedly the proprietor was inquisitive, but he also wanted to give comfort to the lonely one who was condemned to silence. However, he was proud and adhered strictly to the impression that he was a gentleman; and so he kept quiet. Perhaps he remembered a time when he himself was a stranger in some Eastern land. For this reason he conquered his dislike for this countenance which revealed nothing, but, on the other hand, could conceal much.

In the evening that same day, the chief of police was sitting in the large dining room at Askanius's. He was one of the few with whom the proprietor would carry on a conversation over a glass of something or other, when the day's drudgery was over. They were seated underneath the clock, sipping a drink of iced Karlshamn *punsch*, with the crossed flags on the label.

"Well," commenced Askanius, changing the subject under discussion, "you should, of course, know who this newcomer is."

"Oh, that one. . . . Yes, he comes from up north and plans to set himself up here in town as an attorney."

"Ugh!" exclaimed Askanius, "—an attorney, a pettifogger! Until now our town has been preserved from such ilk after I got rid of the last one. You don't remember that rogue, do you? He was a real rascal, I'll tell you. He ate and drank on the credit I gave him, and when I finally took the pains to remind him, he was offended. Then I made a formal demand on him for payment. And what do you think he did? He brought charges against me for unlawful sale of liquor on credit . . ."

"What's that you say?"

"Don't you know the law?" the proprietor quizzed him. He took particular pride in his knowledge of government regulations, especially those that had to do with the sale of liquor.

"Yes, that's right. Anyone serving a customer liquor on credit loses his license. . . . Can you imagine such a wretched character—having fed him for six months! It almost made me lose faith in humanity . . . I came near becoming uncharitable! The only thing that held me back was the remembrance of the many kindnesses people did for me when I was young. Yes, I have had a hard life—a sad childhood . . ."

"So-o . . ." broke in the police chief, "there is such a law, then . . ." paying no attention to the proprietor's sentimental outpourings.

"Don't you believe me?"—and with this, Askanius stretched out his hand and took down a volume of the nation's laws, opened it and promptly proved to the police chief his legal sagacity, after having first adjusted his pince-nez. Whenever he had to read or count, he had to hang his glasses on his nose; they changed his countenance in his favor: his nose took on a more aristocratic shape, the muscles of his face shaped the contours differently, and a look of intelligence, not to say nobility, came upon the man's face.

The police chief's lack of knowledge of the governmental code of laws was richly made up for by his enormous personal information about every character and individual in the community. He was almost all-knowing in the history of the district, its inhabitants, and their goings-on. He knew how much each one of its citizens was worth. With this knowledge he was often able to supply Askanius with valuable information concerning the financial condition of his customers.

"That fellow will never pay you—that one is questionable—that man is dependable; and this scamp belongs in the category that is able to pay, but won't—while this one wants to, but is not always in a position to . . ."

Askanius wanted to learn more about the stranger, with a view to his credit; not that he had asked for any, but because of his personal peculiarities.

"He is an attorney, then—but his father, his family?"

"His father keeps a general store out in the country and is a mess; his elder brother is superintendent of an estate, Torpa, belonging to Count Ecks."

"But the most important thing . . . What is his name?"

"His name is Libotz."

"Libotz. . . . Then he must come from Bohemia or Hungary. . . . He resembles a poor starving musician, come to think of it."

"The name sounds as if it had been adopted. His real name was probably a different one—but he can't be blamed for that. Perhaps his mother was in the circus, or in vaudeville—they are the two that help to blend the races and give birth to his type of cosmopolite. His type never feels at home in our old social order; it's the kind that breeds anarchists and traitors." Here the chief of police stopped short, for he noticed that his host with the Roman name of Askanius began to make faces.

The police chief realized that he had gone astray, and was afraid he would make matters worse if he tried to explain. Luckily a telephone call summoned him to the City Café. Within a half hour he was seated with a new glass of *punsch* before him in the establishment of Askanius's competitor.

Libotz, clerk *pro tempore* of the Circuit Court of Appeals, had previously served in other courts but had realized from the very first that he was lacking in an engaging personality. Unimpeachable, prompt, and able though he was, he found it impossible to gain the confidence of his superiors or fellow jurists. Whether his foreign blood had anything to do with this was a debatable question; perhaps it might rather be attributed to his looks and his appearance, for his destiny was written for all time in his face and figure. He was fated to suffer for himself and for others; and people felt compelled, through some sort of urge or duty, to contribute to the completion of his fate by torturing him. Already in his early days in school he was hacked at by schoolmates and teachers, and when he complained to his parents, he suffered abuse—he, who was the offended one. His long, dark, curly hair served as a constant invitation to hairpulling; and a teacher with blond hair had taken such a hatred to his hair that he could not come near the boy without finding some excuse for mistreating him. The lad never wept. This enraged the teacher still more. One day he came away from the boy with a handful of black hair. As he did not know where to get rid of it, he opened the door to the stove and threw the hair tuft inside. But the wind blew hard that day and swept down through the chimney with a gust so strong that the tuft was blown out again and landed on the floor. Then something very curious happened to the teacher. He disappeared into the boys' coatroom, came out again with eyes showing signs of tears, and then spoke some kind words to the youngster. But a moment later, he tore at the lad's hair again, broke into tears, and left the classroom. He felt *driven* to mistreat this child. Two years later the teacher hanged himself.

The boy must have discovered his fate at an early age, for he soon stopped complaining, became silent and gloomy. His spare time was spent in his father's store, or rather in the storeroom, where he was put to work. His job there was to mix inferior brands with brands of good quality. Coffee, damaged by the sea, had to be disposed of, and therefore it had to be slipped in with the salable goods. Woolen yarn had to be mixed with cotton, snuff with coffee grounds, the poorest grade of cigars was marked at a high price in order to give a better aroma, and so forth. Now and then he was permitted to stand behind the counter, and then he was taught which customers it was safe to cheat, and which not. Counterfeit could always be palmed off on children; and servant girls were to be engaged in pleasant conversation while the scales were being adjusted with the thumb. To give false weight the lad found to be the hardest thing of all. For in the courthouse he had seen the golden scales against a white background, with a bare sword above them, signifying justice. Such was his upbringing.

One day when he had come to realize what a miserable kind of life he was leading, he took a rope and went up to the attic and hanged himself. But he was missed immediately, was discovered and brought back to life. For eight days in succession he was beaten and chastised, and then he was excused from waiting on the customers. He began to study and was graduated from high school; and then things became a little better and brighter. His father decided he was to study law. The law has an attraction for the dishonest. Their liking for it is in proportion to the protection it can give to them against prosecution. And someone has uttered the paradox that he who aspires to be a judge has a certain sympathetic awe for the bench not merely because it is set apart from the benches of the accused, but out of fear of being himself placed in their position.

Edward Libotz became a jurist, practiced in magistrates' courts and circuit courts of appeal; but he did not belong to the right fold. Finally necessity forced him to become a practicing attorney. Out of his small means he rented a couple of rooms, ordered a sign, bought some furniture, and established himself as counselor-at-law in the small, secluded town.

But there still remained something of the father's principles pertaining to doings and dealings; and Libotz exercised a few minor tricks, which in everyday life are looked upon as innocent enough, but are unbecoming to a person devoting his life and career to the defense of justice. Thus he had had his counselor's sign inscribed "Acting Clerk of the Circuit Court of Appeal"—yet he held that position no longer. Therefore he ought to have put *formerly*, etc., instead of *acting*. He used the outer room of the two he had rented and which were on the first floor, for his office. A youth of nineteen, who had formerly been employed at the provincial chancellory, assisted him as law clerk. The first day passed. People would stop and read the sign, and each time Libotz thought it was a prospective client.

"Write," he prodded the youth.

"What shall I write?" asked the lad.

"Make believe you are writing, otherwise they will think we have nothing to do."

The youngster smiled and wrote. It was an innocent trick. But it inculcated in the young man a certain shrewdness; and the attorney was to reap the fruits of his teachings later on.

Not a single client appeared during the whole first week. Libotz was forced to play rich man to his assistant, even though he did not have a penny to spare. He was still able to pay for his dinner, and took his meals at Askanius's. Askanius treated him with a decided chilliness.

Another week passed, and not a visitor. Libotz began to feel anxiety. He went up and down in front of his office and wondered what the reason could be. He thought at last he had found what kept people away. The sign shone like a steel mirror, so that it could only be read from a certain spot on the sidewalk. He had its luster dulled. But even this produced no customers in the third week.

From this time on, he ate no evening meal. He became emaciated, and his face turned yellow as rosin. But when he closed the office at night, and his assistant followed his steps with his eyes, he steered his way toward the City Café and entered the vestibule. There he stood for a while, and then he went for a stroll. He was now down to his last five crowns.

This evening the renowned actor N. from Stockholm was announced to appear in *Attorney Kniving*. This famous artist, who occupied a preeminent position in Stockholm, had never before acted in the provinces. He was unknown in the little town of G. He was greeted, therefore, by a very sparse audience, when Libotz in his dispair went to the theater to seek some sort of distraction. Almost alone on the orchestra floor, he could see how mortified the great actor felt when he discovered the empty seats. It made Libotz ponder the transience of greatness and honor.

But in a loge on the side sat Askanius. His one eye was glued on the stage, the other one on Libotz; and when the misery of an attorney's life was exposed, then he laughed with his face directed toward Libotz. When it came to the scene in which at long last a client appears and attorney Kniving orders his clerks to write like mad, Askanius bellowed with laughter. Libotz, who labored under the impression that this trick had been originated by him, felt as if he were in purgatory. As the play went on and the exposition continued, he felt as if he had been undressed and were sitting there naked.

When the comedy was over, he took a walk past the customs, out into the surrounding countryside. He climbed to the top of the hill in the distance, which had become his favorite place of meditation.

The following day, at noon, Askanius sat at his counter. As he looked in his reflector mirror, he saw Libotz coming up the street toward the restaurant. With his broad knowledge of people, he could at once detect that the sure steps of the approaching customer were trying to cover up for his unsureness; and when the attorney hesitated at the door, turned round, and then started to patrol the street, he was certain that the time for a credit approach had come. At once he prepared his answer, a polite "No, not to persons I don't know," and had it ready. But when the unfortunate man stopped at a lamppost outside, now casting his eyes toward heaven as though pleading for help, now turning them down to earth as if he were looking for a grave, Askanius found himself unable to resist his heart, and changed his mind. He concentrated on the thought that the despairing man would feel that he was welcome.

And, believe it or not, the friendly impulses seemed to have penetrated the windowpane. Libotz straightened up, stepped inside, went directly to the counter, pointed to the slate, and asked with an infinitely sad smile: "May I, Mr. Askanius?"

"Why, certainly, as much as you desire, Mr. Libotz."

Libotz felt an obligation to round out the unpleasant supplication by saying yet another word: "You see, I have had such tremendous expenses getting myself established here. . . ."

"Yes, all beginning is hard, but with courage everything is surmounted . . . Courage only!"

The first thing the attorney did was to take down the innocent circuit appeal court business from the sign. Askanius happened to be passing when the new sign was being put up. The window was open, and Libotz could be seen inside. The restaurant proprietor nodded a friendly greeting and cast an approving glance at the sign as if to say: "You are doing right. That is the way it ought to be."

But still no customers came. At last, at long last, came an old woman. She was wrapped in a shawl that looked like withered leaves and was dressed in a skirt that resembled ash. When Libotz saw her, he did not order his clerk to get busy and write. This was the first lesson he had learned from seeing *Attorney Kniving*.

He asked the woman to be seated and to relate her errand. "Well," she started in, but lost her courage. "You see, I need help, but have no money—no money to pay with . . ."

To Libotz this seemed like mockery. For a moment he felt almost an inclination to invite her to leave, but something held him back. It may have been fear more than compassion; for if anyone was in need of compassion, it was he himself. "What can I help you with, my dear woman?" he asked in his most sympathetic voice.

It concerned a power of attorney for a son in America, and she got it. "All I can give you is thanks. And may your kindness bring you many blessings," said the old woman as she departed.

"It is so little, it isn't worth mentioning. You are very welcome!"

When Libotz came to his eating place later in the day, he noticed that Askanius followed him with his eyes in a peculiar manner. And when luncheon was over, he came up to Libotz and asked him whether he would not care to have a cup of coffee with him down in the garden. This was an exceptional honor, and Libotz accepted the intivation without the slightest objection.

Soon the two gentlemen were seated in one of the pavilions

by the side of the brook, having their coffee and extras. At first Askanius made a few sundry contemplations on life in general, then he passed on to the hardships of life and ended by offering Libotz a generous loan without interest or security.

"In general I don't care for attorneys, when we have judges and courts; but when I see a man struggling honestly and courageously in his chosen profession, I am glad to help him."

The poor attorney wondered what could have so brought him into the good graces of Askanius. He thanked him with a few touching words; and when Askanius answered, he noticed that he used the very same words that he himself had spoken to the old woman.—"It is so little, it isn't worth mentioning. You are very welcome!" Libotz asked himself whether Askanius could have sent the old woman to test him. He could not believe that he had. And he never found the answer.

From that day, however, the wheel of fortune turned in his favor, and clients came. In the beginning it was just one at a time, but soon they came in droves. But Libotz had a fear of luck. He had seen how strictly it was administered and how it could be bought only by sacrifice. Therefore he did not take any kind of case that came his way. He never defended palpable injustice. And when a client pressed him to win a lawsuit, he quickly retorted that this was no play of win or lose, and that he could not bribe the judge. The only thing he could do, he said, was to observe legal procedure and see that the evidence was presented fairly. And if someone came along and suggested a higher fee as an incentive to win a case, he would promptly withdraw from the case with the explanation that he was not to be bought and that he exercised no influence over the judge.

This exceptional conscientiousness made a good impression on the court officials, both in the Magistrate's Court and in the District Court. Libotz also saved the judges considerable work by preparing his cases and questioning the witnesses in advance, and by making a complete inquiry into every phase of the matter in hand. When Libotz refused to act for a litigant or any party to a lawsuit, the court knew at once there was something unsavory about the case. But despite the respect he thus gained, he was a lonely man. No one sought him out or tried to get close to him because of the incomprehensible repulsion he exercised on people. He went his way as if marked by fate, and no one dared touch him. It was as though his fellow beings were afraid of coming under his spell, to have their fate joined with his. He belonged, however, to that group of rare persons who early in life have discovered the secret meaning of life and know which timetable to follow. For this reason he never compared his own lot in life with that of others. Whenever anyone called his attention to some person's undeserved success, he merely replied: "That is their kind of life. And I have *my* way of life." This, of course, was the right manner of avoiding illwill and envy. He had learned how to live his own life. He had learned it by keenly scrutinizing his own experiences in life, even those that seemed inexplicable and which others are in the habit of throwing off, either from laziness or sheer stupidity, labeling them with the word *chance*. As soon as he had realized the connection between events, or the logic of them, no one could persuade him to believe in an illogical or chance happening. Quiet and orderliness became a part of his life; a serene, although sad, submission was coupled with a certain severity toward others. The latter was a direct consequence of his own severity toward himself.

At first he found it difficult to accept the apparently unjust verdicts the courts occasionally rendered. But as he thought of his own dreadful childhood and youth, when he had had to suffer innocently, he would say to the wronged party: "Well, that is something we cannot explain. But I presume it has some sort of meaning."

While in court he had frequently made the observation that as soon as the other party was heard, the halo would disappear from the innocent martyr. The plain truth was that he struck him a blow in the face. But it was still more important to know why he struck him. When a higher court rendered a verdict completely contrary to a decision of a lower court, things seemed pretty bad. But if the minutes of the proceedings were carefully examined and scrutinized, it could be seen that a case was often doubtful, and that it might be interpreted from more than one viewpoint: one could either follow the letter of the law or interpret it humanely. Furthermore, he came across individuals who showed no respect for either rights or justice when their own interests were at stake—yet were constantly screaming out against unrighteousness and injustice. There was one thing that all lawsuits had in common: the plaintiff and the defendant were equally adamant in declaring that there could be no question that justice was on their side. And Libotz thought to himself that justice, like everything else in life, was administered casually, haphazardly: that it had to be done more or less by guesswork.

In order to live he had to take cases for uncollected claims. Such cases placed him in a less agreeable position. People resented it, called him a professional collector, and although he was lenient in his way of going about his task, he nevertheless incurred the quiet hatred that accompanies such a duty as the recovery of money for unpaid debts.

The time passed. Libotz was now out of debt and had money in the bank. In spite of being able to afford it now, he never patronized the City Café, where officials, army officers, and rich farmers held sway. He remained faithful to Askanius. He never became an intimate of the restaurant proprietor, for such a relationship was out of the question as far as Askanius was concerned. But there existed a quiet, respectful understanding between them. Even now Askanius had no genuine feeling for his customer. Yet he was pleased over his show of gratitude, and he thrived on it. Occasionally, when anyone spoke ill of Libotz—and all to whom he was forced to present claims on behalf of clients did so—his countenance froze; but as soon as he himself had to use Libotz to recover payments for an outstanding indebtedness, his face lighted up again. In spite of this, something of disdain remained. He could not help feeling a certain disrespect for a person who performed a job he himself felt to be beneath him.

One evening, at about nine o'clock, Libotz came home to his apartment after his usual frugal dinner. The apartment was fully lighted. As he entered the open door, he was met by a sight that caused him to shudder from head to foot. The room was filled with tobacco smoke. At the big desk sat his father, with his bookkeeping ledgers before him and a bottle of cognac beside him. He greeted the son brutally: "Ugh! There you are at last! I've been looking all over town for you!"

It was the country storekeeper, he who had spent his whole life cheating farming folk, buying and selling spurious wares, palming off counterfeit goods, giving short measure. He had been a success until a year ago, when he bought a cargo of coffee that had been damaged at sea. He had deluged the whole countryside for miles around with this product. Such coffee produces a beverage that smells of sour sweat and tastes of stale vinegar. When people complained, he refused to exchange the spoiled coffee and swore it was first-rate Java. The hatred that had smoldered during the years grew and became like an accumulator discharging itself. The only enjoyment of poor people, and especially of the teetotalers, their beverage had now become unbearably distasteful. The customers came in droves, cursing and spitting at him. The storekeeper, who lacked both shame and conscience and was clever with his tongue, withstood the tempest for a time. But as the storm kept up, he began to languish. He grew emaciated, his face turned yellow. Soon after, he discovered that he had a liver ailment. He had stirred up his customers' bile and now it had come back on him—which, of course, was something he refused to acknowledge. He struggled against the cursing and the scorn and contempt for a year, and then came the final blow at New Year's. A competitor opened a general store with goods that were reputable, and Libotz was dead with one blow.

The once championlike man sat there, a mere yellow shadow of himself. Not only was he emaciated; he had shrunk by half a foot in height. Bitter as bile, base and mean from his very birth, ungrateful and forever looking for gratitude, dishonest and always imputing a lack of honesty to his neighbors, he was not slow in bullying his son into giving him a helping hand—out of filial gratitude, in his hour of need—the son he had once tormented to the point of suicide.

"What is it you wish me to help you with, Father?" asked the son in his softest voice.

"I want you to help me to get out of the attachment of my property and assets."

"Are things as bad as that?"

"The competition is killing me—killing us all!"

The son smiled and had the courage to reply: "But you yourself are a competitor—to the others."

"No! I kept the general store—and then came this competitor, a humbug, who makes the farmers believe he keeps nothing but good stuff. The first thirty days, yes—and then he brings out the substitute stock! Don't fool yourself. . . . There are no decent goods any more anywhere. With all the people in the world to provide with coffee, sugar, tobacco, and so forth, it's only natural that they can't produce enough to give everybody their share. That's why we have to use makeshifts and substitutes, and mixtures. The wholesaler takes care of the mixing, and I sell it. Even the rich man gets coffee that isn't too good; and when some people hit upon the idea to get around this by buying coffee in the bean, they started to sell a substitute. I am not a social-democrat; but nevertheless I think there's a nice thought in this 'equality for all' business —it's real democratic."

The son was unable to follow this national-economical reasoning, and so he asked if he might take a look at his books, and the father said Yes at once.

After an hour's inspection, he realized that his father's position was hopeless, and also dangerous.

"This looks bad. . . . The cash ledger is badly kept; and you have let this thing go much too long. Eight months ago you were in bad shape—it was hopeless already then. . . ."

"Listen to him! You mean I ought to be put behind bars for being a careless debtor. In that case, all debtors should be in jail—for who can tell when to give up hope? . . . You know how luck can turn, you know that! Take yourself, for example! If you had not succeeded, your debts—which you made in anticipation of profits and nothing else—would have brought you to the gallows."

"Yes, but my dear father, your bookkeeping is all wrong. You have entered neither interest nor all your assets."

"Are you saying I've made false entries?" shrieked the old man.

"I am saying your bookkeeping is incorrect. I am sorry—but the courts will call it false."

"The courts, yes. I know the courts. . . . That's why I have come to you. I want you to help me."

The son had a struggle, but his conscience won. He answered: "I can't."

"You are an attorney, aren't you?"

"I cannot do anything dishonest!"

The conversation led to a long debate that lasted until midnight. Then the son suggested in a kindly manner that the father go to the hotel and get himself a room for the night.

"Are you putting me out?" roared the father, who had finished the bottle of cognac.

"No, Father, but I have no place here where you can sleep.

Besides, you would be awakened when my clients come in the morning."

The last reason took effect, and the two went out together.

The streets were fairly empty. Immediately the inebriated father looked for someone to quarrel with. When they had come to the big square and he saw a policeman there, he threw a taunt at him. The constable promptly stepped over to him and led the offender off to the police station.

The atttorney's first impulse was to flee. His very existence depended upon a spotless behavior. But his filial feelings were so strong that he went with the father to police headquarters. He could not very well be a witness against his own father. On the other hand, he could not bear false witness against the arresting constable. He was torn between his feelings, but finally he was saved when the old man became violent and had to be incarcerated.

The only thing the son was able to accomplish was to receive a promise that nothing about the episode would appear in the local newspaper. This over with, he took his nightly walk outside the city and found the mountain, where he was wont to talk with his God. It was a peculiar sight to see this city dweller standing up there on the barren mountain, with a top hat on his head. He bared his head and kept mumbling to himself. Sometimes his words were defiant, complaining, sometimes submissive, resigned. When through, he put his hands in his pockets, paced back and forth as he would sometimes do in his rooms. Then he stopped, started in again, and kept repeating the maneuver, until he finally descended, after having first uncovered his head and made a bow to the Invisible One.

On the way home, it began to rain, and he received the shower as a comforting gift of grace. He let the rain refresh his face like a long-awaited bath.

The following morning the town's lone newspaper carried a news item about the night's happening: Libotz, father and son, intoxicated, coming to blows with the police, and so forth. The son could not, of course, make objections and say that the father alone was inebriated; that would have been to accuse him. Therefore he had to keep his mouth shut and accept his fate without a word in his defense.

"We have to suffer for others," he sighed, "some a little more than others."

When he inquired at the police station, he learned that his father had been fined and let loose. He had not been seen since.

Luncheon time came after a quiet forenoon. The young attorney took the side streets to Askanius's restaurant in order to avoid being pointed out as a police customer. As he entered the dining room, he was met by the proprietor's back and the customers' eyes. The knowledge that he was innocent did not help him; those who were present forced a bad conscience upon him as readily as carbon dioxide takes to the vial. He lost his assurance, became confused like a criminal before the judge. To regain his self-possession, he advanced toward Askanius, attempting to disarm him with a smile. But instead he met a wildly strange countenance, a countenance that tried to make itself unrecognizable.

"What was that?" he asked the attorney, making himself deaf also. His eyes were already blinded; they seemed to be staring far away into the beyond, away from such persons who imbibed too much and yet tried to make others believe that they were sober.

"I merely asked whether my father had been here," repeated the crushed attorney.

"I assume it was he who ate breakfast here with some other men—and was told to leave because of the noise he created."

"May the Lord have mercy. . . . But, of course, I can't be responsible for him. . . . What a pity! What a pity! . . ."

"Certainly it's a pity—it's a pity that one should be so mistaken in people!"

And with this he went toward the pantry window.

The poor counselor lost his appetite and went home hungry.

Of what avail was the position he had gained through sacrifices and drudgery, now that it was all being undermined through someone else's carelessness? What good did it do him constantly to watch his own behavior, to deport himself irreproachably, as long as his fate hung at the mercy of others' opinions? He wondered whether he ought to seek his father at the public bar. But what could he do to instill some sense in such a disorderly and unruly person? It would only make matters worse. Yet if he failed to look out for him, he would be reproached and be called an unnatural son. Thus there was no other way out. . . . "How cruel, how cruel," he repeated to himself. . . . To go to that bar was distasteful to him. Another reason was the innate loathing he felt for the kind of people one met there: men who had no respect for personal feelings and who were always obtrusive and indiscreet in their questions and insinuations. Unquestionably it was, his fate not to be permitted to mingle with the upper strata of society, and at the same time to find it impossible to put up with the lower stratum. He had made the discovery that this was his lot in life. And he suffered from it, for it robbed him of the best in life, social intercourse with his equals.

However, he interrupted his brooding and seated himself at his desk. He dug into his legal papers: everybody complained about everybody else. They had all been done an injustice. There was no end to the accusations, no end to the contentiousness and zeal. If they were not given justice by a lower court, they took their case to a higher court. They would keep their faith right up to the highest court, for *there* were men of *real* intelligence, who would understand them—and who would clearly see that the plaintiff was in the right. It just could not be otherwise in such a clear-cut, self-evident case.

While he was sitting there, the young assistant entered. After reading the morning newspaper, the young man had taken on a different expression on his face, and his shoulders were pushed up. Libotz had kept his assistant at a distance. He had kept him in his place from a natural fear that he might try to worm himself into a partnership, and then find him take over the whole business. The youth had showed himself to be rather familiar during the early days of poverty and insecurity. But after prosperity set in, the attorney had pulled in on the reins; and then the youth seemed to think that he had become overbearing. As an employee, he hated his master, on principle, but when he began to prosper, the hatred became a conscious hatred, striving toward a definite goal. The only thing that kept him in quiet submission was his self-interest, his daily bread and the thought of the future. He knew what he could gain in knowledge here in Libotz's office and through the experience in court. With this in mind, he accepted criticism—in addition to whatever funds he could lay his hands on, and which he hoped would some day help him to take over the reins.

With the advantage of one who is in possession of some unpleasant information, he carelessly threw himself down on his chair; and then, in a tone he tried to make seem indifferent, he uttered: "Now they have sent him back to his own domicile."

"Who?" asked Libotz.

"The old man!"

"You mean my father?"

"Yes!"

The tone used by the youth was a new one: short, superior —but as the fact in itself was something to rejoice over, the attorney overlooked his law clerk's impertinence.

And again quiet came to the peaceful little man, who himself never caused any disturbance, but was always surrounded by the troublesomeness of others.

Although he had passed his first thirty years, Libotz had given no thought to marrying, chiefly because he could not afford to get married. Opportunities to meet a girl to his liking were lacking, to boot, for he was never invited to any home, and he never went away to any bathing resort. Therefore it might be suspected that he would some day attach himself to whoever happened along. It so happened that Askanius's waitresses had more of a reputation for their staid behavior than for their beauty. It was among them—his only contact with the opposite sex—that he had to choose. Karin was a brownish blonde, and her place was in the basement grill. There was nothing attractive about her exterior, but her manner was modest and homey and gave the impression that she was of a domestic nature. When Libotz started to frequent Askanius's restaurant, he never gave her a glance. But one day, as he was paying his check, he noticed the friendliness in her voice. He exchanged a few words with her in order to listen to it. After this episode he began to follow her with his eyes. He measured her figure with his eye, erased here and retouched there. He straightened a sag; and where a line was too straight, he gave it a sweep or a curve. The expression in her eyes secreted certain inequities, and her glances made him forget their lack of color and brightness. In time, he had remodeled her whole slim figure, repainted her complexion, given her hair a new shade of tint, and converted her into a new original of his own.

The girl, who was kindhearted, had at first merely felt compassion for the outcast. She was anything but proud of the attention he gave her. At times she felt offended when he accepted her pity as sympathy; and then she would withdraw for a time. But Libotz, who had had no experience in this territory, still nourished the oldfashioned idea that women were full of artifice and that they had the ability to hide their feelings. Therefore he did not believe that her temporarily retiring manner was merely coquetry.

Her frank, unafraid intimacy, however, stemming actually from his harmlessness, acted upon him as a definite advance. And he began to approach her step by step. One day he had the notion to show her that he was more polite than the other patrons and that he knew how to value the service he received. Thus he doubled the customary tip of the tavern's habitués and placed it on the table after dinner. Karin failed to grasp its import and pushed back one of the coins, briefly commenting that *one* was enough.

Libotz took a walk beyond the city boundaries and felt ashamed. He could not account to himself for his behavior, could not defend his lack of taste. He had committed a stupidity. He always acted stupidly with women.

The following noon he looked so shamefaced that Karin bestowed on him an even greater portion of friendly words than usual. He tried his luck with flowers on her birthday. This time he seemed to have better luck. It was an offering of something of seemingly no value—an object one could not buy something with.

At last Libotz discovered a common interest that could bring them closer together and create a bond between them. Prolonged conversations were not looked upon with favor at the tavern. Karin liked to take long walks, and naturally she preferred to have someone in company when she went outside the city walls, rather than to go by herself. There was always the danger that she might be subjected to attentions from rude and unruly men. She had set aside Sunday mornings for this pastime; and in order not to give cause for gossip, they would mcct outside the customs. Karin arrived, neat and trim, and they set out on their promenade into the spring landscape. The conversation ran smoothly, for there were now no interruptions by any orders from host or guests. Libotz trotted along on the bias in order to be able to look his object in the face. This made his walk seem ludicrous, his speech became choppy, and his figure bent. Karin resisted effectively his every outburst of warmth with light-hearted skepticism; and—that she might properly accentuate the distance between them—she jestingly called him "Uncle."

"Am I so old then?" complained the timid man.

"I haven't thought about your age," answered the girl, dismissing him.

They continued their way, setting their course for Mount Tabor. But this was exactly where Libotz did not wish to go in company with anyone, not even with her. It was there he had suffered his moments of despair, it was there he had wrestled with God and pleaded for strength to bear his heavy fate. He sought to bar her from the path, but she was determined that this was where they should go, and nowhere else. To give in to her desire was, of course, the quickest way to gain her favor—and so he let her have her will.

Libotz's conversation was now aimed at making her displeased with her position at the tavern in order that he afterward might open up the perspective of freedom and independence for her in marriage.

"Don't you find it a little unpleasant to have to breathe all this smell from the cooking into your lungs, day in and day out, without ever getting a chance to sit down?" he asked with a definite expectation that the answer would be Yes.

"No, I don't," replied Karin. "Work brings its own happiness, and, besides, I get my living from it, don't I?"

"Well, but to be one's own master . . . isn't that something to strive after, don't you think?"

"One's own master? Do you really think one can ever be that?" And having said that, she began to sing, jumping over the ditches, and to pick flowers.

All the technique the attorney could master in his attempt to discover some mutual, sympathetic interest was soon at an end; the only thing he found that they had in common was hiking.

Yet Libotz's cleverness to seek out the most dangerous subjects was extraordinary. While resting at the side of the roadway, he commenced to talk about his brother's marriage, and how his wife had gradually learned to become a good housekeeper.

"You see, Miss Karin, there must be order in a marriage, else there will be trouble. When my brother was first married, they had their difficulties. Once, when my sister-in-law complained to me about her husband's bad temper, I told her: 'A bad-tempered husband means a disorderly wife. If you have dinner ready on time, he'll have nothing to upbraid you about.'—And, do you know, Miss Karin, she started to pay attention to the clock, and Adolf lost his bad temper. Now, don't you think that's the way it should be?"

Karin had opened her eyes wide. Then she started to blow with her nostrils like a seal, trying to emit her laughter that way, but the safety valves were not sufficient, and an explosion resulted. Poor Libotz joined in the laughter. At first he did not understand why she broke out like this, but then he suddenly understood. He looked as though he were weeping.

"What were you laughing at, Karin?" he asked at long last—but then she broke out again.

"Did I say something stupid?" . . . and this only made the situation worse.

But this laugh of hers over her silent mental reservations frightened the goodnatured man. He shrank into himself with a feeling that she was false, and his enemy.

In the same breath that he had regained his balance and become reserved, he had won back his dignity. This made a definitive impression on the girl. It commanded her respect. She felt the distance between them and was anxious to diminish it through a new approach. But Libotz remained cool toward her; not in an unfriendly manner—he just buttoned himself up. When they finally reached the mountain, he turned gloomy, took on an air of superiority, spoke darkly of the fate of mankind and the cruel laws of life—laws that were a riddle to all. Karin could not help admiring him; she had never seen the little man like this before. The silly face and stupid smile that a man always presents to a woman when he wishes to make a favorable impression on her were all that she had seen of him hitherto. She had never seen him at his work, or in action before the court.

They were now walking on the flat mountaintop, where Libotz had worn a path through moss and lichen. He recalled the gloomy nights he had tramped there, calling upon heaven for help to bear his wretched fate. For a moment he bared his head, walked a distance away by himself and meditated. He felt again the adverse power that governed his life, sensed ominously new sufferings, greater than any of the past, prayed that he might be spared this cup—yet without any hope. All this was over in a few seconds; and then, again himself, he turned to Karin.

"Now we are going home!" he said. "But by another way— I don't like to retrace my steps. . . ."

He sometimes forgot that Karin's educational level differed from his own. Now and then he would unintentionally slip in some foreign word or phrase. But she never demanded that he explain or translate. On the contrary, she acted as though she understood. True, she would occasionally laugh in the wrong place, in the belief that the foreign words concealed some amusing quip which it was impossible to express in their own native language.

From the mountain they could see the church steeples in the city; and setting his sights for these, he started the homeward march with a commanding: "Forward!"

Their route took them across ditches and roadsides, fallows and meadows. Karin did not wish to fall behind, so she kept pace with him.

But when they came to a field covered with tall heather and brushwood she became afraid of snakes and slowed down.

"You were not brought up in the country, I can see. There are no snakes here."

She admired such courage more than anything else, and treading in his footsteps, she felt secure.

They reached an enclosure where cattle were grazing. Again she became fainthearted. Libotz, however, gave the command: "Follow me!" and with a stick he had picked up on the ground, he passed clear through the herd. The cows soon returned, however, after having separated, gazing at the invaders with curiosity.

"The bull!" screamed Karin—but this time it was Libotz's turn to break into laughter, for there wasn't a male in the herd.

However, when the inquisitive cows began to do a dance

round them, Karin flew straight to the attorney and threw her arms around his neck. "Be quiet, my child," he said, "there is nothing to be afraid of! Be calm! Be calm!"

This was the moment the young lover should have used to offer aid and support for all life. But the opportunity came too suddenly; besides, his desire was to win what to him was an invaluable prize, by slow means. When they suddenly came upon a marsh, Karin was quick to suggest a detour. But the lover refused to yield; he now wished to enjoy his triumph to the last trickle.

"Never give in!" he said, and with this he took the maiden in his arms, like an infant, and ran across the hillocks.

Now he could have asked for a kiss, or he could have stolen one, but he was timid. He wanted to see the fruit ripen on the branch and then fall in his lap.

At the customs gate Libotz took a polite farewell of her.

Hat in hand, he declared he did not wish to compromise her by escorting her into the city. Karin did not know the meaning of the word *compromise*, but sensed nevertheless that he meant something for her own good.

When Libotz was left alone, he felt stronger and more tranquil than usual. He knew that he had come a good way on the road, but regretted that he had not kissed her. That was how certain he was about her feelings now.

"How comical," he said to himself. "The episode with the cows seemed to impress her most. Yes, city children and women—they are in a class by themselves. . . ."

In the afternoon he attended vesper service, and when he greeted Karin there, it was with a nod, as though they were old intimates.

But in the evening, when he had his dinner at Askanius's, he missed her. In his present courageous state of mind, he took the liberty to inquire of the proprietor where Karin was.

After a slight hesitation, the reply came: "She has gone to the theater."

"You don't say, is that where she is?"

And then Askanius bent over toward him and whispered in his discreet manner: "It is not nice to play with a girl's feelings."

"I am not playing!" Libotz burst out with fire in his eyes and in a voice that Askanius had never heard before. This was the first time that the man, the lover, confident of his own strength, had spoken; and Askanius turned pale and drew back. He was evidently impressed.

Libotz immediately felt sorry. For it was not his habit to snap at people. But when he noticed that the proprietor neither showed anger nor hurt but rather became increasingly polite, he meditated with sorrow:

"How strange people are. . . . One has to beat and bite them before they show any friendliness! It's really sad, isn't it?—And I just can't do such things. . . ."

After dinner Askanius asked Libotz if he would like to have a little drink with him down in the beach pavilion . . . he thought it was a long time since they had gotten together for a chat; and the chief of police—who also served as public prosecutor—was expected to join them a little later. . . . No, Libotz had no objection; and not long after, they were seated in the "confidential," as the pavilion was commonly called. Following a prelude, Askanius came to his theme song:

"You see, Mr. Libotz, to take a little drink—there is nothing wrong with that. . . . But to get drunk . . ."

"Now, just a moment. . . . I have never taken a drink too much. . . . All that is nothing but calumny and slander!" Libotz clipped him off promptly, fortified by his newly gained self-esteem.

The restaurant proprietor belonged in that category of persons who can never be corrected, or even accept a piece of information or advice, if they have already made up their mind about anything.

"May I . . ." he broke in, "may I finish what I have to say? . . ."

When Libotz growled, he was again interrupted by gentleman Askanius. "May I . . . may I be permitted to . . ."

He was permitted; and Libotz gave his permission by turning one cold shoulder to him.

"And it is our duty as human beings to forget . . . I have forgotten! Here is to your health, Mr. Libotz!"

Libotz let his glass stand.

"But," continued Askanius, "having committed an offense, and being in need of indulgence—and we all need that—one must not think that . . . that . . ."—and here he suddenly shifted key and went into an *accelerando*—" that it—is—so—

damned—easy—to get—away—from—such—an—incident"—
here he went over into a four-four measure—"which always
has its unavoidable consequences. . . . You see, Mr.
Libotz, humanity is like a piece of fabric, with thread woven into
thread; and if you pull the woof, the warp becomes twisted.
—I don't want to say that your misbehavior . . ."

"I have not misbehaved. I just happened to be with my poor
father, who was drunk . . ." Libotz broke in.

". . . that your misbehavior cannot be excused, far from
that, but its consequences can nonetheless be incalculable.
—The fact is this, namely, that I have a friend who is a bookkeeper on the estate of the Count, for whom your brother
manages the farm. A good name is always a security, but if
your name becomes stained . . . may I—may I . . . !—Well,
now it so happens that the Count has been unpleasantly
affected by this recent police business. He has, so to speak,
taken a kind of rancor toward the name of Libotz, because of
the way it has figured in the newspapers . . . may I finish!
—He now harbors a certain suspicion that his manager may
not be entirely reliable and trustworthy. . . . This is what my
friend writes me—yes, you must not be offended! In a word,
the Count now demands that his manager be bonded, or he
will have to lose his position."

"Why didn't he write to me, who am closest to him?"

"Well, that's another question . . ."

"I know he lost his respect for me when I became an attorney. While I was a circuit appeal court clerk, and he was
a mere bookkeeper in the estate office, then he bragged and
brayed about his brother the appeal court clerk continuously.
But as soon as I became a 'shyster lawyer,' he had to pay for
his past vainglorious boastfulness."

"But, Mr. Libotz, don't you find it only natural that a person
should take pride in his relatives' advancement?"

This was something that had not occurred to the attorney.
But now at once he found it to be quite natural. So he released
his pathos in the *punsch* glass and swallowed it with his drink
in one swoop.

"But where will he get security from?" he reiterated after
a pause the length of a half measure.

"Well, that's something that . . ." Askanius broke in.

"The Count would object to my name on the paper . . ."

"Oh, I don't think so—so long as you are financially sound. The affair with the police has nothing to do with money matters."

"Mr. Askanius, for the last time—on my word of honor—I assure you I was innocent."

"Oh, you mustn't take it so to heart . . . I don't think that a drink or two . . ."

"I was not intoxicated! I was not . . ."

"For heaven's sake, don't get so excited! . . . There are people sitting right near us. . . . But a person should never take more than he can hold. . . ."

"In any case, my brother must pay for his father's sins, and I have to atone for both. . . ."

"Yes, one can never be too careful in one's personal conduct. You, Mr. Libotz, especially. A man in your position owes it to himself to think twice—I mean that any man who can't stand taking a drink, ought to drink less than someone who can. There are people who can stand any amount. Let them drink—it's nobody's business—nobody else's concern. . . . What does it matter to you or to me? Why should we worry . . ."

Unfortunately Askanius belonged to the sort of people that can't stand much. After two glasses he was already on his way—and after the third, he was done for. Once there, he felt inspired to practice oratory. He searched his brain for every synonym in the dictionary, grew sometimes loud and sometimes inaudible, turned himself inside out, rose from out of the graves of centuries past in new and sundry shapes, and at two in the morning came with confessions of illicit doings, that in most cases lead to prison. This was, however, the very reason for Askanius's highly praised sobriety: he just could not drink. And he had a fear of the night, when his heart would open up like a book, and everyone who was able to read could see how he looked inside. This evening he had been seized upon by some demon. He had been denied the opportunity to orate for so terribly long, and now he simply had to get rid of the overflowing accumulation of talkative-ness, stored up in him for months.

Luckily, the police chief–public prosecutor entered at this

very moment, making it necessary for Askanius to recapitulate his first attempt. Libotz had, namely, already grown tired of the accusations and was getting ready to leave.

The chief of police was a man who could withstand anything. His dull "the day after" look was due to the effects of perpetual imbibing. Even after a long night's debauchery, he showed no signs of inebriety. He merely took on the appearance of a piece of statuary. The features were set in a fixed mold: the eyes were frozen, so that neither iris nor pupil could be detected, the tongue was petrified, his mind had ceased to function. This individual had, as the saying goes, no facets to his nature. He was always the same, always dry and always dull, and his personality never varied. In company he conversed by glances and by making faces. He was always attentive, encouraging others to loosen their tongues. Thus he gave the impression of being a sort of hypnotist. He enticed people to unburden themselves, but seldom uttered a word himself. He would merely punctuate with an occasional interjection such as "Exactly!" or "Just what I thought!" or "You hit the nail on the head!"—and "Skoal!"

Askanius admired his police chief, just as he raised all his other boon companions to the rank of nobility—so long as they were his friends and because they were *his* friends. The police chief was a *re-mark*-able man. His knowledge of people was *e-norm*-ous; and as a companion he was *un-sur-passable* —discreet, tactful, and interesting. However, the police chief was in reality nothing of the kind, but Askanius was inclined to exaggerate, and took delight in making over full-grown persons, remolding them to suit his own image of them.

Chief of Police Tjärne was a tall, emaciated person with a head much too small for his body. Created like a snake, it seemed as though he would have no difficulty crawling through any hole if he once managed to slither his head through it. When he rose from his chair to stretch across the table to get a match, it looked as if he crawled through the air. When his long arm swept forward between glasses and bottles without upsetting anything whatsoever, his one concern was to prevent knocking his head against the hanging lamp. This made him twist his head in such a way that his face lay on his back. Otherwise, he was considered to be a handsome man, and he was successful with women. Yet he never boasted about this. He did not even choose to mention it; and this for good reason. In common with his prototype, Don Juan, he found nothing strange in this. He scarcely was conscious of his devastating power. And if he was chided about it, he acted ashamed, as of a weakness. But there was something in his destiny that had brought disharmony into his life. Libotz, who observed everything, had noticed that Tjärne never discussed women, and that whenever divorce or any such irregularity were discussed, he kept a demonstrative silence. He was the son of a former well-known member of the Magistrate's Court, now dead, whose marriage had ended in divorce. He was the image of a certain known army officer; and as a result he was often quite innocently asked whether he was not Baron Platinumcrown. This striking resemblance Tjärne had not become conscious of before he was called to serve his conscription term. His cruel comrades started to call him by the company captain's name. Then a light suddenly went up for him. And he buried his mother's memory forever; but without either accusing or judging. The most desirable inheritance— a birth without stain—he now lacked. Therefore he took to regarding himself early in life as an orphan. They, who knew his hurt, were careful not to allude to it. Having discovered in his young years that a person would be left fairly well alone by people, as long as one left them alone, he avoided any and all temptation to be indiscreet, or to carry on an intimate conversation in company or in public. In his official duties, however, and between four eyes, he did not mince matters. Yet even under such circumstances he displayed a certain timidity, for experience had taught him how demoniacally one can sometimes be led into false conclusions and be thrown off the scent. For this reason he never made any accusations in his reports. His procedure was to "spot" a suspect, leaving it to the judge secretly to examine him before any accusation was made. But he listened willingly. Whenever anyone in company spoke freely, he would sit with mouth wide open and pricked-up ears, and seemingly taking mental notes.

He would spur the gossipy conversationalist on by ejecting detached sputterings of approbation as, for instance, "Just think" and so forth, or by sprinkling the gathering with stray questions. Such questions were always so framed that they concealed the curiosity behind them. He constantly gave the impression that he was interested in everything and every-body, while he himself had ceased to exist.

Askanius received his chief of police like a disciple who had come to hear words of wisdom.

"So-o, you have already had your dinner? Well, then, sit down and have a drink with us. It's a beautiful spring evening, and the crayfish have come into the brook. . . . Soon I shall invite you to a crayfish party, yes, yes. . . ."

The chief of police intercepted with: "Really . . . have they really . . . ?" He didn't bother to complete the sentence, for he knew it would be cut off anyhow.

The attorney offered a polite: "Why, for heaven's sake . . ." —and all the while he was thinking of his brother and the bond he would have to furnish for him.

Askanius, however, felt the dryness from which his audience was suffering. And this evening he had an unquenchable urge to excel, to evoke their interest and admiration. Thus he be-gan with his old *tour de force:* how he had sung before Em-peror Napoleon III at Versailles. As usual, he started with a description of the fountains—which cost *thirty thousand francs* every single day they played—as an introduction. He detailed it as minutely as if his auditors heard them described for the very first time. And curiously enough, both the attor-ney and the police chief had been at Versailles and seen these miracles. But they had never dared to acknowledge this to Askanius for the simple reason that he would not have be-lieved them. He would have considered them as interlopers, as thieves, bent on depriving him of property exclusively his own.

The two culprits exchanged glances now and then; and then Libotz became absorbed in calculations over the cost of the surety bond. But every time his eyes took a downward trend, he was promptly pulled back by Askanius, who forced him to pay attention, with a question uttered in Danish: "Are you listening?" Then Libotz showed his face again, although his eyes were turned inward, for he was making calculations in his mind.

This evening, however, Askanius got tangled up in his foun-tains. It was apparent that his mind was getting foggy, and he sank into a discussion with himself. He could not remem-ber which one of the fountains was the biggest.

"Let me see now? Did I say Diana . . . I don't mean Diana" —and here he began to play drum on his forehead. "What *is* its name now?"

Libotz, who took it for granted that the question was directed to him, was startled out of his absentmindedness and gave him answer.

"Neptune is the biggest."

"No—Neptune is not the biggest—no. . . ." blurted out Askanius with authority.

Now the chief of police forgot himself completely and broke in: "Why, of course, it is Neptune. I have been there myself."

This was entirely too preposterous. Askanius therefore simply took it as some sort of jesting, and continued:

"You see, gentlemen, such fountains you find nowhere else in the world—except in St. Petersburg. . . . Have you gentlemen ever been in St. Petersburg? No! Well, you see there . . . Or in Schönbrunn? Not there either! Oy, oy, oy—that is the very acme of greatness—the most gigantic experience in life. . . . But Versailles—that is one place every human being should see before he dies. . . . You gentlemen should tear yourselves loose some time . . . Drink a little less and save . . . save, be stingy, and say: 'I want to stint, I am going to deny myself even the necessities—but I must see Versailles before I die. . . .' I'll lend you my Baedeker travel guide. . . . I have two: one in French and one in German—the trip costs two hundred francs—that's an even one hundred and fifty crowns . . ."

"One hundred and forty!" interrupted the chief of police who found it impossible to resist Askanius's haughty airs any longer.

"May I—may I? May I finish my sentence!" demanded Askanius.

"Certainly! Certainly!" granted the police chief.

"As I was saying—we sang for the Empress, gentlemen, and believe it or not, she was dressed—in honor of the day—in the Swedish colors, in yellow and blue. . . . Now wasn't that a gracious thing to do? . . ."

And then came the Emperor! From youth Askanius had nourished an indescribable contempt for him, the Sphinx, Badinguet, and whatever he had been called. But from the day that he had sung for the Frenchmen's emperor, he appeared to Askanius as transformed, not to say transfigured. Napoleon III now became a genius, the greatest political figure that ever lived; and as an army leader he was in every respect comparable to Charles the Great of Sweden. The café proprietor was lacking in voice and resonance this evening and he could not get up on his feet; therefore he rang for champagne.

His two victims were dripping from perspiration and were overwhelmed by all this grandeur which was heaped on them like a heavy blanket. Libotz, who never wished to offend anyone, tried to bolster the atmosphere again. But to attempt to speak on any other subject, or about anyone else than Askanius, would have meant death to the proprietor. And so he took up the refrain again by asking a seemingly innocent question.

"What voice did you sing then, Mr. Askanius?"

Askanius acted as if he were searching his memory, masticating a lie on his tongue like a piece of chew. At last he answered diplomatically, his words moderately cutting, but with a finality that brooked no further obtrusive or impertinent questioning on the subject.

"Gentlemen, in a well-conducted quartet for male voices, there exists only *one* voice—one for all, and all for one. . . . And anyone who has the slightest understanding of the great and difficult art of singing, knows that all four voices are equally important—whether they are called first or second tenor, or first and second bass."

Now this was just too elementary, and his manner of leaving his listeners in ignorance of his having sung merely second tenor, annoyed the police chief, who was himself an old quartet singer. The champagne had made them spirited, and now Tjärne felt he could do without further instruction. So, quite casually, he broached the intelligence that he had sung first tenor in the university quartet. This caused a grave silence. Askanius fought with his better self, his pride, his sense of justice. Ought he to stoop to pick up so dangerous a bone of contention? If he did, he would be lost, for it looked as if Libotz was prepared to step in and take the part of the college singing! No, he would not! And without losing ground, he went roundabout, without stubbing a toe.

"Gentlemen," he whispered, "there are two kinds of singing, just as there are many kinds of wines, cigars, entrees, coffees,

and liqueurs. Isn't that so? Very well, we have cultivated singing, and we have natural singing, do you follow me? For my
own part, I prefer professional, artistic singing; and I think
every person who has a cultivated, musical background—he
may belong to whatever social stratum you like—does the
same, as a matter of fact. Therefore, and as a fitting and dignified answer to the somewhat unwarranted remark Police Chief
Tjärne took the liberty to make a moment ago, permit me to
raise my glass in a toast to this art!"

"Bravo!" came a shriek from the police chief, who was altogether too keen about debauchery and too indolent to wish
to waste any effort on a quarrel. And so he drank with pleasure an old nature singer's toast to the art of singing—an ex-
pediency that always brought him an extra glass, filled to the
brim.

Libotz had covered his face with the palm of his hand in
order to wipe away a smile. When he noticed that Askanius
now could neither see nor hear, he turned to Tjärne.

"He is precious just the same," he spoke aloud.

The time was now going on twelve.

"Say something amusing," Askanius spoke up suddenly—
not because he desired to hear anything said, but merely so
that he could get a moment's respite. And with this he placed
himself in position as if he were waiting, patiently and resignedly, for their chatter to come to an end. Meanwhile he played
with his own thoughts, reading over in his mind what to say
next. Tjärne, who was well acquainted with his tactics, now
turned to Libotz and commenced to speak about Paris and got
his answers and a few fresh contributions of information.

No doubt any ordinary person in Askanius's position would
have expressed surprise that the other two gentlemen had also
been in Paris, and with a dash of self-amusement have saved
himself from looking ridiculous a moment ago by passing over
the episode with a smile. But Askanius was no ordinary person. In addition to his good attributes, he was as well possessed of an enormous self-esteem and ego, and he was greedy
for power. He was the center of his little world of hungry and
debt-ridden, who lived by his charity. Singing and Paris were
his particular domains. They belonged to him, and no one else
was permitted to intrude on them. As he now heard that *they*
had visited Paris too—and he knew that already—he was

tempted to strike a blow by interposing with remarks and cor-
rections. But his superiority complex and vanity and megalo-
mania got the upper hand. Puffing vigorously and snortingly
on his cigar, he breathed heavily under the exertion of trying
to find some totally new topic of conversation which would
snip off the thread of their arguments. Several guests who had
just left looked in through the windowpanes; and this gave
Askanius his opportunity. He rose and went over and pulled
down the shades.

"I think it is better with the shade down," said he, as he
seated himself again. Then he asked: "Won't you gentlemen
drink up . . ."

With this the police chief filled his glass to the brim, but he
did not let go of the thread to Paris. Libotz, the altruist, felt
sorry for Askanius, who was suffering the pangs of death. He
interrupted Tjärne's flow of words with the proposition: "Let
us drink to the health of Mr. Askanius!"

This drink became the decisive one; and now commenced a
change of character such as generally occurs in the fourth act
of a polite drama. The chief of police grew loud, malicious,
and challenging. He promptly flew into an argument with the
café proprietor. Askanius was not at a loss for words or answers. Soon the conversation turned into a cockfight over
Shakespeare. The two dialogued simultaneously, trying to
wear each other down and waiting for a chance—*not* in order
to make reply to a question, but in order to be able to drive
forward his own argument at full speed.

Askanius did not listen to his opponent. Every time he
spoke, he turned away from him in utter disgust, the while
making faces that carried the message: "Go ahead and finish
your blabber. I'll soon pick you to pieces."

They had now stumbled onto the broad and open road of
quotations, and Tjärne had stored many in his memory—
while Askanius knew only one. This lone card he now sat
clutching in his brain, to use it at the opportune moment.

"Ah," yelled Tjärne, "this is sublime! It is Macbeth who
speaks it:

> *Life's but a walking shadow . . .*
> *It is a tale . . . full of sound and fury,*
> *Signifying nothing."*

"Pshaw!" hissed Askanius, "this has much more spirit and nobility in it and has much more depth . . . I think it is *Othello*, or *Hamlet* . . . let me think . . ." But here his memory misfired; the question remained unspoken, and the chief of police was not slow to attack the silence.

"This is what Lear says:

> *Down from the waist they are Centaurs,*
> *Though women all above;*
> *But to the girdle do the gods inherit,*
> *Beneath is all the fiend's;*
> *There's hell, there's darkness, there's the*
> *sulphurous pit."*

"Ugh! How can you speak such terrible things!" broke in Libotz, who was presently within the sacred and innermost temple yards of love.

"That's irony," shrieked Askanius. "You see, gentlemen, anyone who does not appreciate irony should never be allowed to discuss Shakespeare. *Par exemple,* I think it is *The Merchant of Venice* . . . but it doesn't matter *who* said it . . . who says that life is woven of the same cloth as our dreams . . . but, of course, this should not be taken literally—he lets some fool say it—to show what a fool he is. That's why we have to be careful when we try to interpret a great poet. . . . The only ones who can interpret him as he *should* be interpreted, are those whom nature has endowed with a feeling of understanding for the great, the beautiful, the true, in life and nature."

This exertion proved to be too much for him. Askanius was now entering a new stage. He closed his eyes, went into a trance, and his soul drifted off to unknown spheres. His hands kept fumbling with his cigar, which he lighted continually, only to have it go out immediately. His body, however, was not fully awake, and the cigar ash kept dropping into his champagne glass.

The chief of police, who had been browbeaten, lost his sense of tact and became brutal. He grabbed the cognac bottle and filled a drinking glass half full. He took a swallow and rinsed out his mouth, downing the rest.

Askanius must have had his eyes in his fingers, for half asleep he stretched out his hands, grasping the cognac bottle by the neck and placing it close to him. He held it with a firm and miserly grip, pressing it against the waistcoat pocket in which he kept his eyeglasses.

Now Tjärne began to speak out of his beard, baring his teeth, and certain that Askanius was dead to the world. "To have to sit and listen to his drivel! Why, it's nothing short of fantastic! Isn't it? And he has the audacity to talk about Shakespeare!"

"Ssh! Ssh!" Libotz warned him. "We must not talk like that. We must be grateful to him as our host."

"It's all very well to be grateful! But to sit and flatter him, and be licking his boots, and have to say 'Yes, yes' to him in everything—that's enough to give the man illusions of grandeur. You'll see—some fine day he'll explode from arrogance! . . ."

Libotz tried to branch away and made a start with the Norwegian question. It turned out to be a long-winded discussion; and finally they got themselves so involved that they annexed each other's viewpoint and ended by arguing both against *each other* and *themselves*.

Askanius seemed to have dozed off, and now he suddenly spoke in his sleep, his eyes shut.

"The national education, gentlemen—the national education does not have its origin in the public school or in universal suffrage, least of all for us Swedes—this may sound like a paradox, but it isn't . . ."

"What's he doing? Is he correcting compositions?" interjected Tjärne.

But Askanius went on without faltering. "Nothing has so contributed to the Swedish nation's education, culturally speaking, as—as the smörgasbord."

Hilarious laughter rang out in the pavilion, in approbation of this entertaining dialogue, even though it was not intended to be amusing but rather something deep.

"It may sound like a paradox," continued Askanius, "but, believe me, gentlemen, I can be sitting at my place behind the counter, making believe I am writing, or counting, or reading —a customer comes in, and . . ."

Here the dramatic situation was accompanied by gestures, and the cognac bottle was set free, so that the chief of police could get himself another drink.

"A customer enters, an unknown, a stranger . . . Now it so

happens that I have a mirror underneath the clock on the wall and I can see—I have my eyes with me even when they are shut. . . ."

The police chief pushed himself back on his chair, amazed that Askanius could prove to be so false.

"A customer has, of course, the privilege to eat as much of the smörgasbord as he wishes, but a gentleman does not abuse the privilege . . . a gentleman makes himself a sandwich, pours himself an aquavit, goes over to his table and sits down, asks for the menu and a bottle of ale. Why does he do this? Because he is well bred, because he has *savoir faire*. A German will never learn to behave like that, even if one should inform him that it is not intended that a customer should eat his fill of the smörgasbord . . . he just is not receptive to instruction. . . . Who is that singing in the garden?"

"Let them sing!" retorted Tjärne, "but skoal to the smörgasbord!"

"There are some who take six aquavits, too, as soon as I turn my back," jabbered Askanius, "but they are people of a lower class . . . and then there are those who eat a cheese sandwich with their oxtail soup . . . there are hypocrites who take a whisky and go and sit down, but the moment I am out on the veranda, they get up and take another . . . but my wife can see from the pantry window . . . and if she isn't there, Karin tells me about it. Karin is a good girl—she looks after my best interests . . . she is loyal to the death and would never give away that my wife—when we arrange a high-class dinner party or banquet—serves ordinary salted salmon for Rhine salmon . . . that is one of the little secrets of our profession . . . and they are not to be given away—but if you put salted salmon in skimmed milk over night, it turns out like fresh salmon; and as long as no one complains—then what difference does it make . . . but I have instructed Karin to inquire of the guests: 'Didn't you think the salmon was good?' —and when they reply: 'Excellent!' my conscience has nothing to reproach itself for. . . ."

Askanius had now arrived at the dangerous stage when he was betraying himself. Libotz, who could disassociate himself from his own self and identify himself with others, and therefore take on and suffer their pains, sat with eyes cast down. He felt ashamed and suffered for Askanius, especially because he saw how Tjärne gloated over the collection of intelligence given him—information which he was later to misuse.

Askanius kept up his crowing that nothing could stop.

"You can't make any money on the food—and you have to do a little cheating in the kitchen—you have to save and take advantage of everything—and change, and use things over again . . . during the winter the customers can sit and eat nettle soup—and sing its praises—and pay more than for kale soup—and yet it's nothing but kale soup . . . it's the same as with the Pilsner at the brewer's—he waters the ale and gets better paid for it—that's nothing but a piece of human folly . . . but the wines, that's my secret—this champagne, for example, is called 'Old England'—but it's not 'Veuve Clicquot Old England'. . . now we have snobs who know that the label should read 'Old England'—but they don't look for the most important thing on the label, which is 'Veuve Clicquot' —for that costs eleven crowns, while this champagne, which is used at balls, only costs two and a half—but that's because of the Monopoly—I am forced to buy from them, and—bang! we are at the core of it! . . . But there will come a day, gentlemen, when the Monopoly will be exposed—I have a newspaper reporter all hooked up—and when the moment arrives—bing, bang! the Monopoly is done for!"

The police chief sat openmouthed, and when Askanius came to the subject of the Monopoly, he crawled forward between bottles and glasses in order to be able to hear every word. For the Monopoly was the little town's great explosive issue.

Askanius expired after his last effort and fell into a real sleep. He was not inebriated now, for he had not touched a drink for two hours. During the sleep his countenance changed again: the mask disappared from his face, and Tjärne—whose eyes were ever on the alert—took a good look at the sleeper.

"I just wonder how that man started out in life, what his past is, what he has done, and if he has ever been in prison. Look at these hairy hands of his . . . they look like a card player's hands . . ."

"One ought never to delve into people's past," interrupted Libotz, who despite his gentleness had a firm character. "For every human being has to suffer for his deeds; and when he has expiated his sins, he is forgiven. And one should try to overlook a friend's weaknesses. Askanius is our friend. He has helped us in moments of need . . ."

"And for this he is now taking payment with interest," broke in the police chief.

"Well, but don't you think we are obligated to pay our debts? . . ."

Tjärne, too, had been given a new face, the face of a murderer; but Libotz's countenance remained unchanged.

Askanius had eventually had sufficient sleep and awakened with a clearing head, but did not recognize his guests. Drunk with sleep, yet not drunk, he addressed himself to Tjärne as if he were the strange customer that he looked like.

"Mister Chester, I would suggest that you go to the docks rather than sit here. Your past is of such a nature that strenuous, regular work in Brooklyn would, I think, do you good."

"He has been in America," whispered the police chief to Libotz.

But Askanius continued with his foreign contribution and gave answer to Mr. Chester's remonstrances, which only he could hear.

"The girl has disappeared, you know, but I am not to blame —not in the slightest! You may say that appearances were against me; but the court exonerated me. I have the decision in my chiffonier . . ."

To save his friend, Libotz now took a daring step, daring for him, timid as he was. He pressed the bell, and within two minutes Karin appeared, somewhat sleepy, for the time was now two in the morning.

It was then Askanius really woke up. With an angry look on his face, he demanded of the girl: "What do you want?"

"It rang, Mr. Askanius . . ."

"Who has the temerity to ring?" Askanius asked imperiously.

In a fit of obstinacy and defiance, and aching to look Askanius in the eye, the police chief answered, "I rang. I want some water . . ."

Askanius scrutinized Tjärne keenly, ran his hand over his forehead, and blurted out: "Heavens, I thought—but it is . . . I must have dozed off . . . Isn't it . . . ?"

"It's Tjärne—the chief of police," filled in Libotz.

"Why, of course—the chief of police—he wants some water . . . Bring some water, Karin. . . ."

Karin left.

"Karin is not as pretty as you think, Mr. Libotz . . ." enunciated Askanius.

"I have never said she was pretty," dared Libotz, "but she is a nice and goodhearted girl. She is far from goodlooking."

"Taste and liking differ, but to say that Karin is a pretty girl . . ." Askanius persisted obstinately.

"I have never made the statement that . . ." stammered Libotz.

"Her features are irregular, her complexion somewhat faded, and her figure so-so; but she is good and well-behaved girl— and anyone who says anything else is a slanderer—yes, that's exactly the word!"

With this, Libotz was given a punishing glance, with which he had to be satisfied, and Askanius trudged on.

"A good and well-behaved girl—those are my words . . ." he reiterated with vehemence, but Tjärne cut him off.

"No! Those are the words Mr. Libotz used!"

"And whoever gets her some day"—Askanius was not to be stopped—"whoever gets her, must be a respectable person and not anyone who boozes and gets his name into the newspapers!"

The full measure of Askanius's instinctive animosity toward Libotz now came out in the open again. He ripped and tore into the poor little man with ferocity.

"Tricks succeed for a short time . . ." he hissed.

"Tub salmon goes farther!" interspersed the police chief dryly.

"And anyone who is no longer a member of the Court of Appeal has no business advertising it on his sign. . . . Honesty is the best policy in the long run . . . and anyone who practices law should be the first to live up to it and respect it," moralized the café proprietor.

By this time Tjärne's patience had run out. Under the pretext that he had to inspect some nonexistent fire-alarm boxes, he thanked Askanius for a pleasant evening and went toward the door, taking Libotz with him. But Askanius, who was drowsy and was getting sluggish in his movements, only succeeded in pushing out the words: "May I . . . may I be permitted . . ."—and then Karin opened the door and brought the decanters with water. This prevented Libotz and Tjärne from departing, for the latter's chronic thirstiness had to be appeased again. He succumbed to the temptation and remained, and then Askanius let go with a long flow of words.

"Fire-alarm boxes? At this time of day? Did you say fire alarm? But the fire station isn't open so early in the morning, is it? . . ."

"I said fire-alarm box . . ." the police chief corrected him.

"The telegraph station may be open nights, but the post office—never!" procrastinated Askanius.

"Good night, brother Askanius . . . now you'd better go to bed," Tjärne flung out as he fled, bringing along Libotz, who wanted to stay and take formal leave of his host.

But when the police chief and Libotz came out in the street, it broke loose. Everything they had been prohibited from saying in there in the pavilion was now brought forward in the light; and a night chat ensued on sidewalk curbs, in the big square, and in the graveyard, lasting away into the wee hours.

Eight days later attorney Libotz exchanged rings with Karin, and after the engagement was announced, the two would take a walk into the countryside every morning. Askanius grew cold toward both, accusing Karin of being ungrateful to him.

During these days Libotz had to fight a continuing struggle. He was overwhelmed with letters from his brother, who requested that he put up the several thousand crowns for the bond. The attorney had explained that he could not sign a bond for an amount he did not possess. "But you can afford to get married," came back from the brother. This sublime utterance of logical egotism steeled Libotz for a few days, though it was too much even for him. For he had to take care of his father, who had gone into bankruptcy. Though he was sick, he could not get into the poorhouse, partly because he was so hated, partly because he had solvent relatives. He was brought to the hospital, where Libotz was forced to pay for his care in a ward. With this, Libotz felt that he had done his duty, and that he ought to be freed from having to furnish the brother's bond. But there were others who did not think so. Askanius was one of these. One day he came over to Libotz at his table and whispered softly: "To leave one's own brother in the lurch! . . . That isn't nice. . . ."

"I haven't left him in the lurch!" replied Libotz resignedly.

"Oh yes . . . he has to suffer for his brother's and father's careless deportment. . . ."

Here was the tower of lies again—built on a lie and impossible to tear down. Libotz sat contemplating the oddity of human behavior, and then he started for home. There he found a letter from his brother, in which he described what he had had to endure because of him. The Count had lost a legal case, in which Libotz had represented his opponent. The Count had let fall some word about the "shyster lawyer" and the manager had then explained that the attorney was his own brother. Consequently the Count took out his hatred on the manager. Next came the newspapers with the drunkenness episode. The Count waved the newspaper under the manager's nose, snapping at him: "Was I right, eh? Drinking goes well with the shyster business!"

All in all, Libotz realized that he, however innocently and indirectly, had been the cause of his brother's awkward and disagreeable situation. So he signed the dangerous paper and sent it off. But as he was candor itself, he confided this to Karin. She quickly expressed her disapproval, as she would be a party to the sacrifice, in future. Libotz was unable to deny that she was right. And so he was torn by a new dilemma.

The engagement was still in effect and had now lasted a month. The first week they talked about their childhood, their parents and relatives; the second week about the future, about marriage and about their housekeeping plans. As Libotz had decided to leave all housekeeping matters to her, they were in agreement on all points. Thus the flat was soon both rented and furnished in their imagination, and nothing remained to add or discuss. The third week they hashed over their first week's conversation, and the fourth week the second week's. Libotz began to notice that the subjects for conversation were diminishing and that no particularly spirited exchange of opinion, capable of animating and giving impulses, ever took place. But so that concord might be achieved, he kept all deviating opinions to himself. Or he hypnotized himself into believing that they were of one mind in everything, that it had to be, if the happiness of their marriage was to be permanent. To him the honor of being loved by a woman was so great that he felt that she, in return, ought to be given the reins to his domain—excepting his legal affairs. Of them he never spoke, for these were the property of others.

One Sunday they were to spend the whole day, from morning till night, in the country. After enjoying themselves there, they were to have dinner. They had planned a real holiday, for Karin was free the whole day from her work at Askanius's. They started out at about nine, and literally flew past the customs gate. At first, they talked about the trivial occurrences since their separation the noon before.

"Well, did you have many at dinner last evening?" asked the fiancé.

"Of course, we always have a lot of people on Saturdays," she answered. And he knew that.

"Was Mr. Askanius in good humor?" (He seldom was.)

"He grumbled as he generally does . . . But he is really a nice man." The word *nice* was most frequently used by Karin, because she knew that she herself was considered to be nice.

"But where were you last evening?" she asked.

"I was at home, writing and working, so that I would be free today, dear child. . . . Oh, look—look at the large bird! It must be a kite . . ." he exclaimed.

"There are no kites around here! Certainly not!"

"Why, certainly, there must be kites here. . . . It must be a kite! It has a cleft tail . . ." insisted Libotz.

"Don't you think it might be a buzzard, the way he cries?"

"It might—but the buzzard hasn't a cleft tail," the attorney informed her.

"But the wagtail over there on the fence has a cleft tail, too," observed Karin.

"Why, of course, I had forgotten about that—but that's the way this bird is described in Berlin's *Natural History* . . . I don't know—but you are absolutely right, Karin dear."

Now that the kite had been dissected and done away with, one could only hear the brisk clatter of their walk. Libotz moved his jaws dryly, felt an emptiness in his head, cast glances across the fields in an attempt to lay eyes on something to talk about. All the while he was plagued by the thought of a pending legal case, which he, of course, could not bring up for conversation.

After he had turned over his professional matters for a considerable time in his head, Karin found the silence improper and began to feel embarrassed by it.

"Say something, Edward! It's awful when you don't say anything!"

Libotz's legal business dropped out of his head, and he could not think of anything to say. In his quandary he said what he should never have said.

"What do you want me to say?"

This was his declaration of bankruptcy. He was insolvent, improverished. The thread was broken. Two strangers walked beside each other and reflected—reflected over each other, over their relationship, over the cause of their dark silence. And one, two, three, their strangeness turned into hostility. Each one felt that the other was faithless. How could anyone be harboring secret thoughts without speaking out? The longer the silence lasted, the worse it became. In his agony, Libotz pulled up a plant from the ground and exclaimed with successful animation: "Look! What a curious-looking plant!"

Karin divined not only the sham of his surprise but as well the morsel of charity that he offered her as pacification. She turned away her head and did not answer. Instead she speeded up her pace, as if she wanted to escape from the whole business.

Libotz followed in her wake. He felt himself disenthralled, dismissed. He was convinced that this was the end. He began to ponder where to take his meals hereafter. He just could not go to Askanius's any more. He wondered whether the newspapers would make a story of it, what the town's gossips would say. He lived himself so thoroughly into the new situation that he let himself fall behind, while Karin forged ahead. Where the road took a turn, she disappeared. Yet he found the whole affair quite natural. She had made the break. That was the end; and the end meant relief. He sat down on a rock, removed his hat, wiped his forehead. But he shed no tears. The thought of being alone again, to be able to get back to normal, now became such a rare delight that he started to whistle softly, while drawing pictures in the soil.

"My heavens! How strange this whole thing seems!" he thought. "Yes, it's very strange, very strange!"

But suddenly a reaction set in, and he was overcome by anguish. He got up and started forward again, for home. And as he came to the turn of the road, he saw Karin standing there, leaning against a tree and crying.

They cried together, first in silence, then in common agony not to be able to be sufficient for each other, not to be able to be happy at all times when together. Finally Karin burst out: "That it could be that hard, I had never thought!"

"This is the hardest of all," Libotz remarked. "But let us separate now, you going your way, and I mine—across the fields . . . then we'll meet by the paddock."

The suggestion was an unusual one, but it was accepted as ideal. Libotz returned to his legal thoughts, was himself again, and expanded into many dimensions. He interrogated witnesses, orated before the court and convinced the opposing attorney that his client was in the wrong—indeed, a rare case that could only happen out in a field, where the parties to the lawsuit were absent.

When he arrived at the paddock and met Karin, he found it only natural that he should release what was on his mind. Therefore, without any kind of introduction, he commenced to give an account of the judicial proceeding. It happened to be nothing but a feud about some property, entailing sundry responsibilities of upkeep, bridges and stone walls; but he really lived when he spoke about his work. . . . He filled the air with his voice and he knew how to expostulate. Karin heard a human voice, and the solitude, to which she was unaccustomed, seemed suddenly peopled—and her fiancé began to show himself to true advantage. She threw in a few little questions here and there that fired him to go on. She encouraged him to the extent that Libotz, when the case was over, was carried away by the triumphant conclusion and immediately brought a second case to trial. But it turned out to be a trifle long and involved. Though it became rather tiring because of the multiplicity of names, he talked himself warm, and then got into his stride, as if marching to drums. Finally they reached Gröndal.

The hour was only eleven, and the inn didn't open until two, at which time they had planned to have Sunday dinner. It was a terribly long time to wait. They walked down to the little lake in the woods. They looked at the carp there, pelted them with pebbles and picked some irises. Yet all this consumed only an hour. And then the tonguetiedness set in again. . . . But having had their awful experience with silence, they chatted about trivialities and nothings and recapitulated old subjects. When they discovered that they were both plagiarizing, they could not look each other in the eye. They felt ashamed for each other, for themselves. But the ghost of silence drove them forward, and it ended by their uttering some involuntary stupidities, touching wounds which they both wanted to forget. Of the two, Libotz suffered the worst set-back.

"It is curious, isn't it, that all shoemakers are named Andersson," he said, merely for the sake of saying something.

"My father was a shoemaker, but his name was Lundberg," chirped Karin with a certain good-natured humor.

"My dear Karin—dear Karin, I didn't know that . . . and I certainly had no intention of hurting your feelings."

"I know you didn't, of course," replied Karin, who was definitely convinced of her fiancé's good intentions. And, besides, they were still living in the Paradise where neither thought evil of the other. Thus there were safeguards against further quarrels—quarrels that generally start when the kind thought and the goodwill cease to exist.

Toward the end, Karin had to go into her storehouse; and her thoughts went to Askanius and the customers at the café.

"That Tjärne is an interesting man, don't you think?" she blurted out.

Libotz might have taken this as a hint that he himself was a bore. But this he did not do. On the contrary, he held up the police chief as a model, a work of art, picking out—with his customary love of humanity—his good sides, and highlighting them with examples from their social intercourse. Karin kept urging him on, as though it was an auction. Tjärne grew into an angel of light, a martyr; his tragic fate and his spurious birth simply forced anyone to forgive him his little peculiarities. . . . Little peculiarities, yes! . . . At this moment they came to a halt, and during the pause, they suddenly became aware of what a terrible scoundrel the police chief really was. They both knew he might do away with Askanius the first opportunity he had. Karin was the first to turn coat, but Libotz was not inclined to go along. Instead he lingered on Tjärne's tragic fate. He gave expression to his horror of a crime, which made counterfeit out of an innocent human being's precious emotional life—a crime that would extend through generations, punishable on the children and the children's children, all the way to the end of the line. . . .

When he had exhausted this subject, he broke into the

Norwegian question, took universal suffrage along in tow, developed the basic concept of proportionateness—but was afraid to look at his watch because this would have indicated that he was impatient.

A church bell in the distance announced the end of the service. It was one o'clock consequently. Still another hour to wait. . . .

Libotz was agonized, perhaps most because he had tortured Karin with lawsuits and politics. To speak about people, who were the most interesting of all subjects, he did not care; and to have to praise scoundrels, he found debasing in the long run—as much as to be slandering people. He was tired and hungry, dry and empty. For a moment he felt an urge to slit his wrist in order to cool off, and to jump into the lake, but instead he made the proposition: "Shall we move about a little?"

They moved about a little. Then they sat down, watched an anthill, wondered how the little ants enjoyed themselves in their tiny world. They tossed pebbles into the lake for the tenth time, gazed up at the pine trees and their branches as though they had suicide in their hearts. They shrank from pursuing the carp again for they had been discussed dry and eliminated as a subject for consideration. The irises had lost their freshness and were likewise cast aside; but the ghost of silence cracked its whip whenever they tired of speaking. The two were, however, sufficiently sensible not to blame the boredom on each other. They found it lay in the very nature of things; yet they were reluctant to discuss the matter, their conduct and relationship, for it was a sensitive subject and had best not be alluded to or criticized.

However, the clock struck two, and their table was set under a cherry tree. No one seemed to be around, and Karin thought it lonely, for she was used to movement and bustle. But Libotz found it ideal to be left in seclusion—yet he did not give vent to what he thought, as his desire was to please her in everything. So he left it to Karin to choose from the menu, and when she saw asparagus, she burst out:

"I wonder how it tastes. . . ."

"Heavens, have you never tasted asparagus?" came from Libotz in surprise.

"Never. . . ."

"Well, then we'll have to have asparagus, even if it is a little dear," said Libotz.

That's the way their Sunday dinner began, and fortified by the meal, their cheerfulness returned. Libotz found everything to be amusing. He was pleased with everything, and Karin was delighted to be waited on by a waiter in tails. First they talked about the food, but Karin quickly broke in with the intelligence that one ought not to discuss what one was eating. Libotz retorted with an attempt to slip out a few jokes in order to entice his fiancée to laugh. And when he noticed the waiter standing behind a door, listening, he flippantly said that the waiter was possessed of X-ray ears.

Karin, however, had no idea what this meant. Therefore Libotz was given the opportunity to speak a short story, which took away the point of the joke. The conversation next turned to precious stones. This was because of a pin Libotz wore in his tie. He had confided to her his discovery that the cheapest stones were the most beautiful, such as garnet, amethyst, topaz, while emerald and ruby gave the appearance of being imitation. Then his fiancée got frightened, thinking that he might be miserly.

"Well, but diamonds—*they* are the *most* beautiful!" she interjected.

"They look like nothing but glass—but they are quite beautiful, you are right. And they are terribly expensive," Libotz admitted.

After dinner came the coffee, but something else came, too. Libotz had accustomed himself to taking a nap at that time of day, and now he found it impossible to resist. He began a struggle for life: a weight, distributed throughout his body, pulled him toward the center of the earth and his consciousness was getting befogged, illusions were shuffled like playing cards, images jeered at him, mirages loomed up, time and place were intermingled, and with eyelids blinking, he ejected somber words from lawsuits, statistics of population, volumes on constitutional law; he mixed up jewels and smoked salmon and called the waiter Askanius and Karin miss.

At first Karin laughed and kept asking him if he had taken one too many, but Libotz answered merely: "Why, of course not, I am only a little sleepy, the air takes its toll when one isn't used to . . ."

And then came the finale: he yawned! Quickly the maiden rose from her seat and Libotz came to, as if after a slap in the face. The moment was a decisive one, and then—a bicycle wheels up; and elegantly—with the movement of a horseback rider—Tjärne dismounts, salutes with military precision, and is received with an outcry as a savior!

Now the conversation really began. The three talked all at the same time. Tjärne had already had his dinner, and he promptly proposed bowling and some Swedish *punsch*. The atmosphere boomed incredibly. Tjärne conversed with Karin until she turned red in the face from glee, and Libotz felt unselfishly happy when he saw how she enjoyed herself. Just as unselfishly he applauded the police chief's strikes and spares, and when he scored a double, was glad when he himself lost, as long as it afforded pleasure for the other two. Soon they began to poke fun at him, and Karin started to prick at all the little weaknesses he had displayed during the day. She even intimated what a dull day they had had, and expressed undisguised joy over the police chief's arrival. Occasionally, however, she would show regret; and then she stroked her fiancé sympathetically on the chin with a soft: "Oh, but he is so nice, so nice. . . ."

The afternoon passed like a wind, and then came a flock of people, and the dancing began.

Toward the evening, the chief of police started to pine away. As soon as Libotz noticed this, he decided on a departure in grand style: they were to drive by carriage to the town and have supper at the City Café, where Karin had never put her foot before.

He disappeared to order the carriage and remained away a short time. When he returned, he found Karin and Tjärne engaged in a rather confidential conversation, which stopped short the moment they saw him. From this he concluded that they had been talking about him. He said nothing, however. He found it quite logical and liked to believe they had said nothing but good about him. And then the carriage drove up. Libotz entered it first, taking a seat with his back to the coachman, thereby forcing Tjärne and Karin to sit next to each other on the rear seat. It never occurred to him that this might be considered bad form.

It was a long trip. Libotz fell asleep, after having first asked them to excuse him; and Tjärne and Karin laughed. Libotz himself smiled at his little indulgence. But when he woke up, he found Karin and Tjärne again absorbed in the same kind of confidential discourse, so low that he could not distinguish their words.

He was evidently not part of the game. He tried to break in, but was shunted aside, then tired and withdrew within himself. Now and then Karin, however, would throw him some jesting remark that smacked of a lack of regard for him. And when she finally snapped out a "Shut up!" he rolled up and became totally inaccessible. He forgot to give answer the next time he was reprieved with a question of no importance, demanding no answer.

The police chief, who exuded neither nobility nor compassion, became incensed over Libotz's sulkiness; and, to make short shrift of him, he flung his death-dealing arrow.

"I hope you are not jealous, old man, are you!" (He and Libotz had been quite like brothers at the bowling alley.)

It was his *coup de grâce*, and it was received without complaint, without any resistance.

The defeated man sat with head bowed, resting against his breast, as if he had spoken his last word in this life: This is the end. As they drove into the town and had come to the apothecary, Libotz stopped the carriage, and with a hasty: "I'm just going to get a prescription," he disappeared through the entrance door.

Both Karin and the police chief had been conducting such a lively conversation that they had paid no attention to Libotz's departure. After a while, however, they found the waiting time too long, and the chief of police stepped out to take a peek through the window at the apothecary's. When he did not see anything of Libotz in there, he went inside and inquired whether the attorney had been there. Then he suddenly grasped the situation; and realizing that he had to save his own skin by ridding himself of the dull and uninteresting role of consoler, he slipped like a snake through the apothecary gateway —disappearing by the same backway across the apothecary backyard as the attorney had used a moment ago. Karin sat alone for a while. But then she began to have misgivings, went inside the apothecary and made inquiry. She got her answer, flew out and—leaving both carriage and coachman—she hastened to her fiancé's abode. He was not at home.

The following morning Karin received a letter, with her engagement ring enclosed. It was not a bitter letter, rather the opposite. Libotz took all the blame, regretted that he had exposed her reputation to gossip, declared that he was not the man she deserved. His gloomy disposition, his taxing work—having to do with all manner of human misery—made him impossible as companion and in social intercourse. Being himself unhappy, he could not bring much light or happiness to someone else. And so it went.

Karin wept, but realized it was as it should be. And so she went back to her job at Askanius's, where Libotz now had ceased to go.

The chief of police, too, remained away for a time; for in the same breath that Libotz let go his hold, the prey had lost all excitation for him. He had merely had a desire to experience his own invincibility and to revel in his rival Libotz's sufferings of a Sunday afternoon.

Libotz kept inside for eight days. He sent out for his meals, turned pale, but attended to his tasks with tranquillity and his usual tenacity.

His demeanor toward the town's inhabitants remained as in the past. Hated by all from whom he was forced to collect claims, suspected, looked down on, he pulled his daily load and completed his duties without stint. If a traveling company of actors, or a circus or orchestra, came to town, he attended —even though it gave him no amusement.

"Well, we have to attend, we who can afford it, or they won't come here any more. And then the theater will stand unused. That would be to the town's shame. And the children's great pleasure is the circus. We have to think about others, too . . ."

But he lent out money also—little pocket loans to the poor. He gave security, had to pay, and in return he was labeled with the disagreeable reputation of being a loanshark. His heaviest duty, however, was his visits to his father at the hospital. Despite his paying for his father in a ward and though he never failed to bring him snuff, port wine, and other little delicacies, he was continuously greeted by complaints.

The old man was hated even within his new domicile. A great many of the inmates had been customers of his and had suffered for years from his spurious merchandise. Consequently he kept out of their way as much as he could. He was afraid to stroll in the yard, suffered frequently from full-fledged persecution mania, which undoubtedly was caused chiefly by the hatred heaped on him. He would suspect that his food was adulterated, the water poisoned, and the bed-clothes impregnated with evil-smelling odors, forcing him to spend the nights sitting in a chair. Hoping that it might make it a little easier for his father, Libotz hit upon the idea of bribing his fellow inmates with little gifts. But then his father showed such envy that his son's exertions were nullified.

One Sunday afternoon, following divine service, Libotz stalked along the sad, interminable street that led to the hospital. To the right lay a chapel, directly across from a huge rock that the authorities had not found time to blast away, and which resembled an intestine from the bowels of the earth. A little further away lay a cholera graveyard, which was a place to stay away from, for fear that the dread plague be stirred up. Here there were children playing hide-and-seek amidst the wild-growing bushes and thickets, or they were climbing the trees that had taken on strange, bizarre shapes and that grew thick, dark, spotted leaves, as if touched by the plague.

One lone cross stood leaning as if about to fall, and standing before it could sometimes be seen an elderly woman, deep in prayer, while the children were boisterously romping about her. The children would use the cross as a target for their stone throwing; and it finally fell. Every time it happened, Libotz would go over and raise it up, propping it with some rocks. There was an inscription on the cross, but it was not the name the woman bore; and Libotz came to the conclusion that it must have been her great love who was now undergoing the transformation down there inside the earth. And the thought of this made him wonder why true mates did not always meet—a thought that made him recall a retort made by the cynical chief of police: "There are no true mates" (except, in parenthesis, those who never get each other).

Close by this gloomy spot stood the hospital. In former days it had first been a government warehouse, then it became a cholera hospital, and now finally a home for misery and sickness. This day Libotz arrived as usual with his black bag. He was searched by the attendant and admitted into the reasonably large room in which his father had been placed together with two other men.

The old man sat by the window, wrapped in his dressing gown. He had his back turned toward his comrades-in-misery in order not to be subjected to their glances. As the son entered, the father promptly took the bag away from him, without giving him either a greeting or a thank you. He immediately disappeared behind a screen and started to eat and drink without saying a word. Moreover, he did all this with a boastful noisiness, merely to irritate the others. He took special pains to make his snuff operation fully audible; and in between pinches he indulged in gossip and slander.

"If everybody could enjoy a pinch of snuff, how would I be able to enjoy it. I don't want you to give any to the others, do you hear, Edward?" the old man said viciously.

Having said this, he snailed over to his son and went through his pockets, knowing that he would always bring along some special surprise. Today he had prepared for him a very great and most endearing one: he brought along two new, fresh decks of cards. Edward detested cards, and he had spent two crowns on this sinful diversion. Therefore the act of love prompting him to this sacrifice was so much greater.

The old man tore off the wrapper round the fresh cards with sensuous pleasure. It was like peeling a peach. The old card-playing addict felt the joy all the way to his fingertips when he glimpsed the ace of hearts, peering out through the jacket's oval cut-out. He wanted to start playing immediately, but the son made objections: "But this is Sunday, and it would not be right. And besides, I don't play cards."

"I'll teach you," the old man was quick to reply.

"No, Father, you can play with your friends here tomorrow."

"Play with *them!* Never! Never!"

"But you can't play by yourself, can you?" pleaded the son.

This turned out to be a terrible problem for his father. It was one of those things one just could not do by oneself. One simply had to have someone to heap abuse on and to wrangle with.

"Sit down!" ordered the oldster, "and don't show yourself

ungrateful to your old father. Don't you think I have enough to contend with!"

Why, yes, the son did think so; and since he found it painful to bring distress to anyone, he discovered himself seated with the cards in his hand in less time than it takes to count to three. They played knock—the only card game the son had ever played. A sense of shame crept over him from time to time. He was disturbed by the thought that the overseer might enter at any moment, and suddenly he dashed the cards onto the table. But his father's influence over him was so powerful that Libotz, at his vigorous urging, picked up his cards again.

"You didn't bid, Father . . ." the son had the temerity to say, although he uttered the words more as a statement of fact than in criticism.

"Are you accusing me of playing crooked?" yelled the old man.

"Why, of course not, I merely wished to call your attention to . . ."

There he was clipped off and the inevitable quarrel was in full swing, managed by the old father exclusively. He not only accused, but also gave the answers.

One of his comrades-in-misfortune had, however, stolen out; and not long after, the overseer came into the room.

"What do you mean by playing cards in the middle of a Sunday afternoon? Have you no shame in you? But—like father, like son!—Put the cards away, or I'll *take* them away from you!"

There was nothing Edward Libotz could say. He sat there in silence, convicted. Out of loyalty to his father, he kept his tongue.

When the overseer had gone, Libotz got up and prepared to leave.

"Are you going already?" the old man spat out.

It was his customary farewell upbraiding. *Already* . . . even when he had stayed for hours! And the son was aware that the father did not miss his company. He merely enjoyed seeing him tormented.

Edward took courage and suggested to his father, with mild reproach: "If you will not obey the rules, Father, I am not coming to see you again."

"That wouldn't surprise me at all, not at all! Didn't you want to see your brother kicked out of his job, and weren't you the cause of my going into bankruptcy?"

How could he answer such an accusation? He merely shuddered at this manifestation of unfathomable evilness, tawdriness, and shabbiness. Crushed, he glided out through the door.

He had to pass through a corridor before he was outside, however; and there he heard abusive words about card-sharks, seducers, and loansharks from every side. The card playing was the hardest, for there he felt that the blame was his alone. He had attended church service in the forenoon and had been comforted by the text: "In this world ye shall have tribulations, but be of good cheer: I have overcome the world." Voices had whispered to him, filling him with faith and hope, consoling him with the confidence that what he was suffering was not a punishment but merely a test; that his was the fate of Job, and that he himself was a comparatively guiltless creature. Yet an hour later, when he wished to consecrate the sabbath by performing an act of love and mercy, he found himself involved in a commonplace game of cards and an argument. . . . There was no doubt he gave the appearance of being a hypocrite—yet he was not. This false semblance, in the glare of which he would forever be snared, these ambiguous situations into which he was dragged against his will—this was the heaviest burden for him to bear. He wanted to do the right and just thing, yet he acted wrongly now and then. . . .

When he walked past the town's church, he found it open and empty. He entered. In here he found tranquility and beauty. Its ceiling was high and lofty, so different from all other spaces and cubicles in the town, and so much roomier. He walked down the center aisle, frightened by the sound of his own footsteps. He stopped by the gate of one of the bench rows, thumbed a forgotten prayer book, and found himself reading the sixteenth chapter of Job.

"My face is foul with weeping, and on my eyelids is the shadow of death; not for any injustice in my hands; also my prayer is pure. O earth, cover not thou my blood, and let my cry have no place, also now, behold, my witness is in heaven, and my record is on high. My friends scorn me: but mine eye poureth out tears unto God. O that one might plead for a man with God, as a man pleadeth for his neighbor!

"When a few years are come, then I shall go the way whence I shall not return."

This was, indeed, his only hope: to meet Death some day; for here on this earth he could expect nothing in future that was good. For this reason all that remained for him was to prepare himself for whatever would come, and to swallow his humiliations like water.

He had never brooded over or doubted his religion. The teachings of the things of the spirit were to him self-evident truths. The only thing that had worried him was his inability to grasp God's goodness, when life was so cynically unkind, and when one was virtually impotent, powerless to resist doing evil, was forced into it.

Seeing how religious people would suddenly reveal themselves as hardened criminals, he grieved that God did not help his faithful in the hour of temptation, but left them to their own fate—thus sacrificing both their friends and the faith for which they suffered. In his own life he never achieved his ideals fully, nor realized his good intentions. For this reason he was afraid of being considered a religious man and did his worshiping in secret.

To go to church every day of the week he looked upon as profanation of God's name. Six days you shall work; but on the seventh, you shall worship the Lord. This was his precept; and he lived up to it, yet never foisted it on others.

After a few moments of meditation, he went home and shut himself in. He used his Sunday afternoons to review his affairs, and to receive diverse visitors. It had come to be his fate, namely, to be pestered by a host of people who came to get confidential advice, to unburden their personal troubles on him, to relieve themselves of their sorrows, their frets and worries and hates.

In this manner he had become a sort of psychiatrist giving free clinical advice and service.

His office was nothing to brag about. He could not keep it clean, since people came and went every day of the week; and on Sundays he did not permit any cleaning to be done.

The misery that was raked up within its walls, moreover, left in its wake an atmosphere, which was suffocating. The moisture of human breath on the windows had evaporated but had trapped the dust, so that the street outside was visible only through a film of dirt and smudge.

Now he seated himself at the big desk and brought out the ledger kept by his assistant. The young man had made progress during the time he had served at Libotz's law office. With the growing clientele, his zeal had increased. He now could be seen as well in Libotz's living quarters during his rest periods, in particular while Libotz was taking his meals. Having in the beginning been frank and open, he had now become evasive and reserved. Armed with this exterior of reserve and stinging brashness, he began to show arrogance, and finally well-behaved animosity. After a period of zeal, he would request a day off now and then and disappear on short trips, always in a mysterious manner. Whenever he was sent to look after a case at one of the district courts, he remained away longer than necessary. As a result of such unpredictable behavior, Libotz lost a number of clear-cut lawsuits which he should have won.

Libotz had long been suspicious of his assistant. But he felt it odious to be snooping on him. Also, he was averse to making a real investigation. The law had now, once and for all, surrounded the criminal with such formidable safeguards that the injured party could only obtain redress with great difficulty; and, to boot, there was always the risk that he himself might be punished instead of the criminal.

As Libotz now started to read in the ledger, he found it far from satisfactory. Debts and claims and collections were jumbled together without rhyme or reason; there were no receipted bills for his assistant's travel expenses, and these were too high. Something was wrong.

Soon after, when he began to read the court decisions in cases that he had lost, he discovered that the opponent had defended himself with the very same words and arguments that he, Libotz, had used in his original brief and that the witnesses on his side had gone over to the opponent's side through admissions, exceptions, and challenges. Sjögren, the assistant, could therefore be suspected of having secretly practiced law on his own initiative and of having betrayed his employer's tactics and manner of presenting his case—and this undoubtedly in return for bribes. It was a sorry discovery, but it made Libotz more downcast than angry, for the young man had shared the hard times with him in the beginning. He had then given proof of patience, had often had to wait for his salary, had offered words of encouragement, and always had helped to dispel any gloomy mood.

Libotz felt no desire to accuse him, for that would mean the end for the young man. But he had to get rid of him, and to do that he had to have in his possession all the facts, all the proofs. To this end he telephoned to the chief of police, requesting that he come over for a confidential talk. Tjärne was not enamored of Libotz, but scenting something that might be of advantage to him, he promised to come without delay. If nothing else was gained, he hoped he would learn some little secret that might prove to be of use to him later.

Tjärne came riding on his bicycle, rushed into the office and promptly stretched his legs across a turned-about chair. Libotz, prudently, as was his custom, opened up with an introduction, which left Tjärne unconcerned. But as he came closer to the subject, the police chief's attention seemed to be awakened.

"But you must not take this as a direct accusation," continued Libotz. "I merely wish to appease my conscience before I notify him that he has to leave."

After this he gave the complete analysis of the case. But as he saw that Tjärne was making notations in his little book, he warned him again.

"You must make no report of this."

"No, I am simply jotting down a memorandum so that I'll be able to make a private investigation . . ." muttered the police chief.

"I can depend on that! But tell me, have you ever heard anything about Sjögren—whether he lives above his means, or spends money around town?" Libotz inquired meekly.

The moment the name Sjögren was mentioned, Tjärne's face was drawn together, as if it had been a bag full of secrets, and in the next moment he answered Libotz.

"I have no definite knowledge, but I think he frequents the City Café, and that there is card playing going on there. And if a fellow plays cards, you can suspect him of anything."

Now it became Libotz's turn to change face. He scrutinized Tjärne's evil eyes, trying to divine whether he alluded to the innocent game of cards at the hospital at noon. He could, however, detect no personal hostility against himself in these sharp, piercing eyes. It was rather as if there smoldered in them an infernal hatred seeking an object far, far in the distance. And he understood now the aggressive onslaught had only been one of those diabolical misfirings brought about by his own thoughts and resulting from their telepathic transmission to him. Yet, at the mention of the City Café, an indistinct recollection of some gossip about a waitress there and a rivalry between Sjögren and Tjärne came to his mind.

"I hope you are not nourishing a grudge against Sjögren?" he asked with the best of intentions, but thoughtlessly.

"Why should I bear a grudge against him? What have I to do with Sjögren, I ask you?" Tjärne delivered with violence, at the same time keenly wishing that he could read Libotz's hidden thoughts.

Libotz realized now that he had touched a sore spot and that Sjögren had actually gotten the upper hand over his rival—something which the irresistible one would never forgive. And he realized too that his assistant was lost; and therefore he began to plead for him. But then Tjärne's hatred fired a spark that set off in his direction. He, Tjärne, was not going to let this little man, whom he had just defeated and put in his place, get the chance to avenge himself by revealing that Don Juan had been conquered by an insignificant little law clerk.

The longer Libotz pleaded the culprit's case, the more of his good sides he brought out. And the more he pleaded, the greater Tjärne's hate against both became. In his panic and agony, Libotz, naively enough, assured him that he had never alluded to any love affair or romantic relationship . . .

"What do you mean?" broke in the police chief.

Libotz understood he had made an error and wanted to retract; but afraid that he might make matters worse, he turned the knife toward himself. He took all the blame on himself, confessed freely to the tricks, the innocent little tricks he had taught the young law clerk.

Tjärne listened with alacrity to Libotz as he slandered himself, encouraged him to unburden his confidences. He plucked his bird, fell into a good humor, enticed him with a few confessions of his own, which he invented for the occasion. And soon they grew quite intimate with each other. Tjärne found the story of Kniving, the attorney in the play, completely superb. The one about Libotz's first free customer he admitted believing wholeheartedly, for he had had similar experiences himself. . . . But when he, in the same breath, questioned Libotz as to what he thought about Askanius and his past, Libotz refused to go along.

"One has to be grateful and loyal," he interrupted, adding that there was nothing so dangerous as to rake in people's past, when they had already atoned for their trespasses.

Tjärne at once became a turncoat. He praised Libotz for his loyalty and spewed out long phrases in praise of Askanius. He gilded his character, although he said he knew little or nothing about his human qualities. He kept up this tirade so gustily that he suddenly was outside the door. Only then did Libotz become aware that he had forgotten to elicit a promise from the police chief not to take any action against Sjögren—but it was too late. Anyhow, Tjärne had left him with the impression that he was favorably disposed toward him. He had spoken so ingratiatingly that Libotz felt completely assured that there could be no danger from that source whatsoever.

When he was alone, he sat down to see if he could bring order in the ledger by entering payments and income in their proper columns—in an attempt to cover up his young law clerk's little indiscretions.

He had now made the definite decision that he would not discharge him; that he would merely give him a friendly admonition. He would make him see his error, would save his future and would thus make a friend of him for life.

Attorney Libotz was a man of keen instincts and broad-minded common sense. After having read an involved brief, he was able to give a clear résumé of its salient points before the court. He never lost his self-possession and composure. He put his teeth into the essential features and never allowed his opponent to talk himself out of an argument or sidestep it. If trivialities were resorted to in order to obscure the main line of argument, Libotz took hold of them, picked them apart, and then returned to the core of the matter—notwithstanding how far afield the digression had gone. Yet despite this strong intelligence, he was naive in his personal relations. He might even have been considered childish, going about as he did, betraying his own weaknesses, furnishing his enemies with both weapons and ammunition—presenting, so to speak, his head on a platter to whomever it might be. But all this could be traced to his credulity, which was not based on a lack of knowledge of human nature, or its evilness, but on his principle of trying to think well of everyone, of believing in thinking good thoughts, and—whenever he was disappointed—of trying to put up with his fellow men's idiosyncrasies and defects, in spite of his disappointments; to forgive wholeheartedly, and to forgive endlessly.

This was in brief his nature: his evaluation of mankind and his own dark fate—an outlook on life he was born with. This was what he called his religion. His friends considered him a dolt outside his profession. People who did not know him called him a hypocrite. They doubted that his professions of these beautiful thoughts about mankind were honest and that he was possessed of an endless patience—a virtue which they characterized as lack of stamina. His expressions of goodwill were likely to draw upon him the accusation of being biased; but he tolerated this as he did all the other slanders and calumnies.

Fon instance, he had on one occasion received a letter from a firm in Stockholm with an inquiry regarding a certain merchant's financial position, for the purpose of ascertaining whether or not to furnish him credit. Libotz had replied that he knew nothing to the man's disadvantage. When the merchant failed in his business, the attorney was served with an insulting letter accusing him of having recommended a cheat and a humbug. It so happened that the man in question was not a swindler, and Libotz had not recommended him. This was the smug, narrow way in which any information he gave was treated. But he had become used to it. And there was nothing he could do about it.

If anyone did him a wrong, he did not get angry but rather felt sorry. He sought no revenge, for he could not find it in his heart to do anything mean. To him the black art of inflicting injury was both odious and unthinkable. He pitied such men; and he was convinced that they themselves suffered most from their malignity, and that the pains they inflicted upon others would come back to plague them. However, after having been alone with himself this Sunday afternoon, he received a visit from a well-known citizen who was about to have his marriage dissolved. For three hours Libotz had to be face to face with all the horrors of a ten-year marriage.

"Why haven't you parted long before this?" he inquired.

"It is not so easy to free oneself, once you get stuck in bird glue. . . . The more you struggle, the more firmly you become imbedded," the client philosophized.

Libotz was bombarded with the quarrels of the two marriage partners and their accusations against each other. He had unrolled before him their intimacies—things he was scarcely cognizant of—all the misery which is brought to the surface in a married life and that had fostered a hatred so unreasonable that it was beyond his comprehension. When Libotz had the temerity to suggest a peaceful settlement, the tanner spouted fire, like a volcano in action, and threatened murder by poison, even at the risk of life imprisonment. When the attorney proposed separation, the unfortunate man began to hesitate, brought up the children, quieted down, lighted a cigar, and ended by breaking into a flow of words in praise of nothing but his wife. And then he went home. . . . Libotz sat there, utterly exhausted. He felt as if he had lived through ten years of an agonizing marriage. He seemed to have aged during these three hours. His face was emaciated, and his skin had dried up. He had taken the sufferings of another so deeply to heart.

But when he went to bed, it was with a peaceful mind. He was glad to have saved the unfortunate clerk, whom he the following morning would bring to his senses again.

Early the next morning, while Libotz was in the throes of preparing the speech he was planning to deliver to Sjögren, Askanius catapulted into his quarters like a handgrenade and exploded in the center of the floor. He was decorated under his eyes with red blooming spots. He was an entirely new and different individual. His dignity was gone. He did not speak in a whisper, as was his custom, but almost shrieked. He moved hither and thither in the room and could not set still. But all that his errand consisted of was to invite Libotz to have luncheon with him at three o'clock at the City Café— at three o'clock on the dot, and just the two. That was all. And then he stormed out.

At the City Café? How curious! Askanius going to the City Café! This foreboded something—but what?

The clock struck ten, when Sjögren was due, but there was no sign of any Sjögren. After a quarter of an hour had elapsed, Libotz started to worry; and at half past ten he was convinced that his clerk had deserted him. In order to obtain assurance, he telephoned the police chief and asked whether he had seen anything of Sjögren.

"Has he run away?" asked the chief of police affirmatively.

"I didn't say that!" sputtered Libotz, afraid of being too hasty. "I merely ask whether you have seen him."

"No," replied Tjärne, "but if he has not appeared at your office, it is only reasonable to assume, after our conversation of yesterday, that he has skipped town."

"Well . . . but wait until noon, before you start making an investigation. It is not a good thing to be too hasty . . ."

"Don't worry!" said Tjärne and rang off.

The forenoon passed, and Libotz kept feeling sorry for the young man who had so ruined his own future. Had he only taken Libotz into his confidence, everything could have been adjusted, but—because he thought only bad of people—things went wrong for him. At three, Askanius arrived like a savage, secretive but aching to unburden himself. In order not to betray what he had in mind, he chatted about the weather and market prices.

As they entered the dining room at the City Café, it was empty of guests. Only the proprietor was there. He was seated at the counter and made believe he was busy with his accounts. The moment he discovered Askanius, his gigantic back shot up and crawled toward the nape of the neck. He greeted his guests by baring his eyeteeth, while his lips remained tightly closed in front.

Askanius had ordered luncheon for two, without mentioning who was coming; and a table was waiting for them at the window—a practice resorted to when business was bad, so that the customers who did appear might be used as window dressing and attract the onlookers' attention from the street.

During the wintertime, the City Café thrived on diverse kinds of affairs: balls, county councils, committee meetings, and so forth, but during the summer months Askanius magnetized all the customers to his garden restaurant. The pro-prietor of the City Café, therefore, had a struggle to keep alive, and he detested his dangerous competitor with an unnatural fierceness. Having been trained abroad, he had introduced a multitude of little innovations, which Askanius had studied during previous visits, and later copied, teaching in turn these secrets to his staff.

This very day, the proprietor of the City Café would have liked nothing better than to dethrone his rival with a piece of crushing news, had he known it was he who was expected; but the telephone had merely announced the visit of two gentlemen. Now the repast was prepared and could not be canceled; thus the inevitable had to take its course.

Askanius was lofty, challenging, and flamboyant; his tone of voice was intentionally loud, and he acted jaunty and quite at ease.

He started in by making complaints about this and that.

"The butter—half margarine! Imprisonment or fine! Take your choice—we are not fussy! Corn gin, eh? It is nothing of the kind—it's distilled from potatoes! I know that everybody palms off potatoes for corn—but in Germany they treat such manipulation as counterfeit."

And in this manner he continued.

"Sherry—three crowns and fifty öre. Chambertin and, let's say, Beaune—well, could be worse—it's drinkable. New pota-toes—that are not new. Woodcock alias fieldfare" . . . and so on and so on.

All through the meal, the café proprietor had remained at his counter. He had blown himself up only to deflate again, he frothed at the mouth, but kept it shut. He no doubt had good reason for keeping his silence, but the thing that made the matter precarious was that Askanius's critical appraisal was acted out in the presence of attorney Libotz.

When the luncheon was over, the two gentlemen marched into a private dining room, which was bare and unpleasant and had too high a ceiling and too many entrances: a living room that had been transformed into a barroom. Here Askanius found fault, too, but when the stage had been set, he commenced by proposing that they call each other by their first names. He was, however, frank enough to motivate this suggestion of his by mentioning that it was merely a means to afford more comfort: it took away the formality, made it easier to converse. And then he broke loose.

"You are ignorant, brother Edward," commenced Askanius, reveling in being given an opportunity to unload his big news, ". . . ignorant of the great things that have taken place, without sound or fury, while you were busy intoxicating yourself with love. Can you imagine—this brazen, arrant rascal has had the audacity to write an article on 'The Secrets of the Cuisine' for the town newspaper . . . in which he covertly points the finger at me. That's what made me give him some of his own poison just now. . . . But wait—that isn't all. I have something else to tell you!"

With this he rose, chose a higher chair instead of the dilapidated spring chair he had occupied. He wanted to ride high, to dominate.

"This brazen arch rascal has, out of pure envy, tried to bring pressure on the Monopoly to have my license revoked. Can you imagine anything so outrageous! . . . For three days I have lived in dread uncertainty. I contacted the mayor, the provincial secretary, and finally the governor—and I am not going to lose my license. . . . But—in order to stop any further attempts in that direction, and as a precaution—I have executed a masterstroke . . . yes, well . . . I presume that sounds a little silly. . . ."

Here he smiled bitterly, self-ironically, and then continued:

"I have struck—a masterful blow—which will prevent any future attempts—in that direction—as I said just now. Many years ago—there was, namely, someone who tried to browbeat and crush me—it was on a steamer between Germany and Denmark—but it doesn't matter. . . . However, I answered. . . ." At this point he must have found his answer less murderous than he thought at that particular time in the past; and sensing the fiasco in the air, he inhibited the quotation and trotted on in his conversation.

"However—I have bought a house—a new, big house—completely unencumbered—no mortgage. . . . Can you guess where?"

Libotz could not possibly imagine where. Therefore the exhausted attorney merely nodded to east and west, signifying a negative reply.

Askanius rose, took Libotz by the arm as if he were about

to arrest him, led him over to the window, and pointed with
a chuckle to the opposite side of the square, saying nothing.
Libotz was obliged to express surprise, of course.

"Yes—Askanius has bought himself a house—directly across
from the City Café—he moves from his old place and sets up
a new, first-class restaurant and café—and the old City Café
ceases to exist!"

"But Askanius, my friend, do you really intend to leave your
old place with the garden and its customers? That's
risky. . . ." the attorney spoke up.

"No—no!" interposed Askanius. "I am not worrying about
that—for it has already been condemned by the Monopoly as
unsanitary and in need of repairs. . . ."

"That may put it in a different light . . . nevertheless I
think you are taking a risk," Libotz said frankly.

Askanius had been given an answer, and this gave impetus
to a long discussion that lasted a full hour. As usual it led to
nothing, for neither one would listen to the reasoning of the
other. Askanius, the dignified, the eternal whisperer, who liked
nothing better than to be flattered and to hear himself spoken
of as a gentleman, sat fixed in his chair, boasting and boosting
himself like an inflated balloon, straining at the hawsers and
ready to fly into the stratosphere. He now occupied the City
Café like a fortress, its proprietor his hostage and prisoner,
about to be decapitated as soon as the time was ripe. In this
manner he kept up his discourse until the break of evening,
when the waiter appeared with the evening gazette, just out.

Libotz opened the newspaper absentmindedly. Then his
arms started to shake, and the paper emitted sounds of whining and irritation.

"What is it?" sputtered Askanius apathetically, although it
sounded as if he was annoyed at something that took the spot-
light away from him.

"This is terrible," came from Libotz. "This is absolutely terrible!"

"Is the Monopoly on the warpath again?" stammered
Askanius.

"No, this is something else! Can you imagine, brother
Askanius! I found some irregularities in my assistant's ac-
counts. To ascertain the facts, I confided my suspicions to
Tjärne—but I particularly begged him not to take any drastic

steps. . . . And now he has done so nevertheless: he has inserted an advertisement, an official notice, to the effect that Sjögren has absconded after having been caught embezzling. . . ."

This was, of course, sensational, but Askanius showed perturbation over being disturbed in his scheming and planning.

"I don't see that that is anything to get excited about! All employees steal . . ." was Askanius's comment.

"But his future . . . his future will be ruined!" remonstrated Libotz.

"Faugh! He'll be given three months, and then he can go to America . . ." was Askanius's verdict.

"How can you talk like that?" pleaded Libotz.

"Do you think the Monopoly treated me with such great affection? Think of it—wanting to take away my license—rob me of my daily bread. . . ." percolated Askanius.

"That you have to thank Chief of Police Tjärne for, my dear Askanius!"

"Say nothing bad about Tjärne—he is my friend—he is entirely above suspicion . . . outstanding in his profession —an in-con-tro-ver-tible connoisseur of human nature—and he possesses an equally astonishing knowledge of what is going on in this town. . . ."

Libotz was certain in his own mind that Tjärne had betrayed the secrets of the cuisine after the long-drawn-out night vigil in the pavilion, when Askanius, drunk and sleepy, had committed treason against himself. But he was not inclined to gossip, so he simply kept quiet, listening to the praises Askanius sang to this Judas, who fabricated a confidence into an accusation. Askanius was much too subjective and egotistical to be receptive to any information of fact; he was beyond reach of any conclusive proof. Although, by nature, he was not a dolt, he had attained the stature of stupidity through haughtiness and by blinding himself to realities.

Libotz was eager to return home, but this desire made Askanius brutal. He flung words to the right, and words to the left, sputtered about card playing and drunkenness, jerked out insults about individuals who went around duping and deceiving young females, about people who came begging for a meal, and much more in this style. In brief, the whole tall tower of lies that had been built up by gossips and slanderers.

While Libotz had made only a vain attempt to defend himself, by emitting the lone word *slander*, Askanius voraciously set upon this as though it were a poor orphan. With an expansive outpouring of definitions and synonyms pertaining to the words *gossip, slander*, and *loose talk*, he expostulated:

"Slander . . . is nothing but the lie itself that I set in circulation . . . it doesn't matter whether it is of my own invention or whether I have heard it from others, or read it in the newspapers . . . for everything printed in the newspapers is a lie . . ."

This brought him by chance back on a previous tack, and he scented his way to the secrets of the cuisine and promptly began to wonder who could have betrayed him—changing the word *betray* to *slander* in the same breath. And suddenly he was bedeviled by the suspicion that Karin had made use of her brief engagement to supply Libotz with confidential professional information, and that his cooking secrets had been given wings by the attorney.

Libotz protested earnestly that Karin had never told any tales out of school, that she had never tattled.

"Did you say tattle? Do you mean to insinuate then that it is true? Do you think that I am in the habit of serving adulterated food like that swindler over there at the City Café?" Askanius had now arrived at the state of insufferableness, and Libotz luckily found, at long last, his salvation in a deadly silence that paralyzed every semblance of initiative in the heroic orator, who little by little dried up from lack of rejoinder and response.

After a prolonged and disagreeable inspection of the check, and an inglorious departure, owing to the miserly tip, the two said goodbye to each other with the mutual assurance that they had enjoyed each other's company—despite the terrible food at the competitor's café.

Libotz went home, five years older. He was reduced to crumbs by Askanius's newly attained greatness. He regretted no end that a human being could change to such an extent in the space of so short a time.

He kept wondering: Is this a new Askanius, or can it be that the old Askanius, the real Askanius, whom we have not known—but of whose existence he has given a hint now and then during his sleep-walking séances at the drinking table—has come to the surface?

The next morning Libotz sat alone in his office, examining the entry ledger once more. As he scrutinized the entries, he found them to be more lacking in orderliness than in good intentions, and, true to his concept of ethics, he sought to make excuses for the offender.

Suddenly the door opened, and a rotund little man of the peasant type strode in. His pate was barren and surrounded by a wreath of shaggy hair remnants. He wore ear-drops of lead. The crowning toupee stood upright on the crest of a low, narrow forehead, and the man's eyes spat red-hot fire.

"Are you Libotz, the attorney?" he asked, giving the lawyer's quarters a scrutinizing, penetrating glance.

"Yes. I am he."

"I have come to notify you that proceedings have been instituted against you in the local Magistrate's Court for slander and defamation of character."

"Well, I'll be . . . How did this come about? And may I ask you who you are?"

"My name is Sjögren, and I am the parish constable here and father of your law clerk, whom you have falsely accused of having run away and of having embezzled funds," the little man shot out.

"Then he hasn't run away?" stuttered Libotz.

"No, he went to the District Circuit Court yesterday morning in your behalf, and then he couldn't get a train back, and was delayed—a lawful excuse."

"Can you prove this?" ventured Libotz.

"I have two witnesses outside."

Libotz peered through the window and saw two strange types standing in the street with his clerk.

"And as far as the embezzling is concerned, it's up to you to prove your case in court."

"Just take a look at this entry ledger," retorted Libotz, who was already beginning to be a little shaky in his speech. The parish constable took more than a peek at the entries, put away the ledger and said: "This proves nothing. It's kept with no special care; but your clerk is not required to know any-

thing about keeping books—and as far as the entries are concerned, there is nothing to indicate any embezzlement."

"I would just like to inform you, Constable Sjögren, that
I have not made any accusation, or reported anyone. I merely
confided, personally and privately, to the chief of police
that . . ."

"The chief of police here is also the public prosecutor. As
such he can receive no confidential information or reports.
Whatever comes to his attention is public property. Besides,
he has withdrawn his report and named you as the instigator
and the source of the rumors," the constable shot back.

"He has withdrawn . . . ?" stammered Libotz slowly.

"Just so—and now you have to face the consequences. At
the same time, the chief of police has announced that—should
there be any falsifications or irregularities—you must take
the blame upon yourself, as you have admitted to having
taught the boy a long list of tricks . . ." the constable said
unfeelingly.

"Harmless tricks, which I have since regretted exceedingly
—been very sorry for—and punished myself for . . ." pleaded
Libotz.

"But tricks just the same!" came like a sword thrust from
the little man.

"Such innocent little things as to be writing, to make believe
he was busy whenever a prospective client came in . . ."
Libotz admitted.

"You can expect a summons tomorrow before twelve. And
we intend to demand the severest penalty according to the
statutory laws—in addition to one year's salary or wages."

"Well, so be it . . ." came meekly from Libotz. "I only wish
to say one thing, Constable Sjögren . . . that it was never
my intention to harm your son . . . On the contrary . . ."

"That's what you say now, yes! But it's too late!"

With these doomsday words, the revengeful constable
walked out, leaving Libotz, blameless though he was, to contemplate the prospect of spending three months in prison.

And now began a court case not unlike many others, where
the scoundrel carried on an action, not alone against the
innocent party, but the injured one: in short, the thief accused
his victim. In self-protection, Libotz without delay engaged a

bookkeeper, who proved beyond a doubt that falsifications had actually been perpetrated. However, as the accused was denied permission to exhibit any evidence, for the reason that he had not prosecuted, this was consequently wasted effort. When he tried to obtain some information about his clerk's actions at the court sessions, he was met by silence. Nobody was anxious to witness; they seemed to take relish in being crooked.

The chief of police was an enigma to Libotz. He hated young Sjögren, his rival, yet—one, two, three,—he turned about face and acted favorably disposed toward him. But Libotz felt it his duty to wash himself clean before Askanius. Thus, bringing along the entry ledger, he placed before him the proofs of his being the one who had been victimized. But Askanius pushed aside the volume, declaring that he was not the one to judge in this matter.

"But I want you to see that I am without guilt . . ." Libotz pleaded.

"I don't care to," answered the egotist. "Besides," and here he had the temerity to repeat the ancient lie: "When two people quarrel, it's never the fault of one."

"This is not a quarrel. It is a court action—with the thief demanding a prison sentence for the victim," explained Libotz.

"Can you prove it?" persisted Askanius.

"The proof is here in this ledger! Read!" begged Libotz.

"I don't want to read! I don't care to have anything to do with the whole business! Go away! You are disturbing me!"

And this was the way he was met everywhere. Libotz presumed that this coldness had its roots in the fact that he was a stranger, an outsider. He was well acquainted with this sort of fraternity, which had something in common with the solidarity exhibited by servants, convicts, and persons wearing some sort of uniform or badge, who would go to any length—even committing perjury—to save a comrade, or rather, a fellow culprit.

The lower court finally handed down its verdict. He was sentenced to indemnify the thief with three thousand crowns. Without complaint he took the case to the Court of Appeal. But he commented to Askanius: "Don't you think it is curious that infamous people are the ones who generally start libel and defamation proceedings?" But Askanius merely derided him.

"Do you still put faith in justice? Do you think goodness prevails?"

"Yes," replied Libotz, "even when things don't look bright."

Askanius could not help admiring him occasionally. He weighed him in his mind, analyzed him, as did the police chief; and when his mind was fresh and at its best, he arrived at the paradoxical conclusion that Libotz was either the slyest, craftiest fox to drag a tail, or an angel. But whenever Askanius was tired and sleepy, he made short shrift of him and executed him with one fell blow:

"He is a boor, a stupid fool!"

Libotz now took the back streets and would walk along with head bowed and with his shoulders raised. His yellow face grew uglier and uglier, and it evoked a feeling of revulsion in people, mingled with horror. As he walked in the streets, he was the target for glances of hatred and detestation, and he did not ward them off but he felt their sting. Reading disapproval in every face he met, he would try to figure out what reason they could have for their hostile attitude. Only then did he begin to react, felt himself guilty of one thing or another, and defended himself in long, silent interchanges. But by occupying himself with their evil thoughts, these fastened on to him like burdocks. Occasionally he was so depressed by this hate that he lost the power of resistance and said to himself: How can I, alone and wretched as I am, be in the right, when I have the whole town, with citizens quite as good as myself, against me? . . . And with this thought he started to accuse himself of all manner of things. Trivialities were magnified into great misdeeds, things forgotten and atoned for were dug up again, and he fancied himself to be the lowest of all creatures. He now began to neglect his appearance also; he had no woman to primp for. He never allowed himself to become completely threadbare. He was not shabby or unclean, but his clothes just hung on him. The tailor took advantage of him and cheated him deliberately. He went through all the preliminaries of taking measure of him but delivered ready-made apparel, while charging for tailor-made. As a result Libotz was forever shifting his shoulders in order to wriggle his clothes into position, buttoning and unbuttoning his coat, which strained across the chest. The hat annoyed him particularly. It kept wobbling to the right and the left, and by continuous tossing of the head he endeavored to keep it balanced.

Sundays he would take his black bag to his father at the hospital, after having first attended church service. By now, the old man was well-nigh hated to death. He was in bed, suffering from three different diseases. In the hospital the son was rewarded with an extra hour of torture. His father would forever accept all lying gossip as gospel truth. Therefore, prejudiced, he opened up on this false assumption with a series of reproaches, warnings, and admonitions. The son had ceased to answer, for it was no use to argue with his unreason. There was only one way out: to lead the old man's thoughts onto a different tack—to the subject of adulterated merchandise. Then he became fluent and started to orate. He commenced by defending such practice from his erstwhile viewpoint as a tradesman, discussing it from a democratic, national-economic standpoint, and developing the theory of conservation of matter. Suddenly, however, he took exception to his original viewpoint, as his present position as consumer occurred to his selfish mind. With this turnabout, there was no end to his complaints, until the time came when the son had to leave. And then came his usual, perpetual complaint: "Do you have to go already?"

"I have to. The visiting hour is over."

"You always have an excuse!" growled the father.

The son felt ashamed, as if he had told a lie; and, strictly speaking, he no doubt had, for he had used a pretext.

His legal business went well, primarily because he was considered a fox who didn't shun any means. He thrived on his undeserved bad reputation and made a very good living out of it. This he realized. And he could read in his clients' eyes how they, as it were, had a sort of secret understanding with this trickster whom they themselves had created out of the evilness that they had grafted onto him. After a time he came to regard this second ego of his as a personality with an independent existence and with which he was constantly at odds.

At this time, the town's gazette began publishing a series of caricatures, and Libotz was the target for one of these. The first time he had seen his distorted image was in connection with *Attorney Kniving*, the play about the lawyer starting out in his profession, and the impoverished old woman. The police chief had turned out to be the traitor in that instance; and Libotz thought he would lose his mind when he first saw his image in the gazette. He was horrorstricken. "Do I really look like that?" he interrogated himself; and he began to think that he did. He regarded himself in the mirror, compared, and saw a likeness. He grew to be afraid of himself, imagined himself to be a hypocrite so saturated with lies and fraud that he was unable to see himself in a true light, felt himself forever doomed . . .

. . . Libotz now turned his steps toward the chapel to pray. But he turned around, took a walk out to the mountain, where he wrestled with his God, and came home with peace in his mind, fortified in his steadfast faith so that he was able to continue living. . . .

During the summer that ensued, the town's population dwindled; and when Askanius's Karin moved away to another city, Libotz returned to his old eating place. This helped to ease his mind, for he could now sit underneath a tree, among flowers, and enjoy the brook flowing by. But he seldom saw anything of Askanius, as the café proprietor was preoccupied with putting his new establishment down by the square in order.

Libotz had now been sitting under his apple tree, which never bore any fruit, for eight days; and every evening he had seen the police chief vainly searching for someone to talk to. Libotz and Tjärne had been avoiding each other, without any attempt at explanation on the part of either, after the incidents in connection with the lawsuit. Tjärne came again today, serpenting his way between tables and trees, looking for someone to talk with. Libotz saw the lonely man's agonized, almost starved countenance and felt compassion for him.

"Don't you want to sit down with me here?" Libotz emitted.

"Why—yes," replied Tjärne; "but I suppose you are angry with me . . ." he chirped.

"No, I am not."

"Well, but I was disloyal to you—and you can blame that on my profession," said Tjärne.

"I expect no loyalty from people. . . . All I look for is someone to talk to," explained Libotz, agreeably touched by the police chief's extravagant confession.

And they began eagerly to exchange repartees by turns, like two shipwrecked men on an uninhabited island—about trifles and nothings, merely to hear their own voices; and for fear that they might collide with the unpleasant past, they avoided everything that had to do with their personal life. Lest they would have to separate and breathe their loneliness individually, they exerted themselves to be agreeable, lent added charm to each other's existence and presence, and exuded magnanimity and nobility. Tjärne was in excellent conversational form, kept his repartee in readiness, as well as in check; and whenever he found himself out of bounds through some extended speech, he generously interrupted himself with an "Oh, but that takes too long to tell"—no doubt recalling to mind Askanius's never-ending monologues. His interest in Libotz's statements showed not the slightest sign of hypocritical attention or interest. He never lacked in sympathetic concern. Unquestionably it was brought about by his need of forgetting himself and his official duties, and was therefore sincere. The urge for reconciliation, too, existed in his make-up; and so he steered clear of the sunken rocks. For instance, when Karin's name inadvertently slipped into the conversation, he immediately bifurcated and branched out to something else. After passing a few agreeable hours together, they ended the reunion by partaking of a light supper in the garden pavilion.

Up to this time they had avoided discussing the subject of Askanius. But there in the pavilion, where everything reminded them of him, his truly powerful personality could not help but press itself upon them. The hanging lamp was lit, the varnished pine walls reminded one of the cabin of a sailboat, and the knots and knags in the boards appeared like so many eyes. The room had the semblance of being peopled, the faces belonging to these eyes being supplied by the imagination. In the beginning they both seemed to be afraid of the subject Askanius. It was as if they had him with them at the table, and as if his eyes were upon them. But after some food and wine, they grew courageous, and soon the dangerous subject came to the fore. The creature was turned inside out, was scrutinized to the seams, analyzed, pondered, and brooded over. In the end, Tjärne broke into the main theme.

"I just wonder how he will make out in his new place. . . ."

"Well, that's hard to tell . . . But let us hope for the best," Libotz answered.

"It's bound to go to hell for him. That's my guess," was the hope expressed by Tjärne.

"Oh, no!" came a suppressed ejaculation from Libotz.

"Oh yes! I know!" the police chief answered back, emphasizing his statement by repeating it, and adding:

"I know! But that is a secret. The City Café is not going to let itself be competed out of business—for the proprietor has the backing of the authorities! . . ."

At this stage, Libotz found it best to withdraw from the forbidding subject; but Tjärne kept hounding him with it. Occasionally the chief of police acted as if he had spoken too freely. Then he seemed repentant. Yet in the next moment he was ashamed of his weakness, accused himself of being a coward, and with the courage of despair, he boldly reacted against any such fear. He took the step clear out and bared in one breath the whole batch of intrigues, hatched by the authorities. Now and then he peered cautiously round for someone who might stealthily be listening. Once or twice he showed real signs of fear. But he swallowed his cowardice with a gulp of cognac from his drinking glass, unlocked the sluices again—and then was suddenly gripped by panic because of Libotz's stubborn silence.

"You are not saying anything, Libotz . . . and I am talking my head off . . ."

"I'll forget everything you have said," swore Libotz.

"You are not planning to give me away, are you?"

"I am not that sort of person," Libotz assured him with simplicity.

The words "I am not that sort of person" probably were a sting in the police chief's side, but he was too indolent to pick a quarrel; and besides he had made up his mind to have a pleasant evening. The words would have to pass, but his volubility had to have an outlet; and so he reveled sensuously in this opportunity to unburden himself. He bared his opinion of young Sjögren's legal action, acknowledged that the law clerk was a swindler, with plans to establish himself independently in his own office in town in the near future, aided by the authorities. He had information that Libotz would lose in the Court of Appeal, but that he might win in the Supreme Court, if he took his case there. Next he invaded the chapter Karin, congratulated Libotz on breaking the engagement, and felt the girl was not suited to him—she was just like the rest. . . .

In response Libotz confessed he had been unworthy of her and took all the blame upon himself: he was entirely too dull in the company of women. When the two had seesawed back and forth for quite a while, Tjärne began to drop behind. After the great performance he had just given in his ecstasy, all chatter about nothings seemed banal; thus he gave up any attempt to be interesting. His conscience and his remorse— which was mostly fear of consequences—made him anxious to depart, the many eyes in the tobacco clouds gazed at him penetratingly, and he got up on his feet, covering the retreat with the brave assurance that he was prepared to stand for every word he had uttered.

"Anyhow, what do I care if the authorities should hear about it. It might do them some good," he said, stalking out.

And so the reunion broke up.

It was the first day of October, and Askanius opened his new restaurant that noon. A gigantic sign on the façade of the building bore only one word, ASKANIUS, painted in gilt letters two feet high. It was self-evident that the intention was to make them readable from the City Café without the aid of glasses. Inside, the decorations were in white and gold, and there was an abundance of mirrors. Libotz had meekly warned against the many mirrors.

"Men use mirrors only when they shave. When they drink, they don't care to look at themselves, for they are not much to look at then."

This remark was cut short by Askanius, who insisted one had to keep up with the times.

And now the great day had arrived, with its table d'hôte dinner and music. It was Askanius's idea to bring people together: not only was his restaurant to be a gathering place for the well-to-do, but for the little people also—and all were to be treated with equal courtesy. In this manner, old-fashioned, unsanitary premises would become superfluous, as Askanius advertised in the manifesto he had published in the town's newspaper. It was also advertised that the cancer of the times, individualism, would here be pulled up by the roots (!), and that people would gradually learn to tolerate one another. This educational method did not appeal to a part of the public; yet people came, out of curiosity.

However, the expected state of cordial relations failed to take place. The well-to-do looked askance at the little people; and the little people felt embarrassed among the gentlefolk. Everything was just too fine and bright for those with threadbare coats; and the men in uniform did not think it was fine enough. Whenever a champagne cork popped at the officers' table, the plain people shuddered, shrank together, and started making remarks. The tailor gabbed about unpaid bills, the shoemaker cast glances at the riding boots. In brief, there were jarring notes.

But there were still other circumstances that contributed to the uncomfortable feeling. The hat-checking business was embarrassing because of the extra tip, the waiters looked like continentals and had an air of haughtiness, and Askanius himself sat as on a throne by the counter, looking as if he was counting every single schnapps. The pantry window was also there; but now the words exchanged were spoken in a far less quiet manner.

There was not a single intimate corner in the café. One could see nothing but one's own image in a variety of poses staring from all sides. And any attempt to indulge in a serious or profound conversation—in which one had the opportunity to speak the last word and "Bottoms up," to throw off the mask and show one's real self—was made impossible by the music.

From his exalted position, Askanius could look out over the square and see the City Café. There he could see Brune, the proprietor, standing with a pair of marine binoculars (he had been a warrant signal officer in the navy) and squinting over at his competitor's. Brune's dining room was empty, and that is how Brune felt inside, but he did not have the courage to show his trepidation.

The dinner concert by the Viennese gypsy orchestra was over and the male customers were seated in the café. Askanius was counting the day's receipts. The cash drawer was bulging with the takings. "Look at this! This is *something,* isn't it?" he chirped to Libotz who was one of those present.—"This means money—and now I won't have to give credit any more!" (The slate had been discontinued.)

On the evening of this great day, at around seven, an incident took place which is still remembered and is inscribed in the chronicles of the town. While the café was filled with guests and the music was about to commence, the doors to the smaller dining room were suddenly blown open, the gas lights were extinguished, and every window and mirror shattered into bits.

It turned out that there had been a gas explosion. The guests fled head over heels. An investigation by the police chief failed to reveal what had caused the explosion, and Askanius was shaken from fright.

During the eight days it took to repair the damage, Askanius walked about like a skipper, giving commands how to maneuver, bribing the workmen and imbuing himself with fortitude.

"My customers will come back—they will be back," he sputtered, cocksure as a man in desperation. Somehow, he could not free himself from a feeling of depression over this unpropitious opening. At times his suspicions would fall on Brune, but Libotz cautioned him then and proved the absurdity of such loose speculation.

When the premises were in order, there appeared again an advertising manifesto, which proved to be a much too explicit reminder of the proprietor's American sojourn. It was in flamboyant taste, reckless, challenging. "The beginning is ever hard," "Success belongs to the bold and the daring," and other similar phrases. Added to this came banalities about hygiene, air, light, the struggle against individualism, and, again, his fixed idea of bringing the classes together, about democracy, and—as a climax—universal suffrage.

This caused the already strained feeling to spread, and after the gala opening benefit—when the curiosity seekers came to "look at the explosion"—the attendance diminished gradually.

Then Askanius became nervous, but he found consolation in the fact that the City Café did not absorb his customers. The male customers began to frequent an improvised club. The little people, who found Askanius's too expensive, cultivated an obscure little basement bar, which grew so rapidly that its proprietor had to rent the floor above and knock a hole in the ceiling and connect it with the basement.

Askanius now began an awesome fight with himself and against his own fate. Being too proud to unbend, he took refuge in humbug. He exhibited himself, partaking of his own meals in the window facing the square, to show that his place was not empty. He instructed the waiters how to busy themselves with the dressing of the unoccupied tables. He invited friends to come in for light suppers in the evening.

But his gayety was merely on the surface and masked his gallows face. His unshakable fortitude had something awesome about it. His hair was turning white, his hands were starting to be shaky. He literally scared away his last customers; and even his private supper invitations were no longer accepted.

Out of spite he spared no expenses. He allowed his hat checker to take a nap—at twenty-five crowns per month—on the shelf reserved for galoshes. The electric light kept burning in the establishment from morning until night; and as a climax he installed an orchestrion at great expense.

The waiters came and went every third day, and he was forced to engage waitresses at fixed wages. Still, no customers showed up.

To cap his misery, his wife became ill from all the frightfulness and the worry. To Askanius this seemed like a reproach, which ought to be fought off and combatted with complete unfeeling. He lived one flight up and never went out, and kept his shades drawn. He never dared inquire whether he had any customers.

Finally the day came when the premises were completely empty of guests. The few tourists and travelers who by chance strolled into the place were frightened away by the loneliness. Besides, as soon as they noticed that most of the dishes on the comprehensive menu were gone or lacking, they decided not to return.

Despite everything, Askanius stubbornly fought against all odds. His greatest joy was to stand gazing over at his competitor's, who likewise stood in the window with *his* binoculars. The two enemies gave spiritual support to each other through such duels.

Askanius's last guest had been the faithful Libotz. He sacrificed his inclinations, pilloried himself at a window table to the ridicule of the passers-by. Askanius felt this gesture was merely done out of sympathy, a charitable pittance of commiseration, and he became brutal. He acquired a hatred toward his one and only friend and plainly told him he need not trouble himself to come unless he really wanted to.

When Libotz advised him to make some changes in the premises: to remove the mirrors, to add a few smaller rooms, to wall up the windows and to make some cozy corners, Askanius responded with a discourteous answer. The loyal friend suffered from the misfortunes of the haughty restaurant proprietor, pondered his fate continuously, brooded over how he could save him—but all in vain.

What staved off the collapse of Askanius's business was the excellent profit he derived from the renting of the other premises in the house.

Christmas Eve came, and Libotz—who had nowhere to go —had arranged to spend the evening with the chief of police, though they had made no plans as to where to go.

As they were leaving, they saw Askanius's place flooded with light. He himself was there, alone, playing a game of billiards. The place looked like a ghost scene; and they decided to go for a walk in order to rid themselves of the impression. But before long, Libotz showed anxiety.

"We must go in and see him. His wife is lying ill, very ill, and he should not be left alone. After all, we are human beings . . . and he has been of help to us when times were hard," said Libotz.

"Very well, let's do it!" acquiesced the police chief. As soon as they came into the deserted restaurant, they saw at once the state of decay there. The curtains were dirty, the mirrors were smeared with dead flies, the tables were covered with dust in which people had scribbled their names. But from within the café came music—the march "Père-la-Victoire"— and as they opened the door, they found Askanius sitting alone among the numberless tables around him, listening to the music and drinking a bottle of champagne. This festive beverage, which demands a mirthful occasion: friends, relatives, or a beautiful woman to toast, seemed here to be used to toast a wake. And the invisible music band with blaring trumpets and martial drums gave the effect of ghost music.

To begin with, Askanius acted high and mighty; but as he noticed that this attitude was not successful, he expressed genuine joy over seeing his old acquaintances, and immediately busied himself by ordering supper and shutting up the place.

While he was still in his exalted stage, he was nevertheless sufficiently crushed to be agreeable. Out of fear of being asked painful questions, he promptly took hold of the conversation and poured forth, uninterruptedly, opinions about politics, the county council, the communal tax, and the railroads. Libotz and Tjärne let him go on. They were afraid to say anything themselves; for the ground was so water soaked that it could hardly support any weighty words. The supper was served. From when it came was a mystery, but the two guests had a suspicion that it had been sent out for, and that it came from the Ditch—as the little basement restaurant which had raised itself up another floor thanks to Askanius's downtrend was commonly called.

Immediately following the supper, Askanius showed how desperately and deeply crushed he was, as he brought up the subject of his misery.

"I was too old," he confessed, "and, besides, 'Pride goeth before destruction.'. . . I am lost. . . ."

"You should have closed a month ago," whispered Libotz in his ear. That was enough to wake up the real Askanius.

"Closed? I am never going to close!" was the proud retort. His soul seemed to move like a swing—now away up in the air, now away down.

"You just wait! Soon the New Year will be here, and then I'll be getting in my rents. . . . Then you'll see!—You'll see great changes here! Do you gentlemen know we will get a railway?"

Tjärne permitted him to boast for a while. He felt sorry for him. But before long Askanius became aggressive and intolerable, and the police chief thought it best to club him, as he was already half dead.

"It's no use trying to put up a fight, Askanius. Six months from now the Grand Hôtel is opening, and then both you and Brune will have to shut your doors."

Askanius fell together like an empty sack.

"What's this you say? . . . Grand Hôtel? . . ."

"It's a hotel the Monopoly is going to build," the police chief said nonchalantly.

Askanius's eyes went hither and thither, as if seeking to find some way out; but finding none, he began to discuss food, criticized the meal, and proposed that they return to the café. There the orchestrion was at once put to work. The weakened man seemed to derive energy from this accumulator: the noise put to sleep so much within him. He now became childish, tra-la-la'd along with the music, stood up on his feet and placed himself before the instrument, made believe he was conducting the band, bellowed out forte and fortissimo, and hummed piano and pianissimo, nodded to the different voice groups to fall in. This was a new incarnation of the former man of dignity, and it frightened them like the vision of some strange person in a room with locked doors.

Now the waitress appeared. She whispered something to Askanius. He gave her a rude answer:

"I don't care about that!"

Soon after, they were brought into a small room, where there were many bottles and drinking glasses. The girl was told to go to bed.

Askanius now commenced one of his Protean acts. He shed his skin; he changed his character and face every ten minutes. Now and then he seemed to speak in his sleep; he seemed to be dreaming. One minute he was in Versailles: the Emperor came forward—he spoke a few words to the singers; the next minute he was in America, in Brooklyn, and it was there that something mysterious took place—something that evoked the police chief's interest and curiosity to a very high degree. But the moment he tried to pry it out of Askanius by putting a question to him, he woke up from his trance, cutting with sober sharpness to the right and the left.

"What's that? What did you say? Did you find out anything? My friends, these fellows are nothing but masqueraders—they are not from the police. . . ."

Tjärne was about to lose his temper, but he figured it was better to sit here than to lie at home, trying to sleep. And so he just laughed an ironic laugh, as when you are amused by a comic or a clown, and let odds pass for even.

Askanius continued with his monologue.

"When a man gets older"—he never used the word *old*—

"his past becomes an incalculable vastness, time ceases to be, and he relives bygone days as if they were today. I can recall my youth . . ."—here his face actually took on the appearance of thirty—"I was exactly as I am now, exactly the same . . . I should say—h'm—not quite the same. Suppose now that a man's character is his fate—for character is inborn—then my fate is also my birthright—then I am without blame, am I not —isn't that right? . . ."

This was intended to be answered with a Yes, but Tjärne was exhausted and wanted a change.

"That doesn't follow at all. . . . Libotz tells me he discovered his fate at thirty, and pulled in his ears and started to develop his character, ending up by tormenting himself."

"I am not tormenting myself," Libotz dared to come back at him. "No one wants to torment himself, for it is human nature to enjoy life. I would like nothing better than to be able to celebrate every night with music, singing, lights, flowers, wine—yet at the same time I should like to spend my mornings working, in order to give me an appetite and to give me sleep at night . . . but I can't afford it. I ought to have the means to live that kind of life, for that's the kind of life I'd like to live. But whenever I seek some enjoyment, I suffer; and the silent commandment of duty bids me to abstain. The fear of a still worse discomfort, a greater misery, repeatedly holds me back . . . and thus I am in the battle again. . . ."

Askanius had been looking sharply at Libotz, as if he had never before heard his voice. He had forgotten the first part of the discussion—the part in which Tjärne squeezed the life out of his paradox about character. This was forgotten, and only Libotz's self-confession occupied him now.

"How curious people are! How strange!" the café proprietor said, as if talking to himself. "They think they know one another, but they don't—they know nothing! I, for example, don't know anything about you, gentlemen. . . . I don't know whether Tjärne is an honest man, or not. And if Libotz really is the person he presents himself to be, then he is not a human being. But, judging by his childish frankness a moment ago, I can only suspect that he is a person who is full of secrets . . . secrets which it is not my business to pry into. For we must respect one another's secrets. That is my maxim . . . isn't that true?"

By scrutinizing personalities so close to the seams, the company was gripped by a secret fear. They all seemed afraid of one another. Their faces took on different expressions, as if they were trying to protect themselves from attack, prepared to parry any charge. They smiled in the wrong places in order to neutralize, by anticipation, an expected sharp sally. Tjärne was fierce to look at. He had downed so much whisky that his eyes had turned yellow, as if he had been crying tears of saffron. He figuratively sat on needles, expecting that Askanius would at any moment disclose him as the originator of the article about the secrets of the cuisine and the revocation of his license. Libotz searched his conscience for some thoughtless, indiscreet word he might have let fall about either of the two men behind their back. Askanius, dissected alive, and desperate, was torn by a desire to commit psychic suicide, with an urge to drag along his companions into the abysmal depths. But he recovered from this and came up on top, feeling himself extraordinary, sublime in his downfall. He had to say something to project himself in an awful, devastating light, so that they would be simply forced, catapulted into admiration of him. And with this in his mind, he began a speech that sounded like nothing so much as a funeral oration.

"Gentlemen, the silence of night enfolds us in a veil of secrecy. . . . We are sitting here, keeping one another company out of fear of our dreams. . . . Gentlemen . . ." (and here it came!)—"I know not with whom I am sitting at this table . . . but you—you have-no-idea-who-*I*-am!"

"Well, tell us then," Tjärne interrupted unfeelingly.

At that moment the waitress entered and said loudly: "Mrs. Askanius is very sick and she asks Mr. Askanius to come to her."

"I can't help that!" Askanius roared in anger at her, who had ruined his great scene—the scene he had had in preparation for so many years. But he quickly regretted his outburst, rose, and asked to be excused.

"Of course, you must go to her," Libotz said, "and we are not going to stay any longer. You go to your wife . . ."

But Askanius found it hard to tear himself away, and he started a long-winded tirade about "The finest woman of all." Then there was a rapping on the ceiling from above.

Whether it sounded to Askanius like the hammering of nails

into a coffin, a remembrance he carried from his childhood, or whether it reminded him of some ghastly omen or premonition . . . whatever it was, he turned pale. With a presentiment of some sort of catastrophe, yet struggling with his vexation over having had to interrupt a delightful pleasure, he took farewell as of life and left through the café, where the countless empty tables stood like white mushrooms in the semi-darkness.

When Libotz and Tjärne came outside, they noticed the physician's carriage before the entrance and they instinctively felt what was in the offing. As they proceeded across the square, the sight of the Christmas trees, still lighted in some of the windows, brought home to them that it was Christmas Eve. Libotz made a sentimental remark about their own lonely life, empty of joy and happiness; but Tjärne's retort indicated he was thinking of something entirely different.

"Who do you think Askanius can be?" Libotz finally inquired, having for years been brooding over this enigma.

"Who he is? Nothing but an ordinary restaurant-keeper, endowed with an incredible arrogance—a fellow who wants to be on top in everything, good as well as bad—a colossal extrovert—a self-glorifier. . . . And his great secret? That he stole a few apples when he was a youngster—perhaps he was mixed up in a brawl in America and put in jail for three days for being drunk—or he may have left a girl in the lurch at one time—or cheated somebody who had put up bail for him. There is not a day we don't hear of such vainglorious fools—and they always boast of having committed the greatest and most interesting of crimes.—Askanius has no dangerous secrets up his sleeve; and he is not deserving of the interest he is trying to cajole out of us."

"So you think people are that simple, do you?" questioned Libotz.

"I don't give a damn about people—let them all go to Hades! . . . I am sleepy and want to go to bed! Good night, Libotz!"

That night Askanius's wife passed away, after her husband had in vain tried to convince her, as well as himself, that what she was suffering from was nothing serious. To him death was something inconceivable, inexplicable, something he kept away from. But having come to pass, he now felt it as something positive, and he literally froze to the marrow, withered down, like some delicate plant in autumn. The source of his tears, too, seemed to have frozen to its very core. He could not weep. He had to find someone to give him sympathy. He had to seek someone outside his own house. And out he went—not to Libotz, but to Police Chief Tjärne; and this despite a warning his wife had uttered against the police chief as his "worst enemy," on her deathbed. She had informed him that it was Tjärne who was the writer of the articles in the gazette and that it was he who had instigated the withdrawal of his license, as well as having originated the idea of putting up the Grand Hôtel. But to no avail. Askanius had taken an incredible liking to Tjärne. And, although he had a suspicion that it might be he who was responsible for his setbacks, he made excuses for him, and let it go at that. His was a kind of animalistic sympathy, the kind that is impossible of explanation or divination. Perhaps something about Tjärne's figure and appearance, or perhaps about his vocal intonations, had something to do with this. Or it might have been that he reminded Askanius of someone he had known and liked in the past. Libotz seemed to recall that Askanius had once made the remark: "That man Tjärne is very like a younger brother of mine—of whom I was very fond. He is dead now." The police chief could be insolent, disloyal, yet Askanius remained steadfast in his liking for him. He continued to dispose of his secrets. And they were at once taken advantage of and misused by the chief of police, not so much out of maliciousness as for personal gain. The circulation of such pieces of information among the authorities attained him their favor.

For two days Askanius went to Tjärne's home and was received, but never remained with him very long. Feigned telephone calls soon interrupted and cut his visits short.

On the third day Askanius sought out Tjärne at the police headquarters and seated himself on a chair beside his desk. The fourth day the chair had disappeared, and the old man was forced to stand. The fifth day was the day of the funeral. Tjärne was absent. The pressure of his official duties kept him away.

This wounded the old man's feelings, and when he now was left alone with himself, and his "best friend" had abandoned him, he saw no other way out of his loneliness than to seek out Libotz.

In the attorney's rooms he was permitted to sit in the sofa and talk on and on, as long as he wanted, about his departed one, her illness, and her last moments. But it could plainly be seen that it was not to Libotz he came, but merely to someone with ears who would listen to him—for the bereaved man never gave his friend a glance; and it suddenly occurred to Libotz that he had never seen him bestow a glance on him—although he had, on occasion, seen his eyes.

As Libotz now, as usual, ended the sitting with the advice: "Close the restaurant!" Askanius replied:

"I shall never close!"

At New Year's however, the City Café closed its doors and bankruptcy followed as a consequence.

Askanius stood at his window with his binoculars, and watched the furniture being removed.

"Why, of course. . . . He had no backbone. One must have a strong back to start a business like that. . . ."

And he added:

"This is Nemesis . . . for he tried to take the bread out of my mouth. You don't have to take revenge on people like him. . . . People of his ilk bring revenge upon themselves."

About the same time, the Court of Appeals handed down its decision. Libotz was exonerated. This was a defeat for the whole town, and its rage at once was leveled at the stranger. It took its expression in a decided, exaggerated sympathy for Sjögren, who generally was anything but liked. Unseen hands helped him to establish himself in a business of his own, a commercial bureau for the purpose of competing with Libotz and driving him out of business.

But the judgment that exonerated Libotz had a very special influence on his character. For he had seen that justice was not extinct. This quieted and consoled him and removed all doubts about the benevolence of the cosmic system. He was cautious not to gloat over his victory. He went his way in tranquillity, and could now be seen again on the town's main streets. He felt himself protected from the evil glances of the inhabitants, immune to taunts and jeers. He refused to hear them. He turned his eyes away from the shop windows, where he could have seen caricatures of himself every week, had he been curious.

In this manner he lived his life. It was as if he had been girded by an impenetrable diving outfit. He sought out neither the little people nor those of means and importance. "I belong to the middle class," was his customary answer, "and I shall remain true to it."

During an election campaign the liberals tried to inveigle him into pleading their cause in speeches. But he declared he was not a liberal in the same sense as they. "The upper class is conservative and the lower liberal, quite naturally. But when the liberal lower class considers itself the cream of society, entrusted with man's destiny, then that is nothing short of nonsense."—And that is why he was rejected: because he could not be used for selfish ends. And he was just as glad.

In the beginning, Sjögren's competition was felt by Libotz. He enticed away some of his clients, and for a time Libotz had his share of difficulties. To boot, he had to pay for his brother's bond—a matter which he, however, had expected. But with time he regained his practice. The authorities then came to Sjögren's aid by assigning to him various commissions and transactions; also he was chosen to represent the Monopoly, was appointed secretary of the City Council, representative of the underwriters, and finally auditor for the Grand Hôtel, which opened the following winter.

Old man Askanius, his hair turned white, stood by his window, drumming on the pane—day in and day out—watching the Grand Hôtel grow up out of the ground. The higher it grew, the more the aging man seemed to shrink. And this could be said literally, for he now reached only to the lower window cornice, and he was unable to open the ventilator, standing on the floor.

The whole day long he would do nothing but play billiards, and evenings he would generally sit by himself in the café, sampling his wines and listening to the orchestrion. The entire restaurant would be glowing with light, fifty blazing bulbs. Saturdays, the police chief and Libotz would be invited, and then the oldster lived his life over again. He recited his old stories, mixing names and dates, made preparations for his grandiose scene, which was forever being interrupted by Libotz, who would not allow Tjärne the ignoble pleasure of having his friend's fate placed in his hands, if there should be any such dangerous secret in his life as Askanius had intimated—something one could not be sure about.

Askanius knew only too well that the moment the Grand Hôtel was opened, his license would not be renewed. But he would not admit it. He did not have the strength to put in a request for a renewal or to make any complaint. He had now come to be regarded as a little foolish, almost on the verge of being ready for the asylum; and, had he had any heirs, they would undoubtedly have had him declared incompetent. He had, in fact, some nieces and nephews away up somewhere in the country, but he refused to acknowledge them as relatives. To this man of subjective outlook it was sufficient not to believe in their existence. He had, however, once in the wee hours of the morning confided this dangerous bagatelle to his "one and only friend" Tjärne; and the police chief had eagerly gobbled up this bit of intelligence with ravenous appetite. In doing so, he had given himself away, for Libotz had observed a look in his eyes which spoke only too plainly the thought: "Heavens, has he relatives! I didn't know that!"

The last days in June a little incident occurred that made Libotz more depressed than he had been for a long time. He was asked to move from his premises. The landlord, a paint dealer, had a glass door leading to his own quarters from the hall, and the pleasant old man had always been in the habit of greeting him in a friendly manner, without any attempt at a closer approach. Libotz had liked the old man for his kindly attitude. For this reason he became a victim of the usual delusion that he, in turn, was looked on with favor by the landlord; and this despite his having heard it rumored that the man was an old rascal. Libotz, however, put no faith in this rumor, thinking it was merely gossip and slander. When he questioned the paint dealer concerning the reason for his having been given notice to move, he replied evasively, giving excuses about reparations, changes, and similar fabrications and falsehoods.

But just as this was going on, Askanius came wobbling in, and after having puffed and panted, he suddenly fell to his knees, exclaiming: "Save me! Save me!"

"What is it? What has happened?" asked Libotz, who was ready to weep.

"They want to place me under a guardianship!" screeched Askanius, quite beyond himself.

For this was the very worst that could have happened to him. He, the proud man, financially independent, to be robbed of property and possessions, to be placed under the thumb of others, and to have to eat the crumbs they felt like feeding him. . . .

Libotz promised to take action in his behalf, and began to collect evidence, which consisted mainly of proof that Askanius was in every respect competent, and retained all his faculties. Having sent the old man home with the admonition not to worry, he went first to get Tjärne's signature. The police chief promptly and stubbornly refused, declaring he was not qualified, that his signature might be challenged. But being pressed further, he gave as his opinion, quite frankly, that Askanius was demented, that his very actions incriminated and judged him.

"It couldn't be you, could it, who is behind all this?" Libotz said quickly, without giving any further thought to what he had said.

"Are you accusing me of intrigues, of being a schemer?" he roared. "Look out! You-had-better-look-out!"

Libotz continued his rounds, but received no signatures. At the same time, he went searching for new quarters. But the advertised premises were always rented; and when he advertised, he received no replies. Then he began to realize that he was condemned to be evicted.

And then the Askanius case came up before the Magistrate's Court. There was no sign of any relatives of the old man; but Sjögren was there, fully empowered to represent them. He had in his possession affidavits testifying to Askanius's mental condition, and these were accepted by the magistrate.

Libotz took the defense in a long statement. He attacked the Monopoly for having caused Askanius's ruin and for having condemned his premises as unsanitary, while the City Café and the Ditch were allowed to continue unmolested, although their premises were in still worse condition. He recalled to their mind, in a long statement, Askanius's garden, its healthful location, the flowing brook with good, clean water. He reminded them of the well-aired dining room next to the expansive glass veranda. In short, he said everything that could be said in rebuttal to the plaintiff's charges. Libotz emphasized as his chief argument that Askanius was a man of means without issue, and that he therefore had every right to engage in a little fantasy, especially after having been so hard hit recently by his wife's death.

The court listened. Sjögren rebutted, reading aloud affidavits corroborating that Askanius was mentally sick, incompetent and in need of care, and that now, since kindhearted relatives had offered to look after him . . . and so on and so forth . . . The case was postponed.

From this day another change could be noticed in the café proprietor's behavior. He commenced to take short trips by horse and buggy to various railroad stations. But he always returned home at night. He visited the bookshop and was engrossed in reading. His subjects were primarily jurisprudence, chemistry, and physics. With the reading, the old character mask from his early days as a tavernkeeper came back. Polished, reserved, and uncommunicative, yet kindly, he did not complain any longer; and he nourished no hope that he would gain victory in court. Yet he did not close his restaurant.

One day in the late summer, while Askanius was sitting alone in the empty dining room reading his newspaper, Police Chief Tjärne came crawling in through the door, his small head first, and the head asked: "Is the proprietor here?"

"Come in, old friend," replied Askanius. "What can I do for you?" Tjärne wormed his way among the tables and showed Askanius a document, heavily decorated with seals and ribbons and sealing wax.

"You forgot to close yesterday, as directed to do . . ."

"I am never going to close!" answered Askanius, who had practiced long and diligently just how to utter this rejoinder.

"Then I shall have to close for you!" said Tjärne.

"You are very welcome . . . But I shall never close!"

This well-prepared dialogue made a success. The police chief laughed loudly.

Askanius went on to his triumph.

"You see now that Askanius is a man of his word! No one is going to get the best of me!"

Tjärne went out into the vestibule, took out the key and

placed it in the keyhole from the inside, locked the door, and his task was completed.

"Now let us drink a little glass—a farewell toast," proposed Askanius, as he brought out a tall, slender bottle, enclosed in basket weave.

"What is this you are offering me?" inquired Tjärne.

"This is my very finest wine—the best I have—and the most expensive. . . ." boasted Askanius.

"What is it?" asked Tjärne tartly, but with curiosity.

"Have you never tasted maraschino?"

"No, I didn't get to that yet," admitted Tjärne.

"It is a cherry liqueur from Dalmatia—seven crowns a bottle."

They drank. They chewed on a macaroon.

"Oh-yes, it's good—tastes of bitter almond—a little too sweet for my taste. I like something a little stronger, you know . . ."

There was a pause. Tjärne, true to his habit of using fictitious telephone appointments at his office as an excuse for breaking away, slithered out between tables, body and head interlaced, his eyes on the telephone.

Askanius was aware of the trick, but did not have the heart to embarrass his friend, so he let it pass and thus saved Tjärne from further explanations.

"I understand perfectly. You are a very busy man, and you have to go. Thanks, however, for everything in the past—and especially for the tactful manner in which you carried out your unpleasant duty," he said graciously.

With these words Askanius had washed out the humiliation of having been locked out from his own premises, so to speak —and with a sealed lock at that. For, as a matter of fact, Tjärne's demeanor had been anything but discreet. On the contrary, he had behaved with cynical mockery.

"I know you realized it is my duty; and duty comes before anything else," the police chief smoothly rounded out his idle talk, trying to slink out through the café entrance in order not to have to go to the trouble of unlocking the main entrance door.

"Go out through the main entrance, Tjärne . . . Nobody will be coming in here anyway!" jested Askanius. But it was too late. Tjärne had already left.

Askanius's was shut, the sign was taken down, the tables were stripped of their covers, the window blinds drawn. . . . And so the town was saved from having to witness the spectacle of the lonely man spooking about behind the dusty panes.

When the old man was seen in the town's streets, and acquaintances greeted him with a roguish: "Well, you did have to close anyhow, didn't you?"—Askanius invariably shot back: "Askanius did not close! Tjärne did the closing!"

And people could not help but admire his equanimity and good sense in the face of disaster.

After the closing, the old man would spend most of his time up in his apartment. He put his papers in order in his bureau-desk, burned old letters in the stove. Often he could be seen sitting reading in his books. He was even and quiet in his temper; and the old housekeeper could find nothing abnormal about him.

Occasionally, however, he would go down into the restaurant and would then spend most of his time in the kitchen. The old woman had expressed the surmise—on being interrogated by the police chief one day when he met her in the square—that her employer was occupied with inventing a new liqueur that would bear his name; and this concoction would forever memorialize him and carry his name to posterity!

Autumn was now approaching.

During this period Libotz had come to realize the impossibility of remaining in the town and carrying on his practice there. Therefore he made no further attempt to find new quarters for himself. He was boycotted. When he visited his father, he was greeted with invective.

"I haven't complained to you, have I?" said Libotz in exchange and in a fit of devil-may-care. But the old man had no comprehension of such humor.

"It's your own fault, and you have no cause for complaint . . ." his father threw back at him.

"I have not complained," answered Libotz weakly.

"You have made your own bed, and now you have to lie in it. . . ." Here the old man turned painfully in his bed, angry over having uttered such a stupidity.

"Very well, go your own way," he continued. "You never were anything but a disorderly, unruly creature, dishonest in your work, given to drinking, obstinate toward the authorities . . ."

The father unloaded all his own vices and faults on the son, who silently let him rid himself of abuse and invective. Weighted down by trespasses not his own, he deserted after having heard the usual: "Are you leaving already?" The lineup in the corridor and entrance hall, the race between taunts, as smarting and punishing as a flogging, made him again ponder his strange fate. "The sins of the fathers," he thought to himself. . . . "Yes, that is what it seems like." And he recalled to mind how he had always been cheated whenever he went into a shop to trade. Now he could only explain this by thinking that it was the father's spurious merchandise that, ghostlike, appeared again, in retribution. He remembered also how everybody envied and begrudged him when he profited from his efforts. If he took a glass of wine some Sunday down at the Ditch, some half-acquaintance would invariably come over to his table, adding spice to his wine with some such remark as: "Well, well! Drinking wine, eh?" Yet he purposely avoided expensive delicacies. Even at his present age of forty, he had never tasted pickled salmon, and he had eaten asparagus only once—when he was engaged to Karin.

But even in little things this grudge and envy came to the fore. It was as if everything was too good and too fine for him. He bought a paper cutter one day; it was embellished with imitation gilt. The price was a mere two crowns, but the object made a showy display. Tjärne came into his office and spotted it immediately. "Why, look at that! Well, well, that's something!"

The whole thing was demoniacal. The moment he began to make a little money, he was able to realize a dream from his childhood: to own a silk umbrella. But no sooner had he bought it than he found it exchanged for one of cotton. Out of spite he bought another silk umbrella; and when this, too, disappeared, he decided to be satisfied with one of cotton.

"It is not for me to wear silk and satin," he consoled himself, as though thoroughly convinced that his fate was being tampered with.

During his engagement period he affected a gayly colored necktie and a stickpin. The town almost went mad. "Just look at him!" resounded from everywhere. He defied the cries for a while. But in the end he was forced to hoist down the flag. Then there was peace in town again.

The falsifications of Sjögren he had reconciled himself with by this time. He had partly transposed them to his old father's debt register, partly assigned them to the accounts of the inexplicable. He had namely made the observation during a great many of his criminal cases that the criminal was given some sort of special protection, that he was beyond reach. He had similarly discovered that his housekeeper had taken for herself the singular privilege of pilfering. He caught her a number of times after setting a trap for her. But invariably she was able to clear herself. After that he decided to close his eyes.

But now, when he was about to move away from the town, he decided to sell his furniture on credit. In the past he had behaved as humanly as possible in all claim cases. He had never sent any communications in envelopes stamped with the name of his legal firm, but always used ordinary plain ones that were not transparent. Following a demand, he would request a private talk, and then suggest arrangements for payment by installments. To persons in need who behaved decently and respectably he would even advance the necessary amount. But now, when he tried to collect moneys and debts owed to him, he realized that he had no promissory notes; and when he sent his debtors courteous letters asking for payment, these were in some cases not even answered. And everyone who owed him money promptly stopped recognizing him from this time on. On the other hand, they were quick to spread the rumor that he was a miser and a bloodsucker.

"Faugh! That there can be such people in the world!" was all that he said. But he said it only to himself, for if he had said it to others, they would have laughed at him.

And he felt ashamed on their behalf. He felt as if he himself had done something wrong; and he sought to make up for their meanness by doing good and by being charitable to them —and so he forgot about his claims.

The first of October had arrived. It was the day the Grand Hôtel was to be opened at noontime.

On the morning of the great day, the chief of police received a telephone call from Askanius's housekeeper. She inquired whether he had seen Askanius. When Tjärne responded in the negative, he was asked to come over to his house at once.

The moment Tjärne entered the building, he received a shock of fright. From inside the closed café he heard the most infernal sounds, resembling music, but in the strangest variety of keys, rhythm, and disharmony. Notes were scrambled together in a chaos of drumming, roaring, bellowing, howling, screeching noises. He realized at once it was the orchestrion, that something must be in disorder, out of joint. He ran up the stairs to Askanius's apartment. He was greeted by the housekeeper, who stood wiping her eyes with her apron.

"What is wrong?" demanded the chief of police.

"I don't know," replied the old woman, "but it has been playing these strange sounds all night. . . ."

"Then he must be down in the café . . . for it can't play longer than fifteen minutes. . . . Come with me, and let's go down there," ordered the police chief.

"But he has locked the door from the inside . . ." wept the housekeeper.

"I can open any door," boasted Tjärne.

When they had come downstairs, the police chief put his pick in the keyhole, turned it, and the key on the inside fell on the floor in the dining room. They hastened into the café and were greeted with the most horrible, piercing, ear-splitting fanfares, interspersed with chorals, waltzes, fragmentary overtures, and military parade marches. And seated at his private table in the center of the café was Askanius, rigid as a statue, white as marble, with an expression of nobility on his regular features. Beside him stood a bowl of silver and a bottle of maraschino.

The chief of police immediately was aware of his duty and started his investigation to the accompaniment of the diabolical music.

"Dead! Peace be with you, old friend!—Maraschino—that indicates hydrocyanic acid—but the case is a novel one—should be taken note of—he was a sly, inventive fellow—he can get a respectable burial—and if he carried insurance, it will be paid. . . . What's in the bowl here?—Ashes—but it has contained burning cognac. . . . Anyhow, he leaves the house—and the heirs will have to do the worrying. . . . How in heaven's name can that infernal noise keep on like this forever and a day?—Oh, I see now—he has connected it up with the electric cable—and the cylinder with the spiked points has become displaced, has shifted. . . . Well, now—let's send for the doctor—then it's up to the relatives to pay for the funeral —they won't like that. . . . Don't touch anything, Augusta, before the doctor comes—I have to get back to the office to write my report."

And with this Askanius was expedited. It was now seven o'clock in the morning.

At nine o'clock that same morning of the first of October, attorney Libotz was seen marching out of the town, past the customs. He had previously sent ahead his two trunks, and had now a desire to hike on foot the few miles to the railroad station, which was situated on the other side of the hills. The weather was gray and dismal, but dry, and the exercise in the fresh air gave the lonely wanderer renewed vigor. He was not destitute. On the contrary, he carried in his pocket a bank draft for his savings. He had also prospects of new fields of endeavor. Yet he felt sorrowful and depressed, and he presented the appearance of a man weighted down by grief and worry, very much like a criminal just turned loose and in doubt of which gate to enter on returning to society. The open fields lay stretched out with fallow land like a vast desert, but the hills in the distance beckoned, and he marched on with eyes lifted up to them. He was in need of something to look up to. He had always had need of it. He never turned to get a last glimpse of the community he had just left—for he did not wish to hate anyone or anything.

Then he heard a vehicle coming up behind him. Two of the town's inhabitants were in it; and as they passed, Libotz heard them emit some jesting words.

"Look, there he goes—the scapegoat!"

It seemed to him an innocent jest, yet it was true. And he recalled to his mind the Feast of the Atonement of the Old Testament, at which a goat, loaded down with the sins of all the people, was driven out into the desert, consecrated to Azazel, or in other words, the Evil One—who thereby regained what was his. This role was neither a grateful one nor an honorable one. But had not Christ carried the same burden of disgrace and dishonor? And did not this have a meaning beyond our understanding?

The outcast, also, felt some of the sting of this, the onus of bearing the hatred of others, being laden with it, with their meanness and maliciousness, which they had grafted onto him.

Could it be that he was the serum animal, who had within him the virus of poison and ills, which through him was to be transmuted, transubstantiated into the curing remedy? As long as he did not return hatred with hatred, he was out of reach of their power. But the moment he let himself be influenced and was roused to anger, he felt the poison. In order to keep his thoughts aloof from bitterness, he kept repeating to himself passages from the Bible that had impressed themselves most on his mind. And these passages had the accumulated effect of the truth of ageless centuries upon his childlike mind.

"My grace is sufficient for thee: for my strength is made perfect in weakness."

"Naked came I out of my mother's womb, and naked shall I return thither."

"And thou, son of man, be not afraid of their words, though briers and thorns be with thee; and thou dost dwell among scorpions."

"Woe unto you, when all men shall speak well of you."

"Ye are bought with a price; be not ye the servants of men."

. . . And when he reached the hilltop, his own Mount Tabor, where he had fought in night and darkness, he ascended it. He now saw the town in the distance, surrounded by the walls of the hills like a prison yard. And it seemed to him as if it were he who had regained his liberty. But in the same breath he could not help but think of the good things he had enjoyed in the little town. And in his thoughts he sent a friendly greeting to Askanius, of whom he had taken leave the evening before— and whose fate was unknown to him. In his memory he now saw his friend only as the quiet, estimable man, who—on Libotz's first visit to his establishment—had made place for him and given him his own, private table. . . .

After a last farewell, he descended the other side of the mountain and found himself in the midst of a different scenery, with hills on the edge of a forest. He continued his walk, and after another hour he was sitting in an inn, drinking a cup of hot coffee.

Here he was unknown; therefore he hoped he would be received in a friendly manner. But the people at the inn needed only to look at him and their faces would darken and their voices be stilled. No one had the courage to speak to him, much less offend him. He was a marked man. And this was his very protection.

Just then was heard the sound of a vehicle coming to a stop, and in came the little town's dispenser. The man did not seem elated over the encounter with Libotz. But he wanted to talk to someone, and so he had to be satisfied to talk to the despised one. They chatted about this and that, and Libotz entered against his will into a confidential conversation with him. Here, separated by a mountain, he now felt the urge to reflect on the happenings in the town.

"Why were people so wrathful against me," he finally asked, requesting bluntly a solution of what had happened to him there.

"That's something that just cannot be explained," replied the dispenser generously. "Your appearance was against you. Your name annoyed people, too. The name Libotz has something offensive about it. It would have been better if your name had been Lobitz—at least it reminds one of something: a railroad station, or a mine. . . . Besides, nobody knows why he loves or hates. . . . This doesn't mean that the townspeople were in love with that swindler Sjögren. Oh, no, their only reason for helping him was vindictiveness: to get back at you. Now that you are gone, he'll sink like a ship. They set their Barabbas loose—now it won't be long before they put him in jail again—but they had to set him free first. And Askanius died just in time. . . ."

"What's that you say? Askanius . . . is . . . dead!" stuttered Libotz.

"Yes—didn't you know?"

"No!" said Libotz, almost in disbelief.

"He died of hydrocyanic acid. . . . But there was no way of proving it. . . . He was a shrewd man, that fellow," testified the dispenser in a tone of admiration.

Libotz shrank together, deep in thought, and the dispenser rose.

"Do you know what they used to call you?" asked the dispenser with something of a sneer on his face.

Libotz knew, but he did not answer.

"The Scapegoat . . . that's what they called you.—And let me tell you something curious. . . . If two persons had a disagreement, they became friends again the moment you became the topic."

"That is, indeed, curious . . ." was all that Libotz could say.

"Yes, they would tear you to pieces, empty their mutual hatred on you and your counselor's service, and they would forget their differences.—I know a married couple, for instance, who were about to be divorced. . . ."

"Could that be the tanner who came to see me?"

"Yes! . . . And no sooner had he come home to his wife than he started to slander you so thoroughly that the wife became ecstatic . . . and in that very moment they were reconciled."

"How strange! How very strange!"

"Yes, damned strange . . . but all life is strange . . . And, do you know, it came to be a proverb in town that whenever it went well for anyone, he could ascribe his good luck to Libotz. No one could succeed in being elected to the Town Council without bellowing about Libotz and saying something derogatory about him. . . . And the editor of the town's newspaper owed his and his wife's and their three children's livelihood to the caricatures he published of you. . . ."

"Did he print caricatures of me so often, then?" queried Libotz.

"Don't you know?" was the astonished answer the dispenser gave.

"No."

"You lie!" spat the dispenser.

"I wouldn't dare to lie. I haven't the courage."

"You are a poor wretched worm, Libotz. . . . And that's why things went badly for you. . . ."

"Not too badly!"

"They say you have saved your money. How about a loan, eh?"

Libotz smiled. This lighthearted, carefree manner of looking at people and at life—which to some was a serious responsibility—yes . . . there was, indeed, a vast difference between the destinies of human beings. . . . Why this should be so was something that could not be fathomed or explained. Perhaps it was meant to be so.

He smiled again but he gave no response to the dispenser's last question.

The dispenser put on his coat, still chattering away.

"That fellow Tjärne—he is a great trickster . . . but Askanius kept his faith in him to the last. Can you imagine what Askanius did? Out of meanness to his heirs, he scratched and defaced every mirror in the place with his diamond, or rock crystal. The mirrors were scribbled full of his inanities and silly platitudes—such as for instance:

> People are not what they seem to be.
> T——e (meant to be Tjärne) is an honest man.
> but L——z (that's meant to be you) is suspect.

"To boot, the police chief was left a considerable legacy by Askanius—for having been his 'one and only friend in this life'!" the dispenser ended his account.

"How strange! How strange!" Libotz uttered contemplatively.

"Would you like to come along with me? I am leaving now . . ." the dispenser offered generously.

"No, thank you, my friend; I prefer to walk."

"Well, goodbye then!"

And Libotz trudged forward again, toward the highroad, and went to face new experiences—which he could not help but foresee, but no longer had any fear of. . . .

Issues for Discussion

The following questions can serve as a check on the accuracy and comprehension of the individual's reading, alerting him to central points he may have overlooked or insufficiently understood. In addition, they may aid both students and instructors in comparing, relating, contrasting, and drawing conclusions from important and illuminating aspects of the material. The questions are intended to be suggestive only; each should generate additional issues for discussion and writing assignments that are here left largely implicit.

1. Does the stress on song, music, and dance in the opening of *The Bacchae* have any relation to scapegoat rituals as described in Part I of this book?

2. If the scapegoat serves to purify society of its sins and ills, what specific sins or faults is the community guilty of in *The Bacchae*? What clues about this appear in Pentheus' opening speech?

3. How is Dionysus' foreign origin useful in adapting him to the role of a scapegoat?

4. Does any character other than Pentheus seem to function as a scapegoat? Who? In what ways?

5. What similarities and differences do you see in Pentheus' behavior toward Dionysus and the latter's treatment of Pentheus? Does the one act as an overture and a forewarning of the other?

6. How would one describe and classify Pentheus' attitude toward religion generally and religion of ecstacy and inspiration in particular?

7. Who are the two Gods that Teiresias claims are mankind's "two supreme blessings"? And what are the purposes of

these blessings? Does Pentheus' reaction to these values indicate a basic philosophical difference in the perception of life?

8. Is there any symbolic significance in Dionysus' being sent down to confinement in Pentheus' dark prison?

9. Why does Pentheus dress as a woman? Is it ironically related to the myth of Dionysus? What purpose does Dionysus have in persuading Pentheus to wear women's clothes?

10. What is Pentheus' response to seeing Cadmus and Teiresias clothed like Dionysus? And what relevance does his attitude have to the later behavior that is manifested toward him?

11. Upon whom does Dionysus cast the spell to bring about the results of his anger? Why inflict the passion on the women so that they become the instrument of his revenge when they worship Dionysus as he desires?

12. Does Pentheus embody Frazer's point about vicarious suffering? What is his ritual relation to the city of Thebes?

13. Does the town itself appear to be a scapegoat? In the overall world of Dionysus' rule is Pentheus the specific leader and scapegoat figure among the people? Does the exodus of Cadmus and Agave from Thebes at the end of the play support the scapegoat theme?

14. What evidence is there in *The Bacchae* that Dionysus is linked with what Murray calls the Year Daemon or the Vegetation Spirit? Does this seem a central aspect of his nature?

15. Murray suggests that Pentheus and other Greek heroes "were essentially like Dionysus." What similarities do you find between them in *The Bacchae?*

16. Murray declares that "the general temper of tragedy moved strongly away from the monotony of fixed ritual." What elements and means does Euripides use to avoid such monotony?

17. How closely does the six-stage ritual of Dionysus as described by Murray fit the structure of *The Bacchae?*

18. Murray says many of the details in the play are taken either from Aeschylus, the predecessor of Euripides, or from the ritual of Dionysus. Does it make any difference to the inter-

pretation of the play which of these was Euripides' immediate source?

19. What evidence does Hoffman present to support his view that Hawthorne's story deals with "the deposition of the Scapegoat King." How would you defend his thesis?

20. Is there any sense in which Robin's "bumpkin" qualities are connected with the scapegoat motif?

21. Which of the characters in the Hawthorne story can be classified as a scapegoat? If more than one, how does the thematic emphasis differ in the individual cases?

22. How are the fancy–reality and the scapegoat patterns related in the story?

23. What are some of the chief differences in psychological emphasis of the scapegoat figure and theme in *The Bacchae* and "My Kinsman, Major Molineux"?

24. Compare the roles of Dionysus and his kinsman King Pentheus in *The Bacchae* to the two kinsmen in Hawthorne's story. If this Dionysian revel and ritual needs to be repeated for the fulfillment of the crops and vegetation rite, could Hawthorne be using this ritual to imply the future fulfillment of American society? Is there any implication that the young boy of Hawthorne's story will fatefully pattern his existence after his kinsman?

25. What means does Lawrence use to make his hero a human being as well as a symbol?

26. What themes apart from that of the scapegoat seem most prominent in the story? How are they related to the scapegoat theme? Does Vickery's essay suggest any relations?

27. Does the fact that Lawrence modeled his characters, especially Egbert, on actual persons affect one's view of the scapegoat motif? Of the general idea of interpreting the work on the basis of the myth?

28. What event begins the development of Egbert as a scapegoat? Does this seem to suggest that Lawrence places a different emphasis on the meaning of the scapegoat than Hawthorne?

29. What similarities of theme and emphasis do you see in Lawrence and Euripides?

30. Does Lawrence relate the scapegoat to sex in the same manner as described by Frazer? What specific differences do you note?

31. What is the relationship between Egbert and Winifred's father? Can it be described in mythic terms?

32. Lawrence emphasizes the theme of pagan versus Christian attitudes in Egbert and Winifred. Does Lawrence imply that Egbert is made a scapegoat because of his anti-Christian values and attitudes?

33. In what ways does Lawrence's communal selection of the scapegoat differ from Pritchett's treatment of the same aspect?

34. What differences are there in the scapegoat rituals of Lawrence and the Bible? How do they differ in the functions they serve?

35. Both Lawrence and Hawthorne explore the personal feelings of the scapegoat figure. To what extent and in what ways can the two sets of feelings be compared and contrasted?

36. The essay on Lawrence suggests that parenthood crucially alters the world of Winifred and Egbert and that this contributes to the development of the scapegoat. Might this view have critical implications for *The Bacchae* and "My Kinsman, Major Molineux" as well?

37. The same essay suggests that Egbert is a *tabu*-figure. Are there any characters in the other stories of whom the same could be said?

38. Which of the scapegoats in other works are treated, like Egbert, as fertility figures, as embodiments of phallic potency? Do the stories treat this aspect differently from the accounts given in Frazer and Bronowski?

39. What features in Lawrence's story suggest he is attaching both pagan and Christian traits to Egbert? Does this affect his consistency as a character?

40. Does Frazer provide any analogues or parallels that help to explain Faulkner's stress on the weather and the time of year?

41. Are there any significant relationships between Miss Minnie Cooper and the female worshippers of Dionysus in *The Bacchae?*

42. What are the implications of rape being used as the basis of the scapegoat selection in "Dry September"? Do Bronowski's remarks about society's concern with authority illuminate the issue?

43. Is Will Mayes the only scapegoat in the story by Faulkner? If there is more than one, how do they differ? What distinguishable facets of society's nature does each reveal?

44. Are there any similarities between the society of "Dry September" and that of "The Lottery"? What is the major difference?

45. What is the structural and thematic function of Part 2 of "Dry September"? How is it connected with the scapegoat motif?

46. Does Part 5 of Faulkner's story have any relevance to the ritual pattern of the scapegoat and the reactions it engenders?

47. Why, in your estimation, does Vickery call "Dry September" an "ironic rendering of the primitive scapegoat ritual"? In what does the irony consist?

48. Can the stories of Hawthorne, Lawrence, Faulkner, Pritchett, Jackson, and Baldwin be differentiated by the characters' degree of consciousness of enacting the ritual of the scapegoat?

49. What part does fear play in the selection of the scapegoat in the stories by Pritchett, Jackson, and Lawrence?

50. What comic features does Pritchett give to the scapegoat theme? Is the ending of the story comic too? In the same sense or a different one?

51. Is any symbolic value to be attached to the description of Lupinsky's physical appearance?

52. Why does Pritchett's story recurrently allude to "Yids"? Is the motif of racial intolerance as prominent as in "Dry September"?

53. The essay on Pritchett suggests that he and Lawrence handle the scapegoat ritual quite differently. What are some of the most important differences you have noticed?

54. This essay also suggests that Pritchett's characters use the scapegoat myth as an expression of cultural values. Could the same be said of Lawrence and Faulkner? Specify the major values each society seems to express or embody.

55. What part do tradition and custom play in society's attitude toward the ritual of the scapegoat in Jackson, Pritchett, Baldwin, and Faulkner?

56. What similarities do you find in the orgiastic dance described by the messenger in *The Bacchae*, the mob's behavior in "The Lottery," and the responses of the people of the street in Pritchett's story?

57. Why do several of the stories make use of more than one character as scapegoat? Does this have anything to do with the ritual's separation from its religious origins?

58. What changes in character and role take place when Lawrence's Egbert and Pritchett's Art Edwards are cast as scapegoats? Are their changes similar or different?

59. How does the Jackson story reflect Frazer's point about the gradual disintegration of religious ritual?

60. What indications are there that the lottery's original purpose was to foster fertility and human life?

61. What symbolic values are embodied in the lottery itself?

62. What is the significance of the villagers' forgetting some of the ritual but remembering the use of the stones? Does Bronowski's essay throw any light on this?

63. Why does Jackson emphasize the date of the lottery?

64. There are certain obvious similarities between the stories of Faulkner and Baldwin. What do you think are the most important relations? Do the two stories differ significantly in their use of the scapegoat figure and pattern? In what ways?

65. What light does Neumann's discussion of the collective throw on Baldwin's story? Do Bronowski's remarks have relevance for the story? In what ways?

66. What signs are there that Baldwin is utilizing Christian symbolism in connection with the scapegoat motif? Does he use the symbolism for a particular effect? If so, what would you consider it to be?

67. To what extent does established religion contribute to the making of the scapegoat in the story?

68. In the death scene do you find any elements similar to Frazer's accounts of scapegoat rituals? What are they? Can they be interpreted in the same manner as Frazer uses or is their meaning different?

69. What are some of the ways in which Baldwin interrelates sex and death? Does this interrelationship have any parallels in the accounts of scapegoat rituals found in Part I? Is Baldwin's purpose in associating the two the same as that in ancient rituals or different?

70. How many scapegoats are there in the story? To what are they being sacrificed, similar or different things?

71. Which version of the scapegoat ritual—the Christian or the pagan—does Strindberg's novella seem closest to? Why? Does it possess elements of both forms?

72. What details of natural setting are important for the author's treatment of the scapegoat theme in Jackson, Faulkner, Baldwin, and Strindberg?

73. What aspects of Libotz's first appearance in the town suggest his fitness for the scapegoat role? What later aspects confirm this?

74. Why does Strindberg include the account of Libotz's teacher? And of his family upbringing?

75. Is there any motivation for Askanius' initial generosity to Libotz?

76. In what ways is Frazer's principle of vicarious suffering presented in Strindberg's novella?

77. What similarities and differences in the theme of money as related to the scapegoat are there in Lawrence, Pritchett, and Strindberg?

78. How do Faulkner, Jackson, and Strindberg make use of social conventions and attitudes to develop the theme of the scapegoat?

79. What adaptations do Lawrence, Pritchett, and Strindberg make in the traditional role of the woman in the scapegoat ritual? How do they compare with Euripides' treatment of the same issue?

80. Women play an important role in the scapegoat theme of *The Bacchae*, but they play an almost non-existent role in Strindberg's novella *The Scapegoat*. Considering the female or male as a function or aspect of each human being, discuss the relevance of these aspects in the nature of the theme in each work. Explain the strong relevance of women in Euripides and their strong lack of relevance in Strindberg.

81. What relation does the drinking scene and the conversation between Libotz, the chief of police, and Askanius have to the central scapegoat motif?

82. Why does Askanius criticize Libotz's attitude to his brother? What evidence is there that Strindberg uses Libotz as a scapegoat to explore the ironies of human responsibility?

83. Is there a functional connection between the scapegoat theme and the Sunday-in-the-country episode of Libotz, Karin, and the police chief?

84. What role does Askanius' new restaurant play in the structure and thematic development of Strindberg's novella?

85. In what ways does the Christmas Eve scene underscore the differences in character of Libotz and Askanius? Do any similarities emerge as well?

86. What is the function of the novella's final scene and the conversation between Libotz and the dispenser?

87. In Euripides a spell has been cast which causes much of the action, both Dionysus' freeing himself, the destruction of the palace, and the eventual destruction of Pentheus himself. How is cause and effect different, for example, in the contemporary scenes of Strindberg, Shirley Jackson, and V. S. Pritchett? Use different examples and deal with the influence of the gods, fate, or determinism upon the situations. Does the use of scapegoat ritual depend upon an unknown force greater than man can fathom?

Literary Works
for Further Study

The idea and the figure of the scapegoat are of such complexity and possess so many distinctive versions that it is obviously impossible to represent all of them in a single collection. What follows therefore is a suggestive list of works that seem in one fashion or another to be related to the scapegoat theme. The list is by no means exhaustive. Nevertheless, it aims to bring to the attention of student and instructor literature that may profitably be read in conjunction with the present volume and on which essays of various kinds may be based. The list is alphabetical by author and includes a descriptive classification by genre and the date of first publication.

Barth, John   *Giles Goat-Boy*, Novel, 1968

Bellow, Saul   *Dangling Man*, Novel, 1944; *The Victim*, Novel, 1947; *Henderson, the Rain King*, Novel, 1959

Bronowski, Jacob   *The Face of Violence*, Drama, 1955

Brooke, Jocelyn   *The Scapegoat*, Novel, 1949; "The Scapegoat," Poem, 1946

Clark, Walter Van Tilburg   *The Ox-Bow Incident*, Novel, 1940

Crane, Stephen   *The Red Badge of Courage*, Novel, 1895

Du Maurier, Daphne   *The Scapegoat*, Novel, 1957

Eliot, T. S.   "Sweeney Agonistes," Poem, 1932; *The Family Reunion*, Drama, 1939; *Murder in the Cathedral*, Drama, 1935

Ellison, Ralph   *Invisible Man*, Novel, 1947

Faulkner, William   "Red Leaves," Short story, 1930; *Light in August*, Novel, 1932; *A Fable*, Novel, 1954

Fitzgerald, F. Scott   *Tender is the Night*, Novel, 1933

Golding, William   *Lord of the Flies*, Novel, 1954

Gordon, Caroline   *The Garden of Adonis*, Novel, 1937

Graves, Robert   *King Jesus*, Novel, 1946; "In the Wilderness,"
Poem, 1916; *Seven Days in New Crete*, Novel, 1949

Hardy, Thomas   *Jude the Obscure*, Novel, 1895; *Tess of the
D'Urbervilles*, Novel, 1891

Hawthorne, Nathaniel   *The Scarlet Letter*, Novel, 1850; "Young
Goodman Brown," Short story, 1835; "The Maypole of
Merry Mount," Short story, 1836

Hemingway, Ernest   *The Sun Also Rises*, Novel, 1926; "The
Killers," Short story, 1927; "The Short Happy Life of
Francis Macomber," Short story, 1936; "The Snows of
Kilimanjaro," Short story, 1936

James, Henry   *Daisy Miller*, Novel, 1879

Jones, LeRoi   *The System of Dante's Hell*, Novel, 1965

Joyce, James   *Ulysses*, Novel, 1922

Ibsen, Henrik   *The Enemy of the People*, Drama, 1882

Kazantzakes, N.   *Zorba the Greek*, Novel, 1952

Kesey, Ken   *One Flew Over the Cuckoo's Nest*, Novel, 1962

Lawrence, D. H.   *The Woman Who Rode Away*, Novella, 1928;
The Man Who Died, Novella, 1931; *The Plumed Serpent*, Novel, 1926

Lowry, Malcolm   *Under the Volcano*, Novel, 1947

McCullers, Carson   *The Ballad of the Sad Cafe*, Novella, 1951

Melville, Herman   *Billy Budd*, Novella, 1924

Plato   *Euthyphro, Apology, Crito, and Phaedo*, Dramatic dia-
logues

Shakespeare, William   *Henry IV, Parts I & II*, Drama, 1598,
1600; *King Lear*, Drama, 1608

Shelley, Percy Bysshe   *Prometheus Unbound*, Drama, 1820

Steinbeck, John   *The Grapes of Wrath*, Novel, 1939; *Of Mice
and Men*, Novel, 1937

Woolf, Virginia   *Mrs. Dalloway*, Novel, 1925

Wright, Richard   *Native Son*, Novel, 1940